Students and External Readers	Staff & Research Students
DATE DUE FOR RETURN	**DATE OF ISSUE**
10.MA	-2 APR 79
30.	WITHDRAWN
	30.JUN 87 6043

Any book which you borrow remains your responsibility
until the loan slip is cancelled

60 0080624 2

D1615208

Studies in Child Development

Advice, Guidance and Assistance

Studies in Child Development

Titles in this series
Four Years On
11,000 Seven-Year-Olds
Adoption – Facts and Fallacies
Family Advice Services
Foster Home Care – Facts and Fallacies
Residential Child Care – Facts and Fallacies
The Community's Children
The Hostage Seekers
Caring for Children
Street Club Work in Tel Aviv and New York
Directory of Voluntary Organisations
Able Misfits
The Challenge of Thalidomide
The Handicapped Child: Research Review Volume 1
Deprivation and Education: Second Edition
Advice, Guidance and Assistance

The National Children's Bureau

Advice, Guidance and Assistance
A Study of Seven Family Advice Centres

ARYEH LEISSNER
K. ANGELA M. HERDMAN
ELIZABETH V. DAVIES

UNIVERSITY LIBRARY
NOTTINGHAM

LONGMAN
in association with
THE NATIONAL CHILDREN'S BUREAU

LONGMAN GROUP LTD
London

*Associated companies, branches and representatives
throughout the world*

© *The National Children's Bureau (formerly The National Bureau for Co-operation in Child Care)*
1971

*All rights reserved. No part of this publication may be reproduced,
stored in a retrieval system, or transmitted in any form, or by any means
electrical, mechanical, photocopying, recording, or otherwise without
the prior permission of the Copyright owner.*

First published 1971

ISBN *0 582 32451 3*

*Printed in Great Britain by
William Clowes & Sons Limited
London, Colchester and Beccles*

Contents

Foreword

In his foreword to Aryeh Leissner's report on the exploratory study of Family Advice Centres carried out by the National Children's Bureau in 1966 (*Family Advice Services*, Longman 1967), the late Derek Morrell stressed the need for the development and the ongoing assessment of easily accessible social services which are designed to meet the needs of people in a rapidly changing society. Now we are given a meticulously detailed report on a study of seven different working models of Family Advice Centres. The study, jointly financed by the Home Office, the Rowntree Trust and the Van Leer Foundation, is yet another practical demonstration of the effective and close working relationships which the National Children's Bureau has established with local authorities and voluntary organisations in recent years as part of a continuous programme of action projects designed to describe and evaluate preventive services. The fund of practical experience, factual information and theoretical knowledge thus made available makes a valuable contribution to practitioners, policy makers and planners in the present dynamic situation of the personal social services.

The publication of this report on the study of Family Advice Centres, soon after the setting up of the new unified local authority Social Service Departments, could not be more opportune. Since the passing of the Local Authority Social Services Act 1970 the minds and energies of those concerned with the planning and development of the new unified approach to the personal social services have, inevitably, been dominated by the wide range of organisational problems and the professional issues involved in the unification and the deployment of social work skills and supporting services into a single coherent administrative framework. Moreover, the upheaval of established traditions and working relationships, and the consequent stresses and strains inherent in a major reorganisation of this kind, will undoubtedly continue for some time to come.

This report may, therefore, serve as a timely and salutary reminder that the new Social Service Departments are faced with more than merely organisational and administrative tasks in bringing about the major objectives of the Seebohm Committee. The task of providing a 'community based and family oriented service which will be available to all', which will 'reach far beyond the discovery and reuse of social casualties', demands new methods as well as new attitudes. A more flexible approach and more accessible provisions will be needed to prevent social distress and to enable 'the greatest possible number of individuals to act reciprocally, giving and receiving service for the well-being of the whole community'. The wealth of practical experience and the insights gained by the family advice centres which participated in the National Children's Bureau study must be regarded as a very significant contribution to the ongoing search for new and effective ways of meeting the goals of the new Social Services Departments.

It is in the implementation of this wider concept of a social service in which the community is itself involved that this study will be of the greatest value to practitioners and planners in local authorities and voluntary organisations. The wealth of material which the report makes available confirms the Seebohm Report's emphasis on the need for accessibility, and for on-the-spot advice, guidance and assistance for the many people who find it increasingly difficult to make constructive use of the complex network of services and provisions. The report shows that the key function of the family advice services of providing 'on-the-spot, no-strings-attached' practical help and support is, especially in the detached, community based centres, successful in bridging the accessibility gap between the providers and the consumers of social services, and in improving communication and co-operation between the different social service agencies themselves. Perhaps most important of all, the report shows that the pioneering work of the detached centres proved the validity of the community work approach within the statutory local authority setting.

The study highlights the prevalence of unmet needs in community integration and it provides new scope for experimentation and for flexible and imaginative responses to social crisis. Most significant is the report's account of the many ways in which the community itself can and does become involved in identifying its needs and in devising effective ways of meeting them. The practical experience in community participation gained by the detached Family Advice Centres deserves the close attention of all those now engaged in planning community based services. It is in the crucial area of community work in areas with a high incidence of social problems and unmet needs that the

Family Advice Centres clearly have an important contribution to make
to the processes of change and to the need for innovation in the social
services.

Perhaps equally important for the future is the wide range of opportunities for further study and evaluation which the study reveals. It is
especially gratifying to know that the National Children's Bureau is
now engaged in a further action research study based on the experience
already gained in this field, which will investigate the potentialities
of intermediate treatment services for children and youth based on
detached Family Advice Centres in high need areas.

April 1971   SEROTA

Acknowledgements

We would like to acknowledge our debt of gratitude to all the many people, chief officers, supervisors, F.A.S. workers, youth work staff, ancillary and indigenous workers and volunteers, who gave so generously of their time and co-operated so wholeheartedly with us in carrying out the Family Advice Services Study. We regret deeply that, in order to preserve the confidentiality of this report, we cannot give their names. Each one of them contributed very materially to the success of our endeavour.

We also express our gratitude to the Home Office, the Rowntree Trust and the Van Leer Foundation for granting financial support to enable the National Children's Bureau to undertake the Family Advice Services Study.

ARYEH LEISSNER
K. ANGELA M. HERDMAN
ELIZABETH V. DAVIES

Introduction

The family advice service can be regarded as one of the responses of local authority children's departments to the growing awareness of the need for preventive approaches, an awareness which went hand in hand with a gradual shift in the emphasis from statutory, administrative concern with the individual child to professional social work focus upon the family as the client unit. The two developments complemented one another. The increasing preoccupation with prevention led to the search for ways in which to make the existing services more accessible to those who had not yet entered the stages of acute crisis or chronic malfunctioning, and for new methods which would enable child care officers to reach out to people who, for various reasons, were not availing themselves of the help and guidance they needed. The broadening of the child care officer's functions to include all members of the family made it possible to experiment with new concepts and settings which could offer a range of social work services not only to children, but also to the adults who play important roles in the shaping of the child's environment and the moulding of his personality.

We do not know when the term 'family advice service' was first used. However, at least one children's department reported that its staff offered 'advice, guidance and assistance' to families as early as 1952 (Oxfordshire County Council, 1964). Official impetus to the concept was given in 1960 by the Committee on Children and Young Persons, under the chairmanship of Lord Ingleby, which suggested the setting up of family advice centres in its report. The Ingleby Report as such came in for some criticism at the time, but this particular concept fell upon receptive ears in some circles. Peggy Jay, then Vice-Chairman of the L.C.C. Welfare Committee, took the report to task for its insufficiencies, but wrote: 'There was, however, one gleam of light in the main part of the report where the possibility of setting up statutory centres for advice and information on family matters was discussed.' Using the term

'Family Bureaux' to describe the proposed centres, Mrs Jay thought that 'the Ingleby Committee may eventually be remembered as the birth place of this concept'. Precipitating the questions we began to examine in the exploratory study, and which we shall seek to answer in this report, Peggy Jay asked: 'How are these bureaux to be run, who is to staff them, where are they to be sited and with what problems are they to deal?' The author made some remarkably accurate predictions of the goals and functions the new advice service would adopt. She wrote of 'filling the gap in the statutory services through which at present so many families fall', of accessibility as a major prerequisite of centres 'whose whereabouts are as well known as the local Post Office, and at which a call need cause no more neighbourly comment than a visit to the doctor'. Pointing at the model of the Citizen's Advice Bureau, Mrs Jay listed referral, provision of information on social service resources to other agencies, diagnosis of the deeper facts of personal trouble and not just the apparent symptoms, and 'a personal counselling service' as among the potential functions of the family advice service (Jay, 1968, pp. 11–15).

The functions of family advice centres were outlined as those of 'advice, guidance and assistance' in the context of an overall preventive approach by the Children and Young Persons' Act 1963. In the years that followed the publication of the Act a number of local authority children's departments set up family advice centres or offered advice, guidance and assistance as part of their services, but these attempts varied widely from one local authority to the other and the basic concepts, functions and goals of the new approach remained largely undefined. Wide interest had, however, been aroused, especially among those people in the social welfare field who had long since been exponents of change and innovation. One booklet published in 1965, for instance, contained the following passage:

The phrase 'advice' in the new Act gives authorities a chance to experiment with Family Advice Centres. The door on which to knock—a known door and a friendly door—could be the key to real preventive work. Here could be born the concept of families taking responsibility for their own well-being by seeking help and advice at an early stage, rather than waiting at home for problems, and social workers finally to overwhelm them. The pre-requisites of a Family Advice Centre are availability (pram pushing distance), a friendly reception by qualified staff and a cheerful domestic setting. The white tiled public lavatory decor of too many local authority offices is not conducive to confidential comfort. A further development could be an appointments system for meeting experts in a variety of fields such as Education Psychologists, Probation Officers and Marriage Guidance Counsellors (Hastings and Jay, 1965, pp. 9–10).

The same year the Director of the National Bureau for Co-operation in Child Care wrote:

Whether prevention can be translated into reality by reorganising existing services, both statutory and voluntary, or whether some new structure or organisation is required, is still an open and controversial question. Those who believe that the existing machinery is adequate may be either too optimistic or take too narrow a view of prevention. It is possible that a new framework needs to be created. This has been put forward by the L.C.C., the Fabian Society, the Fisher group (in their report to the Ingleby Committee) and the Home Secretary (to judge from his foreword to the most recent report of the Children's Department). Various labels have been suggested for such a new preventive service: family bureaux, family consultation centres, family welfare clinics, or family advice centres (Kellmer Pringle, 1965a, p. 277).

In 1966, just when the National Bureau began its exploratory study of family advice services, an American investigator commented: 'As the result of the 1963 legislation, local authorities have begun to expand their child welfare services in the direction of prevention-oriented Family Advice Centres. Several modes of operation are being tested for these centres and the trend is not clear' (Kahn et al., 1966, p. 44).

The Seebohm Report, published in 1968, recommended far-reaching changes in the social service field. While the report omitted any specific discussions of family advice services, it emphasised some of the basic concepts by pointing out that: 'For those it is intended to serve, "effectiveness" implies a service which is accessible and which meets the need promptly; that is, a service which is as far as possible community based'. The emphasis on a community-based service highlights what could, perhaps, be regarded as the most important development of recent years, namely the growing interest in community work. Local authority children's departments were, as yet, slow to respond to the new challenge, but a few hesitant first steps were taken. For the family advice service approach the growing interest in community work meant new scope for experimentation. There were the first signs that the children's departments, many of them having already accepted the broadening of their statutory functions to include the family, were now ready to look at the social environment of children and families—the community—as their future field of operations. As our report will show, the family advice service approach was, in certain instances, able to further this development.

In 1966 the National Bureau for Co-operation in Child Care carried out an exploratory study of family advice services. The study was sponsored by the Children's Department of the Home Office and a report of its findings was subsequently published. The Director of the National Bureau, wrote in her introduction to the report:

The Children and Young Persons Act, 1963 makes it possible for local authorities to initiate preventive work so as to make available help to children from socially handicapped families at a much earlier stage than hitherto. Among the ways for doing so, the idea of Family Advice Services has aroused considerable interest; and a number of local authorities are beginning to set up such services. However, there are few models to follow and, indeed, the concept of prevention itself is being interpreted in many different ways. It is likely, therefore, that different methods and structures will evolve, not only because of these differing concepts but also to meet the needs of different localities (Leissner, 1967, p. ix).

In our report on seven family advice centres we shall attempt to describe and to evaluate several of these different structures and methods. In the words of Derek H. Morrell we shall endeavour to provide 'a description of this pioneer effort, both to inform further development of the idea and as a means of identifying problems which require study in depth in the wider context of the children's (and family advice) service as a whole' (Leissner, 1967, p. vii).

The goals and methods of the study

Margaret Stacey (1969a) said that 'there are two main reasons for doing research: one is to try and solve a practical problem, and the other is to find out how something works just because it is interesting to know' (p. 12). Our attempt to find out about the family advice service began with the exploratory study carried out by the National Bureau in 1966. The present study can be regarded as an extension of the exploratory investigation, continuing the process of finding out how family advice centres work through observation, and contributing to the solving of the many practical problems through action-research.

The exploratory study provided the basis by obtaining information about the ways in which family advice services carried out their work in a variety of existing settings. This first look at the family advice service showed the need for the clarification of concepts, goals and methods. It made apparent the need for the definition of roles and functions, and it raised a number of significant issues.

The goals and basic concepts which needed clarification were those of *prevention, accessibility, the earliest possible detection of problems*, and the '*no-strings-attached*' character of the service.

Definitions were needed for the *role of the F.A.S. worker in the statutory setting* and *the worker's role as seen by the clients of the service*. Furthermore, definitions were needed for a range of functions which were already carried out by F.A.S. workers in the existing family advice centres, but which were being applied and interpreted in a variety of different ways. These functions included the provision of *advice, guidance* and *assistance*, the functions of *referral, co-ordination of services, liaison and mediation*, and *community work*.

The issues raised were those of the possible *conflict of functions* between the roles of F.A.S. worker and statutory officer, the *duplication of functions* between the family advice services and other existing services, and *confidentiality*.

A number of questions were raised explicitly, or were implied by our findings. These questions were related to the goals and concepts of the family advice service, the roles and functions of the F.A.S. staff, the issues raised by the experience of F.A.S. work, the specific requirements of the different types of F.A.S. settings and a number of practical problems regarding staffing, administrative procedures and resources.

The exploratory study identified four different types of family advice service settings. These were family advice centres set up by children's departments as

(a) integrated units of children's department central or area offices;
(b) family advice centres serving two or more statutory agencies;
(c) family advice centres under the auspices of voluntary agencies, but financed by and supervised by the children's department;
(d) 'detached' family advice centres serving a specific neighbourhood or community.

The aim of the study of family advice services was a detailed examination of representative examples of these four different types of F.A.S. settings. The study was intended to be carried out over a period of two years; however, mainly due to the difficulties encountered by the participating local authorities in making the necessary arrangements, (such as obtaining committee approval, financing, accommodation and staffing), the individual projects joined the study at different times. As a result only two family advice centres participated in the study for the full period of two years, two centres were observed for a period of eighteen months and three centres for only one year.

The study was carried out in two concurrent parts. Part 1 consisted of an *observational study* of four family advice centres, each of them representative of one of the above listed four different types of F.A.S. settings. Three of these centres had been in operation for some time before the onset of the study period, while in the case of one of the centres its opening coincided with the beginning of the National Bureau study. Part 2 consisted of an *action-research* study of three detached family advice centres, set up specifically as experimental projects for the purposes of the F.A.S. study.

The methods of investigation used were essentially the same for both parts of the study, although we tried to adapt them to the specific requirements and characteristics of each of the centres. The difference between the observational and the action-research approach was mainly one of the degree of involvement of the research staff in the planning, the formulation of policies and the daily work processes of the centres. It was stipulated that the research team would adopt the role of 'passive observer' in the centres which participated in Part 1 of the study. In the centres which formed Part 2 of the study, the research team participated in the planning of the centres, the formulation of policies and acted as consultant to the F.A.S. staff and the children's departments throughout the study period in all matters pertaining to the work processes of the centres.

It should be pointed out that, in practice, the clear distinction between passive observation and more active involvement could not always be maintained. It has been said that the agencies which co-operate in investigations of any part of their services have to 'face the fact that the research will in some measure affect the day-to-day work of the organisation' (National Council of Social Service, 1965, p. 12). This became apparent in both parts of the study. In a few instances, the staff of the action-research projects and the children's departments showed signs of resenting the intervention of the research team or did not always respond to the team's suggestions regarding changes in policies and practice. In the projects in which we sought to assume the role of observer, on the other hand, questions we asked for clarification often resulted in intensive discussion which influenced policy and practice. In some cases we were asked to give advice and found it difficult to refuse. We must also admit that, from time to time, we succumbed to the temptation to offer unsolicited advice or expressed critical opinions which resulted in modifications of policy and practice. In both parts of the study we were constantly aware of the dictum that: 'Research ought not to prejudice, by its intervention, any treatment or service which the organisation may be providing. Nor ought it to create or exacerbate problems that the user of the service has to face unaided by any further help' (N.C.S.S., 1965, p. 13). We tried to act accordingly, although the time required for recording, at the request of the research team undoubtedly reduced the time available for services to clients.

Our methods of investigation in both parts of the study consisted of the following:

(a) Participation in the supervision meetings and (where these existed) in the meetings of consultative committees.

(b) Analysis of family case files maintained by the F.A.S. staff.

(c) Analysis of agency contact files maintained by the F.A.S. staff.

(d) Analysis of selective summaries and reports drawn up by the F.A.S. staff, including observations by clerical staff, volunteers and indigenous workers, as well as diaries and card indexes maintained by the F.A.S. staff.

(e) Analysis of the use of the F.A.S. worker's time based on a categorised time sheet drawn up by the research team.

(f) Interviews with a small sample group of the clients of the centres.

(g) Interviews with a small sample group of representatives of other agencies, various professionals and other interested persons who had been in contact with the centres during the study period.

Interim reports at three or six month intervals were submitted to the children's officers, the children's department supervisors, the F.A.S. staff and the Director of the National Bureau.

In applying these methods of investigation we encountered a number of difficulties. The quality and consistency of recording varied widely in the different family advice centres. In some instances adequate clerical staff was not consistently available and this affected the recording procedures. On one occasion records and a card index file were destroyed by youngsters who broke into the centre. The interviews of clients posed problems, a significant proportion of the sample selected could not be found and time did not permit us to interview additional sample groups. We were also led to conclude that the inherent difficulties of communication between interviewer and F.A.S. clients cannot be overcome in one, relatively brief, 'chat', but need the comfort and security of an established relationship. In several cases the staff of the centres felt that the interviewing of clients would have detrimental effects upon the future relationships between the clients and the family advice centres and in one centre the staff expressed their objections to the interviewing of representatives of other agencies. In all these cases we deferred to the wishes of the staff.

On a number of occasions members of the staff of one or another of the participating centres disagreed with our interpretation of specific processes and events. We tried to provide some safeguards against misunderstandings and factual errors on our part by submitting detailed confidential reports on our observations and findings to the children's officers, the supervisors and to all members of the F.A.S. staff, asking for their comments and critical observations. As far as possible the opinions expressed by the workers with regard to the individual reports were taken into account in the writing of the final report on the F.A.S. study.

Over periods ranging from one to two years we established relationships with a considerable number of workers of different backgrounds and personalities, all committed to their work and faced with a multitude of demands and problems to which the requirements and interventions of research were not always welcome additions. In trying to find out

what all these workers were doing, thinking and feeling we soon learned
how true it is that: 'People will talk more freely of past struggles than
those in which they are at the moment engaged, and an outside observer
risks degenerating into a gossip-monger if he tries too insistently to
unravel the personal conflicts of those about him' (Marris and Rein,
1967, p. 2).

The action-research approach applied to the study of three detached
family advice centres may bear some further discussion:

Professor Donnison (1970) defines action-research as 'the professional-
isation of social reform', but thinks that 'planned and tested innovation
in social policy' might be a better description. He tells us that action-
research '. . . calls for good research workers, but it is not, properly
speaking, research. It is inquiry and innovation and its success should be
measured by comparison with that of other procedures which have the
same purposes'. And he points out that action-research:

by posing and clarifying the social problems and policy questions that call for
attention, and producing an urgent demand for ideas and theories that will
assist people grappling with these issues, may help to promote more useful
research of conventional kinds and encourage those who do it to present their
conclusions in a form which helps practitioners.

This may help to see action-research through the eyes of conventional research and in the wider perspectives of social policy. Marris
and Rein (1967) outline the distinctions between conventional and
action-research more concretely:

Research requires a clear and constant purpose, which both defines and precedes
the choice of means; that the means be exactly and consistently followed; and
that no revision takes place until the sequence of steps is completed. Action is
tentative, non-committal and adaptive. It concentrates upon the next step,
breaking the sequence into discrete manageable decisions. It casts events in a
fundamentally different perspective, evolving the future out of present opportunities, where research perceives the present in the context of a final outcome.
Research cannot interpret the present until it knows the answers to the ultimate
questions. Action cannot foresee what questions to ask until it has interpreted
the present. Action attempts to comprehend all the factors relevant to an immediate problem, whose nature continually changes as events proceed, where
research abstracts one or two factors for attention, and holds to a constant
definition of the problem until the experiment is concluded (p. 205).

This passage provides us with a very useful explanation of the
dichotomy inherent in action-research. We did indeed concentrate
upon 'the next step' and sought to evolve 'the future out of present
opportunities'. We decided to do so by the methods outlined above,
and to refrain from any direct contact with clients (except through
incidental observation when we visited the centres), so as to avoid

distorting the picture by including in it our own (the research team's) particular skills and methods. Our approach was to set processes in motion, while observing and reporting the effects of what is happening (Leissner *et al.*, 1967, p. 51).

As our list of methods will have shown, we did not make use of questionnaires in either part of the study. It has been said that: 'Fixed choice questions preclude the possibility of obtaining un-anticipated definitions of the situation which might reveal a respondent's private thoughts and feelings' (Wakeford, 1968, p. 118). We tend to believe that this also holds true to some degree for open-ended questions. No doubt questionnaires are useful tools for research in many situations, but, by definition, they do ask questions which demand answers in circumscribed areas of relevance and from prescribed sources. In our situation we wanted not only to elicit answers, but to encourage questions which we had not known enough to ask. Moreover, we wanted answers and questions not only from expected sources, but from others, still unknown to us, which we perhaps had not perceived as significant or relevant. We relied to a great degree upon 'informants' in both parts of the study. These were all the members of the F.A.S. staff, as well as anyone else directly or indirectly involved with the family advice centres and willing to talk to us, answer our questions or write down experiences and impressions for us. In some cases, especially in the action-research part of the study, this led to the merging of the 'guided informant' of whom it has been said that he 'is not only led to introduce topics which may seem to him personally as of little interest, but he may even adopt attitudes and pretend to beliefs which he would not have expressed if he had been free of the investigator's influence' (Madge, 1965, p. 89).

We found no way of avoiding this widely known phenomenon, but, aside from certain safeguards provided by the availability of several informants in every centre, we may also say that the men and women who staffed the centres were not 'guided' too easily.

Finally, the question may be asked as to the hypotheses upon which we based the study of different types of family advice service settings. The answer was partly given by Margaret Stacey (1969a), who wrote:

Some people consider that a piece of social research is not scientific unless it has a clearly defined hypothesis which it sets out to test. This would appear to be too narrow a view. In any unknown field it is not possible to set up sufficiently clear hypotheses for testing to form a basis for research (p. 89).

In this, and in the lack of control groups, for which we saw no practical possibilities, the study assumed the characteristics of a concurrent series of 'demonstrations', a research approach which has been described as being used 'to appraise action either through informal observation or systematically gathered evidence'. This form of investigation has also been described as useful for 'discovering new ways to do things' and as serving to 'reduce uncertainty about the intended and unintended consequences of action' (E. J. Thomas, 1960, p. 291).

In summary, it may be said that while we had no sufficient basis for clearly defined hypotheses, we started out with the general assumption that family advice services can make a valuable contribution to helping people who find it difficult to make use of the existing services for a variety of reasons about which we hoped to learn more. We assumed that there are gaps between the existing services, and that these gaps could be bridged by family advice services. We assumed that the accessibility and the specialised functions of the family advice services could serve to bridge the 'us-and-them' gaps between the statutory services and certain sectors of the population, and that the F.A.S. approach could serve to prevent social malfunctions by establishing the kind of image of no-strings-attached service which would encourage 'hard to reach' people to seek help with their problems at the earliest possible moment. We set out to find out whether our assumptions were valid in general, and to what degree they were justified in each one of the different types of settings. At the same time we had the task of defining and, where necessary, formulating, the goals, concepts, roles, functions and methods which we assumed to constitute the family advice service approach.

1 The observational study of four family advice centres

A family advice service as a unit of an area office; the 'A' project, 20 May 1968 to 20 May 1969

The area served by the family advice centre

Plans to decentralise the borough's children's department and move the area teams out from the central office in the heart of the city began to materialise early in 1968. On 20 May of that year the 'A' project area office and family advice centre opened. The area office was located in a large, three-storey Victorian house on a wide, treelined main road running out from the city centre to the eastern boundary. The population numbered approximately 175,000, consisting of working-class and middle-class groups, a relatively recent influx of immigrants among them. The housing varied considerably throughout the area, a high proportion was owner occupied and council estates consisted of semi-detached housing and high-rise blocks.

The setting

As indicated by its official designation the area office and family advice centre was planned from the outset to make the family advice service an integral part of this children's department area office. A room on the ground floor, adjacent to the reception office and waiting area, was designated the family advice centre.

Staffing, administration and supervision

Of the fourteen staff members of the area office a team of five child care officers was assigned to man the family advice centre in rotation. Each member of the team spent one day a week in the family advice centre and attended to their routine child care work during the rest of the week. The team consisted of one senior child care officer and four child care officers. Two members of the team were professionally qualified, the work experience of the other three included teaching, child care and youth work.

One member of the team was seconded to a training course three months after the start of the project and was replaced by another child care officer. Four months later, in December 1968, the senior child care officer left the children's department; her position remained vacant, reducing the team to four members.

The senior child care officer assigned to the F.A.S. team supervised two of the team members as child care officers, as well as in their F.A.S. functions. The two other members of the team were supervised by a senior officer who was not directly involved in the work of the family advice service.

A clerical assistant was appointed to the family advice centre for four hours a day from 20 May 1968, with the task of assisting the F.A.S. staff with recording and filing.

The family advice centre was opened to the public five days a week from 9.00 a.m. to 12.30 p.m. and from 1.30 to 5.00 p.m. When the senior child care officer left the department opening time was reduced to four days a week, maintaining the same hours.

After some initial confusion it was decided by the F.A.S. staff that all the clients who did not ask specifically for a child care officer, or presented a problem (such as a request to have a child taken into care, adoption, etc.) which was clearly the responsibility of the children's department, would be directed to the family advice worker by the receptionist. In cases of doubt the receptionist was instructed to ask the administrative officer, or the senior child care officer on the F.A.S. team, for guidance.

Financing[1]
The family advice centre was financed by the children's department from the rate fund within the Children and Young Person's Act 1963. Expenditure covered by the children's department amounted to approximately £1,994. This sum included costs due solely to research requirements.

Publicity
In April 1968 the deputy children's officer wrote to the chief officers of all statutory departments informing them of the setting up of the family advice service at the area office. The letter asked for the co-operation of the statutory departments, pointing out that the family

[1] Information provided by the children's department.

advice service would call for multidisciplinary co-operation and that the family advice centre would be available for referrals. Letters announcing the date of opening of the area office and advice centre were sent to other agencies including schools, general practitioners and the public library.

After the area team had settled into their new premises they held an 'open house' party in September 1968. Representatives of several local statutory and voluntary agencies, headmasters, general practitioners and others attended. The functions of the family advice service were explained to a number of the guests in informal conversation on this occasion.

DATA AND COMMENTS

The first client came to the area office family advice centre in May 1968, the last on 24 February 1969. The data presented below cover this period of the research project.

Number of contacts with clients

'Contact' as used below means any relationship between the family advice service worker, and members of the community which includes any or several of the categories of advice, guidance, assistance, liaison/mediation and referral.

Families	33
Children, 0–12 incl.	3
Teenagers, 13–19 incl.	4
Young adults, 20–29 incl.	10
Adults, 30–49 incl.	22
Adults, 50–65 incl.	5
Old people, 65 and over	0

Thus the workers established contact with 44 individuals of all ages. These were all members of the 33 families listed above. This does not necessarily imply that the workers established contact with all members of each of these families.

Sources of referral

Of the 33 families who made use of the service, 15 came to the family advice centre of their own accord, 4 were referred by relatives or friends, 1 was referred by another F.A.S. client. The other 13 clients were referred by other agencies and professionals including a health

STUDY OF FOUR FAMILY ADVICE CENTRES

visitor, a local councillor and a probation officer, 3 clients were referred by school teachers.

Types of problems

The 33 families asked for help with regard to a range of 17 different types of problems. Requests for help with matrimonial difficulties ranked highest with 6 requests; teenage problems, child minding and general family problems followed. In total 43 requests for help covering a range of 17 different, though often related and sometimes overlapping, presented problems were received and dealt with by the F.A.S. workers during the twelve month period.

Referrals to other persons and agencies

During the year the F.A.S. team established contact with 43 other statutory and voluntary agencies and individuals, 49 referrals to other agencies regarding specific problems were made by the F.A.S. workers. The highest number of referrals, 11, was to the area children's department. Of these 10 involved complete referral of client families to the department, 3 of these 10 families were already known to the children's department. Other referrals were made to the following agencies: a children's department in another county, the home help service, the mental health department, the department of health and social security, the police and general practitioners, a housing association, the housing department rent rebate scheme, a marriage guidance council and a citizen's advice bureau. Under certain circumstances a family or individual client was referred to several different agencies.

Use of worker's time

The members of the F.A.S. team found it somewhat difficult to categorise the use of their time according to the time sheets provided by the research team. This is reflected in the fact that 90 per cent of the working hours were listed under 'miscellaneous'. This inordinately large proportion also reflects the fact that there was only a relatively small number of clients, and that apparently most of the workers' time was spent waiting for things to happen.[1]

Out of the remaining 102 working hours, 47 were listed under 'formal contact with clients', 16 under 'home visits' and 7 under 'referrals to other agencies'. We noted that 6 of the 33 families were visited at home by the F.A.S. workers. One client was visited because

[1] The workers used much of this time to attend to paper work and matters concerning their routine duties as child care officers.

she failed to keep an appointment at the F.A.C. and lived very close to the office. Two families lived four miles away, and the F.A.S. worker gave his reason for visiting both families at home as 'the difficulty of public transport from this housing estate to the advice centre'. Two other families were visited at home as the F.A.S. worker wished to see the teenage children who were either at work or school during the day. Another F.A.S. worker visited a family in which one member was regarded as an F.A.S. client, while another member of the family was her client in her child care officer's role.

Role confusion and other difficulties

Situations such as this reflected the problems faced by the family advice team in maintaining the distinction between the roles of F.A.S. worker and child care officer. It became quite clear in discussions that the difficulties were largely caused by the, somewhat artificial, separation of the F.A.S. and child care functions, which had to be imposed by the research team. The situation was aggravated by an undercurrent of frustration caused by the fact that the staff as a whole, and the F.A.S. team in particular, felt that there had not been sufficient consultation or preparation about the setting up and the methods of operation of the family advice centre.

The members of the team were understandably confused and frustrated about being in a position where they had to 'switch off' their child care officer role one day per week and present themselves in the more flexible, diffuse role of the F.A.S. worker.

The technical difficulties of the rotation system of manning the family advice centre also became apparent. Some members of the group felt that it was difficult to maintain the feeling of continuity between worker and client, when the latter would find a different person behind the desk of the family advice office on returning the following day. To establish the necessary relationship with the client it was suggested that, in some cases, the client could be asked to return for the next interview the following week, on the day when the worker who had established the initial contact was on duty. At the same time, members of the team felt uneasy because one of their own child care clients might have to be turned away, or see a colleague who had not established a relationship with this particular client, because the client's 'own' child care officer was on F.A.S. duty.

Towards the end of 1968 the feeling of uneasiness about the family advice centre had spread throughout the area office. Tensions about the work itself, and the burden placed on the rest of the staff by the fact that five officers were exempt from routine duties for one day of each working week, became more and more pronounced. The F.A.S. team came to the conclusion that arguing and complaining led nowhere and that something more constructive had to be done. They discussed the matter among themselves, consulted the rest of the area office staff, and finally formed a working party to draw up a statement which spelled out their views.

The paper submitted by the working party stated that:

An effective 'caring' Centre must inevitably go out of the centre to meet the community, and encourage the community to come to us. This is not being done, and the only overt recognition of this need was in having an 'Open Day' which, although useful, did not meet the community on its own level, in its work and play areas.

The working party concluded that the rota system of operating the family advice service should be discontinued, and that one person should be assigned permanently to the family advice centre.

The statement of the working party was discussed with the children's officer and the recommendation, that one suitably trained worker should be appointed to the area office staff and assume the post of F.A.S. worker, was accepted.

The post of F.A.S. worker was advertised in February 1969 and a statement drawn up by the area children's officer sent to all applicants. This showed clearly how the understanding of the tasks of the family service had increased and gained in depth since the opening of the project. It stated: 'The family advice centre has been working so far firstly, as a referral agency and secondly filling in any gaps due to shortcomings of agency functions. A need has been recognised for a third function, in giving support to groups within the community.'

To everyone's regret, no suitable applicant for the post of family advice worker could be found. The operation of the centre was therefore suspended for the time being. It can be safely assumed that the matter will not rest there, but that a family advice centre set up in accordance with the recommendations of the working party and functioning as defined in the statement to the applicants for the post, will eventually become part of the area office.[1] Our year of study at the area office has also convinced us that the F.A.S. experience broadened the scope of the staff, had some effect upon all aspects of their work, and made the staff more fully aware of their preventive functions, and of the need to explore the possibilities of group work and community work.

[1] At the writing of this report the children's department has taken steps to set up three new family advice centres in other areas.

A family advice service operated jointly by two statutory agencies; the 'B' project, 1 April 1968 to 31 March 1969

The area served by the family advice centre
The 'B' project family advice centre was located in a small market town of approximately 5000 inhabitants in a rural area to which many middle-class people retire. Many of the younger people leave home to live and work in the large cities.

Agriculture and tourism provide most of the employment opportunities, both being affected by seasonal variations. Pottery and lace making, the traditional industries, thrive on a small scale. An army camp just outside the town provides a considerable amount of employment as well as some social life for the teenage girls.

Most of the town's people live in privately owned, early twentieth-century terraced houses. One third of the population, the lower income group, live in local authority housing. During the summer months there is something of a housing shortage when the summer visitors take over much of the privately-owned rented accommodation at a higher rent than that paid during the winter by local people.

The setting
The family advice centre is above a supermarket on the main street. The entrance is in a narrow side street which leads to the local secondary school and the health clinic.

Staffing, administration and supervision
The family advice centre was opened in October 1964 as—

the result of a local authority decision in a rural and small town area. Here a policy decision to integrate the services of the Children's Department and the Welfare Department brought about a setting up of a Family Advice Service. The clerical staff deputise for one another during holidays etc. A common card index is maintained. Although the goal of this particular setting is an integrated Family Advice Service pooling the resources of the two participating departments, it appears (as expressed by the Staff) that both departments function in fact as separate units, each offering advice services according to the statutory duties and working conditions of its own service. This it is thought will continue while the two central organisations remain unintegrated and responsible to different spending committees. (Letter from the children's officer, November 1966.)

The family advice centre is shared by the area office staff of the children's and welfare departments. The staff members directly involved in the family advice services study were:

the area children's officer (one quarter of her time),
the senior area welfare officer,
one child care officer,
one trainee child care officer (one sixth of his time),
two welfare officers,
two full-time clerk-receptionists,
one half-time clerk-receptionist,
one part-time clerical assistant (two hours daily) especially assigned
to the family advice services study.

The qualifications of the staff of the centre included diplomas in
social studies, applied social studies, social administration and mental
health. Professional experience ranged from medical social work,
residential child care, mental health social work, youth work, home
teaching for the blind, to statutory welfare and child care work.

The child care staff received supervision from their area children's
officer and from senior staff of the central office of the department.
The welfare staff was supervised by their senior area welfare officer.
They also met together regularly with a senior member from central
office to discuss co-ordination and consultation between themselves,
the field work staff, and the central office staff. For the purposes of
research, the research staff initiated monthly meetings with all the
participating staff of the family advice centre.

Financing
Neither department made any extra financial allocation to the family
advice centre apart from the salary of the part-time clerical assistant
especially appointed for research purposes and appointed only for the
period of research.

Publicity
The health clinics and some of the general practitioners in the area
had been informed of the availability of the family advice centre,
but the F.A.S. functions were not explained in detail. Some other
agencies had been told informally. Through the group meetings
with the staff the researchers learnt of mixed feelings about the
desirability of publicity. Several members of the group felt that to
publicise such a 'wide-open' service could have undesirable results:
a possible influx of clients asking for help outside the range of the
statutory functions would impinge on the workers' statutory caseloads;
other agencies might refer all 'difficult' clients to the family advice
centre and thus avoid giving a service to which these people might be

entitled. Someone wondered whether it was 'right' to encourage people to seek help, whether this could not in fact prevent people from using their own resources in coping with their problems.

DATA AND COMMENTS

In the discussions that took place between the researchers and the participating staff of the family advice centre, the basic concepts of advice, guidance and assistance available in an easily accessible form, were examined in an attempt to find out if, and in what way, this service was being provided by the family advice centre. In the following pages, the most salient facts arising out of these discussions are summarised.

The first question to be examined was whether there existed any identifiable difference between the F.A.S. functions and the routine work of the child care and welfare officers. The researchers were told: 'No, we can't see any such difference. Child care and welfare staff both work on the basis of understanding that most of their clients' problems, no matter what kinds of problems or the age of the person, involve the family. The staff of both departments sharing the work of the area office make use of Section 1 provisions of the Children's and Young Person's Act 1963. The workers co-ordinate their activities concerning specific clients as the need arises and informally.' It is interesting to note that the welfare department uses powers under the 1963 act. This approach can be further illustrated by citing the example of a welfare officer taking the child of a family on his caseload to a children's home rather than making a formal referral to the children's department.

Trying to find a definition of the F.A.S. client, as distinct from that of the children's and welfare department clients who seek the help of the family welfare centre, a member of the group could only offer a negative definition: 'I suppose that F.A.S. clients are people who seek help or advice in matters which do not fall under the statutory obligations of either one of the two departments.' However, all were agreed that there were not many cases in which child care and welfare officers wouldn't stretch a point, even if they have never heard of the all-inclusive approach of the family advice service.

Next to be discussed was the possible 'reaching-out' function as a special contribution of the family advice service. The workers had similar feelings towards this as they did towards the question of publicity. They did, however, conclude that it might be useful to make themselves more accessible to some of the more isolated groups in the rural population—a gypsy camp was mentioned, and a house converted into flatlets, where many of the families were constantly getting into some kind of trouble. The welfare department made itself more available once a week when a welfare officer would be present at the health centre of two outlying communities and work, in fact, as a family advice service worker mainly making referrals.

The discussion turned to the relationship with other agencies. The workers feared that the all-encompassing functions of a family advice service might put other agencies on the defensive. Some said that the F.A.S. functions were already being carried out by the health visitors, 'the real grass-roots workers'. This may have been particularly relevant in the rural area. The statistics obtained on sources of referral of clients show that the majority of clients visited the family welfare centre on the advice of health departments, hospitals or G.P.s.

The question was asked whether the area office for the children's and welfare departments could actually be regarded as a family advice service, or include this specific service among its other functions. The significant role of the clerk-receptionists who often dealt with cases of 'simple advice' was recognised. Fairly frequently they were able to deal with simple enquiries and sometimes chat with someone in momentary need of relief from distress. However, the clerk-receptionists stated that they were not able to deal with more complex cases and sometimes, when these did not fall within the statutory functions of the two departments, they had to be turned away. Everyone agreed that it was always regrettable to refuse help, but the staff of both departments pointed out that their statutory caseloads must have first priority.

The meetings which followed were taken up with examining the policies of the two departments and the needs of the clients. The staff became aware that many of the 'inappropriate' requests for help (in that they did not fall within the statutory duties of the two departments) were made by people who were trying to test the attitude of the family advice centre towards them. Some members of the group said that, not only was it possible that people did not know that they would receive help and advice at the centre for a wide range of problems, but it could be that people have had the experience of not receiving the kind of service they expected when they did ask for help. Someone said: 'Perhaps we don't know what service people want because we don't try hard enough to find out by going out and asking them.'

The year's discussion ended with members of the group stating that both the child care and welfare officers had become increasingly flexible in the range of clients they accepted and in the variety of problems they handled. However, the fact remained that it was the duty of each of the social workers to give the statutory caseload first priority.

2

The possibility of creating a special F.A.S. post within the area office, manned by a worker whose specific tasks would be intake and referral, was raised.

It will now be apparent that it was not possible to make a valid separation of family advice service work and the overall work of the children's and welfare sections. The data presented in the following pages do not constitute the entire caseload of the centre, but only a representative sample. This sample was selected and examined in order to throw some light upon the family advice service aspects of the overall work. The sample taken for the twelve month analysis was as follows:

All welfare department case files[1] opened since the start of the period of research.

Ten per cent of welfare department miscellaneous files[2] opened since the start of the period of research.

All children's department 'preventive' case files[3] opened since the start of the period of research.

Agency contact files relating to the above sample of case files.

Number of contacts with clients
'Contact' as used below means any relationship between the family welfare centre workers and members of the community which involves one or several of the categories of advice, guidance and assistance, liaison, mediation and referral.

	Welfare dept.	Children's dept.	Total
Families	50	30	80
Children, 0–12	9	57	66
Teenagers, 13–19	3	11	14
Young adults, 20–29	8	18	26
Adults, 30–49	39	20	59
Adults, 50–65	9	5	14
Old people, 65 and over	65	3	68

Thus, in the sample taken the workers in the welfare department were in touch with 133 individuals of all ages: all but 26 of these were

[1] Files of those clients who presented problems within the statutory functions of the welfare department.
[2] Files of those clients whose presented problems did not fall within the statutory functions of the welfare department.
[3] Files of those clients categorised by the Children's and Young Person's Act (1963).

members of the 50 families. The workers in the children's department were in touch with 114 individuals of all ages: all but 2 of these were members of the 30 families. In the sample there were 8 families with whom no contact was made—the work being done by letter or through other agencies. Defining the family as a 'client' and adding the individuals with no apparent family connections, the welfare department sample consisted of 76 clients. The children's department sample consisted of 40 clients.

The data illustrate that the staff of the two departments served mainly those age groups most relevant to their statutory functions.

Sources of referral

Of the 76 clients who asked for help from the welfare department, 36 were referred by health departments, hospitals or general practitioners. Twelve clients visited the centre of their own accord and 8 were referred by relatives, friends, neighbours or employers.

Of the 40 clients who asked for help from the children's department, 19 were referred by health departments, hospitals or general practitioners, 7 clients were referred by the courts, the probation service or the police, 6 clients visited the centre of their own accord.

Types of presented problems

In the welfare department, of the sample taken, the 76 clients asked for help with regard to a wide range of different, though often related and sometimes overlapping, types of problems. As could be expected, the highest number of requests for help were with those problems falling within the statutory functions of the welfare department; 37 requests for help with problems connected with old age, 24 for problems connected with mental and physical handicaps and 23 for housing problems. In the children's department, of the sample taken, the 40 clients asked for help with regard to 12 different, though often related and sometimes overlapping, types of problems. Children 'at risk' and child-minding difficulties were at the top of the list with 10 and 8 requests for help respectively.

However, there are indications that the close co-operation between the staff of two different departments led to some degree of flexibility with regard to the statutory boundary lines. Both departments dealt with a number of matrimonial problems (welfare 4 and children's 6) and both offered help in cases of financial difficulties (welfare 8 and children 1). The welfare officers intervened in cases of clients experiencing difficulties with other statutory officials (4 times) and the child care officers helped clients to obtain legal advice (3 times).

One client may have asked for help with more than one problem. The sample shows that the workers in the welfare department received and dealt with 124 requests for help. The children's department received and dealt with 44 requests.

Referrals to other agencies
The welfare department referred the 76 clients to a wide range of agencies. In total, 81 referrals to other agencies were made during the twelve months. The highest number (29) were made to other welfare departments or other area offices; (28) referrals were made to health departments, hospitals or general practitioners.

The children's department made 11 referrals; 6 of these to the health department, hospitals and general practitioners.

In many cases one client may have been referred to more than one agency for help in different matters. A referral to another agency did not necessarily mean that the family welfare centre discontinued its own service to the client.

Use of worker's time
Time-sheets were completed by all participating social work staff for a period of six months.

Home visits, including travelling time, took up the greatest amount of the worker's time: 469 out of a total of 1968 working hours for child care officers and 1102 out of a total of 3695 working hours for members of the welfare department. It may be assumed that this is characteristic of a rural setting in which many clients live at a considerable distance from the area office.

The two time-sheet categories of special significance for the family advice service, 'simple advice' and 'informal contacts' with clients or groups of clients, showed a low number of working hours for both departments. However, the time spent by the clerk-receptionists on this type of work was not recorded.

On the whole it may be said that the staff of the family advice centre took a realistic view of the practicability of a family advice service in the setting of an area office. The child care and welfare officers agreed that their services to clients should be as flexible and wide-ranging as possible, but emphasised that their resources must first be allocated to their statutory caseloads. To summarise their views and feelings about the concepts and methods of family advice service work we quote extracts from the comments of two child care officers:

There is unlikely to be a vast number of people coming here for unspecified advice. The town itself is small, only 5000 population in the immediate vicinity, and I think people in the town itself are fairly quickly routed to the appropriate agency. Similarly, in the country area, health visitors, educational welfare officers, G.P.s and solicitors are more likely to hear of difficulties and either refer to us for home visiting, or to ask for consultative advice that they can use in continuing their service to the client.

If I had my way, I would like to be more outwardgoing. But to do that I would need considerably more time and energy. I ought to spend half a day per week in each health clinic and secondary school—probably not doing anything at all for the first few months, but just being available. I ought to have more contact with the youth clubs. All this would be 'preventive' in the real sense of the word. What I am doing now doesn't even scratch the surface. But I have to remember, that as a C.C.O. I have many statutory duties, and my time is considerably taken up by routine home visiting.

A by no means negligible amount of work which could be classified under the advice, guidance and assistance functions of the family advice service was carried out, much of it by the clerk-receptionist. Nevertheless, we came to the conclusions that the area office could not be regarded as constituting a family advice service *per se*, or as offering a family advice service as a specialised service within the structure of the children's and welfare departments area office.

A family advice service in a voluntary agency setting; the 'C' project, 15 November 1967 to 15 May 1969

The area served by the family advice centre
The neighbourhood in which the 'C' project family advice centre was located is a city area of redevelopment and shifting population. The area is changing rapidly and tower blocks loom up between the rows of small terraced houses. While many of the local people and their parents were born in the neighbourhood, there are newcomers from other parts of the city and immigrants from the West Indies. Many of the young people are forced to leave the area because of the lack of housing and employment opportunities. There is a mood of depression among the older population, who feel that 'people who make good get out of this area'.

The setting
The family advice centre, set up in January 1965, was located in one of the rooms of a settlement house which provides a range of services and activities such as a boys' club, a club for old people, a literacy scheme, a voluntary social work scheme financed by the welfare department and a legal advice centre. During the period of research, a community worker was appointed and the community development activities of the settlement are being expanded.

Staffing, administration and supervision

From February 1967, two part-time social workers worked between them a forty-hour week in the family advice centre. They had the following work experience and qualifications:

One social worker held a certificate in social studies and had attended courses in family casework and marital interaction. Prior to her F.A.S. appointment, she had done settlement house work and casework with Family Service Units. The other social worker held a B.Sc. in sociology and also attended the marital interaction course. She had secondary school teaching experience, had worked as a child care officer and did part-time work with pre-school children in an adventure playground.

Throughout the period of research, the family advice centre was open for six sessions during the week: two mornings, two afternoons, and two evenings. In defining the role and responsibilities of the family advice service, 'it was agreed that, although the money was provided by the children's department, the case-worker herself should be a member of the settlement's staff rather than the department's; this is in order not to deceive the public by concealing the brawny arm of authority under the soft sleeves of (the settlement), and in order to achieve genuine confidentiality'.[1]

It was emphasised, however, that there should be a close link between the family advice centre and the children's department. A senior child care officer was made available as consultant to the family advice service workers.

The family advice service shared the waiting room and reception facilities with the legal advice centre. In an introductory letter sent to other interested agencies, the head of the settlement wrote: 'The service is envisaged as an expansion of the Legal Advice Service already available and use will be made of the facilities there.'

Financing

The Borough financed the settlement house family advice centre under Section 1 of the Children's and Young Persons' Act 1963. Grants covering the period of research were made as follows:

	£
April 1967–March 1968	2100
April 1968–March 1969	2210
(excluding an additional grant of £190 for research expenses)	
April 1969–March 1970	2442[2]

---

[1] Annual Report, 1965, issued by the Settlement House.
[2] Information obtained from the children's department.

The centre was 100 per cent grant-aided and the amounts were intended to cover all expenses directly arising from the family advice centre (salaries and all running costs).

Publicity
The text of a leaflet distributed to the public in 1967 was as follows:

FREE CONFIDENTIAL ADVICE given on family and personal problems by a qualified family consultant.
ANYONE of any age with a problem, especially one to do with the family, can call during the hours shown below or ring for an appointment.
FURTHER HELP available from other experts or specialists. Home visits can be arranged if wanted.

DATA AND COMMENT
The data presented here may serve to provide the reader with the essential facts and figures with regard to the 'C' project family advice centre during the period of research.

Number of contacts with clients
'Contact' as used below means any relationship between the family advice service workers and members of the community which involves one or several of the categories of advice, guidance and assistance, liaison, mediation and referral.

Families	280
Children, 0–12	113
Teenagers, 13–19	29
Young adults, 20–29	115
Adults, 30–49	198
Adults, 50–65	34
Old people, 65 and over	6
Adults, age not established	8

During the eighteen months of research, the workers in the family advice centre were in touch with 503 individuals of all ages: all but 13 of these individuals were members of the 280 families. Defining the family as a client and adding the 13 individuals with no family connections, the family advice service workers were in touch with 293 clients during the period of research.

The relatively small number of young people within the 0–19 age group seems to indicate that the family advice centre attracted a much wider population group than it would have done had it been part of a children's department. This is no doubt related to the well-established image of the settlement house.

Sources of referral
A substantial number of clients, 111 out of a total of 293 clients, visited the centre of their own accord or were referred by friends or relatives. This suggests that the centre was successful in establishing its image as a place to which people could safely bring their problems. The close co-operation with the legal advice centre is shown by the fact that 66 people were referred from it to the family advice centre; 22 clients were referred by the citizens' advice bureau, only 2 clients were referred by the children's department.

Frequency of visits to the family advice centre
Out of a total of 293, 178 clients visited the centre only once and 52 visited twice. No data was collected by the research staff with regard to home visits except that the two workers between them spent 15 hours a month visiting people in their own homes. Ten clients visited the centre on five or six occasions; 1 client visited more then 6 times.

We reached the conclusion that there was some emphasis on simple advice, short-term guidance and assistance cases that only required one or two visits to the family advice centre. This can be said to reflect the accepted roles and functions of the family advice centre.

Types of presented problems
During the eighteen-month period of research, the workers in the family advice centre received and dealt with 424 requests for help covering a range of 31 different, though often related and sometimes overlapping, problem situations. The greatest number of presented problems (143) was in the area of marital difficulties; 77 requests were for help with housing problems. The high incidence of marital problems may have been partly due to the interests, abilities and experience of the workers, but may also have been connected with the legal advice centre next door to the F.A.C. from which many clients were referred. One of the F.A.S. workers said, somewhat despairingly, that the centre seemed to be used as a 'place of last resort', especially concerning housing and marital problems. This we observed to be true of all the F.A.C.s in high-need areas and to be caused largely by the widespread lack of sufficient services to which referrals could be made.

The comparison of the incidence of marital problems with the data on frequency of visits to the centre by clients raises some questions. It must be assumed that for the majority of clients presenting marital

problems one or two visits to the centre and, in a few cases, one or two
talks with the social worker in their own homes, could not have brought
about a satisfactory solution. In some cases simple advice or one or two
prolonged talks may have been sufficient, and some clients will have been
referred to other agencies. But, as the figures in the next paragraph show,
this would not have accounted for all of the 143 cases of marital problems.
In other cases, the presented marital problem may have been diagnosed
as a 'cover' for other, more easily and quickly dealt with matters such as
debts, illness, the need for legal advice, etc.

Referrals to other agencies
The family advice centre made 146 referrals to other agencies during
the eighteen-month period. Any one client may have been referred to
more than one agency. The special relationship between the legal
advice centre and family advice centre is underlined by the fact that
the former heads the list of agencies to which clients were referred
(17 referrals). Eleven referrals were made to the children's department
and 11 to the welfare department. The majority of referrals, 77 out of
the total of 146, went to local authority and central government
departments.

Use of workers' time
The two social workers in the family advice centre completed time
sheets for a period of twelve months. The total working hours for both
workers came to 1746. The largest proportion of worker's time was
used in contact with other agencies (481). The next largest block of
time was used for formal contact with clients (397 working hours);
180 hours were spent making home visits. One of the workers spent
49 hours in 'informal group contact' when she helped organise and
maintain a play scheme on the G.L.C. estate opposite the settlement.
It is, however, doubtful whether this was regarded as part of the F.A.S.
work, or rather as one of the services provided by the settlement house
as part of its community service approach.

A family advice centre in a detached setting; the 'D' project, 1 February 1968 to 31 July 1969

The area served by the family advice centre
The 'D' project family advice centre is situated in a city area which
some years ago had achieved notoriety as a 'red-light district', frequented
by seamen from the nearby docks. In recent years, however, redevelopment has significantly changed the character of the area. When the

family advice centre opened, the neighbourhood consisted of several new local authority housing estates and some small privately owned housing scheduled for demolition.

Accommodation in the local authority housing estates was largely allocated to local residents, regarded as 'respectable working-class', who had been on the waiting list of the housing department for a considerable length of time. There are relatively few immigrants in this area, compared with other parts of the borough, but there are some Pakistanis and a small Maltese community.

The setting
The family advice centre occupied two rooms of a former town hall. During the period of research, another room was allocated to the centre. The 'official' impression of the town hall was reinforced by the presence of the maintenance section of the borough housing department and the rent assessment panel on the premises.

Staffing, administration and supervision
The staff directly involved in the family advice services study was as follows:

one full-time F.A.S. worker;
a part-time F.A.S. worker who resigned her post on 30 April 1968;
an F.A.S. worker, appointed 27 May 1968, who worked at the centre for four days a week and continued her child care duties in the department on the remaining day of her working week;
a clerical assistant, provided by the children's department on two half-days a week;
a clerical assistant, added to the staff on 14 April 1968;
an ancillary worker, seconded to the F.A.C. for one half-day a week from March to September 1968;
an ancillary worker, seconded to the F.A.C. for two and a half days a week from 1 January 1969.

The two F.A.S. workers who staffed the centre during the study period had the following work experience and qualifications: One held a Bachelor of Commerce degree and a post-graduate diploma in social work. He worked as an accountant, labourer, docker, cook and probation officer before his F.A.S. appointment. The other held an M.A. degree in psychology and philosophy and the Home Office letter of Recognition in Child Care. She had working experience in teaching and child care.

During the period of research, the assistant children's officer was responsible for supervision and consultation and met the F.A.S. staff once a week at the centre. The research staff attended these meetings every week for the first eight months of the study and thereafter fortnightly. To ensure that the two adjacent children's department sectors would continue to be involved in the F.A.C., a consultative committee was set up to meet once a month for the first ten months of the project and every three months thereafter. This committee consisted of the children's officer, the assistant children's officer, the two senior child care officers, the two family advice service workers, the ancillary worker and the National Bureau's research staff.

Financing[1]
The authority for setting up the 'D' project family advice centre was provided under Section 1 of the Children and Young Persons' Act 1963. The total cost of the operation during the research period was £6300. This figure includes salaries for two F.A.S. workers, part-time supervisor, ancillary worker and clerical assistant.

Publicity
A letter, signed by the children's officer was sent to all former clients of a family advice centre in a nearby neighbourhood which had been closed in May 1967. There are indications that the children's department did not explore all the available possibilities of publicising and explaining the family advice service to the inhabitants and to all the other statutory and voluntary agencies and other professionals in the area.

DATA AND COMMENTS
Number of contacts with clients
'Contact' as used below means any relationship between the F.A.S. workers and members of the community which involves one or several of the categories of advice, guidance and assistance, liaison, mediation and referral.

Families	316
Children, 0–12 incl.	259
Teenagers, 13–19 incl.	41
Young adults, 20–29 incl.	131
Adults, 30–49 incl.	231
Adults, 50–65	19
Old people, 65 and over	9
Adults, age not established	6

1 Information provided by the children's department.

Thus, the workers were in contact with 696 individuals of all ages during the eighteen-month period of research. All but 19 of these were members of the 316 families. If the 19 individuals who appeared to have no family connections are added, a total of 335 'clients' were in contact with the F.A.S. workers.

The large proportion of young people (300 out of a total of 696 individuals came from the 0–19 age group) underlines the child-focused character of the service. At the same time, the significant number of adults of all ages indicates that the range of clients served may be somewhat wider than that of the children's department. Also, the range and variety of groups and individuals served by the community work aspects of the family advice service was undoubtedly wider.

Frequency of visits to the F.A.C.
The total number of 1118 visits represents an average of about 62 visits per month. This is an impressive number if we bear in mind that, in addition to this, the two F.A.S. workers dealt with home visits, telephone calls and correspondence, allocated a significant proportion of their working time to contact with other agencies, recording, other administrative work, supervision, consultation and a wide range of community work.

Sources of referral
The large number of self-referrals and referrals by friends, neighbours and relatives, 202 out of a total of 335 clients, confirms the marked success of the centre in establishing its image as an easily accessible, confidence-inspiring service. The 59 referrals by health visitors em-phasises the close links with the health clinic situated in the immediate vicinity. Several sources of referrals (tenants' associations, ancillary worker, a pre-school playgroup, voluntary playleader, a nearby Methodist Church) show how the advice, guidance and assistance and the community work aspects of the service complemented each other.

Types of presented problems
Requests for help totalling 569 and covering a range of 47 different, though often related and sometimes overlapping problem areas, were received and dealt with by the F.A.S. workers during the eighteen-month period of research. There was a relatively small number of problems which can be said to fall clearly within the category of child care, but most of the listed categories of presented problems can be related to the prevention of a wide range of social problems which directly affect the well-being of children. One-fifth of the total number of

presented problems (119) was related to housing difficulties: 57 of these were cases of inadequate accommodation; 25 were cases of homelessness or potential homelessness. Financial difficulties were presented as the problem in 71 cases. The 18 teenage problems, 18 applications for playgroup places and 12 cases of lack of play facilities show the need for facilities in these areas. There were also 15 requests for legal advice.

Referrals to other persons or agencies by the F.A.C.
A total of 349 referrals, slightly more than one referral per client, were made. The relatively high number of referrals to the children's department reflects the close ties between the family advice centre and the department. Other referrals were related to the preponderance of certain 'presented problems', such as housing and financial difficulties. Some referrals, for instance the 15 referrals to the pre-school playgroup, are a further indication of the complementary relationship between the advice, guidance and assistance and the community work of the service. The 16 referrals to local firms of solicitors, and to a barrister and solicitor offering their services voluntarily, have relevance to the development of a neighbourhood legal advice service.

General contact with other agencies
The wide range of agency contacts—meetings or communications with certain agencies initiated by the family advice service worker regarding a specific client—matches the range of problems that clients brought to the centre. Thus, it can be concluded that the 'D' project centre demonstrated clearly that this type of service not only attracts people who need help in areas of their social situation, but also functions effectively as a source of relevant contacts with other agencies as a mediator between these agencies and people who need help, advice and information. The F.A.S. workers also met with members of other agencies to discuss matters that had no immediate reference to particular clients: meetings with local agencies to examine the ways of working together in the community and with agencies outside the locality who shared interests with the F.A.C.

Use of worker's time
Time sheets were maintained by the F.A.S. staff in accordance with time-use categories specified by the research team. Though the figures can only be regarded as approximations, they indicate that most of the staff's time was spent in formal contact with clients in the office. We do, however, know that a substantial number of casual contacts

with a wide range of people during community work activities remained
unrecorded.

The family advice centre and the community
The family advice centre added to the variety of F.A.S. functions
by offering a range of services to the community, and made some
important strides towards combining the advice, guidance and assistance functions with community work. The F.A.S. workers acted
as consultants and resource persons to the tenants' associations, an
adventure playground, a play project, a housing estate, a parents'
group and a pre-school play group. The initiative taken by the centre
in introducing a neighbourhood legal advice service is especially noteworthy because it grew out of the recognition of specific community
needs. Throughout this work, the F.A.S. workers gave priority to
the development of self-help capacities and indigenous potentialities
in the community. They took special care not to use their influence,
skills and knowledge in any way that could deprive the community
from drawing upon their own resources and from gaining the necessary
experience.

2 The action-research study of three detached family advice centres

A family advice centre in a loosely defined area of 'mixed' housing; the 'E' project, 1 September 1967 to 15 October 1969

The area served by the family advice centre

The target area was selected because of its geographical distance from the children's department. As little was known about the neighbourhood it was hoped that the family advice centre would eventually provide more detailed information about the needs and characteristics of the population of this area, which consisted of a cluster of small streets facing the centre on the opposite side of a main road.

The area contained large, semi-detached, early Victorian terraced three-storey houses, many owned by private landlords, a few owner-occupied. The inhabitants included a long established working-class population, some middle-class families and West Indian and other immigrant families.

Small industrial premises, such as clothing factories, garages and a foundry, were tucked in among houses at the end of the streets. Directly opposite the centre, in a row of assorted shop premises, was a large café owned by a Greek Cypriot, nearby on the corner a pub, on the opposite corner a bank, further along the road a pawn shop. An infant welfare centre was nearby. A general practitioner had his flat and his surgery in the immediate vicinity and three general practitioners had clients in the target area. Infant and junior schools were located nearby, two secondary schools some distance away and a pre-school play group was accommodated in a nearby church hall.

The setting

The family advice centre was accommodated in a three-storey terraced Georgian house. The building, set back from the pavement by a small untidy garden, contained a basement, two ground floor rooms

divided by large double doors. Upstairs the large front room overlooked the street and at the back a small room with an old cooker
and stone sink served as a kitchen. There was a toilet under the stairs
by the back door. On the first floor the front room was designated as
reception and waiting room, and the other room served as the F.A.C.
office. The rooms on the second floor and in the basement were later
used as a club room. The top storey attic rooms were boarded up as
unsafe.

Staffing, administration and supervision
A child care officer was appointed as full-time F.A.S. worker shortly
before the opening of the centre.

He had previously worked as a coal miner and in the building,
engineering and shipbuilding industries. He worked as family case
worker, responsible for case work supervision and training, with
family service units, and as child care officer. He attended courses
in social administration, social and liberal studies, held the Home
Office Letter of Recognition in Child Care, and a diploma of the
Institute of Group Analysis.

A sociology student worked as a part-time playground leader in
June and July 1968. He was appointed full-time youth worker in July,
but resigned in August.

Mr J. was appointed as full-time youth worker in August 1968.
He held a National Diploma in Design from Carlisle Art School, and
a teaching diploma. He had worked as a painter and sculptor, freelance
designer and photographer.

Miss L., a twenty-seven-year-old former youth centre worker,
had a degree in history and had worked as an administrator at the
Friends International Centre. She was appointed full-time youth
worker in October 1968 but resigned after one month because the
pressure of the work and the unstructured setting were too demanding.

Mrs C. was appointed part-time playgroup leader in November
1968. She had lived in the area for many years and knew it thoroughly.
She worked previously with a mother and children group at the
Family Services Unit. Mrs C. had also managed a small sweet shop
and had worked as assistant to the headmistress in a primary school.
Skilled in arts and crafts activities and drama, she had written articles
and was in the process of publishing a book.

Mr H. was appointed part-time assistant family advice worker
in June 1969. He had been employed in the engineering and building
trade, and also had a long standing interest in jazz and folk music.
He had been an area organiser for Oxfam and attended social work

courses, gaining some practical experience through a fieldwork placement with the Family Service Unit. He was employed as a child care officer before he joined the staff of the family advice centre.

A part-time clerical assistant was seconded to the centre from the children's department staff for two hours per day in October 1967. This assignment did not meet the needs of the centre adequately, she resigned in August 1968, and the centre remained without a clerical assistant for about two months. Another part-time clerical assistant was appointed in October 1968 for fifteen hours per week. The following April her hours were increased to full-time and she was able to participate more fully in the work of the centre.

A cleaner was appointed for two hours a day in October 1967. She left in October 1968 and was replaced by a former client of the centre in November 1968.

Mr R., the senior child care officer responsible for the children's department sector, was appointed as liaison officer to the family advice centre. He resigned in February 1968 and Miss J., the senior child care officer who succeeded him, assumed the task of supervising the centre. Supervision meetings, attended by all F.A.S., the supervisor and the research staff, took place once every two weeks. In addition to this the F.A.S. worker met with the supervisor once every week.

Financing[1]

The children's department cited an expenditure of £15,917 for the 'E' project family advice centre from its inception in September 1967 and including estimated expenditure to 31 March 1970. These figures gave an approximate average expenditure of £525 per month, or a total of £12,600 for the two-year study period. About one-third of this sum may have been used for rent and repairs. Two-thirds of the remaining sum was used to pay the salaries of the staff.

In addition to the money provided by the children's department, the 'E' project Playground Management Committee raised a total of £1120 from various sources. This money was used for repairs, petty cash for club activities, a record player, a film camera, football equipment, reimbursement for stolen cash and other incidental expenses, as well as for the following salaries:

part-time salary for Mr J. for three weeks in August 1968 and for a five-month period between September 1968 and February 1969;
full-time salary for Miss L. for one month in November 1968;

part-time salary for Mrs C. for a six-month period between November 1968 and May 1969;
payments for twelve evening work sessions by Mr G., a West Indian Youth Worker.

£1 was donated by a local grocer for the adventure playground. In August 1969 a group of teenagers raised £8 10s. in a jumble sale for football team equipment and expenses.

Publicity
Prior to the opening of the centre in August 1967 the children's officer notified the chief officers of all statutory agencies of the intention to open a family advice centre and explained the purpose of the centre. During the first weeks following the opening of the centre, the F.A.S. worker contacted a number of statutory and voluntary agencies and discussed the goals and functions of the centre. A leaflet stating the times of opening, address and telephone number of the centre was distributed to each house in the area by the worker in October.

DATA AND COMMENTS
The data presented below cover the two-year period of study and the clients listed here are those persons of all ages who have been in contact with the centre with regard to advice, guidance and assistance. They do *not* include the large number of children and teenagers who benefited from other services provided by the centre.

Number of contacts with clients
'Contact' with clients as used below means any relationship between the F.A.S. workers and members of the community which involves one or several of the categories of advice, guidance and assistance, liaison, mediation and referral.

Families	69
Children, 0–12 incl.	29
Teenagers, 13–19 incl.	36
Young adults, 20–29 incl.	15
Adults, 30–49 incl.	42
Adults, 50–65 incl.	5
Old people, 65 and over	7

Thus, the worker was in contact with 134 individuals of all ages during the two-year period of research. All but 2 of these were members of the 69 families. Two individuals appeared to have no family connections and therefore defining the family as a 'client' and adding the two individuals, a total of 71 clients were in contact with the F.A.S. worker.

Sources of referral
Of the 71 clients who came to the family advice centre, 36 referred themselves, of these 10 were members of the youth clubs, 2 clients each were referred by neighbours, friends, another F.A.S. client, a health visitor, a general practitioner, a social welfare officer and the headmistress of a local infants school. (The latter also referred three schoolchildren to the adventure playground.)

Other agencies who referred clients to the centre included a local shopkeeper, a garage mechanic, a medical social worker and the youth worker. The children's department referred one client to the centre and three to the club and adventure playground. The family service unit and the court officer each formally referred two club members to the centre.

Of the total of 71 clients 25 came from inside and 42 from outside the target area. Of the latter, 3 clients lived outside the borough, the addresses of 3 were not known and 1 had no fixed address.

Types of presented problems
A total of 100 requests for help covering a range of 28 different, though related and sometimes overlapping problem areas was received and dealt with by the F.A.S. worker. Any one family or individual may have asked for help with one or several problem situations.

Teenage problems ranked highest in number with 16 requests, and 5 or more clients came to the family advice centre with the following problems: matrimonial difficulties, housing, children at risk, conflict with neighbours, legal advice, adjustment problems for immigrants and day care for children under five. Single problems presented by 7 clients included tracing a relative and receiving anonymous letters.

Referrals to other persons or agencies
A total of 49 referrals to other persons or agencies was made by the family advice worker. One or more clients were referred to the children's department, local infant welfare centre, mental health section of the health department, housing department and solicitors.

General contact with other agencies
Agencies in general contact with the worker, but to whom no referrals had been made, numbered 81. These contacts included discussions with schools, playgroups and the youth service with regard to the adventure playground and clubs, as well as with voluntary services,

local councillors and a wide range of social workers with whom meetings
were held concerning the work of the centre.

Use of worker's time
Time-sheets were maintained by the worker from October 1967 to
February 1968. The majority of his time during these first four months
was spent in contact with other agencies, either making general contact, making referrals or accepting referrals from other agencies.
Almost as much time was categorised as 'miscellaneous'. This included
a wide range of technical and administrative matters, a child care case
left over from the worker's duties as a child care officer before the
start of the project, and one afternoon a week attending a group dynamics
course.

The family advice centre and the community
Initially the worker spent a great deal of time contacting other agencies
in the area and explaining the functions of the new service. The need
for community services for old people and for pre-school children
were mentioned by many agencies, and the possibility of organising
a playgroup was followed up by the family advice centre, though without success, during the first six-month period. The provision of a
room in the centre for a group of West Indian teenagers to use as a
clubroom one evening each week was the first service to be given in
response to group need. The F.A.S. worker's own initiative led to the
opening of an adventure playground on vacant land behind the centre.
The demand for indoor club activities by the children and teenagers
who came to the playground led to the renting of a vacant house adjacent
to the centre for use as a club house. The F.A.S. worker and the youth
workers acted as consultants to the playground management committee.
A mother and children's group was held one day a week by child care
officers and the playgroup leader after the family advice centre had
moved to new premises towards the end of the study period. Free legal
advice sessions were also started at the new centre, and were held for
one evening a week to serve the growing number of clients in need of
this service.

A family advice centre in a redevelopment area; the 'F' project, 9 September 1968 to 9 September 1969

The area served by the family advice centre
The area selected was a lower-class housing district near the centre of a
city. The neighbourhood's back-to-back, three-storey, red-brick

terraced houses were built in the 1870s and were originally occupied by tenants of private landlords. The paved backyards, or small gardens, shared by three to eight households, are accessible to the street by narrow alleys between the houses. The traditional working-class pattern of large families, dependent for existence on the small tool-making and metal industries in the adjacent area remained unaltered until the housing department purchased large sections of the housing stock at the beginning of this century and the character of the area gradually began to change.

During the twenty years following the Second World War the housing shortage grew to be a cause of anxiety in the city. In 1959 there seemed to be little prospect of reducing the waiting list of 30,000 families. Areas within the inner ring of the city were designated slum-clearance areas and the 'F' project area was scheduled for demolition between 1967 and 1969 as part of the city's rebuilding programme. The existing houses, now almost a hundred years old, almost 90 per cent of them without bathrooms or hot water, had only outside sanitation and only a few had adequate damp courses. They were designated by the medical officer of health as unfit for habitation.

Many families applied for rehousing to other areas of the city or moved away of their own accord, and consequently accommodation was left free for the rehousing of other families who were 'temporarily' accommodated in these 'patched-up' houses within the slum clearance areas. The families rehoused in the area within the past ten years were those who were not considered by the housing department to have a sufficiently strong claim to warrant the allocation of new council house accommodation.

The population of the area according to the 1966 10 per cent census was a little over 2000. In September 1968, when the twelve-month study of the family advice centres started, the population included a few long established families and a few coloured immigrants (West Indian, Indian and Pakistani). The majority of the inhabitants were families rehoused temporarily by the housing department, their incomes low and their needs many and various.

Almost a year after the opening of the family advice centre the worker and the parents' association initiated a series of interviews with forty people from families in the neighbourhood, carried out by university students. While the material gathered cannot be regarded as conclusive, some of it may serve to illustrate the problems existing in the area. Twenty of the interviewed families had lived in the area less than six years, ten had lived there for more than twenty-five years. Almost everyone questioned felt that the area had deteriorated greatly during the past years. This, they said, was due to an influx of multi-problem families, bad housing conditions (not one of the families interviewed lived in a house with a bathroom), fear for safety of children, break-up of the old community, an increase in violence and a high percentage of unemployment. Most of the husbands were employed as unskilled workers. Thirteen families had never gone away for a holiday, ten said they went away for one day each year and ten said that they took a week or fortnight's holiday every year, but of these three families said they would not take their holiday this year because they were afraid to leave their homes unoccupied.

Ten families barely managed to exist on their income but could not save money for emergencies, eight families said they were able to save small amounts. Twenty families could specify instances in which they had no money to buy food for their children. All parents stressed the lack of play facilities in the area and many found it impossible to obtain nursery school placements for their children. The children of five families had been victims of traffic accidents, twice in the case of one of the families.

By the time the family advice centre opened the initial phase of slum clearance had begun. Some houses, some small shops and factories were already empty and boarded up, and feelings of anxiety about rehousing prospects were added to the tensions already prevalent among the families in the neighbourhood.

The setting

The family advice centre was accommodated in one of the terraced houses. The front door opened to the street into the reception cum waiting room linked by a doorway to the family advice worker's office, beyond which was a small scullery with a sink and cold tap, looking onto the backyard where there was an outside lavatory. In March 1969 two additional upstairs rooms, accessible by a steep wooden stair leading from the office, were made available for use as interviewing and storage rooms at the worker's request. Renovations and repairs were undertaken by the housing department and the homes section of the children's department. That same month a large shop in premises at the corner of the street was acquired by the centre to be used as a community arts and crafts centre.

Staffing, administration and supervision

Mr R. was appointed family advice service worker by the children's department and attached to the staff of the west area office. Born and educated in South Africa, Mr R. served in the army during the

Second World War and, after his return to South Africa, became secretary to an ex-serviceman's association in Port Elizabeth. He was instrumental in the building of two blocks of flats for ex-servicemen and served as full-time secretary for the Trades and Labour Council for one year. He was responsible for the founding of the Eastern Provinces Distressed Areas Council and Welfare Organisation in Port Elizabeth, and took a leading part in the wide range of voluntary community work carried out by this organisation. As a result of his work with African and 'coloured' communities, he was imprisoned after the state of emergency (Sharpeville) regulation in 1959 without charge or trial. While in South Africa Mr R. worked in commerce; after his arrival in England he worked as a child care officer. He attended a two-year child care course.

One month after the opening of the centre, a clerical assistant, Mrs C., was appointed for four hours a day from 10.00 a.m. to 2.00 p.m.; as the volume of work increased she was requested to work an extra hour each day from February 1969 onwards. It must be noted that her role was not limited to secretarial work; she frequently assisted clients with simple advice, helped with telephone calls, occasionally made home visits to clients and assisted members of the self-help sub-committee with their work in the community. The mother of three children, Mrs C. was brought up in the area adjacent to the family advice centre and knew the neighbourhood well. She was trained as a secretary and had previously worked in business and industry.

Mrs A. mother of three young children and living two doors away from the centre, was appointed domestic help on 14 October 1968. Having lived in the neighbourhood all her life, she too was well acquainted with the area and took a keen and active interest in the work of the centre.

During the year of study the centre employed a number of people for a variety of tasks. Four indigenous workers were employed from August 1969 onwards as 'community helpers' and 'children's attendants'. Three of the women lived in the neighbourhood and all were mothers of several children. All four had initially become involved in the activities of the parents' association and the self-help sub-committee and had done voluntary work for the centre. These workers were paid for four hours per day by the children's department. The student son of a local vicar worked voluntarily at the arts centre in the summer holidays and in September was employed by the children's department as a temporary worker. One adult and several teenagers, all living in the target area, did occasional part-time repair work and other odd jobs for the centre. These workers were paid partly by the children's department and partly from arts centre funds raised by the parents' association.

Mr W., a senior child care officer (later assistant area officer), was assigned as supervisor and liaison officer to the centre. The deputy children's officer, assumed overall responsibility. The F.A.S. worker met with the research team and the supervisor for consultation and supervision sessions once a fortnight and had alternate fortnightly meetings with the area office supervisor.

The centre was open all day, every day, and the times of opening were posted on the front door. Each day was spent seeing clients who called at the centre, making home visits, contacting other agencies and recording the work. In addition, the front room was made available for use by the children as an art room three afternoons a week from 3.30 to 5.30 p.m., under the supervision of the F.A.S. worker and one or two mothers, until the opening of the arts centre in the corner shop. On one afternoon a week the old people's group met, and on Friday evenings parents' association meetings were held at the centre.

Financing
The 'F' project family advice centre was financed by the children's department from the rate fund within the Children and Young Person's Act 1963. Expenditure covered by the children's department amounted to approximately £3400.[1] This sum included costs due solely to research requirements.

In addition to the above sum, £400 was raised by application for grants and contributions from private funds and charitable organisations and through the fund-raising activities of the parents' association. In some cases the needs of the centre were supplemented by gifts of equipment and materials. Expenditures met by private funds included electricity and repairs for the arts centre, part payment to British Waterways for a canal narrow boat, payments to helpers at the arts centre and small grants to families.

Publicity
Prior to the opening of the centre a letter was sent to chief officers of the departments of health, education, housing and welfare. The letter announced the proposed opening of the centre and described its purpose and functions.

DATA AND COMMENTS
The data presented opposite cover the one-year period of the research project, 9 September 1968 to 8 September 1969.

[1] Information provided by the children's department.

Number of clients in contact with the centre
'Contact' as used below means any relationship between the family advice service worker and members of the community which involves one or several of the categories and advice, guidance, assistance, liaison/mediation and referral.

Families	166
Children, 0–12	154
Teenagers, 13–19	40
Young adults, 20–29	47
Adults, 30–49	90
Adults, 50–65	26
Old people, 65–80	15
Old people, 80 and over	6

During the twelve-month period of research, the family advice worker was in touch with 378 individuals of all ages: all but 8 of these individuals were members of the 166 families.

Defining the family as a 'client' and adding the individuals with no apparent family connections, the family advice service worker was in touch with 174 clients during the period of research; 16 of the client families were in contact with the children's department *before* the opening of the F.A.C.

The relatively large proportion of children (154) indicates that the focus on services to children was preserved in the community-based setting of the family advice centre. It should be remembered that a considerably larger number of children benefited from the services provided, as the data presented here do *not* include the community work aspects of the family advice service.

The significant proportion of teenagers (40) should also be noted. Mainly due to staff limitations, work with adolescents remained marginal. There is no doubt that a far greater number of youngsters in this age group needed the service and would have been 'reached' if a youth worker had been available. The fact that the number of families served increased from 16 (served by the children's department area office) before, to 166 after the opening of the family advice centre, also has some important implications. This seems to confirm the widely held view that the conventional statutory services do not 'reach' all those in need of help. Furthermore, the figures indicate that the detached F.A.S. worker may provide a satisfactory and economical solution to the problems of an unmanageable influx of clients resulting from a concerted effort to 'reach the unreached'.

Finally, the wide distribution of age groups among the clients confirms the view that the type of service offered by the detached, community-based family advice centre regards the community as the client unit and can, therefore, not restrict the service to families with children.

Distribution of clients

The geographical distribution of the 174 clients showed that 138 clients lived inside the target area; of these approximately 70 per cent lived in the street where the F.A.C. was situated or on the main road and bus route which ran through the area; 33 were from outside the area and about half this group lived in the area adjacent to the target area where the housing and living conditions were similar. These clients came to the family advice centre towards the latter part of the twelve-month period after some of the client families had already been rehoused in the area. The rest of the clients from outside the target area were scattered some distance from the centre; they had either been rehoused from the centre's target area or had friends or relatives living in the area. Three clients had no fixed address.

Frequency of contacts

Out of the total number of 174 clients, 167 clients had 312 formal contacts with the F.A.S. worker over a period of one year; 6 formal contacts of 1 client were spaced over a three-month period; 7 formal contacts of 1 client were spaced over a seven-month period.

Of the above listed clients 78 families were rehoused and moved from the area during the one year period. Of these 78 families 9 had formal contact with the worker after their departure from the neighbourhood. At a Christmas party held at the centre in December 1969, all the families with young children who had been rehoused were invited; 29 of these families with 96 children attended the party.

Sources of referral

Sixty-seven per cent of the clients referred themselves to the centre, and a further 20 per cent were referred by a relative, friend, neighbour, or member of the parents' association. Three clients were referred by the children's department, 2 by health visitors, and 2 by councillors; 1 client each was referred by each of the following: welfare department, education welfare office, public health inspector, building works inspector, the old people's visiting service—the council of social service, a member of the social survey team, a local shopkeeper and a landlady.

In the first three-month period of the study 61 clients were referred or referred themselves to the centre, 29 in the second, 37 in the third and 47 in the fourth three-month period.

Types of presented problems

During the period of research the family advice worker received and dealt with 270 requests for help covering a range of 30 different though often related and sometimes overlapping problem areas.

As all the families were being rehoused from the area prior to, but in many cases during, demolition of all housing in the area, it can be said that *all* families had some problem with rehousing. The 54 clients who specifically sought help with this problem had particular anxieties, the predominant concern was the need to know the dates when they would be rehoused; other problems concerned the health of members of the family, the size of the family and the need to be rehoused quickly because of conflict with neighbours. Problems with rent, rates or fuel arrears numbered 32; non-support by fathers 17— this problem overlapped with 'husband in gaol' in 5 cases. Illness in the family ranked fourth with 16 requests; 15 client families had problems with inadequate sanitary conditions, blocked drains and lavatories, rising sewage in the backyards, and damp throughout the houses making some rooms unusable, causing plaster to fall off the walls and food to rot. Other problems concerning 7 or more clients included accidents, conflict with neighbours, old age, employment, financial problems, teenage problems and the need for second-hand clothes or furniture.

Referral to other persons or agencies

The number of problems referred to other agencies by the family advice centre totalled 138. In many cases one client was referred to a number of different agencies.

The incidence of referrals reflects that of the different presented problems. Referrals with regard to housing problems headed the list with 56 referrals, followed by referrals concerning financial difficulties and health problems: 20 clients problems were referred to the department of health and social security, 6 to the health department, 3 to hospitals, 6 to the children's department and 5 to the welfare department, 16 referrals were made to the gas and electricity boards, others included referrals made to the Salvation Army, youth employment officer, solicitors, general practitioners, a local housing trust and the R.S.P.C.A.

General contact with other persons or agencies

Requests for information and/or co-operation regarding a specific client initiated by the F.A.S. worker, and discussions initiated by the agency or the F.A.S. worker were recorded as 'general contact'. The family advice worker established contact with 53 agencies, professions and interested persons; among these were the following local authority departments: children's, housing, education, public health and welfare. Contact with voluntary organisations included Child Poverty Action Group, and the Family Service Unit.

Contact was also made with 21 agencies which involved *no* referrals of client problems. The family advice worker met monthly with local social workers, teachers, clergy and councillors to discuss matters of importance in the community. Other contacts included a meeting with the chairman of British Waterways Board with regard to purchasing a canal narrow boat for the arts centre, discussions with students and social workers on their visits to the family advice centre, and talks by the F.A.S. worker about the centre at schools and colleges.

Use of worker's time
The pressure and constant variety of the work process made it difficult for the worker to maintain exact records and as a result not all the working hours were recorded on the time sheets which were maintained for the first five-month period. The figures indicated that a significant proportion of formal and informal group contacts reflected the important role of meetings and group discussions at the centre and the demands on the worker's time were considerable.

The F.A.C. and the community
The encouragement of community group activities by the worker started within a month of the opening of the centre. First to form was the parents' association and its activities were carried out by three subcommittees: the self-help subcommittee, which was formed to assist families in special need, a working party to assist fatherless families and old people with their domestic repairs, and a management committee to supervise and operate the arts and crafts centre. These specific community needs were defined and responded to by the sixty or more adults directly involved, in consultation with the F.A.S. worker.

A family advice centre on a council estate; the 'G' project, 18 July 1967 to 31 July 1969

The area served by the family advice centre
The selection of the 'G' estate as the area in which the family advice centre was to be situated was made by the children's department in

consultation with the housing department. The estate was regarded by the two departments as a 'high need, multi-problem' community. There were 139 families living on the estate, and there was a certain amount of turnover during the course of each year. The 139 flats are built on four sides facing each other over a concrete courtyard. There are 31 five-roomed flats, 99 four-roomed flats, 1 two-roomed flat and 8 one-roomed flats.

In March 1967, 43 of the families were on the active case files of the children's department and an additional 12 families had been brought to the attention of the department by local schools. At the end of the financial year 1965/66, 51 tenants were in arrears with their rent not counting those owing one week or less.[1]

The people of the estate were regarded as 'working-class'. Some of them were said to maintain good standards, but many were thought to be inadequate families of the type unofficially classified as 'bad tenants' and 'rent delinquents'.

Children's and housing department staff familiar with the estate made the following observations: The families on the top floors of the estate feel more isolated than the rest and there appears to be some degree of social distance between them and the lower floors. The women seem to be the dominant element whenever there is trouble, while the men tend to remain uninvolved. There is a certain amount of friction between different groups and cliques. There is some teenage delinquency, and many of the younger children remain unsupervised for much of the day. Hostility and distrust towards agencies representing 'authority' is pronounced. There are vestiges of a tradition of mutual aid in times of crisis, especially with regard to young children and old people. A tenants' association which had been fairly active some years ago has become defunct for all practical purposes although it still exists in name.

Immediately before the opening of the family advice centre, the F.A.S. worker organised a programme of visits to other agencies in the borough to introduce herself and the family advice service. A deputy chief nursing officer described the estate as being 'full of problem families'. The principal medical officer saw the estate as 'a dumping ground for families with special problems who have been chucked there because they needed rehousing', and spoke of the lack of playing space and the severe difficulties of mothers with subnormal children and children with behaviour problems. The principal mental health social worker said that the estate was a place to which many of her patients had been rehoused and from which they were waiting to be rehoused again.

---

[1] Statement in a survey of the estate conducted by the housing department in 1966.

The principal social worker in the welfare department said that the problems that the family advice centre would encounter would be 'major and multiple—in fact, they will be a right shower'. Officials of the housing department described the estate in some detail. It was built in 1939 'for the relief of overcrowding' and was respectable and sought after, but from the late 1940s it became known as 'Dartmoor' by the introduction of so-called 'problem families' there. This was not a deliberately planned policy, but families not normally (i.e. via the waiting list) eligible for rehousing but referred from other departments had by an 'unwritten tradition' tended to be 'shoved into the estate'. The housing welfare officer described the estate as '139 families: 139 of them wanting transfers'.

The setting
On 18 July 1967 the family advice service worker moved in to a small one-room brick bungalow in the centre of the courtyard. Formerly the rent office, this was to be the family advice centre until October 1968 when the housing department made available a three-roomed ground floor flat on the estate to be used as the family advice centre.

Staffing, administration and supervision
Mrs D. was assigned as full-time F.A.S. worker. She held a diploma in sociology, a diploma in social studies, and had probation service training. She had nursing experience, and had worked with the Child Welfare Society in Orlando Township, Johannesburg, where she organised a 'Place of Safety' for non-European children, a children's home and a day nursery. She was also responsible for the training of African staff. She was organising secretary of the Institute of Race Relations (Cape Western Region) in South Africa where she helped to set up and run evening classes and health clinics for Africans. Between 1956 and 1961 Mrs D. worked in Southern Arabia. Here she gave help to the Aden Children's Society and worked in liaison with welfare and probation officers. Upon her return to England she worked as a probation officer and as child care officer. In the course of her work as a child care officer, she was assigned to the welfare department Part III accommodation, and helped initiate a peripatetic housemother scheme. She was founder member of a housing trust set up to provide housing for unsupported mothers and their children.

An assistant child care officer participated in the preliminary explorations preceding the opening of the centre. She was to be appointed as F.A.S. assistant, but left the department during the summer of 1967 to attend a social work course. An untrained worker was appointed F.A.S. assistant in October 1967. He worked part-time (20 hours a week) and resigned his post in August 1968. No further appointments were made.

Clerical and typing help were not provided on a regular basis until towards the end of the project when twelve hours a week of typing help were made available.

A young Dutch lawyer on a British Council scholarship to gain experience in the British social services was assigned to the family advice centre for two months at the beginning of 1969. Scheduled to work at the centre one day a week, her interest in the work led her to give some additional time to the project.

The senior child care officer responsible for the sector which included the estate, acted as supervisor to the family advice service worker in consultation with the senior research officer. Supervision meetings attended by the research staff were held in the sector offices once a week. In addition, the senior child care officer met with the family advice service worker as the need arose and at the worker's request.

A consultative committee was formed at the start of the project. Representatives from the following agencies took part: the children's department, the health department, the housing department, and the welfare department. Representatives from a university research unit (who were doing research in the borough), the Council of Social Service, the Youth Service and the estate's Tenants' Association attended some of these meetings. All meetings were chaired by the children's officer or his deputy and were attended by the F.A.S. staff, the senior child care officer/supervisor and the research staff. The consultative committee initially met once a month, but after the first three months started to meet once every two months.

Financing[1]
The family advice service was given a special allocation in the budget of the children's department and all costs including salaries, rent of the premises, maintenance, and administrative costs were met from this. The total cost of operation of the family advice service for the two year period came to £4840.

Publicity
It was not necessary to publicise the family advice centre to the community because of its location in the middle of the courtyard of the estate. A small notice was pinned to the door of the centre giving the times of opening. In the first two weeks of the centre, the family advice

[1] Information provided by the children's department.

service worker made contact with 21 families including 18 mothers, 3 fathers and 17 children. She also met 2 elderly people.

During the two weeks before the opening of the centre, the family advice service worker made a series of visits to other agencies in the borough to inform them of the family advice centre.

DATA AND COMMENTS
Number of contacts with clients
'Contact' as used below means any relationship between the F.A.S. worker and members of the community which involves one or several of the categories of advice, guidance, and assistance, liaison, mediation and referral.

Families	143
Children, 0–12	173
Teenagers, 13–19	54
Young adults, 20–29	55
Adults, 30–49	104
Adults, 50–65	29
Old people, 65 and over	34

Thus, the worker was in contact with 449 individuals of all ages. All but 18 of these were members of the 143 families. Of the 143 families 30 lived outside the estate. If we regard each family as one client unit and add to this the 18 individuals without known family connections, we arrive at the total of 161 clients in contact with the family advice centre during the two years. Even if we deduct the 30 clients who lived outside the estate, it appears that the family advice centre had established contact, usually involving some form of helping process, with one or several of the tenants of nearly every flat on the estate. This is, however, due to a certain amount of turnover during the two years. In fact, there were 26 families on the estate who did not use the services offered by the centre at all. These 26 families were mainly middle-aged couples with grown-up children. On average they lived in better conditions and had somewhat better incomes than most of the other tenants. Most of them had moved into the estate shortly after it was built. Their standards and aspirations were higher than those of the other tenants and they tended to hold themselves aloof from the rest of the community.

As far as could be ascertained, all clients came to the centre of their own accord or were advised to seek the help of the centre by friends and neighbours.

Frequency of contacts

Due to pressure of work and the priority given to descriptive process recording for research purposes detailed data on the frequency of contacts with each client are not available. Contacts with clients involved simple advice, guidance and various forms of assistance. Frequency of contacts with clients ranged from sporadic meetings over the entire study period in which simple advice, information and/or immediate assistance was provided, to sustained series of meetings in which a guidance process took place. In a number of cases the F.A.S. worker met with a family or an individual client once or twice a week for periods ranging from six months to a year. In a few cases clients visited the centre almost every single day for the entire two year period. Based on an analysis of the process records we arrived at a figure of 1135 meetings between worker and client over the two years, or an average of slightly over 60 meetings a month. These meetings occupied anything from five minutes to two hours of the worker's time and took place in the family advice centre, the client's home, or the courtyard of the estate. These figures do not include group contacts in which the worker met with a number of clients together to discuss common problems or community matters, nor do they include informal meetings in which the worker exchanged casual remarks with members of the community.

Types of presented problems

A total of 433 requests for help, covering a range of 36 different though often related and sometimes overlapping problem areas, were received and dealt with by the F.A.S. worker over the two years. Of these 68 were for help with housing problems and more than half of these were requests for rehousing out of the estate; 23 requests for help with removals were received during the last few months. Insanitary living conditions were the problem in 16 cases. Financial difficulties brought 38 requests for help with general financial problems, 32 for help with arrears and 24 concerned with social security payments. Conflict with neighbours (36), teenage problems (21), and lack of play facilities (20), were also recorded.

Any one family or any one individual may have asked the worker's help with one or several different problem situations. In many cases the initially presented problem led to the identification of other problem situations.

Referrals to other persons or agencies

A total number of 353 referrals to 85 different agencies or persons were made during the two-year period, an average of over 2 referrals

3

per client. The incidence of referrals reflects that of presented problems to a marked degree. The housing department tops the list with 47 referrals, followed by the department of health and social security (43), the children's department (37), and the health department (33). The range and number of voluntary agencies, professionals not connected with any social service agency and private persons to which problems were referred is noteworthy and shows the resourcefulness of the worker in identifying and making use of sources of help outside the statutory system and, in many cases, in the immediate area of the estate.

General contact with other agencies
The F.A.S. worker had general contact with 28 different agencies, bringing the number of agencies, professionals and private persons with whom the family advice centre was in contact during the two years to a total of 113. This confirms our view of the importance of the liaison, mediation and referral functions of the family advice centre.

Use of worker's time
For a six-month period from 1 August 1967 to 31 January 1968, the F.A.S. worker maintained a time log according to a set of categories provided by the research team. A substantial part of the F.A.S. worker's time was spent in formal contacts with clients and home visits, and, as could be expected from the wide range of agency contacts, the worker spent a great proportion of her time in contacts with other agencies. Because of the demands of research, a significant amount of time was spent in recording. Indeed, the research benefited greatly from the very full descriptive recording of the F.A.S. worker. The informal image of the centre is shown by the large proportion of time spent in informal contacts with clients and informal group contacts. The percentages of time spent on these various activities were as follows: 29 per cent on recording; 22 per cent on contact with other agencies; 22 per cent on formal contacts with clients and home visits; 11 per cent on informal contacts with clients and informal group contacts.

The family advice centre and the community
The community activities stemmed from the problems presented to the family advice centre by members of the community. As has already been shown, the major problem confronting people was related to the housing situation. The F.A.S. worker helped to initiate community action with regard to housing problems and rehousing procedures. She

acted as a resource person to the tenants' association, provided, or attempted to provide, services for the community's children and teenagers and stimulated interested, better understanding and mutual aid with regard to the estate's elderly tenants and immigrant families.

Concluding remarks to Chapters 1 and 2

The preceding pages will have shown that we were not able to obtain data on the work process of every one of the seven family advice centres with the same consistency and degree of detail. This was mainly due to such factors as difficulties encountered by F.A.S. staff in some of the centres in maintaining records, or the special characteristics which differentiated several of the centres (The 'A', 'B' and 'E' projects) from the others. This 'imbalance' of factual data makes it somewhat difficult to draw valid comparative conclusions. Such comparisons are, however, possible if we restrict them to the four family advice centres which provided the most easily comparable sets of data. These were the 'C', 'D', 'F' and 'G' projects. In the following pages we shall, therefore, present some comparative data which may serve to summarise the first two chapters of the report.

Sources of referral
The most significant comparison with regard to sources of referral seems to be that between the figures for self-referrals, referrals by friends, relatives and neighbours, and referrals by other agencies. These data are shown below in percentages of the total number of referrals for each centre.

Project	Self-referrals (%)	Referrals by friends, etc. (%)	Referrals by other agencies (%)
'C'	31	7	62
'D'	33	27	40
'F'	67	24	9
'G'	100	—	—

The figures for the four family advice centres seem to show that the incidence of self-referrals and referrals by friends, relatives and neighbours rises in direct relation to the proximity of the client community to the family advice centre. The figures for the 'C' project are relatively high, because the settlement house in which the centre was located was well known as a source of help in the area. The 'D' project family advice centre achieved a marked success in establishing its image in a fairly large area, as evidenced by the high percentages of self-referrals and referrals by friends, relatives and neighbours. The 'F' project centre served a fairly cohesive population group living in the immediate vicinity of the centre and, as a result, most of the centre's clients availed themselves of its services of their own accord or because someone in the community advised them to do so. (We include referrals by the parents' association in the referrals by friends, relatives and neighbours.) In the case of the 'G' project centre, the family advice service was located literally on the doorstep or in sight of the courtyard windows of almost all its clients. It is not surprising to see that all the centre's clients used its services by direct personal contact, without intermediaries. On the other hand, it should be pointed out that the two centres which served a wider area, and whose clients were not clustered closely around their offices, provided a wide range of other agencies with an address to which they could refer clients. The two more definitely 'community-based' centres did not provide this service to other agencies to the same extent. These two centres did, however, co-operate with a range of other agencies in providing services for the latter's clients.

Presented problems

The classification of presented problems caused some difficulties, mainly because in the majority of cases a presented problem was either the pretext for discussing some other more serious troubles, or else it was 'the tip of the iceberg' beneath which spread a conglomeration of other matters that needed attention. The data given below are therefore somewhat misleading. We selected the most frequently presented problems, those concerning housing and financial difficulties, for comparison. However, our observations showed that in the 'F' and 'G' projects where rehousing was the main cause of concern, housing problems were at the core of, or connected with, a far greater number of cases than shown here.

Under 'housing problems' we included the following: rehousing—inadequate sanitary conditions—homelessness—removal problems.

Under 'financial problems' we included: rent, rates or fuel arrears—other financial problems—social security benefits problems—debts (other than rent, rates and fuel arrears)—budgeting problems—income tax problems—rent rebate queries—rent tribunal applications.

Project	Housing problems (%)	Financial problems (%)	Other presented problems (%)
'C'	19	12	69
'D'	21	26	53
'F'	27	18	55
'G'	25	22	53

While housing and financial problems ranked highest in the lists of presented problems recorded in the three detached family advice centres, the 'C' project centre listed the greatest number of presented problems, 34 per cent of the total, under 'matrimonial conflict'. This stands in marked contrast to the figures for this problem category provided by the other centres. It can be inferred that the specialised training in marriage guidance of the two F.A.S. workers had something to do with the high percentage of clients who sought help with marriage difficulties.

Finally, it may be of some interest to take a glance at some comparative figures relating to the number of clients served by the centres, the number of requests for help presented by these clients and the number of referrals to other agencies.

Project	Period of study (months)	F.A.S. workers	No. of clients	No. of requests	Referrals to other agencies
'C'	18	2	293	424	146
'D'	18	2	335	569	349
'F'	12	1	174	270	138
'G'	24	1	143	433	353

In the case of the three detached centres it must be remembered that the considerable amount of community work carried out is *not* reflected in the above figures.

The observation of seven family advice centres, representing four different types of F.A.S. settings, did *not* provide conclusive information about all four of the different types of settings we set out to investigate. While we were provided with valid examples of detached family advice centres and of a family advice centre operated by a voluntary agency, financed by the children's department, the centre selected to represent a setting in which two statutory services co-operated in the provision of a family advice service, did not provide conclusive information. The centre which was intended to represent an F.A.S. setting functioning as an integrated unit of a children's department area office encountered planning and staffing difficulties and could *not* be regarded as providing a valid example of an F.A.S. setting of this type. The 'E' project centre, while providing a very valuable range of services for children and youth, did not make full use of its potential in offering advice, guidance and assistance and community work. While this centre made a very significant contribution by pioneering imaginative and daring experimental services for children and youth in the statutory services, it could *not* be regarded as a valid example of a detached, community oriented family advice centre of its type. Nevertheless, all seven centres provided us with a wide range of pertinent information, and all contributed to our understanding of the goals and concepts, the functions and the methods of the family advice service approach.

3 Goals and concepts

In the Children and Young Persons' Act 1963, Section 1, Part I, it is stated that: 'It shall be the duty of every local authority to make available such advice, guidance and assistance as may promote the welfare of children by diminishing the need to receive children into, or keep them in care . . . or to bring children before a juvenile court.'

The exploratory study carried out between 1 April and 30 September 1966 was able to elaborate on the goals of the family advice service. The report on the study listed the following objectives (Leissner, 1967, pp. 18–19):

(*a*) the prevention of family breakdown;
(*b*) the prevention of children coming into care and/or appearing before a juvenile court;
(*c*) the provision of an easily accessible source of help for all those in need of advice, guidance and assistance;
(*d*) the earliest possible detection of families and children at risk;
(*e*) the initiation and improvement of field-level co-ordination between the staff of relevant statutory and voluntary agencies;
(*f*) the provision of a community work service.

The experience we gained in the subsequent study of seven family advice centres enabled us to formulate a number of additional objectives:

(*g*) the identification of community problems and the meeting of community needs;
(*h*) the fostering of better relations and understanding of each other's potentialities, resources, problems and limitations between the recipients of social services and the services themselves;
(*i*) the bringing about of changes, modifications and innovations in the policies and methods of existing services through interpretation of the community's needs, resources and limitations;

(*j*) the identification, recruiting, employment and on-the-job training of suitable members of the community ('indigeneous workers') to participate in the work of the family advice service.

In comparison, it may be of some interest to cite the goals of six neighbourhood service centres in five American cities (Boston, Syracuse, New Haven, New York and Washington D.C.) set up with the support of the United States Office of Juvenile Delinquency and Youth Development. A report on these centres states:

The neighborhood service centers in these projects do not conform to one simple description. They differ considerably in their stated goals, their structures and their actual operations. Despite these differences, they share certain general purposes and features which are summarized in the following working definition of a neighborhood center:

1. It provides information and referral services to assist people to use established agencies. In some instances, a reaching-out operation brings 'information and referral' to the neighborhood resident in his home or on the street.
2. The center acts as advocate to protect a client's interests and rights with respect to another agency. It may also seek a change in another agency's procedure or policy that will become a precedent for similar situations.
3. Concrete services are provided directly to individuals and families. The list varies from project to project and may include one or more of these: legal aid, day care for children, employment counseling, training and job placement, casework, assistance in homemaking, recreation and group work, health services, and help with housing problems.
4. The center organizes and mobilizes groups for collective action on behalf of the residents of the neighborhood. This ranges from facilitating two-way communication between residents and local institutions to assisting groups to confront and challenge those who make decisions affecting conditions and services in their neighborhood. (Perlman and Jones, 1967, p. 1.)

Prevention

The dominant concept, the alpha and omega of the whole range of goals of the family advice service, is that of prevention. This all-inclusive term is perhaps most relevantly defined as a range of activities and processes

to help families through periods of temporary strain and crisis: to improve and, where necessary, supplement the quality of care and education of children considered 'vulnerable' or to be 'at risk', and to prevent the disintegration of the family unit. The keynote must be early and constructive intervention (Kellmer Pringle 1965b, p. 133).[1]

1 For further discussion of prevention see Kellmer Pringle (1965a), *Deprivation and Education*.

While the term is a commonsense one and self-explanatory, the measurement of prevention, the quantitative assessment of *how much* of *what* has been prevented, is notoriously difficult, if not impossible. We cannot state categorically that so-and-so-many families have been prevented from disintegrating through the intervention of the F.A.S. worker, that x number of children have been prevented from coming into care or appearing before the courts as delinquents. Moreover, the boundaries between preventive work, which occurs *before* malfunction becomes manifest, and rehabilitation, which takes place *after* a problem situation has arisen or has reached the crisis stage, are often impossible to define.

More often than not what is described as preventive work actually takes place when rehabilitation has already become necessary. As a recent discussion of current social work practice points out: 'Children's departments and other social agencies undertake preventive casework mainly with individuals who have already shown to the social service some warning sign such as truancy or rent arrears' (Holman and Radford, 1969, p. 1312).

Methods and techniques of prevention have also posed some problems of definition:

The schools talk about 'bad homes', youth workers speak vaguely of so-called 'un-clubbables'; social caseworkers refer to a rough category of 'problem families'; local government officers fulminate over 'unsatisfactory tenants'. Many of these often identical households produce a crop of deprived and/or delinquent children. These are par excellence the kinds of families which those responsible for the Children's Act of 1963 must have had constantly in mind. The Act stressed the necessity of preventive work being undertaken on behalf of such families, but, significantly, offered hardly any clues as to how this should be attempted (Mays, 1965, p. 76).

It can be said that, while prevention as a concept and as a goal has become widely accepted, there is reason to believe that the degree to which the preventive approach necessitates profound changes in attitudes and greatly increased flexibility has not yet been fully realised. As an experienced social worker, who has at one time supervised a detached family advice centre, pointed out: 'The child care service has been invested with a preventive function in which no defined relationship is possible, where the worker has to structure the relationship in the shape that he sees as most useful to the client' (Rae-Price, 1967, p. 414). It is perhaps one of the most valuable contributions of the family advice service in its range of different settings, that it allowed for experimentation with various approaches to prevention, and that it afforded a wealth of opportunities to gain experience in preventive work and to observe the dynamics and processes of the preventive approach in almost all types of social work practice.

The Seebohm Report (para. 427) emphasises 'the prevention of social distress' as the foremost task of an overall preventive approach. The Report distinguishes between 'specific prevention', which it defines as 'action directed at helping families or individuals who are recognised to be at particular risk, whose problems are likely to generate further and more profound difficulties' (para. 435), and 'general prevention', to be achieved 'by those universal services or policies which together reduce social and economic risk throughout the community' (para. 440).

By describing and discussing the work of the family advice centres we hope to show the many different ways in which the family advice service can and does function as a means of 'specific prevention' for individuals and families, for parents and children, teenagers and elderly people, for people who come to the centres with their many different personal problems, and for communities whose very existence constitutes social problems. We hope to show that the family advice service can make a special contribution to the task of prevention by helping to identify needs and priorities and by helping other social services to take a critical look at established attitudes and methods which fail to meet the needs. We hope to show that the family advice service can serve as one of the means of bridging the gaps between the consumers and the distributors of social services; that it can help the former to articulate their needs more clearly and to make their demands more forcefully; that, in doing so, it can make a significant contribution to the continuous evaluation and adaptation of existing policies in order to make these more truly preventive in their methods and objectives.

Accessibility, and reaching the hard-to-reach

Accessibility of a family advice service is determined by two factors. One of these, the most obvious, is the geographic location and the physical setting of the centre. The second factor is a somewhat more subtle, psychological one, largely related to the staff's ability to create an image which inspires confidence, stimulates interest in their work and offers a comfortable reassuring atmosphere which enables even the most distraught or uncommunicative individuals to establish good relations with the workers and to express themselves freely and honestly.

Accessibility must be regarded as the *raison d'être* of the family advice service. Obviously, there is no need to add yet another service which is geographically and socially distant from the people who need it most, the use of which demands considerable know-how and strong motivation, and to which many people only come under the pressure of severe crisis. Accessibility is one of the most effective ways of bringing about early prevention by making it easy and comfortable for people to seek advice and help with their problems before the crisis stage has been reached. The degree to which a service can be deemed accessible can be measured, at least partly, by its success or failure in reaching those individuals, families and groups which have been found to be 'hard-to-reach' by several or all of the existing services.

Because the question as to whether a family advice service is able to reach a significant number of 'unreached' or 'hard-to-reach' individuals, families and population groups is clearly related to the concept of physical and psychological accessibility, we have to examine the issues involved in some more detail.

The admittedly awkward and inexact term 'unreachable' can be defined in two ways. The first is that of the individuals, families or groups who have become inaccessible to the social services and institutions because of their own geographic and/or social isolation, the latter being manifested by such attitudes as distrust of those who seek to help, apathy with regard to social malfunctions, hostility towards all forms of outside intervention etc. On the other hand, these people may be inaccessible to the services because of the latter's own lack of resources, insufficient or not suitably trained staff, or attitudes and methods which are not geared to the needs and to the socio-economic and socio-cultural norms and traditions of the people whom the services seek to reach.

The second definition of 'unreachable' can be described as a situation in which a great number of statutory officers, social workers and other social service personnel are involved in often intensive and costly attempts to help certain individuals, families or groups, but their efforts remain largely ineffective. Here, too, the causes may be sought in the advanced deterioration of the social and psychological state of the clients, or in asocial or apathetic attitudes. The reason may also be identified as inadequate services, wrong methods, unsuitable attitudes and lack of co-ordination on the part of the helping agencies. The questions raised by an American writer and the answers he gives are relevant here:

Is it the client who is 'hard to reach' or is it the service? Are the non-participants truly 'drop-outs' or are they 'push-outs'? We were taught by hard and sad experience that to assume a priori that the case failure is always an instance of client pathology, incapacity and lack of motivation is to engage in modern day 'poor law' social analysis, or in what we think of as 'Social Darwinism' (Kahn, 1969, p. 5).

Quite often the client who is regarded as 'unreachable' or 'hard-to-reach' is in reality the client who seems 'incurable', who defies all efforts at rehabilitation. Every social work practitioner has, at one or another time experienced the feelings of helplessness and frustration, and sometimes of anger and resentment, engendered by this type of 'unreachable' client. The ensuing self-defeating situation is analysed and put into perspective in a recent article which deserves careful reading:

Because their own perspectives are likely to be so very different from those of most agencies, clients often see the kind of help they are offered as inappropriate to their immediate needs. Their inability to be self-sufficient leads to a perception of being dependent, and this dependency has a demoralising effect on their images. Dependency is often stigmatised, and one of the ways to evade the unpleasantness of being dependent is to avoid the getting of help at all. Families in trouble often hide away when they need help most.

The most important effect of this discrepancy in the perspective of both sides is that much help is offered these families in accordance with standards which they neither understand nor support. There are many examples of the way this discrepancy leads to incomprehension. The medical and psychiatric services and the complexity of their systems of referral, are often improperly understood. The securing of many forms of financial assistance can be a humiliating experience and sometimes deliberate rudeness is aimed at discouraging difficult or troublesome clients and making the pressures on the agency more manageable. The complex rules governing many applications for help often assume a level of sophistication that is unrealistic of many of the applicants. The need to provide supporting evidence of wages from employers for certain benefits means that the help applied for cannot be kept secret and one's own self-respect thereby maintained. The subjective and often unpredictable decisions of social workers make it difficult for some clients to know what the end result of seeking help will be. Caseworkers who withhold from the clients the nature of the diagnosis they have made may create anxiety in clients and often appear to be conspiratorial. For some families in distress all these factors combine to place their economic and material foundation completely at the mercy of those quite incomprehensible agencies. Thus, by virtue of their situation they tend to be more dependent than other groups on a larger number of organisations which are themselves unclear about the bases for their criteria, and very unpredictable in their decisions, and render the poor even more helpless by condescending or hostile attitudes, and explicit verbal communications, which imply the inferiority of the poor. This enforced dependency can be very destructive (Kemeny and Popplestone, 1970, p. 13).

The causative relationship between 'unreachability' and lack of communication between recipients and providers of services is clearly implied. Apart from the important factor of its own accessibility, it is in improving these communications through its mediation/liaison function that the family advice service makes its most significant contribution to 'reaching the unreached'.

The Seebohm Report stated:

Many of those submitting evidence stressed the difficulty which the public and members of other services found in approaching the local authority personal social services. People are often unclear about the pattern of services and uncertain about the division of responsibilities between them. Initially a person's true need (sometimes a matter for expert diagnosis) may not be clearly recognised; sometimes the person seeking help may be confused or inarticulate and unable to make plain what particular help he requires. In such circumstances it may be difficult for him to get straight to the right services and the delay and further referral this involves may be discouraging, particularly if the local offices of different services are a considerable distance apart. Furthermore members of the public are often diffident about approaching the services, either on their own behalf, or on behalf of relatives or acquaintances. They may doubt whether help is available or they may fear officials to be remote and bureaucratic (para. 83).

The experience of the seven family advice centres confirmed the findings of the Seebohm Report. Our observations also showed that the family advice service, especially in the detached community based settings, is able to bridge the accessibility gap between the client and the social work practitioner, as well as to make a significant contribution towards improving communications between the client and the social services and between the services themselves.

The earliest possible detection of problems

Early detection of social and personal malfunctions is logically related to prevention and must, therefore, be regarded as an essential F.A.S. function. 'Prevention . . . consists of *early discovery*, control, and elimination of conditions which *potentially* could hamper social functioning (Rapoport, 1961, p. 4). However, early detection, involving a certain amount of 'probing' and 'investigating' is also one of the statutory duties of the children's department and may, as such, come into conflict with the no-strings-attached quality of the family advice service. This was discussed in the report on the exploratory study.

That the issue of detection and probing poses problems for all social workers is indicated in a chapter in Anthony Forder's (1966) authoritative book on case work and social administration. This author points out that:

One of the aspects of the work of social caseworkers that gives concern to many people, and not least to students of social work, is the reluctance that they often evince to accept simple requests for help from clients at their face value. The implication is that social caseworkers use the authority of their position to make a client's need for a simple service the excuse for going into deeper aspects of the client's personal life against the latter's wishes (p. 58).

While Forder implies that, on the whole, the importance of this issue has been overstated, he goes on to say:

> One must recognize that it is often very difficult for social caseworkers to know how far in particular situations it is appropriate for them to go in exploring and helping clients with problems related to that with which they have originally asked for help. One limit is set by the clients themselves who have many ways of defending themselves against unwelcome intrusions, and of showing their resentment if the boundaries of propriety are exceeded. If the social caseworker is not sensitive to these, there will be a deterioration in the relationship which will make co-operation impossible (pp. 60–1).

What is most important, however, is that the client may defend himself or show his resentment by staying away, and by refusing to make any further use of the service. In the case of the statutory agency this may result in a simple closing of the file on the grounds of non-co-operation or lack of motivation, or else, in more serious cases, official pressure may be brought to bear to ensure the client's co-operation, if necessary under the threat of sanctions. The family advice service cannot react in this way. For this service the withdrawal of the client means a clear failure in achieving the goals of the service and it might be said that any action or attitude which runs counter to the principles of accessibility and no-strings-attached service is self-defeating and inappropriate. Mr Forder makes a further observation which F.A.S. workers, as other social workers, do well to bear in mind:

> There are occasions when clients are rendered particularly defenceless by the extremity of the crisis that has struck them, and they will pour out a great deal of material about themselves which they will afterwards regret having told. These occasions are not so common as might be thought, but social caseworkers do have to be on the look-out for them. They are easier to recognize in retrospect than at the time, because either the client misses the next appointment, or his attitude is quite different at the next meeting (p. 61).

So far we have spoken of the problems and the pitfalls of early detection with regard to the individual client and the client family. Our conclusion with regard to this kind of detection of problems and malfunctions is: (1) the earliest possible detection of malfunction is necessary and commendable as a first step to prevention but, (2) it should *not* take precedence over the worker's respect for the stated or implied wishes of the client and even the best-motivated probing should not be permitted to endanger the image of the family advice centre as an easily accessible place to which anyone can bring his problems and receive a 'no-strings-attached' confidential service. (3) The earliest possible detection of problems should and, as our observations show, *can* be expected to grow out of the relationship formed between F.A.S. worker and client, and occur as a result of the positive, confidence-inspiring image of the family advice centre in the area which it serves. We may add that the process of problem identification and detection of malfunctions often demands not only diagnostic skill, but also considerable tact. As Golan (1969) observed:

A quietly desperate applicant . . . clinging to shreds of denial and determined not to give way to panic, may successfully mask a true crisis. Or a usually adequate person, confronted with the unexpected inadequacy of his customary problem solving methods in a crisis, may withdraw in the face of the probing information gathering process of the intake interview. Moreover, a nonverbal client may be unable to describe his predicament adequately and be turned away before it is even investigated as a possible crisis (p. 389).

It was for the very reasons spelled out in the above passage, that it became a foremost rule of the family advice centres *not* to press a client to divulge information, and *never* to turn a client away.

There are, however, other forms and areas of detection. One of these is implied in an address by Frederick Seebohm in December 1968:

It was depressing for us to find, when we talked to people in general practice—doctors—how little they knew about the social services which were available; how few of them, in fact, ever referred for help to the social services, although they knew their clients needed them. In the case of one enquiry to which replies were received from general practitioners about their patients who needed some sort of social care, 81 per cent of the families reported had in fact not been referred or had not gone to the local authority, and were not even known by the local authority as being in need of care (Address to the Seebohm Report Study Conference, p. 7).

What holds true for general practitioners has been seen to be relevant to many other professionals, such as lawyers and clergymen, in contact with people who may need help. Here the F.A.S. worker's ability to establish relations with a wide range of professionals in other disciplines, and to make use of these relations in his mediation/liaison role, may provide an early identification of need or malfunction and may effect prompt and appropriate referrals.

But perhaps most important of all is the identification of needs and the detection of malfunctions which affect a whole community, whether these be lack of play space for children, lack of recreational facilities for adolescents, disinterest or outright discrimination of a statutory service with regard to a certain population group or area, or gaps in the existing services which leave certain categories of people without anyone to turn to for help.[1] Especially in the detached, community based family advice centre, this type of detection of malfunctions and inadequacies which may precipitate hardship becomes a very important function indeed.

The Seebohm Report pointed out that effective preventive work

is determined by our ability to recognise early those who are at particular risk. Again there is too little knowledge, although it is not impossible to identify some individuals and groups who are known to be specially vulnerable to social distress. They may be recognised by the environments in which they live (for example, new communities or dilapidated central urban areas); by individual behaviour or history (truants or ex-prisoners, for instance); or by the characteristic of their families (that they are, for example, fatherless or large). There are, furthermore, certain developmental stages at which many people are likely to be in greater need of help than usual (in adolescence, for instance, or during the early period of family formation). Particular critical events such as birth, retirement, serious illness or bereavement can also impose strain and create unfamiliar problems for an individual or family (para. 429).

[1] Soon after the termination of the family advice services study we had occasion to observe the case of a homeless elderly couple, both of them former patients in psychiatric hospitals and financially destitute, who did not seem to have a right to the services of any of the existing social welfare agencies. One of the statutory agencies which was approached on the couple's behalf stated that they could not help because the couple, whose most immediate problem was homelessness, had no permanent address. Emergency accommodation was offered by the local authority on the condition that the couple agreed to live apart. The two elderly people refused to be separated. The family advice centre found accommodation for them.

4 Functions and methods

Advice

Advice can be broadly defined as 'simple advice', consisting mainly of the imparting of straightforward information, explanation regarding the best ways of using this information, and the consequences which may result, e.g. what the client should expect to happen when he takes certain steps. (See also Leissner, 1969b, p. 120.)

We regard this type of advice as one of the key functions of the family advice service. It may take the form of answering a client's questions over the telephone, a five- or ten-minute conversation in the centre, an informal chat at a street corner on the way to an appointment or during a group activity in the community. 'Simple advice' can become one of the means to establish the centre's image as an easily accessible, 'no-strings-attached' preventive service, and may play an important role in establishing the centre's relationship with the community. On the other hand, the degree to which members of the centre's target population take advantage of the availability of this service depends largely upon the centre's initial success in making itself known to the community. While simple advice may be limited to the imparting of information, it is often extended to include explanation, interpretation and, quite frequently, a certain measure of reassurance and support.

The need for this type of service is confirmed by the experience in many areas of social work. A brief report on an advice centre in Edinburgh, for instance, states:

Looking at the problem from the point of view of the client . . . there is a danger of assuming that he or she is informed and understands the administrative structure of the Welfare State. Some people *are* very well informed but the average individual or family—especially if under stress—is more likely to be confused. Many people under stress lack the motivation to seek help and so it becomes doubly important that the means of achieving it are straightforward and simple (Short and McCulloch, 1968, p. 108).

This observation draws attention to the very important indication that the no-strings-attached availability and easy accessibility of simple advice may in itself serve to encourage people to seek help at the earliest possible stage, and motivate them to confront their problems and to take action to resolve them. This has important implications for preventive social work and for the search for effective methods of reaching the hard-to-reach.

The experience of the seven F.A.S. projects showed that the, by definition, unpretentious and straightforward 'simple advice' function must be regarded as the starting point for the entire range of F.A.S. functions, and as that aspect of the overall service which continues to provide a basis and point of reference for all other approaches and activities. In its simplest form, that of straightforward information, the advice function often provides people with an opportunity to have a closer look at the family advice centre and its staff without committing themselves. People may use a request for straightforward information to test the attitude and the competence of the F.A.S. worker before asking for help and advice in more complex matters. In the many instances in which simple advice is coupled with more detailed explanation and interpretation, it often becomes the first step in the guidance process and may necessitate various forms of assistance. Requests for advice frequently relate to the services of other social service agencies, and therefore may involve the mediation/liaison function of the family advice centre. If a pattern of requests for advice and information regarding specific services, the availability of resources and/or the rights of citizens, emerges, this may lead to community work which in turn may result in various forms of community action.

The key role of the advice function emerged only gradually during the study of the seven family advice centres. Because of the frequent merging of simple advice and information with assistance and guidance processes, the workers found it difficult to make clear distinctions between simple advice and other functions, and there was, consequently, a marked tendency not to record instances of simple advice and information. Although there is no doubt that in most centres, especially in the detached, community-based ones, simple advice played a major role and took up a significant proportion of the staff's time, this was not reflected in the categorised time-sheets filled in by the workers.

Our observations indicate that the number of clients who come to a family advice centre requesting advice and/or information may provide a measure of the accessibility of the centre both in the geographic and the psychological sense. The incidence of requests for simple advice and/or information was lowest in those family advice centres which were least involved with the community.

It is also important to note that in those centres in which clerical assistants had been appointed, the latter usually functioned as receptionists and often themselves answered simple straightforward requests for information.

The clients of the family advice centres asked for advice with regard to any conceivable subject or problem.

● A woman was sent to the centre by her husband to show the F.A.S. worker two boxes of chocolate cigarettes which one of her children had bought in a nearby shop. Five of the sweets were mouldy and the parents felt that something should be done about this, as a child might become ill by eating the chocolate. The worker took the matter up with the environmental health department and an inspector was sent to caution the shopkeeper. Another time a neighbour came to tell the worker that a bedridden elderly lady had told him that she wanted to send a telegram to a relative. He himself had never sent a telegram to anyone and did not know how to go about it. The F.A.S. worker went to see the old lady, obtained the necessary information from her and showed the helpful neighbour how to send the telegram.

● Mrs N, the young immigrant mother of a one-year-old child, separated from her husband, came to the family advice centre with a neighbour. Both lived side by side in basement flats in a privately owned building. Mrs N was concerned about the dampness of her flat, which she feared would affect the health of her baby, and was also worried because she was in arrears with her rent. The F.A.S. worker found out that Mrs N had agreed to rent the flat as furnished accommodation, although the landlord had provided only a few shoddy pieces of furniture. She paid £3 10s. a week rent and felt that this was an unfair amount. After discussing the situation with the public health inspector and with the valuer's department of the G.L.C., the F.A.S. worker referred Mrs N to the borough rent officer who arranged for a rent tribunal officer to visit the flat. Shortly after this the landlord received a letter from the rent officer stating that the rent had been reduced to £1 6s. and that this ruling applied retroactively to the beginning of the tenancy. At the same time the public health inspector visited the flat and assured Mrs N that he would order the landlord to make the necessary repairs to alleviate the dampness.

As already mentioned, simple advice and information was, in some cases, provided by the clerk receptionist. In the 'B' project centre, for instance, the clerk-receptionist reported the two following examples:

● A woman came into the office to ask for advice. She had recently been separated from her husband and wanted to do something that would occupy her and add some interest to her life. An informal chat brought out the fact that she had a number of spare rooms in her house. The clerk-receptionist suggested that she might like to take in lodgers, foster children, etc. After the woman had left, the clerk-receptionist gave the information to a child care officer who visited her home for further discussion.

● A young man came to the office and told the clerk-receptionist that he needed money and accommodation. Chatting with him the clerk-receptionist found out that he was on probation. She persuaded him to let her call his probation officer, then handed him the phone, and let him discuss his problems and make an appointment with the officer.

The important contribution a clerical assistant who fully regards herself as a member of the team can make is graphically illustrated by the following incident which occurred in the 'F' project centre.

● One morning, while the F.A.S. worker was out, Mrs K, a young mother of five children, came to the centre in a state of near-hysterical agitation. She told the clerical assistant that she had just hit a housing department officer who had visited her home for the seventh time. The housing officer had said that the kind of accommodation the Ks had requested could not be provided because of the family's short-term tenancy in their present home. Pressed by Mr K, the officer added that the Ks' flat was dirty, and that this was another reason why the housing department was reluctant to accede to their request. Mr K had become angry and said that the department was just looking for excuses to force the family to accept accommodation without an inside bathroom. Mrs K, already distraught because one of her children was in hospital at the time and a second child was ill at home, had attacked the officer and threatened to kill her.

Mrs K, obviously frightened of the consequences of her behaviour, asked the clerical assistant whether she could contact the building works inspector in whom she had a great deal of confidence. Unfortunately, the inspector was on leave, but his secretary put the clerical assistant in touch with the head of the housing visitor's section. This officer had already been informed of the incident. He was very concerned about the member of his staff who had been physically attacked and threatened, had no sympathy for Mrs K and said that she might be in a great deal of trouble because of her behaviour.

Mrs K's state of mind became steadily worse. She was sobbing uncontrollably and saying that she wished she were dead, and that there was no future for her and her children. The clerical assistant tried to calm her down. As the F.A.S. worker was not available, she called the supervising senior child care officer at the area office. He came to the centre shortly afterwards accompanied by the area officer. Between them they succeeded in calming Mrs K and she let her husband take her home. At Mrs K's request the two senior child care officers visited the Ks' home and reported that they considered it reasonably clean for an overcrowded flat accommodating two adults and five children.

Some time later Mrs K returned to the centre to thank the clerical assistant for 'pulling her out' of the state she had been in. There was some further discussion of the incident with the F.A.S. worker, and a member of the community self-help subcommittee accompanied Mrs K to the housing department where she was given the opportunity to explain her behaviour, and it was suggested to her that she write a letter of apology. During her interview at the housing department Mrs K was very upset and broke out in tears, but she said that she felt much better afterwards. She wrote the letter of apology at the centre.

Less than a week after this the K family were offered spacious new accommodation with an inside bathroom and a garden. Mr and Mrs K and their five children were all very happy and seemed much encouraged. Rather than postpone the move, Mr K did all necessary repair work in the new house himself. The centre's community home helper visited the Ks in their new home and reported that the house was clean and well kept and that the family were very proud of it. The family continued to visit the family advice centre. Some time later the F.A.S. worker referred the family to the children's department for assistance with an adoption problem.

In many instances a request for advice required immediate action to relieve a client's anxiety, and often such cases afforded the F.A.S. worker an opportunity to gain insight into the situation of a problem family.

● Mrs A came to the 'G' project centre one morning: 'You'll excuse me coming in but I want to discuss something personal with you. To tell you the truth—well, I might as well—I went over to that woman over the other side and asked her what sort you were. You can't tell your business to everybody and I wasn't sure if you were the sort of woman you could talk to. I'm in trouble with the children's department and out of my mind with worry. They might arrest my husband. The rent's in arrears and, what with one thing and another, I don't know which way to turn.' Mrs A produced a demand for £22 from the assessment section of the children's department which she owed from the time when her children were in care. 'To tell you the truth, my kids were in care when we hadn't a place to go. God forgive me. I deserted them. But my husband is a terribly funny sort of man. Sometimes he never speaks and you don't know how to take him.' In agreement with Mrs A the worker contacted the children's department. She telephoned the assessment section and established that the final demand was only a routine notice and that Mrs A would be given time to pay. The worker pointed out to the officer that the curt and somewhat threatening notice had caused anxiety to this family, and that a personal interview might be preferable in such cases. Mrs A was greatly relieved and asked the worker to go and see two of her friends who 'are often crying their hearts out'.

● The young mother of a one-year-old baby came to the 'D' project family advice centre at the suggestion of her health visitor. Mrs B's husband was in gaol awaiting trial and needed legal advice. A solicitor she contacted was not able to take the case and the probation officer had told her that he could not be in court on the day of the arraignment. Mrs B was also anxious about a number of hire purchase payments which were overdue. The F.A.S. worker helped Mrs B to obtain legal advice for her husband and to sort out her debts. A number of letters were written on her behalf. Four months later Mrs B returned to the centre to seek help. Her husband was now out of gaol, but the marriage had broken up after a series of violent quarrels in which the police had intervened and this situation had greatly upset her parents in whose flat she lived. She wanted to find a flat of her own and needed advice on how to obtain a separation order. The F.A.S. worker helped Mrs K to establish contact with the probation department and with a child care officer. When a flat became available, the worker assisted Mrs B to make the necessary arrangements with the gas and electricity boards and to obtain some additional money from the Department of Health and Social Security. Some time later the health visitor informed the F.A.S. worker that the young woman's situation was now satisfactory.

Sometimes the F.A.S. worker can do no more than help a harassed client to gain some perspective on his problems by talking about them to a sympathetic listener, and perhaps make certain that the appropriate agencies are aware of a problem situation:

● Mr O came to the 'C' project family advice centre and asked the worker to help him find temporary accommodation until he sorted out his affairs. He used to be a docker. He gave this up to take over a pub but this did not work out, either for the children or for Mr O himself, who found the responsibility too much. On his doctor's advice, he gave up the pub—this not only meant giving up his work, but also giving up the accommodation for him and his family. Mrs O enquired for help at the children's department, but eventually was able to find accommodation with friends in Kent. Mr O was separated from his family and staying with friends in Southwark. He had been to see the local housing department, but was told that he could not put his name on the housing list for another four years.

Mr O had capital to put towards the purchase of a house but could not secure a mortgage until he had a regular job. He had been to see the employment exchange and was offered a driving job for £18 per week. He would be able to start this when his driving licence came through. He was anxious to find temporary accommodation for himself and his family. His wife and children were living in a rather overcrowded situation—the friends they were staying with had three children of their own and could not put them up for many more weeks. Mr O was not hopeful about finding a flat locally, but the worker made some suggestions about where to look and urged him to continue his search. A few days later Mr O returned to the centre. He seemed in a better frame of mind. He now had a mortgage arranged and would know within three or four days if it was final. Within four to five weeks the family hoped to move into their own home. His wife was no longer worried as their friends said they would put them up until they moved. Mr O felt things were satisfactory and that there was no need for him to return to the F.A.S. He said he had been very depressed going to different local authority departments seeking help and advice and finding that no temporary accommodation or council mortgages were available. The worker told Mr O to return to the centre if there was any difficulty.

Four days later, Mr O returned. Negotiations for the purchase of the house had been proceeding without a hitch, but Mrs O was finding it difficult to cope in an overcrowded situation. Mr O asked if the worker could speak to his wife on the telephone and advise her who she should consult locally. The worker telephoned Mrs O who sounded a little harassed and eager to contact someone for advice. The worker gave her the telephone number of the local children's department, then telephoned the children's department and explained the situation. A child care officer promised to visit Mrs O to see if there was any need for help. Three weeks later the worker telephoned the children's department again. They had visited Mrs O and found the situation to be very troubled—Mrs O was very unstable and had continuous rows with her friends and her husband. She had suddenly 'upped and gone' to her mother's home with her children. The children's department were contacting the children's department where her mother lived to tell them about the situation.

Very often simple advice entailed some immediate practical assistance, as in the following cases:

● A young woman came to the centre and told the worker that her husband was ill. She wanted to contact the family doctor but hesitated to do so because her husband had not kept a previous appointment at the surgery. The F.A.S. worker telephoned the doctor for her. The latter was indeed annoyed about the patient's lack of co-operation, but he spoke to the young woman on the phone and arranged for her to collect a prescription at a local chemist. As the young woman felt anxious about leaving her husband alone, the F.A.S. worker picked up the tablets at the chemist and delivered them to her flat.

The ancillary worker brought Mrs M to the 'D' project family advice centre. Her seven-year-old son had been suspended from school three months before because of violent and disruptive behaviour. The boy, at home all day, caused distress to the entire family and his behaviour had deteriorated. Mrs M had not been able to get any information as to what would happen to the child's education. The F.A.S. worker made a written referral of the case to the Inner London Education Authority. The case was investigated. A home tutor was assigned immediately and arrangements were made to admit the boy to a residential school as soon as a vacancy became available.

● When demolition workers were pulling down houses in the area served by the 'F' project centre they noticed a vast crack in the side of the house at the end of the street. They notified the building works inspector who came to the family advice centre to inform the F.A.S. worker and to ask for his assistance, as the house was occupied. The F.A.S. worker asked Mrs S, a member of the self-help subcommittee, to accompany the inspector to see Mrs T, a seventy-year-old widow, the sole occupant of the building. Because of the obvious danger, the building works inspector and the F.A.S. worker communicated their concern to the housing department and requested that Mrs T be rehoused immediately. The following day the building works inspector called at the centre with keys and an offer of rehousing for Mrs T. He and Mrs S visited her again and explained the necessity for her to move to alternative accommodation. They took her to see the house which was offered and she accepted this. The F.A.S. worker contacted the electricity board asking them to connect the electricity, and Mrs S helped her move her belongings. This urgent rehousing problem was dealt with in one day.

While in many instances simple advice was offered in relatively brief interviews or even by telephone, this service was, especially in the detached, community-based family advice centres, quite often provided during informal chats outside the centre or during a community activity involving a group of people. There were occasions in the 'G' project when a woman would see the F.A.S. worker crossing the courtyard and yell her question from a second-floor window. Quite often the worker simply shouted her reply and the matter was settled there and then. Or else a client would corner the worker on the stairs when the latter was on her way to visit one of the flats. From time to time a client phoned the worker at home after working hours or at weekends. Usually this happened only in cases of great urgency and the privilege of having the F.A.S. worker's private telephone number was rarely abused. In the 'D' project centre the staff frequently met people they knew when they walked through the neighbourhood and, on such occasions, were sometimes asked for advice. There were also requests for advice before and after tenants' association meetings and other community and group activities in the area, and there were times when the worker helped someone to sort out a problem over a drink in the pub. Much the same situation prevailed in the 'F' project centre, where the F.A.S. worker responded to requests for simple advice and/or information at a street corner, outside the door of the centre, in the shop in which he bought his groceries, in the arts and crafts centre or after a meeting of one of the community committees. The 'E' project F.A.S. worker also had occasion to provide this informal on-the-spot service to clients over a cup of coffee in the café across the road, while supervising the activities in the adventure playground or during the meetings of the youth clubs. This informal on-the-spot availability of advice becomes especially important in high-need areas of the type which were served by the detached centres.

The on-the-spot availability of a wide range of authentic information and knowledge upon which people can draw, even the unsolicited intervention with a word of advice or caution: 'Listen, you can't do that. It'll get you in trouble'; or 'You're going about this the wrong way, let me tell you a better way'; or 'I can see that something's bothering you. Maybe I can help you if you tell me about it' became a valuable source of support and helped to ease tensions. Moreover, in many communities of this kind there is an abundance of rumours, wishful thinking, unwarranted fears and misinformation. The simple advice provided by the F.A.S. worker often consisted of a mere stating of the facts, thereby helping people to gain perspective on their own situation and to enable them to look at their needs, fears, wishes and problems more realistically.

As has already been pointed out the advice function was, more often than not, interwoven with many other F.A.S. functions. In the detached centres a request for advice concerning a problem often grew out of the community work context and, in turn, could lead to one or another form of community involvement.

• Mrs D, the energetic and usually cheerful mother of a large family, had helped the staff of the 'D' project centre to establish and equip a playground for the children of the estate on which she lived. Her own children, especially the three oldest ones, had participated eagerly in getting the playground ready and had, on occasions, led groups of other children to the centre to discuss the playground with the workers. In recent years Mrs D had found it increasingly difficult to cope with the needs of her aged parents who lived nearby. Mr and Mrs E were both in their seventies, Mr E had recently been in hospital for treatment of lumbago and sciatica, and his wife had become partially paralysed. The two old people found it very difficult to get about and were quite unable to communicate their needs to the relevant authorities. Mrs D talked about her parents and her own anxiety about them to fellow members of the estate's tenants' association who advised her to seek the help of the F.A.S. worker. After discussing the situation with Mrs D, and after visiting Mr and Mrs E at home, the F.A.S. worker entered into negotiations and discussions regarding the old couple with their doctor, their health visitor and the housing welfare officer of the G.L.C. who had promised to do someting about providing better accommodation over a year ago. The worker's objectives were to obtain a wheelchair for Mrs E and special handles for the bath tub which would enable them to bathe unassisted (for this purpose the couple had to be registered as 'handicapped' with the welfare department), and to obtain a suitable flat for them.

• The 'F' project F.A.S. worker was called one morning to a nearby street where Bill, nineteen years old, had been knocked down by a car. He had not suffered badly, but his ear was bleeding and the worker brought him, the driver and a witness to the family advice centre. There Bill was given first aid, and John, another teenage boy who had called in to see the worker, made coffee for everybody. One evening, a month later, Mrs L, Bill's mother, came into the centre when a group of children were drawing and painting. She told the worker that her youngest son, Ronny, had also had an accident, he had been knocked down by a car, in the same street as his brother, and had been taken to hospital. He was suffering from head injuries which Mrs L feared were serious. Mrs L used the telephone to call the hospital, and after that came to the centre frequently to use the phone and to talk to the worker. Two of her sons, Richard, 16, and Martin, 10, began to attend the arts centre when it opened. She came with Bill, the eldest boy, to the parents' association meeting fairly regularly, at first shy but later able to participate in group discussions.

At her request the F.A.S. worker wrote to the housing manager asking if he would consider the family for rehousing 'as Mrs L complains that her house, especially after this last accident, has many unhappy associations for her and her family'. As there were five sons in the family, the Ls needed a fairly large house or flat. Mrs L also sought advice about claiming insurance from the driver who had knocked down Ronny. The worker wrote to a firm of solicitors asking for advice on motor accident claims, and they returned a claim form for Mrs L to complete. The worker helped her with this as it requested a detailed account of the accident, the expenses she and her husband had incurred in visiting the hospital and an account of the money her husband had lost through being off work at the time. The solicitor recommended that Mrs L apply for legal aid.

Mrs L took a part-time cleaning job to supplement the family income. Her eldest son Bill had continual difficulty in finding and keeping jobs and the workers helped him several times to obtain employment. Throughout the year Mrs L was in continuous contact with the family advice centre. Her youngest son Ronny recovered from his accident; the legal system was slow in taking action and numerous letters passed between the solicitor and the F.A.S. worker on behalf of the L family.

Towards the end of the year a rehousing offer was made by the housing department and a member of the self-help committee helped Mrs L, who was at work, by taking her rent book to the housing department so that Mrs L could obtain the house keys. At first the clerk said the offer would have to be withdrawn as the rent book showed arrears of £6, but he was persuaded to hold the keys until Mrs L came next day with the rent arrears. The F.A.S. worker urged Mrs L to raise the rent money immediately and the keys for the new house were obtained.

After Mrs L had seen the house, she described it to the F.A.S. worker, crying with happiness, especially delighted because her family's new home was very spacious and had a garden.

In all the centres the first hesitant question: 'What do you think I should do . . . ?' often turned out to have been the first step in the helping process we have termed 'guidance', involving the client who has sought advice and the F.A.S. worker who seeks to respond to the client's needs, in a helping relationship in which both sides have to learn to work together towards practical and lasting solutions to problem situations. In quite a number of cases, however, the worker has to limit his expectations and accept the responsibility for long-term supportive guidance which, while unlikely to bring about any radical changes, will prevent further deterioration and may bring about improvements in at least some areas of social functioning.

● John, an eighteen-year-old who had left the home of his father and stepmother and was lodging with a family in the vicinity of the 'F' project centre, approached the F.A.S. worker soon after the centre had opened. He told the worker that he was unemployed; he had been to the labour exchange but was not willing to accept the jobs he was offered. The labour exchange official had written on his form 'he is unwilling to take work and so is unable to register'. The F.A.S. worker encouraged John to go to the centre almost every day and to help with any odd jobs of work which were necessary, such as making shelves, cleaning the back yard or the outside lavatory, or helping to decorate the downstairs rooms. To help John find work, the F.A.S. worker contacted the labour exchange and urged them to continue their efforts on John's behalf. The worker also contacted various employers in the area. Meanwhile he referred John to the Department of Health and Social Security for unemployment benefit. Eventually a factory job was found for him which he kept for some time.

John told the worker that he had been in the care of the children's department under a fit person order when in his teens. His mother had died when he was a child and his father had remarried. The F.A.S. worker consulted John's landlady who told him that John's father had prevented him from attending school and had insisted that John be taken into care. John had refused to go back to live with his father and stepmother, but his landlady stressed that he always expressed loyalty to his father. John's contact with the children's department had ceased when he was seventeen; the F.A.S. worker was not able to gain access to the children's department records. Throughout the year contact was maintained with John, if he did not call in at the centre for a while the F.A.S. worker wrote a short note to him and he came to have a chat.

Although John knew many of the groups of youths in the locality, he was always on the perimeter of their activities, rarely in the midst. For a time he was in touch with a group of youngsters who were sleeping rough in the empty houses. Whenever he lost or left a job he came to the centre to see the worker. When preparations were being made for opening the arts and crafts centre he helped with this, and the worker felt it would help John's flagging self-confidence and prevent him from establishing a habit of loafing about if he offered him regular paid employment as an odd-job man at the centre. Payment for John's work was made from a special grant provided by the children's department for this purpose. At times John showed no interest in the work whatsoever, other than receiving payment; at other times he was very willing to do anything to help. When the arts and crafts centre fund was established, payments for temporary work in the centre by members of the community were made from this fund.

The F.A.S. worker enabled John to improve his relationship with his father and eventually he went to live with his father and stepmother. The worker met John's parents on several occasions, when they came to the family advice centre to seek advice concerning housing problems.

● Mrs B came to the 'G' project centre to ask what she could do about a note someone had pushed through her letter-box. The note said that if her electricity arrears of about £10 were not paid immediately, the electricity would be turned off. She said that she had mentioned the debt to the housing welfare officer some time ago and he had told her to see the F.A.S. worker about it. The worker tried to contact the housing welfare officer, but he was not available. She then called the electricity board who agreed to delay action until they had heard from the housing welfare officer.

Mrs B stayed in touch with the family advice centre, and during the next few days the F.A.S. worker learned more about her circumstances: Mr B worked as a porter earning £11 per week. The Bs had four children. There was five-year-old Brian at a 'health school'. Sandra was ten, and there was a set of twelve-year-old boy and girl twins. The boy had been in an approved school and there was £30 owing to the children's department. Margaret, the other twin, had epileptic fits.

The Bs paid £1 9s 4d in rent per week. The housing welfare officer was sympathetic: 'They try their best, but always need special attention, special schools, special holidays. They just can't think out anything for themselves and seem to live by imitating others.' The F.A.S. worker felt that this family needed relief from the growing pressure of debts. She used her good relations with a private trust to obtain a grant of £5 which was given after a conversation with the worker and a brief descriptive statement in writing, without the need to fill out forms or lengthy investigation. The worker had a talk with Mr B, a small, pale man. When the worker apologised for questioning him about his income, he said: 'That's alright, we're used to telling people. Don't worry about that.' The worker wrote to the Mayor asking for help and received a cheque for £3 by return mail. The electricity arrears were now paid in full and the worker asked the electricity board to install a pre-payment meter in accordance with Mrs B's wishes.

Two weeks later Mrs B came to the centre to ask the F.A.S. worker to help her fill out a form concerning the change-over to a slot meter. On that occasion Mrs B mentioned that she was paying 8s a week to the children's department under a court order. The F.A.S. worker asked whether she could ask the department to reduce this sum, but Mrs B was afraid that the payment might be increased if she drew attention to herself. She said that her daughter would soon be sent to a special school because of her epileptic seizures.

Ten days later Mrs B was at the centre with another bill from the electricity board, this time for £3 19s 3d. The slot meter had not yet been installed. The F.A.S. worker had £1 11s 8d left over from the last fund-raising activity and helped Mrs B to write to the board, enclosing this amount and asking them to calibrate the slot meter upward to pay off the debt. Mrs B expressed her relief and her emotional stress in a gush of words: 'It's nice to be able to come to somewhere like this. People can help you. I don't believe that people should be ashamed of asking someone to help them. People are very cruel here. Just because my children go to the special school the other children call them "silly" and say they go to the "silly school". I tell people they might have children themselves that are not so bright. It could happen to anybody—that's what they don't understand.'

Some weeks later Mr C, one of the older tenants, had to go to hospital. He told the F.A.S. worker that he was worried about Mrs Y, an elderly lady who lived next door to him and who could not manage on her own. He had looked after her for some time, but now she would have no-one to come in and see that she was all right. The F.A.S. worker contacted the Good Neighbour Service of the health department and arranged for Mrs B to look after Mrs Y. For this service Mrs B received 10s a week. The F.A.S. worker helped Mrs B to fill out the necessary forms. The following week Mr C died in hospital. Mrs B and the F.A.S. worker broke the news to Mrs Y who was terribly upset and cried bitterly. This upset Mrs B who became angry with the old lady 'for carrying on so' and had to be reasoned with by the worker. Mrs B cleaned Mr C's flat and continued to look after Mrs Y. She complained to the worker that she had to do a lot of work and felt that she should get some more money. The F.A.S. worker contacted the health department to ask whether Mrs B's fees could be increased, but was told that this was not possible. A few days later the caretaker called the centre and said that Mrs E, an 84-year-old lady, had moved into one of the flats. It was a Friday and the geriatric service had no one available to send over. Mrs B agreed to visit Mrs E and look after her needs.

Mrs B continued to look after Mrs E until one of the other neighbours took over. Some weeks later Mrs B came to the centre to say that the welfare van had not arrived to take Mrs Y to her club and that this had happened on several occasions. The worker called the welfare department to make a complaint, but on later occasions Mrs B contacted the welfare department herself and took them to task. By now Mrs B was paid £2 per week for her work and an extra 10s for looking after Mrs Y on weekends. Whenever there were difficulties Mrs B came to the centre for support.

Nine months after Mrs B had first asked for some advice about her electricity bill, Mrs B saw the F.A.S. worker about a rent arrears bill which she said she did not believe she owed at all. The worker contacted the housing welfare officer, who said that the B family had been taken off his list of 'special cases' because they were doing so well. The F.A.S. worker attended to the rent arrears matter herself. The debt turned out to be valid and an arrangement for paying it off in instalments was made. Meanwhile Mrs Y had shown marked improvements since Mrs B had started to look after her.

In June Mrs B told the F.A.S. worker that she would be rehoused in an area close to her husband's place of work and was worried about what would become of Mrs Y. The worker, who had already been informed of the plan to rehouse Mrs B by the housing department, suggested that the department should be asked to rehouse Mrs Y in the same area, so that Mrs B could continue to look after her. Mrs B was pleased about this.

Towards the end of the year Mrs B resigned from the Good Neighbour Service. The F.A.S. worker thanked her warmly for her help which had resulted in a marked improvement in Mrs Y's state of health, but Mrs B was rather angry about the abrupt way in which the Good Neighbour organiser had accepted her resignation 'with never a word of thanks'. She was nearly in tears when she talked about it.

The reader will have noticed that the record presented above shows a number of gaps in the information available to the worker about the B family. We believe that this is characteristic of, and necessary for, the no-strings-attached approach of the advice function. The client was not asked to fill out any forms or provide any details about her family which were not relevant to the immediate request for help. The F.A.S.

worker did not carry out any investigation and did not engage in any prying. This has obvious drawbacks which are, however, outweighed by the advantages. These are mainly that the client enters a relationship which is free from the constraints and tensions of the 'official' approach. The client is shown that the family advice centre is a place where help is given unconditionally. The all too prevalent diffuse fears of ominous consequences of seeking help are dispelled. The relationship between worker and client becomes one of mutual trust in which the worker conveys to the client the fact that her main interest is to help, while the client learns that the help she is offered is not given on condition that her life and her feelings become 'an open book' and that if the worker does ask for information, this is done solely in the interest of more effective help, and that it is the client's own responsibility and decision to provide the worker with sufficient details to enable the latter to carry out her task.

Finally, it should be noted that the family advice centres provided advice either directly, in the form of information and interpretation, or indirectly, through initiating new and imaginative approaches to problems, to the field workers and the senior staff of a number of statutory and voluntary agencies in the area. This was often immersed in the network of formal contacts and informal relationships with colleagues and not identified as a specific function. Nevertheless, an important and useful service was provided in this manner, at times initiating and helping to maintain good working relationships with obvious implications for the F.A.S. worker's functions of liaison/mediation and co-ordination of services. The following example may serve to illustrate this aspect of the advice function:

● A health visitor discussed with the F.A.S. worker her concern about Mary, a five-year-old girl who seemed to be suffering greatly from a highly inadequate relationship with her mother. The health visitor had already referred Mary to a child psychiatrist, who felt that the child should not be received into care. Mary and her mother had been put on the waiting list of an out-patient child guidance clinic.

The F.A.S. worker contacted Mrs L, Mary's mother and, after discussion with the health visitor and the psychiatrist, referred the case to the children's department. On the worker's recommendation the children's department arranged for temporary day care for Mary at a local children's home. Some time later Mrs L and Mary began to attend treatment sessions at the clinic, and the F.A.S. worker introduced the clinic's social worker to the health visitor. The latter continued to provide support for Mrs L and Mary, while the F.A.S. worker remained in contact with the family, the child care officer assigned to the case and the health visitor, keeping informed of the progress of the situation and being available for any additional help needed.

Our observations showed that in a substantial number of cases social workers, statutory officers, various professionals and officials sought the advice of the family advice service staff with regard to specific difficulties or general problems which had arisen in their own work with their clients. Many of them acknowledged the fact that they had benefited from the F.A.S. workers' advice, gained better perspectives and new insights and had been helped to improve their relationships with the people they served. This was especially noticeable with regard to housing department officials, child care officers, health visitors, Department of Health and Social Security officials, police officers and teachers. It should, of course, be added that this process was usually reciprocal, and that the F.A.S. workers often benefited from the advice offered by colleagues in other fields.

The potentialities of the advice function for prevention have already been emphasized. It should also be pointed out that the on-the-spot availability of advice was frequently observed to provide opportunities for intervention in a crisis situation. In such cases the situation had passed the stage in which a crisis could have been prevented, but further deterioration could be halted. As a report on another type of advice centre stated:

Intervention and support during a period of crisis are important, especially since persons whose whole life situation is punctuated by periods of stress, which are onerous, are more willing to accept advice and help during an acute phase. Caplan[1] has pointed out that where the reaction to crisis is to evade it, ignore it or treat it unrealistically, the mechanism for coping with crises will progressively become so weakened that, eventually, the person or family becomes overburdened and unable to escape except by taking refuge in mental ill health or asocial behaviour (Short and McCulloch, 1968, p. 107).

Considerable diagnostic skill may be needed to recognise a crisis situation and to offer the appropriate help. Parad (1966) suggests that 'Crisis intervention may be most applicable for the very strong or the very weak, for those requiring only short periods of help, and for those not motivated for continuing service' (cited in Golan, 1969, p. 394). All this is highly relevant for the F.A.S. setting. Our observations showed that in all the centres the staff did, from time to time, recognise a crisis situation hidden behind a seemingly simple, or even trivial request for

[1] G. Caplan is the author of *An Approach to Community Mental Health, Prevention of Mental Disorders in Children* and *Principles of Preventive Psychiatry*.

4

advice or information. The degree to which clients can be 'reached' in such situations so that crisis intervention can take place, depends largely upon the accessibility and the image of the family advice centre. In the detached, community-based settings the informal relationships the workers established with people, even if the latter had not yet made any use of the service, and the workers' awareness of community patterns and dynamics was often decisive. Quite frequently the F.A.S. workers were alerted to the need for help in a crisis situation by neighbours, the caretaker, a colleague or official from another agency or even a bit of gossip overheard while having a cup of tea with a group of mothers or while supervising the play activities of a group of children.

The opportunities for offering easily accessible advice in times of acute crisis were most frequent in the detached, community-based settings. Perhaps it can be said that this availability of on-the-spot advice aimed at helping people to cope in emergencies and at arresting the self-defeating processes of evasion, deviant reactions and, finally, apathy, is the most valuable service provided by the family advice service in a high-need community.

Guidance

Guidance may mean being available for an occasional chat to help a troubled person to gain some insight and better perspective with regard to relatively minor problems. It may take the form of more structured short-term counselling aimed at 'working through' some difficulties or changing certain irrational attitudes. Guidance may also entail the process of enabling a client to understand the need for referral to more intensive, specialised treatment services, and to prepare the client for the referral (Leissner, 1969b, p. 120).

We used the term 'guidance' in the above sense. For all practical purposes 'guidance' can be regarded as similar to the familiar method of counselling described by Murray G. Ross (1955):

Counselling, whether conducted with an individual, with one or more family members, or with a group, has certain common features. As has been indicated, the overall goal of counselling is to help the individual enhance his capacity for satisfactory social functioning. One means of increasing such capacity is to help the person acquire information and knowledge that he can use in his day-to-day affairs. The counsellor, therefore, must be well-versed in the area of functioning under consideration. He may utilise specialists to augment his contribution, but he, himself, must be able to recognise specific problems with which the person may be having difficulties and to appraise the merits of possible solutions. He must be able to provide relevant information that will be of use to the client (pp. 227–8).

Professor Ross's description of the goals and processes of counselling indicates the close relationship between 'advice' and 'guidance' and the relevance of referral to the latter.

What we learned about the F.A.S. function of guidance (or counselling) raised some other questions: What is the difference between guidance and case work? Need there *be* a difference? Is the difference a methodological one, purely semantic or related to how much time the worker spends in helping the client in a problem-solving situation? We have to try to answer these questions in order to obtain an accurate description of the functions of the family advice service. In order to do so we looked for a definition of case work generally accepted in Britain. Here we encountered some difficulties. Timms (1964) tells us that

within social work and in more public allusion, criticism or defence, casework has rarely been defined to anyone's satisfaction. It remains elusive and even its sympathizers are forced to admit that attempts to describe it often reveal—to borrow a phrase of Oscar Wilde's—'all the utility of error and all the tedious-ness of an old friend' (p. 3).

Stroud (1965) states that:

The Child Care Officer is always doing casework, whether he is attending a Court or interviewing prospective foster-parents or moving a child in his car (p. 168).

He then describes casework as

the way in which one person helps another through a relationship based on mutual respect and made effective because professional knowledge of human affairs, and professional skill in making them comprehensible, help the client towards solving his own problems (p. 173).

This is the kind of definition usually offered and it is vague enough to include all methods and approaches of social work. In order to differentiate between the various methods, a more precise definition is needed. But the same writer tells us:

It really is rather extraordinary that, although the word has been extensively used for at least fifteen years in this country and appears almost ad nauseam in any book about social work, there is still no universally accepted definition. Attempts have been made, ranging from 'ego-enablement' to 'well, commonsense really'; and perhaps the very variety of these attempts gives us the clue to the difficulty. It is a word used by different people in many different ways; and because this concept, or rather the methodology which it represents, has been comparatively recently introduced but has been modified and remodified very rapidly, practitioners active in social work have met the word in different circumstances. A person trained, for example, before 1950 will not have met the word at all in training and will retain to this day a suspicion and distrust of it, perhaps seeing a person trained after 1960 as representing a complex way of working, akin to psycho-therapy. People's ideas may well depend upon the tutor they studied with, the book which most influenced them, the degree of insight they possess, the level of their own intelligence. Further, almost the whole output of descriptive work in this field has been by the most voluble, verbose, and psychoanalytically oriented practitioners who have cultivated a jungle of words which can frighten off a normal human being (p. 169).

This seems to sum up the prevailing situation and leads to the conclusion that *no* generally accepted definition of case work is, at present, available.[1]

We did, however, enter the research situation with the assumption that the family advice service must have some demarcation lines at which the F.A.S. worker, rather than exceed his functions of advice, guidance and assistance, must take recourse to referral to obtain the necessary help for his client. To enable the worker to determine a boundary line, there has to be some definition, some criterion as to what lies beyond the guidance function, which is by our definition the most continuous and intensive part of the range of F.A.S. functions. There are, of course, many specialised services which are not included in the counselling or guidance process, such as psychiatry, prenatal care, legal representation, vocational training, etc. which the client may obtain through referral. The definition of these services poses no problems. We are here mainly concerned with the wide range of services covered by the vaguely and variously defined term 'case-work', and which are carried out by many different agencies, such as children's departments, family service units, welfare departments, settlement houses, etc. To provide the family advice service with a frame of reference, we propose the following three criteria as demarcation lines between guidance and case work and as determinants for referral: (1) length of treatment or support needed; (2) depth or intensity of service necessary, and (3) expertise required to provide the needed service.

In accordance with these criteria the F.A.S. worker would make a referral at the point where he reaches the conclusion that the client either needs long-term support, possibly for an indefinite period of time, or needs intensive, in-depth treatment which involves frequent treatment sessions and/or home visits by a caseworker and discussion of deeply rooted personal problems and severe social and psychological malfunctions; or else the client's problems require a specific expertise which may involve intensive, long-term work, such as a severely damaged

[1] It is of some interest to note in this context that Timm's *Language of Social Casework* (1968), while discussing a wide range of commonly used terms, and while indeed seeming to regard the term 'casework' as being synonymous with 'social work', does not propose any generally accepted definition of case work. Nor is there such a definition in Forder's *Social Casework and Administration* (1966).

marital situation, or may be resolved by a short-term help, as for instance, when an adoption has to be arranged.

This frame of reference should, of course, be applied with some degree of flexibility. However, we find that there *is* a need to differentiate between guidance and casework in a way which permits the family advice service to focus on advice, guidance and assistance and other relevant functions, while making the best possible use of referral.

The matter is greatly complicated by the often encountered lack of adequate resources. The worker may find it relatively easy to limit his guidance function to three to six sessions with a couple who are trying to reach a decision regarding the adoption of a child, and then refer the couple to a child care officer who specialises in adoption procedures. He may find it much more difficult to locate a highly trained experienced worker in any agency who is willing, and who has the time needed, to provide long-term intensive treatment and support for a highly neurotic, self-destructive father who has ceased to fulfil his social functions adequately, whose emotional state is precarious, whose behaviour has aroused the hostility of the community and whose family has begun to disintegrate. In all too many cases the worker may not be able to find anyone within reasonable distance who can accept a referral of this type. It must be concluded that, if this is the case, and if it is apparent that even long-term support and guidance by the F.A.S. worker alone cannot meet the needs of the client, the worker may have to acknowledge that the client cannot be helped by the family advice service. This kind of situation is hard to accept and even harder to convey to the person who is asking for help. The fact that the family advice service is not omnipotent, and that the available services are not always sufficient to meet the needs which become known to the family advice centre, must be confronted realistically and honestly.

On the other hand, we found that the family advice service can, quite frequently, provide a kind of supportive, continuous guidance service which is not (as we assume case work to be) based on a treatment plan which leads to a satisfactory overall adjustment or 'cure'. This process, while perhaps involving a less intensive, intimate worker-client relationship than 'intensive case work' has in some cases been found to be an especially taxing and demanding procedure.

In the supportive guidance approach any treatment plan will often have to be a day-to-day affair. The guidance and support provided by the F.A.S. worker depends mainly on the client's recurrent requests for help and the F.A.S. worker's continuous availability and accessibility. In fact we found that this type of guidance process consists largely of a series of responses to requests for advice and assistance, as well as involving most of the other F.A.S. functions from time to time. It seems essential that the worker does *not* confront the client with unrealistic expectations and demands, but regards the recurrent need for guidance and support as one of the routine tasks of the service. Any gratification the worker may derive from his work will have to come from very modest achievements and the knowledge that the worker's patience may be of some benefit to the children of such families.

Some excerpts and summaries from the files of the seven family advice centres may serve to illustrate the range and variety of guidance work which took place. The first of these is taken from the case records of the 'A' project family advice centre:

● Mr and Mrs D had adopted a fifteen-year-old girl, Betty, when they were both in their early fifties. Now the girl was seventeen years old, working in an office, and causing them concern. They came to the family advice centre to seek guidance about how to deal with the girl who, as they said, did not live up to the high standards of behaviour they sought to maintain. Betty had left her adopted parents' home for a while and lived in lodgings, but had been permitted to return when she said that she wanted to live at home again.

In the ensuing discussion of the situation, in which Betty participated at the worker's suggestion, it became apparent that the tension between the girl and Mr and Mrs D was largely due to Betty's insistence to attempt to find her 'real' mother. The Ds seemed to be threatened by this and resented the fact that the child care officer of a children's department, who had originally placed Betty in Mr and Mrs D's care, was encouraging and helping the girl in her search for her mother.

Having convinced Mr and Mrs D that the girl had a right to find out who her mother was, the F.A.S. worker obtained the Ds permission to discuss the matter with the child care officer who had arranged for the adoption. This made it possible for the worker to find out some facts about the girl's mother, and, although it was ascertained that the girl's mother could not be contacted, the information Betty was given seemed to put her mind at rest. Mr and Mrs D became more relaxed about the matter and more accessible to the worker's advice that they would be wise to accept Betty as a person in her own right, and not insist on complete conformity to their own standards. After a series of talks all three left the family advice centre in a better frame of mind, saying that they had gained in understanding of each other and thanking the worker for her help.

In certain circumstances guidance becomes primarily a supportive process and expectations are limited to effecting very minor changes at best, or to maintaining the *status quo* at worst. The experience of the community-based centres showed that this not only fills a wide gap in the range of social services available, but that a supportive, unconditional helping approach has the important secondary function of bringing about an easing-up of community tensions and conflict by relieving some of the pressures. The F.A.S. worker using professional skill, not only provides sustained, consistent support through the guidance function, but is available for on-the-spot advice, practical and immediate assistance in recurrent crisis situations, and, perhaps most important of all in this kind of situation, the F.A.S. worker functions as mediator and liaison person between the client family and the many social workers, officials and agencies who are usually involved in fragmented and overlapping efforts of helping this type of client.

The following summarized account of long-term supportive guidance may serve to illustrate our point:

● Mrs P lived on the 'G' project estate with her fourteen-year-old daughter June and her eight-year-old son Tommy. She contacted the F.A.S. worker by calling from the window of her second floor flat a few days after the opening of the family advice centre, asking the worker to come up and see her. She remained a client of the centre for the next two years.

Tommy had sustained serious burns on his legs in an accident a year before. Ten months after this Mrs P's husband collapsed suddenly and died. Her daughter June was involved in a variety of delinquent activities and the relationship between mother and daughter was steadily deteriorating. Mrs P lived on a widow's pension and family allowance, together amounting to £11 10s 6d per week; she paid a weekly rent of £2 3s 7d and was under pressure from the housing department because of £80 in arrears which her husband had accumulated. About six months after her first contact with the family advice centre Mrs P's pension was reduced by £3 10s, her rent was raised by 17s and she began to draw social security benefit payments. Mrs P suffered severely from arthritis and was unable to work and neither she nor her daughter had as yet been able to cope with the emotional shock of Mr P's sudden death.

During the two-year period of supportive work with Mrs P the F.A.S. worker helped her to obtain legal aid and start a long process of litigation for compensation for her son's accident. She helped her on several occasions to obtain clothing for her children, helped June to look for employment and intervened on several occasions to settle violent quarrels between mother and daughter. In a series of long, searching discussions the worker helped mother and daughter to face the reality of Mr P's death and to improve their relationship with each other. The worker provided play activities and support for Tommy and did some intensive work with June when the girl started to steal from local shops. She helped Mrs P to fill out the necessary forms and obtain her social security benefits and applied on her behalf to voluntary organisations for small grants on several occasions. The worker intervened on Mrs P's behalf with the housing department in order to 'write off' the substantial rent arrears accrued before her husband's death and assisted Mrs P to budget realistically and to pay her rent promptly. She looked after Mrs P during a period of illness, arranged for her to register as a handicapped person in order to get her television licence paid by the welfare department, and intervened when bailiffs removed Mrs P's furniture on a court order regarding debts incurred by her husband for which she was not legally responsible. The worker discussed June's employment problems with the youth employment officer, and arranged for Tommy to see a specialist about the effects of his accident. She cut Mrs P's nails for her when she was unable to do so herself because of her arthritis and helped her over several bouts of severe depression. She arranged a recuperative holiday for Mrs P, and boosted her self-confidence and her financial position by obtaining part-time work as a 'good neighbour', looking after an elderly neighbour. The worker spent many hours with Mrs P after she collapsed when some youngsters played a cruel hoax on her by telling her that Tommy had met with an accident, and made all the necessary arrangements with the police and a solicitor when June was run over and slightly hurt. The worker arranged for a holiday for June and persuaded Tommy to go to school when the boy had become truant. She helped to improve Mrs P's standing in the community and to give her some new interests by encouraging her to take part in the activities of the tenants' association and by enlisting her help in running the clothing exchange. When June, now fifteen years old, became pregnant the F.A.S. worker arranged for an abortion and helped the girl and her mother to face the situation, but had to intervene periodically when a feud between Mrs P and the family of the teenage father broke out.

Throughout the two-year period the F.A.S. worker mediated between Mrs P and the social security benefits officials and obtained a number of supplementary benefit payments to which Mrs P was entitled; in one case she applied for a tribunal hearing and acted as her client's advocate. Gradually she succeeded in improving relations between the harassed officials and her demanding and sometimes unreasonable client, and eventually Mrs P was able to negotiate with the Department of Health and Social Security officials on her own, 'putting on her posh voice', as she described it, and stating her case clearly and rationally. The worker's mediation also resulted in better relations between Mrs P and other social service workers, such as the housing welfare officer, the school care worker and the health visitor. The F.A.S. worker obtained a supplementary allowance under Section 1 from the children's department for Mrs P, helped her to press her case for rehousing and with the problems of moving and adjustment in the new neighbourhood.

Mrs P continued to come to the centre to see the F.A.S. worker after she had left the estate. When the family advice centre closed down at the end of the research period in July 1969 the F.A.S. worker discussed the family with a colleague in the children's department who agreed to take over the supporting role and remain in close contact with the family.

The case of Mrs P and her children will have shown the reader the kind of pressures to which the F.A.S. worker becomes subjected in carrying out long-term supportive guidance work with families whose situation is one of perpetual crisis, whose attitudes and abilities to establish relationships are highly inadequate and whose own resources and potentialities are very low. During the two year study period the 'G' project family advice service worker provided this type of long-term supportive guidance to approximately twenty multi-problem families.

Ideally we would insist that, while remaining available for on-the-spot advice and assistance, and while possibly functioning as liaison with other agencies, the F.A.S. worker cannot be permitted to allocate such disproportionate slices of her working time and energy to any one family. Mrs P and other families with the same incidence of problems and paucity of resources should be referred to the appropriate agency for intensive long-term supportive case work. Realistically we must admit that the F.A.S. worker's decision to accept the responsibility and the immense burden of providing *the* key service for such clients was the only possible one in the circumstances. These circumstances not only include the fact that it would have been impossible to find adequate case work services for these families which would have been able to supply the quality of service provided by the family advice centre, but also the very real possibility that the F.A.S. worker's relationship with the community would have remained tenuous and her image would never have become that of the trusted, down-to-earth, understanding and resourceful friend she grew to be regarded as by the tenants of the estate.

The importance of community involvement is, perhaps, even more pronounced in the following example of guidance work which was recorded in the 'F' project family advice centre:

● Mrs J, a woman in her mid-thirties, mother of five-year-old twin daughters and an eight-year-old son, had become well known at the centre before she drew the F.A.S. worker's attention to her problems. Mrs J came to the centre with a friend shortly after it opened and participated in the activities of the parents' association from the very outset and with great enthusiasm. She and her friend, Mrs I, took the initiative in visiting a number of elderly people who had come to the attention of the centre. The parents' association noted in the minutes of one of its meetings: 'This work was greatly appreciated, particularly in view of the fact that several of these elderly people are not visited very often, either by members of the community or by social work agencies.' Both women recorded the details of about a dozen such home visits for the centre. Mrs J was also interested in the activities of the arts and crafts centre. Her own children participated and she helped to supervise the activities of twenty to thirty children.

While Mrs J undoubtedly made constructive contributions in the parents' association and the arts centre, her personal problems became a source of concern to her and others. The children at the centre sometimes teased her about her obesity and she would become very upset, and the F.A.S. worker often had to stop whatever he was doing to calm her down and talk to her. On a theatre trip with fifty children and nine other adults from the community, other parents expressed resentment about her somewhat hysterical and embarrassing behaviour. On the return trip the children made up a ditty deriding Mrs J, and while she laughed about it at the time, she later broke down and cried in the F.A.S. worker's office. However, when she fell ill the following weekend, two members of the parents' association brought groceries to her home and cooked meals for her and her children, for which she was very grateful.

Mrs J's husband had left her some time ago and she found it very difficult to manage on the social security benefits which she received. One afternoon she came to the centre in a very distraught state, saying that she felt faint, had a sore throat, her nose was bleeding and one of the twins was ill. When the F.A.S. worker had calmed her down, she told him that she only had 3s 6d of her social security money left until the next payment was due, two days hence. The F.A.S. worker gave her a small loan and took her home, where her elderly father was taking care of the children. He was angry about her prolonged absence and complained that the children were misbehaving. There was no reason to believe that any of the children were ill, the house was untidy and dirty, and Mrs J seemed embarrassed about this. Characteristically, she sought to cover her embarrassment by giving the worker a carton of secondhand clothes which she had collected for the parents' association clothing exchange.

To alleviate her financial situation, the F.A.S. worker contacted the Department of Health and Social Security on her behalf, asking them to provide her with a clothing grant and discussing some difficulties which had arisen with regard to her milk token book. A visit from a D.H.S.S. officer to Mrs J's home was promised, but this visit was delayed for some time. She did, however, receive a £13 grant and deposited part of this sum with the F.A.S. worker as 'emergency money'.

A local police sergeant with special responsibility for road safety in the area was invited to one of the parents' association meetings in January. The group suggested this as they were very concerned with the prevention of road accidents in the area and wished to discuss with the police how the traffic could be regulated. He offered three mothers, one of them Mrs J, jobs as 'lollipop-women'. Mrs J wrote a lively description of the responsibilities and fun of the job, and although her duties prevented her from being with the children in the centre after school hours, she continued to visit the centre frequently.

In the spring of 1969, Mrs J was rehoused. Mrs M, a member of the parents' association, had moved to the same neighbourhood and the F.A.S. worker asked her to stay in touch with Mrs J and visit her from time to time. Two months after her move, Mrs J came to the centre to ask for further help. She said that the house to which she moved had not been properly cleaned before they moved in and the entire family was suffering from scabies. The F.A.S. worker wrote to the housing department, drawing their attention to the situation and requesting the fumigation of the house. The department complied with this request. Shortly after this, Mrs J informed the worker that her husband had returned to live with her.

Both short-term guidance, aimed at helping an individual or a family to resolve a specific problem or to find realistic, constructive ways of adjustment, and long-term supportive guidance geared to helping people to cope with personal inadequacies and socio-economic deprivation without much hope of decisive changes and lasting solutions, is carried out by the family advice centres and benefits many people. For obvious reasons, short-term guidance in which discernible results could be obtained was, on the whole, a more rewarding, less emotionally and physically taxing experience than long-term supportive guidance. Nevertheless, we were led to conclude that the latter may, in communities with severe and widespread socio-economic problems, become the more essential, effective service. This type of social work demands a very high degree of non-judgmental acceptance and competence on the part of the F.A.S. worker. It also demands an understanding, realistic, supportive attitude by the agencies which employ the workers in the family advice centres, an attitude which finds expression in the policy decisions and the administrative practice of the agency, and which is constantly alert to the pernicious echoes of poor-law philosophy which can still be heard.

The experience of the family advice centres, especially in the detached, community-based settings, has shown that the social work profession can and does produce workers who meet the high standards required by this type of work. It also became apparent that, while there is still much to be learned, and many adjustments of professional attitudes and administrative practice must still be made, the local authority children's departments are well able to provide the leadership and the support needed.

Assistance

Assistance may consist of a simple service, such as helping a person to fill out some forms or write a letter of complaint or application. It may involve emergency help in cases of immediate need of money or essential facilities, such as lighting and heating, furniture etc., either to relieve a momentary distress before the underlying problems are tackled, or else in cases where it seems that the relief of the immediate need is all that is necessary, and that the client will be able to cope from there on (Leissner, 1969b, p. 120).

We found that it is only rarely that this form of assistance is provided as a completely separate function. In most cases assistance is part of the advice and guidance process. In theory it could be assumed that there should be provision of 'simple assistance', similar to that of 'simple advice', in other words, that a client should be able to ask for assistance of a specific and immediate kind without having to explain his reasons for the request and without having to enter into any form of worker-client relationship. In practice the 'no-strings-attached' approach to assistance could be maintained only in a few relatively trivial cases. With regard to what we might call 'technical assistance', the F.A.S. workers did, at times, provide such simple services as helping a client fill out a form, type out a letter or even picking up groceries for a client without asking questions and without probing for further information about the client's situation and needs. In most instances, however, even filling out a form or taking a child to a playgroup because the mother could not do so herself, became part of an evolving relationship between worker and client. In almost all cases clients accepted this without difficulties. Financial assistance, with the occasional exception of a casually given sixpence for a phone call or a shilling for the gas meter, always entailed a certain amount of discussion and probing and the expectation of a continuing worker-client relationship. As unconditional giving of any significant amount of money is quite alien to the established norms of our society, this was generally expected and accepted by clients and workers. But beneath the overt acceptance of the fact that financial assistance could not be provided without some, no matter how subtly expressed, conditions and obligations, there were some undercurrents of discomfort or resentment on the part of clients and some instances of frustration, doubt or guilt feelings on the part of the workers.

As part of the overall service, assistance in all its forms was in no way less important or time consuming than other F.A.S. functions. For the clients it was often, at least initially, the most important proof of the F.A.S. workers' sincerity and capability. F.A.S. staff became aware of the potentialities of assistance in all its forms as an effective, practical way of relieving distress and, quite frequently, of preventing a temporary, acute crisis from becoming a lingering, chronic one. Especially with regard to financial assistance, the workers were also aware of the dependence-fostering propensities of assistance and the powers with which it might imbue the worker in the eyes of the client.

The exploratory study of family advice services noted that:

The Family Advice Service can, where circumstances warrant this, provide financial assistance under Section 1 of the Children and Young Persons Act 1963. All F.A.S. settings we observed offer such financial assistance in the form of grants or loans in cases of debts, rent, rate or services arrears, fares, removal costs, and household necessities. In a number of cases Children's Department funds are supplemented by donations from voluntary agencies. There appears to be no questioning of the relevance and usefulness of this type of assistance. It is, however, not always clear whether financial assistance should be made available directly through the Family Advice Service or whether the client should be referred to the Children's Department in cases where material aid is indicated. Most departments take the latter course. In some instances F.A.S. staff may provide financial assistance directly, but in consultation with the senior officer in the department (Leissner, 1967, p. 40).

This observation was confirmed in the experience of the seven family advice centres under discussion here. A number of generally applicable conclusions could be arrived at.

There are instances in which it is not only possible, but advisable to refer a client in need of financial assistance under Section 1 to the children's department. In some cases the referral may be made because the matter is not so urgent as not to allow for the referral procedure to run its course. In other cases the referral may be a means of demonstrating to the client that the family advice centre is a unit of the children's department, and that this statutory service can be regarded as a source of concrete help in times of trouble. There may, conceivably, also be instances in which the quality of the worker's relationship with a particular client leads him to prefer to provide financial aid through official channels rather than, for instance, reinforce a client's tendency to become over-dependent by risking to strengthen an illusion of personal gifts or favours offered by the worker.

There may be reasons which lead the F.A.S. worker to draw upon the resources of voluntary agencies or charitable funds. There may also be valid reasons against this procedure. The judgment must be that of the worker whose relationship with the client and whose firsthand knowledge of the situation determines his decisions in such matters. It should *not* be a matter of expediency only.

Furthermore, we have noted a number of cases in which the best course of action leading to the most effective and immediate relief of a crisis situation would be for the F.A.S. worker to make an on-the-spot grant or loan. This is especially important in neighbourhoods of the type served by the community-based centres, in which financial crisis is a recurrent phenomenon for many families. A survey carried out by volunteers from Birmingham University under the supervision of the F.A.S. worker, showed that thirty of the forty families who were interviewed in the 'F' project stated that they lived on the borderline of their income and were not able to put aside any reserve funds for emergencies. Twenty families described instances in which they were left completely without funds and had to go without food for one or two days.

It has been said that 'the simplest and possibly the cheapest, but by no means the best way of helping families is by the immediate payment of debts which are hindering proper functioning of the family' (Birmingham Report, 1967, p. 11). While this type of financial assistance is certainly not always the best way, it is often the first essential step towards establishing a relationship with the client which may enable the worker to explore the reasons for this all-too-prevalent malfunction and to help the client to prevent recurrence.

It should also be pointed out that the relatively short frustration span of people in a high need area, and the experience of complex bureaucratic procedures and long delays in obtaining help from statutory agencies, can be identified as one of the sources of apathy, distrust or open hostility towards official institutions. The demonstration of immediate, non-judgmental, practical assistance by the family advice centre may serve to break this pattern most effectively and introduce the educational tasks of fostering a more realistic understanding of administrative structures and financial limitations to which official bodies are subject. It would seem that this breaking of established patterns of apathy and distrust would justify the risk of occasional errors and instances of manipulation.

Because of the exposed position of the family advice service, especially in the case of the detached, community-based centres, and because of the possible effects on the image of the service and on relations with clients and other agencies, the family advice service function as regards financial assistance requires close scrutiny and constant critical evaluation. In fact, financial assistance has been a subject of concern to statutory and voluntary social service agencies for some time. One of the most experienced practitioners and teachers of social work in Britain stressed the importance of material assistance in the context of the overall goals of social work:

The real purpose, the real social function of social workers, is to use the contagious nature of human relationships in such ways as to lower the negative stresses which result from too much anxiety, fear and hostility and to increase the positive experience of actual achievement. To say this is not to deny the importance of material goods and services. Sometimes the material goods and services may be the essential means of bringing about the desired results (Younghusband, 1964, p. 122).

Another author draws attention to the dangers of unrealistic expectations by social workers when he points out that:

How those on the borderline of poverty ought to spend their money is a very different thing from how they do spend their money. It would be unrealistic to expect them . . . to be skilled dieticians with marked tendencies toward puritanism (Townsend, 1954).

An American observer draws attention to the explicit and implicit conditions imposed on clients who seek material assistance by the statutory services:

The children's department stands in a very powerful position vis-à-vis the client. The agency is a dispenser of rewards and benefits (which includes the staving off of more serious sanctions) that the families sorely need. These rewards and benefits are levers that the officers use in the casework plan. The casework plan means changing behaviour to conform to what the child care officer thinks is proper (Handler, 1968).[1]

The assistance function can be regarded as a variant of 'simple advice and information' with a clearcut emphasis on immediate and practical solutions for concrete needs. The aim is usually a tangible and effective result, whether as a simple service of the kind a neighbour might render, a bit of special expertise in doing something the client

[1] See also discussions of financial assistance in family service unit and family welfare association settings in Irvine (1967) and Greve (1969).

finds difficult to do himself, an intercession on a client's behalf, the procuring of an item of clothing, furniture or equipment or the provision of hard cash. The approaches used in the centres consisted of : (1) direct action in which the worker gives someone a lift in his car, repairs an electric plug, picks up a broom to help clean a flat, etc.; (2) provision of on-the-spot help in writing a letter, filling out a form, explaining an official document; (3) drawing on available resources to provide a pair of shoes, a push chair for a toddler, a bed, an electric heater, etc.; (4) direct intervention with a creditor to cancel or postpone a debt or to arrange for manageable payments; (5) the provision of small on-the-spot loans, special grants from statutory or voluntary agencies and funds, or supplementary payments from the appropriate agencies. There were also many instances in which F.A.S. workers helped clients to find employment or interceded with an employer to prevent a client from losing his job. In the detached, community-based centres material assistance was also provided through the setting-up of clothing exchanges and fund-raising activities and neighbourly practical help was provided through the fostering of better neighbourly relations, self-help committees and the employment of voluntary and/or paid indigenous home-helpers.

An example of practical and effective assistance is provided by the following case which occurred in the 'E' project family advice centre:

● Mr G rang from his home seven miles away to ask whether the F.A.S. worker could help him to trace a relative with whom he had not had contact for fifteen years. The relative, his aunt, moved to the area fifteen years ago but he had never known her address. Her name is Mrs H, she is about seventy years old. The F.A.S. worker agreed to try to trace this relative for the client. The worker telephoned the children's and old people's welfare departments to see if they had a record of Mr G's relative. They were unable to help. The worker then contacted the Health Service Executive Council and was told that there was only one woman of this name on their records. They provided her address, stipulating that the worker must ascertain whether she was indeed Mr G's relative before passing on her address to him. The F.A.S. worker found the woman's name in the telephone directory. He rang up Mrs H and told her that Mr G had been enquiring for her address. After asking for some details about Mr G, which the worker checked with the latter, Mrs H asked the worker to give Mr G her address. Three days later a letter from Mr G was received by the centre saying: 'I would now like to express my deepest thanks for all the help and kindness you and your good office have given in tracing my aunt.'

There were other cases in which assistance was a relatively simple and straightforward process:

● Mrs E, a mother of eight children, came to the 'A' project family advice centre to ask for help with her debts. Her husband worked for a contracting firm and his wages were irregular, varying from £11 to £15 per week. Now and then there were weeks without work. Over a period of time, the Es had accumulated £27 in rent arrears and they owed £5 for electricity bills. They were managing to pay off the latter, but the housing department had demanded the current rent plus £5 weekly arrear payments. Mrs E said that she was unable to meet these demands. The F.A.S. worker contacted the housing department and obtained their agreement for reduced arrear payments over a longer period of time. Mrs E was satisfied with this arrangement and left the office saying that she was glad she had come for advice.

In a number of instances the F.A.S. worker helped to overcome a debt problem by arrangements in which the worker shared the responsibility for repayment with the client, thereby helping the client to accept a certain degree of self-imposed discipline as in the case of Mr B, a Pakistani immigrant and his English wife, parents of three children and owners of a local grocery shop on the edge of bankruptcy.

● The F.A.S. worker occasionally did his own shopping at the Bs' store. He became acquainted with Mr B and found out that the shop was not patronised by the majority of the local people and that Mr B made a precarious living by selling goods to the few Indian and Pakistani families in the area. The worker encouraged Mrs B to become involved in the community activities sponsored by the centre. She came to some of the meetings of the parents' association, but usually was very reticent and did not participate in any of the group activities, apparently self-conscious because of her husband's ethnic origin. However, her three children attended the arts centre frequently and participated in an outing in a nearby park which was organised by the parents' association and the F.A.S. worker.

Mrs B came to the family advice centre in March 1969 with a letter she had received from the bailiffs, saying that if the £38 rate arrears on the shop premises owned by her husband were not paid within seven days, or if alternative arrangements for paying this sum were not made, a distress warrant would be served. The F.A.S. worker contacted the bailiffs who agreed to accept payments of £2 a week towards the rate arrears; Mrs B agreed to this. It was arranged that she would bring a postal order of £2 to the family advice centre each week, which the F.A.S. worker would then send to the bailiffs.

The contributions of £2 a week towards the rate arrears were paid regularly. Three months later Mr B received a letter from the housing department announcing that the department were going to take possession of the shop which was to be demolished as part of the redevelopment plan for the area. An offer of compensation was made by the housing department provided that Mr B gave up the shop and moved with his family to a council-owned house. Mr B accepted the offer and the family left the area.

In the 'G' project estate, as in many other communities of its kind, the recurrent financial crisis to which most of the families were prone, was at the root of many cases of personal maladjustment and was often dominant among the causes of general tension, of family and community conflict. Material needs were almost always the first priority in helping people to cope with a wide range of problems. In a significant number of cases these needs were so dominant, that all other considerations receded into the background and the worker had to give most of her time and attention to providing immediate practical assistance. The 'marginal existence', the state of constantly teetering on the brink of disaster, in which many of the estate families lived, resulted not only in deprivation and debts, but also in a variety of deviant activities such as pilfering, 'doing the meters', all sorts of rarely successful attempts at fiddling or manipulating the authorities and, in some cases, in money-lending at usurer's rates. The assistance provided by the family advice centre became one important means through which this destructive and demoralising network of 'shady' activities was counteracted, and through which people were helped to deal with their material problems more realistically.

In order to give immediate support in instances of momentary crisis, the 'G' project F.A.S. worker made small *personal* loans to clients in a significant number of cases. In our view this procedure was justified in the prevailing circumstances and entirely consistent with the worker's image as a helping person as perceived by the community. With very few exceptions these personal loans, rarely exceeding the sum of 10s or £1, were repaid promptly. The following summary of the F.A.S. worker's records may serve as an illustration of the kind of situation which did, on occasions, induce the worker to reach into her own pocket:

● I met Mrs J soon after the family advice service opened. She greeted me in the courtyard one day: 'Hello! I've seen you around.' I explained that a family advice service had opened in the old rent office: 'Oh, that will be all right for those with problems, but at the moment I haven't any.' Mrs J is a young woman in her late twenties with six children under the age of eleven. Throughout the two years that I knew her (and I would see her or her children almost every day) her Greek Cypriot husband was in jail. Towards the end of the two years, she gave birth to another child by her co-habitee—I was delighted that she invited me to the christening.

I was able to be of some help to Mrs J in a number of ways: by generally supporting her whilst her husband was in jail; by arranging playgroup places for her two youngest children (they regularly attended the Little People's Playgroup); by giving her some support in managing her oldest daughter; by arranging for her to be a 'Good Neighbour' to a widower and his family who lived in Montague Tibbles; by arranging for her two youngest children to be looked after when she was admitted to hospital to have her seventh child. (I was originally planning to refer the two children for temporary reception into care by the children's department, but when Mrs T of the Little People's Playgroup heard about this she offered to look after the children. I referred to the children's department for a Section 1 grant to finance Mrs T); by helping to sort out bills from the gas and electricity companies and to sort out rent arrears (through Section 1 and through Save the Children Fund).

Mrs J received £13 8s from Social Security and £2 8s in Family Allowances. She paid £4 0s 8d in rent plus 5s a week off arrears that had accumulated. Not long after I had first met her in the courtyard, Mrs J came over to the centre to ask me 'to help with the electricity'—it had been cut off because of non-payment of the account. I referred her to the Social Security for a special grant: 'Thanks very much. I'd never have thought of it myself—didn't know we could get extra grants like that.' Later the same day, Maria, Mrs J's eldest daughter, knocked on the door of the centre with a note:

'Dear Mrs Madam—I don't know your name. But could I borrow £1 off you till Monday please. I know I should not ask you. Could you possibly just this once. Please. Thanking you. S.J.'

I said to Maria that I'd be up to see her mum shortly. Mrs J told me that she was 'skint' and that she 'would not ask anybody round here'. I produced £1—she said she'd let me have it back on Monday without fail. 'Thank Gawd for that—now I can get me dinner,' she said. I wrote down my name for her.

On the Monday morning, Mrs J appeared at the centre at 8.45 a.m.: 'Here's your £1. Thank you very much. I'm all right now. Terrible weather ain't it? Bye—thank you.'

Three weeks later Mrs J came to the centre again to borrow 10s. 'Betty, do me a favour will you—lend me ten bob till Monday. I'm skint.' I said that I would, but asked her to keep it to herself as there are so many people in The Estate who are hard-up and I couldn't do it for all. 'Thank you, Bet. You're right about people being hard-up here. God knows how I'd manage without my sister bringing me over an occasional tin of fruit or cakes. You know I'm ever so careful, but what with the kids being home from school, and they ask for ice-creams and you can't refuse them all the time.' Again first thing on the Monday morning, Mrs J returned the ten shillings to me.

This continued to happen quite regularly over the two year period— I would lend Mrs J £1 or 10s on a Friday and it was always paid back on the Monday.

We might add that this kind of helping someone out with a small loan was customary among the tenants of the estate and the worker's occasional conformity with this custom helped to reduce the distance between client and worker to the minimum required for this type of social work setting. Nevertheless, we feel that the F.A.S. worker should *not* have to draw on her own funds in such cases, but should be provided with an emergency fund for the explicit purpose of providing small on-the-spot loans.

As we have already pointed out at the beginning of this chapter, the special powers of the children's departments to grant material and financial assistance under Section 1 of the Children's and Young Persons' Act 1963, provides the F.A.S. worker with some very useful resources, but also poses some problems. In all the family advice centres the workers did, from time to time, obtain Section 1 grants for clients by applying to the children's departments through the prescribed channels. In a number of cases, however, the workers found that voluntary sources, such as various charitable funds and organisations, offered grants and loans with less procedural delay and with fewer 'ifs' and 'buts'.[1]

Cases in which the F.A.S. worker obtained Section 1 grants for clients included a woman whose handbag containing £3 (set aside for the payment of an electricity bill) was stolen. A £3 grant was received three days after the theft. The mother of four children who attended the 'E' project adventure playground had been deserted by her husband and had accumulated £31 arrears in electricity payment. The F.A.S. worker applied to the Department of Health and Social Security

---

1 This observation does not necessarily hold true for the large, well-established voluntary organisations. For a relevant comparison of such an organisation with the statutory services see Greve (1969).

who paid half the amount and the other half was obtained through an application for a Section 1 grant from the children's department. An assistance case in the 'G' estate necessitated a combination of helping activities:

● Mr and Mrs Z, the latter an Irish immigrant and the mother of eight children, asked the F.A.S. worker for help when her husband became unemployed. Two of the children needed shoes urgently and these were supplied by the clothing exchange. The F.A.S. worker then asked Mrs Z to clean the family advice centre at the rate of 5*s* per hour. Shortly after this Mr Z found a job, but Mrs Z had accumulated a £10 grocery debt. The F.A.S. worker obtained a grant of that sum for her from a charitable society and helped her to find shops where she could buy less expensive food. Soon after this Mr Z became ill and the worker obtained a £10 Section 1 grant and a £4 grant from the Save the Children Fund for the family to pay for a pram and for a television licence. An additional £12 Section 1 grant was made by the children's department two months later when Mr Z's illness had become chronic and Mrs Z began to show signs of emotional and physical exhaustion. She was nearing complete breakdown when two of the children fell ill. In consultation with some of the Z's relatives the F.A.S. worker arranged for a holiday with her family in Ireland for Mrs Z. At the worker's request the children's department provided £10 for the fare and £10 to pay a cousin to take care of the children during Mrs Z's absence. Things were better for a while after Mrs Z's return, but six weeks later she had to undergo a hysterectomy. Her cousin agreed to look after the children for a period of three weeks and was paid £24 from Section 1 funds. About a month after the operation the Zs were rehoused and the F.A.S. worker obtained £35 from the Department of Health and Social Security for removal and furnishing expenses.

Our observations showed that the precarious economic conditions in which many families in high need areas find themselves bring about a perpetual chain of requests for material and financial assistance. In many instances it became apparent that a significant proportion of these requests would not have become the concern of the family advice centres and, through conditions of social malfunctioning greatly aggravated by economic deprivation, of many other social service agencies, if the privileges, rights and resources provided by central government and local authorities were more widely known and more easily accessible. In addition to this, many people would find it easier to manage if the established system of payments for the essential services were flexible enough to take different styles of life and modes of income into account.

These facts have been raised again and again. One recent article, for
instance, commented that:

There are officials who still fail to appreciate that the majority of wage earners
are paid and budget weekly. It is no good sending manual workers quarterly
accounts and expecting them to reach for their cheque books. How far can you
get from reality? (Owens, 1969, p. 32.)

A report on an investigation of supplementary benefits concluded:

This small Enquiry confirms the hypothesis that there is, even among the long-
term disabled and chronic sick, who may be thought to arouse sympathy
on the part of officials, a lack of information about discretionary grants and
allowances which are within the power of the Supplementary Benefits Commission. There is an apparent arbitrariness in the decision, and the basis for
refusals is unclear (Owtram, 1969, p. 88).

A study of a high-need area in Liverpool emphasised 'the need to work
through the community more and offer more direct access to information
on benefits' (Moss, 1969, p. 26). All the different types of family advice
service settings which participated in our study provide opportunities
for making information on sources of material aid and financial assistance
available to the public. There is, however, no doubt that the community-
based family advice centres are the most advantageously placed for the
dissemination of this essential information where it is most needed.
We also found that the detached F.A.S. workers, if they did not know
this initially, were very soon made fully aware of the need for down-to-
earth, practical responses to the problems their clients face. As two
experienced social welfare workers aptly put it:

The need for sheer hard cash in the solution of family problems is sometimes
overlooked in an excessive concentration on what are described as 'problems
of relationship'. The filling of an empty purse can greatly improve family
relations (Hastings and Jay, 1965, p. 10).[1]

Referral and follow-up

We regarded referrals as:

the result of a direct request by the client, or of a diagnostic decision by the F.A.S.
worker. In both cases a painstaking process of preparation with the client,
as well as with the person or agency to which the client is being referred, may be
demanded (Leissner 1969b, p. 120).

Professor Kahn described referral as:

a specific form of advice involving the suggestion that the person in need of
service or information go to a specific agency or facility. The interviewer

[1] For a searching discussion of the social work aspects of statutory financial assistance
see also Stevenson (1970).

establishes the contact and might make a specific appointment, send a report or explanation and even escort the person in need of service (Kahn *et al.*, 1966, p. 34).

It must be emphasised that referral in professional social work *cannot* be regarded merely as the act of telling a client where to go for help. There are, of course, instances in which a person simply wants to obtain an address or a telephone number and is well able to take care of things himself. We would not regard this as a referral, but classify this type of service as the provision of information.

Referral is a professional process which demands skill, patience and time. It may involve helping the client to understand that he *needs* help with a certain problem, explaining to him the functions and responsibilities of the agency to which he is being referred, his rights and responsibilities in the matter, and what he can realistically expect of the specialised service to which he is referred. The referral process may further necessitate a thorough explanation of the client's situation and needs to the agency to which he is being referred. In addition to this, the F.A.S. worker may have to take the necessary steps to ensure that the client gets to the right person in the right place at the appointed time and presents his problem in the right manner. Furthermore, the F.A.S. worker may have to ascertain, as far as this is possible, that the colleague to whom he has referred the client, receives the latter with a sympathetic understanding attitude.

Duration and intensity of the referral process does, of course, depend in any one case upon the state of mind and the personal resources of the client, as well as upon the competence and readiness to co-operate of the agency to which the client is being referred.

Referral may become an objective in itself once a client's specific need for service has been established, or the preparation for referral may become part of a guidance process which consists of 'working through' various problematic aspects of the client's situation. A referral may transfer the responsibility for helping an individual or a family to another agency, or else it may only enlist the services of another agency in helping to alleviate or resolve one specific problem among several others faced by the client. In both cases, but more frequently in the latter, the client may continue to seek specific advice, guidance and assistance at the family advice centre, or may continue a generally supportive relationship with the F.A.S. worker.

The issue of the termination of service after referral must be examined in relation to the specific role and image of the family advice service. Such termination is, in certain circumstances, advisable in the interest of the client, as well as of the agency to which the former has been referred, to enable the agency to establish the necessary relationship and carry out the treatment plan. One of the basic precepts of the family advice service is, however, that the staff is available and accessible to anyone with any kind of problem. The F.A.S. worker would, therefore, find it difficult to turn away a client who has been referred to another agency, even if the client and worker have agreed that all necessary services would henceforward be provided by the agency which accepted the referral. The F.A.S. worker may even hesitate to inform his colleague, who is now the key worker in the case, of the client's visit and of the reason for it, if the client objects. To do so might be regarded as a breach of confidence and could be detrimental to the image of no-strings-attached service and confidentiality which the family advice centre seeks to maintain.

Such difficulties can be handled flexibly and can usually be overcome. There may, however, be instances in which a client has to be told firmly and clearly that the F.A.S. worker is obliged to share information regarding the client with the agency which has accepted the referral, and that he cannot enter into any discussion with the client unless he agrees to this. This rule must, of course, be applied judiciously, so as not to deprive people of the opportunity to seek advice or to voice a legitimate complaint if they feel that they are not receiving adequate services.

In some instances a referral includes an agreement between all parties that the F.A.S. worker will continue to function in a general supportive role, and will continue to see the client. In this situation there is always a possibility that, unknown to either, the agency to which the client has been referred and the family advice centre will work at cross purposes. Here continuous mutual consultation with the knowledge and agreement of the client is essential.

On occasion the F.A.S. worker has to refer a family to two or more different agencies for help with a range of specific problems. In some cases the family was already in more or less sustained contact with one or more additional agencies. More often than not the burden of co-ordinating the actions and policies of the different workers falls upon the family advice centre. In some cases this is unavoidable or even desirable. There are, however, times when the F.A.S. worker could and should make the appointment of a 'key worker' from another agency, who then functions as co-ordinator, part of the referral procedure. Referral and follow-up are, in our view, two stages of the same process.

Follow-up should be regarded as an integral part of referral. Good liaison with colleagues in the field is a pre-condition for ensuring that the F.A.S. maintains consistent follow-up procedures which ensure that referred clients have, in fact, made contact with the relevant agency and that the required service is being provided. In addition to this, the follow-up procedure assures the client and the agency to which he has been referred, of the continued interest of the F.A.S. and of the latter's availability in case additional help is needed (Leissner, 1969b, p. 120).

In order to fulfil his obligation to the client and to meet his professional responsibilities, the F.A.S. worker must make every effort to ensure that adequate follow-up procedures are maintained after every referral. Kahn and his colleagues (1966) put it even more strongly when speaking of the need 'to follow through (aggressively if necessary) until the enquirer has his needs or his rights recognised' (p. 116). No doubt this makes great demands upon the worker's time, not to mention the need for considerable diplomatic skill. The same source points out that:

It is clear from investigation in the United States and Britain that there always is a price to be paid. Agencies that are objects of pressure and attacks in connection with some cases might become less accessible in what should be the 'simple' situations. Since aggressive follow through is needed at times if people are to be helped, its form and extent become an issue (p. 116).

We would argue that social service agencies would be more willing to be amenable to follow-up procedures if these were applied as a matter of routine in even the 'simplest' cases, and if generic social work training were to establish once and for all that follow-up is the responsibility of any social worker who refers a client. At present follow-up procedures are neither widely known nor practised in the social services. An investigation of Citizens' Advice Bureaux in Britain, for instance, concluded that: 'There is no systematic follow-up; and when asked about this, there is often some surprise that such follow-up might ever be considered' (Kahn *et al.*, 1966, p. 45).

A glance at some of the relevant data we collected may serve to give some indication of the role of referral in the overall service of the family advice centres:

Project	Years	No. of individual clients	No. of families	No. of referrals
'D'	$1\frac{1}{2}$	696	316	349
'C'	$1\frac{1}{2}$	503	280	146
'G'	2	449	143	353
'F'	1	378	166	138
'B'	1	247	80	92
'E'*	2	134	69	49
'A'	1	44	33	49

* These figures do *not* include the large number of children and youth served by this family advice centre.

The most significant feature of these figures is the fact that they denote referrals of problems, *not* of clients. In other words, when we listed 353 referrals during a two-year period of F.A.S. work with 143 client families on a high-need council estate, this means that on 353 occasions the F.A.S. worker enlisted the services of the appropriate agencies in helping to alleviate or resolve one or several problems faced by any one of the families. It does *not* mean that in any of these 353 referrals the entire responsibility for helping an individual or a family was transferred to another agency. The figures presented above therefore represent *problem-referrals*, in distinction to *case-referrals*.

While the F.A.S. workers made a substantial number of problem referrals (in one of the detached centres averaging more than two such referrals per client family), the number of case referrals, in which the responsibility for an individual client or a family was transferred to another agency and the services of the family advice centre were terminated, was so low as to be insignificant. There were, of course, many instances in which clients who had been advised as to the appropriate sources of help with certain problems did, for a variety of reasons, *not* return to the family advice centre. These cannot be regarded as referrals. In most instances of problem referrals the clients continued to use the services of the centres sporadically or continuously. In two of the detached centres, both of them serving relatively small and cohesive high-need communities, it can be said that *all* the centres' clients continued to use the family advice service, if not directly through requests for advice, guidance and assistance, then indirectly, through the centre's community work activities.

It must furthermore be pointed out that a great number of problem referrals did *not* involve intensive processes of preparation and formal procedures, but were made by simply telling a client where to go, making a phone call to the relevant agencies and/or equipping the client with verbal instructions or a brief written note.

There were fairly wide divergencies of the incidence of referrals not only between the different centres, but also in the ratio of the number of clients served and the number of referrals made. Obviously this is due to a number of factors, but mainly to the availability of services and the attitudes of the different F.A.S. workers towards the referral function. We made a number of observations which are relevant in this context:

It seems that the ability and/or willingness to accept referrals varied considerably in the different areas and between the various agencies in any one of the areas. The diagnostic concept of 'lack of motivation' which is often another way of categorising an individual or a family as 'unreachable', is of considerable significance here. For example, an F.S.U. worker engaged in community work reported that:

On two occasions in the past families were referred to FSU for intensive family casework help but it was agreed we should not accept them as we felt that the prognosis was so poor for their being able to use casework help constructively (Fitzwilliams, 1969).

All the statutory and many of the voluntary agencies do, of course, carry heavy case loads and, in some cases, stated frankly that they would be glad to leave the family advice centre to deal with a problem, even if it was clearly within their own area of jurisdiction and competence. In one of the areas the children's department asked the F.A.S. worker on several occasions to take the department's heavy case load into account and not to refer clients if the centre could deal with the matter independently. Other statutory agencies also pleaded full case loads from time to time, but some agencies were simply evasive and, while seeming to accept a referral, more or less ignored the case. As a result F.A.S. workers and clients alike were led to regard referrals to one or another agency as a waste of time. In one area a welfare department exhibited a somewhat ambivalent attitude by firmly insisting that all cases within this agency's jurisdiction be referred to it, but frequently having to plead staff shortages and large case loads when a case was referred and the agency was unable to attend to it. The speed with which different agencies reacted to referrals also determined the readiness of F.A.S. workers and clients to consider referrals.

The range and depth of the F.A.S. workers' knowledge of the services was impressive, and was constantly supplemented by the experience gained in daily practice. Their confidence in the services was not always easy to maintain.

Of equal importance were the views different agencies held with regard to the functions of the family advice centre. In quite a number of cases overworked and understaffed agencies found it difficult to understand why a case should be referred to them when a trained social worker who could deal with it was available on-the-spot. While this was only on a few occasions expressed openly, it was apparent in the attitudes of social workers and officials and affected the F.A.S. workers who, in consequence, often felt somewhat guilty about making a referral.

The attitudes of clients influenced the F.A.S. workers' decisions with regard to referrals. In many cases people, especially those who already had been repeatedly sent from one agency to another in the past, expressed some degree of suspicion or resentment when a referral was suggested and thereby induced the worker to deal with their problems himself.

The attitudes of the workers also differed fairly widely and were influenced by their own interests, backgrounds and training. Some workers simply found it difficult to 'let go', especially if the case was challenging and interesting, or a close relationship with the client had developed. In some instances F.A.S. workers were reluctant to relinquish the case work role to which they had previously been accustomed. F.A.S. workers also at times felt under pressure to 'justify their existence' by doing all the work that came their way themselves. Last but not least there were the workers' special interests. In one centre, for instance, we felt that the staff, who had attended a marriage guidance course, spent an undue amount of time in providing long-term marital counselling, often with cases of great complexity and severe conflict which could have been referred to the appropriate agencies specialising in this type of counselling.

Some examples from the records of the 'E' project centre may serve to illustrate the work done in this area of service and some of the difficulties encountered:

● Mrs L visited the family advice centre and told the worker that she had left her husband three months ago because he was irresponsible and difficult to live with, having left her twice for other women. She came to the centre to seek reconciliation with him and to return to her two children. Both Mr and Mrs L lived in an adjacent borough, and Mrs L agreed to the F.A.S. worker's suggestion to refer her to the borough's children's department for intensive casework. The F.A.S. worker rang the children's department who were reluctant to accept the referral. The referral was made by telephone.

● Mrs M, a young West Indian, telephoned the centre to ask if she could be helped to find a private foster parent for her four-year-old son. She told the F.A.S. worker that she was a nurse and found that her hours of work prevented her from looking after him. The worker suggested that it would be better if she came to see him and she agreed to visit the centre the following morning.

Mrs M did not keep her appointment and the worker visited her at her home a week later. Mrs M explained that she was separated from her husband. Her son had been privately fostered twice and the last foster placement broke down when the foster mother died. Mrs M was a nurse and was to start work at a hospital in a week's time. She asked whether the children's department could provide a foster home for her son. The worker explained to Mrs M that this was not possible and also explained how the children's department uses its foster homes. The worker and Mrs M discussed whether she could stay at home to look after her son or whether it would be possible to find a daily baby-minder who would accept her hours of work. She told the worker she earned £15 per week plus £2 maintenance from her husband for their son and she did not want to have to exist on the money from the Department of Health and Social Security. She agreed that to foster her son for a third time could be damaging to the child and the worker offered to approach the infant welfare clinic for a daily baby-minder.

The following day the worker rang the superintendent of a local health clinic and explained Mrs M's problem. The clinic was unable to provide a daily baby-minder who would accept a child at weekends. The worker then contacted Mrs M to tell her that he had been unable to find a daily baby-minder for her, but suggested she should ask the hospital to allow her to work hours which would enable her to apply for a nursery placement. He suggested that in the long term a change of hours was desirable, so that Mrs M would be available when her son started school. She agreed to ask the hospital, but did not sound very hopeful. The worker felt that she would probably end up finding a further private foster mother.

In many cases referrals were relatively simple and straightforward:

● The headmaster of a local school contacted the 'D' project family advice centre with regard to Mr H, the father of two girls who attended his school. The headmaster was deeply concerned because the girls' mother had died suddenly, leaving Mr H, who was deeply upset over the death of his wife, to care for the children. The F.A.S. worker immediately visited Mr H. He found that he and his children lived in highly inadequate conditions in a slum-clearance area. Besides giving Mr H all possible support to help him cope with the emotional shock, the worker prevailed on the housing department to rehouse the family immediately, several months in advance of the scheduled rehousing. As Mr H's depressed state of mind made it difficult for him to cope fully with the care of his children, the worker introduced him to a child care officer who assumed the responsibility for sustained, long-term support for this family.

Duration and intensity of the referral process does, of course, depend in any one case upon the state of mind and the personal resources of the client, as well as upon the competence and readiness to co-operate of the agency to which the client is being referred. There are, however, many other, often unpredictable, factors in the community-based setting of the detached family advice centre which add to the complexities and hazards of referrals.

A persistent, though unsuccessful effort to help a family through referral was made at the 'E' project family advice centre:

● Mr and Mrs N, their five children and Mr N's brother Dennis came into the centre at 7 p.m. after youth club activities had started and while the F.A.S. worker was interviewing a client. They had noticed the F.A.S. sign on the door when they drove by in Dennis's car.

Mr N and his brother had been living and working in the building trade in Stafford. This firm's contract ended some weeks before and Mr N and his brother were offered a transfer to a construction job in London. Dennis was sent ahead to find accommodation and when he reported that he had found a room for himself and a flat for the N family, Mr N followed. Three days ago the family had arrived in London and found that their flat was suddenly not available when the landlord realised that there were five children. For the next few days the Ns and their children crowded into Dennis's room against the objections of the landlord. This morning they had been ordered to leave. From the first day of their arrival Mr N and his brother had taken turns working in the new job and looking for accommodation. The only place they found demanded £230 as an advance payment and the Ns did not have that much money. They continued the search while Mrs N and the children found refuge with friends for one night and spent the rest of the time in Dennis's car. Last night they had spent in a welfare department hostel but had been told they could not stay there.

The family was tired and bewildered and afraid that they would have to spend the night in the car. The F.A.S. staff provided tea and some comforting remarks. One of the children had a sore throat and was given some lozenges. The teenagers of the club crowded around and some went out to enquire about accommodation in the neighbourhood. The F.A.S. worker contacted the welfare department which had put up the Ns the previous night after several attempts. He was told that the department had no further responsibility as the family was at present in another borough. After some futile arguing the F.A.S. worker contacted the reception centre for homeless families in the borough in which the centre was located. The warden said that, as the Ns had spent last night in a hostel in another borough it was that borough's responsibility. Further telephone calls to officials in both boroughs finally resulted in an agreement to permit the family to spend the night at a hostel for homeless families in the 'E' project borough. It was 10.15 p.m. when this arrangement was finally made.

The following morning the F.A.S. worker was told by the warden of the hostel that the Ns had been sent to the welfare department and would not be permitted to stay a further night. A welfare department official said that the family had waited at the department for some time and had then left without having been seen by anyone. The official expressed the view that Mr N had shown disinterest in his family as he had left them alone at the department. The F.A.S. worker explained that Mr N had gone to work in order to keep his job, and had left his brother with the family. The latter had taken Mrs N and the children to continue to search for a flat.

Dennis came to the centre the next morning and said that the Ns had been told at the welfare department that there was no accommodation for them and that their children may have to be received into care. After he had to go to work Mr N had taken his family to the police and they had sent them back to the welfare department. The F.A.S. worker contacted the welfare department and was told that hostel accommodation for Mrs N and her children could be provided, but that Mr N would not be permitted to join them, as this might encourage him to stop looking for accommodation. After lengthy arguing, and after the F.A.S. worker had repeatedly assured the official that Mr N was a responsible working man who was not out to scrounge on the Council the F.A.S. worker was told to have Dennis bring the family, which had left to search for a place to sleep for the night, to the welfare department. He promised that the family would be admitted to a hostel. A few hours later Mr N's brother called the centre and said that the Ns had been refused the promised accommodation and were continuing their search. He promised to return to the family advice centre with the family, but there was no further contact with him or the N family, nor did the welfare department have any information about them.

A referral may also be of a very different, much more informal kind in the community-based setting of the detached family advice centre. For instance, the 'G' project F.A.S. worker found out that a man in his forties whose family had asked for her help many times, and who in his turn had often been helpful and full of useful information about the community, was illiterate. The man was embarrassed about his inability to read and write and though he rarely needed these skills in his work, he regarded his lack of elementary education as a serious handicap. The F.A.S. worker discussed this with him and he was somewhat astonished when she told him that there was no reason why he should not make up for lost time. The worker introduced the man to a teacher who was one of her personal friends. This teacher visited Mr X's flat regularly as his tutor. Made to feel welcome by the entire family and pleased with the eagerness of her 'mature student', she soon reported to the F.A.S.

worker that Mr X was making very rapid progress. After a few months Mr X proudly showed the worker his 'written work': 'The Story of the Estate'.

The informal, accepting atmosphere which is a prerequisite for the detached, community-based family advice centre raises some issues with regard to the referral function. Informality and acceptance are without doubt essential. It is also understandable that it is difficult and demanding for even the most experienced worker to find herself in a situation where she has to switch roles rapidly and frequently. Nevertheless, we find it important to point out that the informal, non-judgmental, compassionate and accepting attitude which makes it possible for a troubled and apprehensive mother to confide in the F.A.S. worker and become receptive to advice and guidance, may not always be suitable or effective when dealing with other professionals, officials and agencies. In making a referral (or in following up a referral) the F.A.S. worker has to deal with other professionals as a professional in her own right, and with officials of other agencies as a statutory officer of the children's department. The warm, spontaneous, outspoken, don't-stand-on-ceremony approach which is the very key to the worker's success in the kind of community represented by a council housing estate is, unfortunately, not always acceptable or effective in dealing with other professionals and officials. In order to ensure a competent service for the client, the worker must not only demonstrate her professional experience and competence, but also her authority. She must, however tactfully, demand that her approaches on behalf of her client be met with professional responsibility. A sound and effective referral procedure seems to demand a somewhat formal, structured approach from both sides; the worker who makes the referral, as well as the agency which receives it. It is our view that this would be facilitated by a more structured initial approach. We therefore suggest that referrals from the family advice centre be made in writing on standardised forms, especially devised to meet the requirements of the family advice service, and that these forms should be accompanied by a referral-acceptance form, to be returned by the agency to which the client has been referred. This referral-acceptance form should briefly state the reason for the referral, the conditions, if any, under which the referral has been accepted and the action the agency intends to take. It should be signed by the official who has interviewed the client and/or the official who has assumed responsibility for providing the requested service. We suggest that these forms should bear the family advice service address under the children's department letterhead.

Our recommendation is influenced by the prevailing lack of adequate referral procedures in many statutory and voluntary social service agencies. Due to pressure of work and/or insufficient emphasis given to this social work process in training, one finds all too often that even the most confused and distraught people are simply told where to go for help and then left to their own devices. In many cases a telephone call (often received by a clerical worker or receptionist) is made to the agency, or the client is given a brief note and the matter rests there. In the case of the family advice centre the client is usually able to return to the F.A.S. worker and ask for reassurance, complain about any lack of attention by the agency referred to, or ask for further help. In many other cases the client is left in doubt as to why he is being sent somewhere else, why the agency to which he has been sent has not been adequately briefed as to the reasons for and the purpose of the referral, why he is received with an unexpectedly punitive attitude, or why he is confronted with demands and conditions which he is either unable or unwilling to meet.

Our observations showed that in many cases social workers and officials from other agencies extended their co-operation with regard to referrals readily and promptly. There were, however, all too many situations in which it proved to be difficult for the F.A.S. workers to locate the appropriate officer or to have messages passed on promptly. Hard-pressed colleagues were not always able to allocate the time needed for thorough discussion of the referral, or were not able to offer the client the accepting, understanding attitude which is essential for the helping process.

The following case summary shows the persistent efforts of an F.A.S. worker in 'following through' on behalf of his client, and the frustrations encountered in the process:

● The health visitor advised Mrs J to visit the family advice centre and ask for help in sorting out her housing situation. Mrs J lived with her five children, all of them under the age of six, in a one-room flat without running water and with inadequate heating arrangements. She had applied for rehousing some time ago and received an offer of a two-bedroom flat without a bathroom which she refused to accept. She did not know which housing authority made the offer. The fact that she remarried recently, changing her name (her new husband had since left her), added to the confusion, as she did not know under which name she appeared on the housing list.

The F.A.S. worker first cleared up the matter of the name on the housing list. This done, the worker discussed the matter with the borough housing department. The worker found out that the records

5

concerning Mrs J's rehousing were sent to the G.L.C. by the borough housing department some time ago, but apparently contained incorrect information. Due to this error, Mrs J was offered a flat which was too small for her needs. The worker contacted the G.L.C. housing department and the latter decided that Mrs J's records would have to be returned to the borough housing department for correction, and a G.L.C. official would visit Mrs J's flat to obtain further details of her situation.

Three days later Mrs J told the worker that she had not heard from anyone and was becoming very anxious. She was advised to wait a little longer. She returned to the centre a week later. She had still not heard anything. Winter was drawing near and she was greatly concerned about the effects of the inadequate heating conditions (paraffin stoves) upon her children. She also told the worker that a new landlord was due to take over the building in which she lived. She had been told that the new owner intended to install water and gas in her flat, but that this would entail a rent increase from £3 to £4, a 25 per cent rise. The worker explained to Mrs J that she could contest this increase with the rent tribunal, but she was reluctant to do so, fearing the effects of such a step upon her relations with the landlord.

The F.A.S. worker contacted the G.L.C. district office once more. He was told that Mrs J's need for a five-bedroom flat had been established. Her records had been returned to the G.L.C. central office from where they would be returned to the borough housing department with a request to make the necessary amendments. Trying to speed things up, the F.A.S. worker called the borough housing department and passed on the information he had just received. The borough official to whom he spoke was surprised about the offer of a five-bedroom flat and said that the records showed that the G.L.C. and borough housing department had agreed a week earlier to provide Mrs J with a three-bedroom flat. Further discussion between the borough housing department and the F.A.S. worker involved a senior officer of the borough department. The latter said that he was not at all happy about Mrs J's application and that an investigating officer would be assigned to the case in order to clarify the situation. The F.A.S. worker told Mrs J that she would have to wait another week and that a borough official would visit her during this time.

That week Mrs J's oldest child had to enter hospital for an operation. The school care committee showed concern and the matter was also discussed with the health visitor. The F.A.S. worker found out that a child care officer had applied for priority rehousing for Mrs J the year before, but that this had been turned down by the children's committee.

The health visitor now renewed the application pressing for acceptance on medical grounds.

Nearly two weeks passed and no investigating officer from the borough housing department contacted Mrs J. An enquiry by the F.A.S. worker received the reply that the matter was under review and that an investigator would visit Mrs J. The child care officer, who had been contacted by the F.A.S. worker, also called the borough department and received the same reply. Mrs J was told that she would have to wait.

Ten days later Mrs J had still not heard anything. In the meantime her youngest child had also been admitted to hospital with an acute respiratory disorder. Mrs J felt that this illness was due to the paraffin stove fumes. She was very upset. The F.A.S. worker contacted the borough housing department once again and was told that the matter was under consideration under the medical priority quota, but that, at present, there were no suitable flats available. The worker contacted the health visitor and the child care officer and asked both to inform the housing department of the urgency of this case. This did not bring about any change in the situation.

The worker continued to give all possible support to Mrs J, but he himself felt rather hopeless and frustrated. Another two weeks passed and Mrs J, who had by now given up all hope of being rehoused in the foreseeable future, told the worker that she was ready to apply to the rent tribunal with regard to the substantial rise in her rent. The worker sought the advice of a solicitor and helped Mrs J take the necessary steps and fill out the application forms. A week after this Mrs J told the worker that the landlord had been upset by her application. At the worker's invitation the landlord came to the centre and the matter was discussed. Although rather angry at first, the landlord agreed to specify the details of the alterations he intended to make and to reduce the rent increase to 10s, so that Mrs J would have to pay £3 10s instead of the originally demanded £4. Mrs J agreed that the alterations were desirable and that she would pay the increase. She withdrew her application to the rent tribunal. About a month later Mrs J informed the F.A.S. worker that her landlord had completed the alterations in her flat and that she was somewhat more comfortable now. She had still not received any word about her chances of a larger flat, but felt that it was easier for her now to wait.

The kind of referral cum follow-up procedure which became a routine pattern in the 'G' project centre is described in the following example:

● The F.A.S. worker referred an unsupported mother to the Department of Health and Social Security for a special grant for removal and furnishing expenses. The reasons for the request were spelled out by the worker in a letter which the client presented at the D.H.S.S. office. The client returned to the family advice centre a few hours later to say that she had been told that she would receive the requested help from the borough council where secondhand clothing and furniture was available. The F.A.S. worker contacted the relevant D.H.S.S. official and explained that he had apparently been misinformed, and that there were *no* stores of used clothing or furniture available at the Borough Council. The worker also pointed out that the children's department could not disburse Section 1 funds in cases where a client was clearly entitled to a supplementary D.H.S.S. grant. The D.H.S.S. official accepted this explanation. He also listened sympathetically when the worker told him that the client had now made several futile visits to the D.H.S.S. offices and at every occasion had to wait for a considerable time. On one recent occasion she had waited several hours and was then told that she would have to return the following morning because her file could not be found. The officer acceded to the F.A.S. worker's request to visit the client at her flat. The home visit was made and the client received a £20 grant.

The special conditions and requirements of those of the detached family advice centres which were situated in the midst of a relatively small and cohesive community, such as the 'G' project and the 'F' project centres, appeared to affect the F.A.S. workers' effectiveness in follow-up procedures very favourably. The easy accessibility of these centres and the workers' images as helping persons to whom one could return again and again without encountering attitudes of impatience, evasion or rejection, were factors which were also present to varying degrees in the other family advice centres. However, in these two centres there was also close physical proximity to the client population and this resulted in frequent informal contacts which made it as natural and unavoidable for clients and workers to exchange the latest news about a referral procedure, as it was to engage in the national pastime of discussing the weather. Quite often neighbours also told each other what had or had not happened when someone had 'gone to the social security' or had 'been to the housing', and it was not unusual for an F.A.S. worker to receive follow-up information from the neighbour of a client, before the client herself reported to her or, if the client did not come to the centre, before the worker rang the client's doorbell to enquire how things had turned out.

In conclusion we suggest that a more formal follow-up procedure, in line with our recommendation with regard to referral procedure, should be maintained by family advice centres. We suggest a follow-up form under an official letter-head which would be sent to the relevant agencies at a suitable interval after a referral was made. The referral and follow-up forms should, of course, be used at the F.A.S. worker's discretion, mainly in those cases in which the worker has *not* succeeded in establishing the kind of co-operative working relationships which would make formalised procedures superfluous. We wish to emphasise that we do *not* regard official forms of any kind as satisfactory substitutes for mutual understanding and good co-operation between agencies.

Co-ordination, liaison and mediation

On the subject of co-ordination of the intricate network of services it may be said that a family advice centre cannot be expected to succeed in a period of two years where all others have failed over many decades.[1] It should, however, be added that experience shows that in many cases co-ordination of services becomes an integral part of the liaison/mediation function. More often than not, the F.A.S. worker's efforts to mediate and liaise between clients and agencies and between the agencies themselves remain at least partly ineffective if some degree of co-ordination cannot be brought about. On the other hand it became apparent that almost every skilful mediation/liaison effort can be regarded as a step forward in co-ordination.

In trying to bring about even a minimal level of co-ordination the F.A.S. worker must, more often than not, adopt the roles of liaison person and mediator between the clients, who may only see their own needs and problems, and the many different social service workers and officials, whose perspective may be narrowed by professional traditions, accustomed methods, agency rules and regulations and, last but not least, their own values and expectations. Before applying his skills to effecting the co-ordination of services of, let us say, health and housing

[1] This is by no means a situation unique to Britain, a fact which was widely acknowledged at the Fifth European Symposium of the International Council of Social Welfare on the theme 'Social Welfare in Integrated Development' in Berne, Switzerland, July 1968, which was attended by the National Bureau's senior research officer responsible for the family advice services study. The latter wrote in his report to the director of the National Bureau:

'Having established the fact that in all European countries there exists a complex and intricate network of social welfare services and organisational structures, it was generally agreed that the co-ordination of these services in all the twenty countries attending the conference ... leaves much to be desired. The lack of co-ordination and co-operation, two interdependent processes, has detrimental effects upon planning, economy of service and effectiveness of service to the client.'

department officials with regard to the needs of a family who have sought the centre's help, the F.A.S. worker may have to interpret the norms and attitudes, or even the language and questionnaires of his colleagues to the client. He may have to interpret the client's expressions of confusion or hostility to the two officials in a manner which is acceptable to them. He may even have to interpret the approaches of the two officials and their agencies to each other. This process obliges the F.A.S. worker to make every effort to understand the functions and methods, the attitudes and the language of a wide range of different agencies, professions and indeed of different persons. This applies to all aspects of family advice service work, including community work. It is perhaps most complex and demanding in the latter function.

A recent study of community work observes that:

Fundamental to all problems of interpretation in this work are the difficulties that arise from the differences in objectives of the various field-work elements. These differences affect both their ability and willingness to understand one another's point of view, and to consider the situation objectively.

The differences in objectives, interests and concerns of the various field-work elements give rise not only to different ways of working (e.g. formal and informal, short-term and long-term procedures), but to differences of viewing, explaining and rationalising their work to and among themselves and to and with outsiders. The same situation is therefore seen by each element in a different context and is fitted into a different frame of reference.

When the same situation is seen from different points of view, and judgements are made from within different frames of reference, the participants are likely to fear, distrust or shy away from any attempt at full interpretation of the situation. They fear that they might have to change their presuppositions or their institutional set-up and this might involve losing cherished privileges, prerogatives and status. This applies to individuals, groups and agencies (Goetschius, 1969, p. 106).

This may seem somewhat harsh. Our experience showed that it represents a quite realistic view.

An American analysis of social welfare in modern society stated:

We need guides . . . through a new kind of civilized jungle. Social work is an example of . . . the liaison function, a large part of its total activity being devoted to putting people in touch with the community resources they need but can hardly know, let alone locate (Wilensky and Lebeau, 1965, p. 286).

In the range of functions of the family advice service, liaison and the usually concomitant function of mediation does, indeed, play a major role and it is, in most instances, an integral part of all other functions. It could even be said that all the other functions—advice, guidance, assistance, referral and follow-up and community work—depend largely on the worker's skill in liaison and mediation. One of the most essential ingredients of this skill is the ability to interpret attitudes, language, norms, traditions, expectations, resources and limitations.

The staff of the family advice centres faced a wide range of different local conditions, attitudes and reactions with regard to the issues of inter-services co-operation and co-ordination in general, and the F.A.S. function of mediation and liaison in particular. The workers themselves brought with them different backgrounds and personalities which determined their work in the mediation/liaison function to the same degree as in all other areas and aspects of their practice. Last but not least, the F.A.S. workers' attitudes towards co-ordination, liaison and mediation were influenced by the type of setting in which the family advice service work was carried out. Some noticeable differences between the different types of settings became apparent.

In the setting in which the family advice service functioned as a more or less integrated unit of the children's department, the F.A.S. staff found it somewhat difficult to make distinctions between their routine work as child care officers and their F.A.S. assignments. The possibility that, as F.A.S. workers, the staff would have to carry out the duties of another statutory service, and have to interpret this necessity to colleagues from other agencies, aroused some concern. During a discussion with the research team, one of the group of child care officers assigned to F.A.S. work cited the example of a health visitor who asked a child care officer to visit the home of a pregnant woman and enquire into her needs. When the worker arrived at the woman's flat he was received with surprise and distrust. She had not been told that a child care officer would visit her. Was it, in a case of this kind, the F.A.S. worker's function to point out to the health visitor that she should have explained her reasons for involving the children's department, or the family advice service, and that she should have obtained the consent of the client before requesting a visit by the child care officer? The F.A.S. workers were not too eager to assume this responsibility.

In another setting the fact that the family advice centre was one of the services of a voluntary agency, namely a settlement house, did in some instances serve to free the F.A.S. workers from the more marked constraints which affect the relationships between some of the statutory services. On the other hand, the relationship between the voluntary setting and its long-established traditions and the children's department, which financed and supervised the family advice centre, posed some problems. In this setting the settlement house warden determined the policies of the family advice centre in consultation with the children's officer and the children's department did not at any time exert any pressure to make the centre adapt its approaches and priorities to the requirements of the statutory service. This had the advantage of permitting the centre to function in the informal, easy-going atmosphere which is traditional in the settlement house. On the other hand, no effort was made to bring about some degree of integration of the centre with the overall work of the children's department, and the latter did not take the initiative in helping the F.A.S. workers to arrive at clear definitions of their functions, methods and goals. One might also say that, while the family advice centre had the children's department's financial support, it did not benefit fully from the department's professional experience and its influence and status in the local authority scheme.

The tendency of voluntary social service agencies to regard themselves as a kind of benevolent 'third force' which offers people an alternative to the statutory services 'on neutral ground' in some cases, and functions as an agent of social reform in others, also has some bearings upon the relationships between statutory services and F.A.S. workers who are members of the staff of a settlement house. It may be added that this alternative role of the voluntary agencies, while certainly of great value in some of its aspects, contains some inherent dangers: if not carefully and responsibly controlled it may lead to a deepening of the all-too-prevalent 'us' and 'them' attitudes between clients and the statutory services, which, after all, operate the machinery and wield the powers of the welfare state. Needless to say, such widening of the 'us' and 'them' gap runs directly counter to the goals of the family advice service concept.

The F.A.S. setting in which two statutory agencies, the children's and the welfare departments, shared the same premises did, of course, bring about closer co-operation between the staff of the two departments. However, this co-operation did not become as close as might have been expected. The statutory functions and priorities of the two services remained dominant and the different training backgrounds and service traditions of the two staff teams did not easily lend themselves to merging into a unified F.A.S. approach. On the whole, it can be said that the members of the two staff groups remained child care and welfare officers and did *not* become F.A.S. workers to the same extent that this rapid transformation took place in the detached, community-based settings. The workers in this setting continued to have doubts about the F.A.S. functions which affected their views of their own responsibilities with regard to co-ordination, mediation and liaison. They felt that too much emphasis on the F.A.S. approach might put other agencies in the area on the defensive, and that the local health visitors were already fulfilling the need for the kind of service a family advice centre could offer.

The mediation/liaison function seemed most appropriate and relevant to the F.A.S. workers, and its goals were most vigorously pursued in the detached, community-based or community-oriented family advice centres. In the 'F' project centre the F.A.S. worker did not have to start 'from scratch'. He not only found a ready response from colleagues in several of the statutory and voluntary agencies he contacted, but he also discovered that through the initiative of a local vicar, a 'social workers' luncheon group' had been formed some two years before the opening of the centre. The aim of this group, which consisted of about twenty-five members, was to facilitate communication between social workers in the area. The group's organising committee consisted of the vicar, a family case worker, a welfare officer, a local headmaster and an education welfare officer. The group met at intervals of one to two months to listen to talks by invited speakers on subjects of common concern. The F.A.S. worker was well received when he addressed the group and explained the goals and functions of the family advice centre to them.

Perhaps even more important was the support the F.A.S. worker received from the children's department in his efforts to bring the relevant social service agencies together to discuss and examine ways and means of improving services to the people of the area. Members of the children's committee were encouraged to visit the family advice centre and the F.A.S. worker was invited to address the committee in formal session. The children's officer explained the goals and functions of the centre to other chief officers and enlisted their co-operation. Shortly after the end of the year of study the deputy children's officer was instrumental in arranging a meeting of a consultative body with the aim of discussing and supporting the family advice service. This meeting was attended by senior officers of the children's, education, housing and welfare departments. The representative of the health department was unable to attend, but assured the meeting of the department's interest and support. Unfortunately, the Department of Health and Social Security did not send a representative. The reasons for the exclusion of this key service were not made clear, but it was said that one of the statutory agencies had objected to their presence.

In the case of the 'G' project family advice centre, a consultative committee was set up for the dual purpose of ensuring the represented agencies that they would be informed and consulted with regard to the policies and the practice of the family advice centre, and of affording the F.A.S. worker the opportunity to consult a group of senior staff members of key agencies with regard to specific problems or wider issues arising in her work. The committee consisted of representatives of the children's, welfare, health departments, the borough's Council of Social Service, the F.A.S. worker and the National Bureau's research team. On certain occasions the education department youth officer, a member of the borough architect's department, members of another research organisation which carried out a study in the borough and the chairman of the Tenants' Association attended the meetings. Our observations showed that the consultative committee provided the F.A.S. worker with some useful information and enabled her to discuss some problems and to clear up some misunderstandings. However, the committee could *not* make the worker's task of fostering co-operation and co-ordination with other agencies, including the agencies represented on the committee, significantly easier. This seems to confirm our own assumption that co-ordinating and liaison/mediation work is most effective when carried out on the field-work level, where co-operative working relationships and mutual understanding between the field workers of different services grow out of the shared efforts and agreed-upon goals in the process of helping the client.

In the 'E' project centre the intensive work with children and teenagers, many of them delinquent, presented the F.A.S. staff with special challenges and posed some specific problems:

The liaison/mediation function is as essential to effective work with youth as with adult clients, all the more so if the socio-cultural and educational background of the youngsters and their parents leaves them ill-equipped for understanding the responsibilities and for making effective use of the rights which society prescribes for its members. In the process of helping young people the worker may have to liaise and mediate on behalf of his clients with numerous agencies and institutions, social service workers and officials, teachers, shopkeepers, employers, etc. The worker's objectives are to help the youngsters 'to deal with the complex and intricate processes of modern society through educating, counselling and direct intervention'. His task is guiding them towards the establishing of 'positive relations to their community and to societal institutions and mediating between them and their social environment' (Leissner, 1969a, p. 134).

In the process of helping youngsters who have become involved in delinquent activities, the role of liaison/mediation becomes especially important with regard to the police and the courts. In the worker's dealings with the police:

The degree of understanding and co-operation which the worker obtains depends upon a number of factors: his ability to explain his professional functions and to convey his understanding of the responsibilities and complexities of the policeman's job; the personal attitudes of the individual officers with whom he deals; the attitudes of the commanding officer of the precinct and, last but not least, the public pressure exerted upon the police at any given time due to dramatic incidents of youth crime, press campaigns against 'young hoodlums' etc. (Leissner, 1969a, p. 199).

The support provided by the worker when a youngster has to appear in court can be of immense value to the boy or girl in a time of severe crisis, as well as being of benefit to the court authorities who emphasise the rehabilitation of the young person, rather than his punishment.

No one expects the . . . worker to be an amateur lawyer or psychologist, but he is expected to know what he is talking about when he describes the boy's attitudes and behaviour, his role in the group, the milieu in which the youngster and his group exist, conditions and prospects of employment, education, family relations, housing conditions, etc. (Leissner, 1969a, p. 210).

The staff of the 'E' project centre was able to help a number of young people through establishing contact with the relevant agencies and persons, and through the judicious use of these contacts on their behalf. On several occasions the F.A.S. worker or the youth worker provided support for boys who appeared in court. Some beginnings in establishing relations with the police were made, but still needed much improvement at the termination of the research period. The juvenile liaison bureau of the police showed a co-operative attitude, but there were instances in which the local police refused to co-operate with the family advice centre.[1]

The number of contacts with other agencies, professionals and helpful and/or influential private persons established by the F.A.S. workers on behalf of their clients was fairly high. The range of such contacts included not only all the statutory agencies and the larger voluntary services, but also many smaller, not generally known voluntary organisations and charitable funds as well as doctors, lawyers, business firms and employers. Some examples from the files of the family advice centres may serve to show some of the practical applications of these contacts and their relevance to the tasks of co-ordination, liaison and mediation.

In the 'E' project centre, for instance, the F.A.S. worker provided guidance and assistance over a six-week period to a young mother with two children who was in severe financial difficulties because her husband had left her and did not contribute to the support of the family. The worker obtained the co-operation of the divisional school care officer, the Department of Health and Social Security, a social welfare officer, two mail order firms and a solicitor acting on behalf of a mail order firm.

In another case, in which the F.A.S. worker helped a family to 'work through' a range of problems which included marital conflict, debts, non-support by husband, housing problems, emotional and physical

[1] For a discussion of the functions of the Police Juvenile Bureau see Bilton (1970).

illness and attempted suicide, the F.A.S. worker liaised with two hospital medical social workers, a mental health clinic, a probation officer, the Department of Health and Social Security, the children's department, two housing trusts, a moral welfare officer and the headmistress of a school. A medical social worker commented that for the first time in two years' work in the hospital she had found a way of co-ordinating her work with a family with other agencies and of obtaining the full co-operation of other workers. She said that she wished there were more family advice centres of this kind available.

The 'C' project family advice centre recorded a case in which a young mother of three children and a history of mental and physical illness asked for help and advice about her urgent need for rehousing, the threatening break-up of her marriage, and an accumulation of debts. Besides providing the kind of supportive guidance this client needed, the F.A.S. worker took the following steps:

1. The worker discussed the client with her general practitioner who described the young couple as 'noisy' and 'extrovert', said that the young woman was 'obsessional' and 'compulsive' and that her present state of mind was 'constitutional' rather than due to her environmental pressures. (The F.A.S. worker described the living conditions of this family as follows: two adults and three children share a small flat consisting of one bedroom, a living room and a small kitchen; the toilet is situated five flights downstairs from the flat and shared between six adults and nine children. The ceiling of the flat has been leaking for some time and the landlord has so far refused to make any repairs. There are no play facilities for the children.)

2. The worker contacted the public health inspector who promised to put pressure on the landlord to repair the leaking roof. He suggested that the couple should apply for a rent reduction and advised the worker to discuss the case with the housing inspector. (On the health inspector's intervention the landlord started to repair the roof a week later.)

3. The F.A.S. worker contacted the housing inspector who promised to send someone to look at the family's flat.

4. The worker contacted the children's department to ask for help in rehousing the family. She was told that the department's priority rehousing list was full, and that it had become impossible in some cases to send children in care home because of the lack of adequate housing. The senior child care officer advised the worker to get in touch with the housing department.

5. The worker contacted the housing department. They told her that the family had 'lapsed from the housing list' and said it was difficult to understand why this had happened. They gave the worker information about rehousing in New Towns, but said that the fact that the husband was an unskilled labourer reduced the family's chances for rehousing in a New Town. (When the worker discussed this with her clients she was shown a postcard from the housing department addressed to the client which stated that further enquiries would serve no useful purpose.) The young couple spent an exhausting day trying to find out what had happened to their housing list number. They went to three separate housing departments as they had previously lived in another local authority area. Some papers were found which proved that their names had been transferred to their present borough housing list in 1965. The borough housing department had sent forms to the client and returned them as 'not completed'. The clients insisted that they had returned the forms completed, but the housing department stated that they had not received the forms and the name of the family had, therefore, been removed from the list.

6. The F.A.S. worker discussed her clients with the health visitor. The latter expressed the opinion that this family would not be helped by rehousing, and that there were many families who were worse off.

7. The worker contacted two housing trusts, but received negative replies.

8. The worker again discussed the possibility of rehousing in one of the New Towns with the housing department. She was told that housing in six New Towns was available, but it was very difficult to get unskilled workers admitted to these. The housing department also said that they were awaiting a report on the family by the health department and that they could do nothing about the lost forms and reinstatement on the housing list and that no exceptions could be made because this sort of thing happened so often. The worker then wrote to the housing department, restating the urgency of the case and asking for the department's co-operation in solving the difficulties of this family. Shortly after this the worker found out that the repairs made by the landlord had been ineffectual and that the ceiling in her client's flat was leaking worse than ever. Because there had been heavy rain the bedroom had become uninhabitable. The youngest child had acute bronchitis and the mother had become severely depressed and refused to talk to the worker. The F.A.S. worker informed the housing department of the worsening situation.

9. The F.A.S. worker discussed the case with her children's department supervisor. On the latter's advice she asked the department to send a child care officer to visit the family and offer them some casework support. The worker wrote to her client to announce the visit of the child care officer. She sent written applications for priority rehousing for the family to the children's department.

The children's department assigned a child care officer to visit the family and arranged for them to be offered a three-bedroom maisonette. The clients rejected this offer because there was no play space for the children. Rejecting the worker's advice to accept the new flat, they decided to wait for another offer. The young mother told the worker that she had overcome her depression and that her marriage had been saved because of the F.A.S. worker's help.

● A young married mother with one child, the mother a diabetic and in very bad physical condition, were referred to the 'D' project family advice centre by the nearby health clinic. They arrived at the clinic in a somewhat hysterical state. The couple had applied for an extra allowance at the local office of the Department of Health and Social Security the previous Friday as, perhaps due to mismanagement, they had been left without a penny. The D.H.S.S. officer had given them £4 and spoken to them severely, saying that if they could not manage, their child would be taken into care. The officer has asked the couple to return the following Tuesday, leaving them to subsist on £4 for five days. When Tuesday came, the couple were too frightened to return to the D.H.H.S. office, as they had taken the threat to remove their child seriously. Instead they went to the health clinic. A health visitor spoke to them and, after a rather angry and futile telephone conversation with the D.H.S.S. officer, referred them to the family advice centre. The F.A.S. worker calmed them down somewhat, assured them that the D.H.S.S. officer had no powers to put children into care, and drove them to the children's department to arrange for a Section 1 grant, leaving them after she had introduced them to a child care officer. About two hours later the health visitor called to say that the couple had returned to the clinic, having walked the considerable distance from the children's department. The child care officer had told them that they were not eligible for a Section 1 grant. At the clinic the family was given a meal. In response to the F.A.S. worker's enquiry, the children's department said that the family was apparently eligible for additional D.H.S.S. benefits and would have to obtain their money from that source. It was explained that the children's department could not use

Section 1 funds to provide grants to people who had a right to D.H.S.S. payments. This policy is undoubtedly correct. For the moment, however, the family was left destitute and, consequently, a child could be regarded as being 'at risk'.

The F.A.S. worker was left with the immediate task of getting the couple some money from whatever source. As a next step the D.H.S.S. officer had to be persuaded to make a grant, and do so without unwarranted threats. Later, perhaps, there would have to be an attempt to establish the kind of relationship with this officer which would enable the F.A.S. worker to point out to him that clients ought to be treated according to their statutory rights and that it was not his function to threaten and sit in judgment. A chat with the health visitor about the case was also in order, and a talk with the colleague in the children's department who had refused the grant. It would have to be pointed out that as the family had been referred to him, he should have informed the family advice centre immediately of his decision and would be expected to follow this procedure in future. At the next opportunity the policy of the department would have to be discussed with a senior officer. The worker would point out that in another recent case, the centre had referred a destitute client to the Department of Health and Social Security, giving her a letter explaining her situation. This client was also frightened of confronting the D.H.S.S. officer and had asked a health visitor for help. The latter had sent her to the children's department where she received an immediate emergency grant. The worker would point out that there was an inconsistency in the department's policy, which was confusing to him. He would suggest that the family advice centre be given a small reserve fund from which emergency grants under Section 1 of the Children's Act could be made in similar and, unfortunately quite frequent, cases.

Other types of difficulties arise when the F.A.S. worker has to advise a client who objects to a colleague from another agency on specific personal grounds. There was, for instance, the case where a woman awaiting trial on a morals charge told the F.A.S. worker that she could not discuss her situation with the probation officer who had been assigned to her, because the officer was a young girl, a fact which embarrassed the older woman. This should be regarded as a legitimate objection, acceptable to a professionally trained social worker. The F.A.S. worker found it difficult to interpret the client's needs to the probation officer. He did, however, find full understanding when he referred the client to the children's department and asked that a suitably mature officer be assigned.

Finally, another example of the centre's role in liaison and co-ordination:

● A man who was under treatment for alcoholism at the outpatient clinic of a local hospital came to the centre to ask for advice with regard to a housing problem. The F.A.S. worker helped to establish contact between the hospital and the housing department and asked a school care worker to visit the family to look into some problems affecting the client's children. The school care worker came to the centre to discuss the case and to seek guidance after she had visited the family and found the man's wife in a highly upset state. The F.A.S. worker helped the school care worker to establish contact with the psychiatric case worker at the hospital in order to discuss the situation of the man's family with her. As a result of the centre's intervention this client and his family became the focus of a co-ordinated helping process by three social workers who each dealt with specific and relevant aspects of the overall situation.

In the 'F' project centre a good deal of the fostering of better mutual understanding between the community and the services was brought about through the parents' association. Representatives of the children's and housing departments and the police were invited to parents' association meetings. They had the opportunity to explain the policies and methods of their services, to answer questions and engage in discussion. These officials as well as members of the community who met with them told the F.A.S. worker that they had acquired new understanding, and saw the needs of the area and their own approaches to meeting these needs in better perspectives, as a result of these discussions. One of the most beneficial practical results was the agreement of the housing department to make an officer available to answer questions and advise the local inhabitants once a week at the family advice centre. At the end of August 1969, the F.A.S. worker wrote in a letter to the housing manager: 'Mr R [a housing inspector] has been interviewing clients with housing difficulties every Wednesday afternoon for the last three months and the parents' association has asked me to inform you that this arrangement has been very useful.'

A few out of many examples which could be cited may serve to describe some of the ways in which the F.A.S. worker sought to meet the requirements of the liaison and mediation goals in the daily practice of the centre.

Shortly after the opening of the 'F' project family advice centre a local school-teacher dropped in. She had heard about the centre from some of the youngsters in her class and wanted to see what it was all about. What she saw were about a dozen children, some of them sitting at a table, others running about, a few sprawling on the floor, all of them busy drawing pictures. While she talked to the F.A.S. worker youngsters interrupted excitedly to show him a picture or to ask for crayons; a mother came in waving a printed form: 'I got this in the mail, Mr R, what's it mean?' The telephone rang and while the teacher watched a little girl get tangled up in sticky tape trying to patch up a torn sheet of paper, she heard the F.A.S. worker say: 'I am quite certain that this debt will be paid, but you must give us a little more time, the old gentleman is coming out of hospital tomorrow, and we must given him a few days to settle down before raising the matter with him.' When the worker put down the phone, apologising for the interruption, the teacher was reprimanding a little girl who had pulled one of the desk drawers open and was rummaging through its contents. She was surprised and looked a bit sceptical when the worker told her: 'We are very permissive with the youngsters; you see we want them to feel accepted and to be able to express themselves freely. They get their fingers into everything and we don't interfere, once they've satisfied their curiosity they lose interest in my desk.' Teacher and F.A.S. worker discussed the pros and cons of permissiveness, the differences in children's behaviour in the classroom and in the centre, the need for youngsters to find things out for themselves, to experiment, to express their feelings about themselves and their environment. When the teacher left she said that she would like to visit the centre again and that she wanted to introduce the F.A.S. worker to her headmaster.

● In October 1968 the parents' association discussed the hazards presented by a derelict factory near the centre. The children chased each other and climbed about inside the factory, and they might get hurt. The week before a little boy had come out of there with acid burns on his hands. One of the fathers thought there might be remnants of petrol in some rusty tin cans in the cellar. The F.A.S. worker called the housing department several times to ask that the factory be made secure. Weeks passed and nothing was done. The worker asked for an appointment with Mr E, senior housing department official responsible for the area. He explained the goals and functions of the family advice centre and Mr E listened, asked pertinent questions and promised his support.

The following day Mr H, another housing department official contacted the centre and discussed the situation with the F.A.S. worker. The worker used the opportunity to point out that much of the anxiety of the people in the area and their hostility towards the housing department was due to the lack of information regarding the department's redevelopment and rehousing plans. Was it not possible for the department to tell the people what was going to happen to them? Mr H said that it was difficult to give any definite information as the department itself was not certain about the plans for this area. The worker said that perhaps the department should tell people this. Could someone from the department come to the centre and talk to the parents' association? Mr H said that it sounded like a good idea. He suggested a request for such a meeting should be made in a letter to the housing manager. He told the worker to contact another housing department official with regard to the securing of the factory. The meeting between the parents' association and a housing department official was arranged. The worker's continued efforts to get the factory secured did not meet with success. Eventually the parents' association formed a working party of fathers who boarded up the door and windows of the factory.

One afternoon a member of the children's committee visited the centre. He was introduced to the chairman of the parents' association. After a few minutes the F.A.S. worker was called away to deal with a client's request for help and the councillor and the parents' association chairman talked for almost an hour about the rehousing problems in the area. The councillor later expressed his appreciation for the opportunity to get some firsthand information about the feelings of the community.

●   In December 1968 a voluntary organisation offered to give a Christmas party to fifty neighbourhood children. The organisation offered the use of a large hall, transportation to and from the party, refreshments and gifts for the children. A list of fifty children was drawn up by the parents' association and submitted to the president of the organisation by the F.A.S. worker. It was agreed that several members of the self-help subcommittee would accompany the children and help to supervise the activities.

A few days before the event an official of the organisation called and withdrew the offer, saying that, due to unforeseen circumstances, the hall would not be available. There was an angry reaction from the parents and great disappointment among the children who had eagerly anticipated the party. The F.A.S. worker explained the feelings of the community to the voluntary organisation and pointed out that they had assumed a responsibility when they made a definite offer to provide the party. At the worker's suggestion the organisation agreed to send the promised refreshments and gifts to the centre, so that substitute arrangements could be made. A local school agreed to make a hall available and the parents' association organised the preparation for the event. The party was attended by well over double the number of children originally invited and by many parents. It was a great success. Members of the voluntary organisation came, were pleased and impressed, and returned to visit the centre on several other occasions. The organisation became a valuable supporter of the centre from then on.

A meeting between the F.A.S. worker and officials of the housing department and the Department of Health and Social Security was arranged with the help of the deputy children's officer. There was a useful discussion of the interrelated problems of rehousing and financial assistance in the area. The suggestion that an official of each of the two agencies be available to interview members of the community at the family advice centre once a week was accepted by the housing department, but rejected by the Department of Health and Social Security. A week later the housing department lettings officer and a senior inspector visited the centre, talked to members of the community about blocked drains and other problems and visited the home of one of the families with the F.A.S. worker. Some weeks later a delegation of mothers came to the centre and told the worker angrily that they were 'fed up' with not knowing what was happening with regard to their rehousing. They said that they were organising a protest march to the housing department. The F.A.S. worker discussed the proposed march with them and suggested that an attempt should be made to communicate the frustration of the group to the housing department before a march took place. The group agreed. The worker called the housing department. Within the hour a housing department official with a clerical assistant arrived at the centre. They brought the files on the area with them, interviewed fourteen families and made some direct offers of rehousing. One of the mothers told the worker afterwards: 'We feel much easier in our minds now.'

The F.A.S. worker's continuous emphasis that all the social services must be asked to combine their efforts to improve the situation of the area did not fall on deaf ears in the community. The degree to which the people of the neighbourhood had learned to understand the need for such a combined effort is reflected in a letter sent to three statutory departments by a group of sixteen families in May 1969. The letter asked explicitly for a co-ordinated effort by the housing, health and children's departments to 'take the necessary and immediate action to prevent us and our children from having to live in the present conditions . . . which are disrupting family life'.

The following example from the files of the 'G' project centre may serve to show the recurring need for the F.A.S. worker to explain her functions and to reassure other services that she was supplementing their own work, rather than interfering needlessly:

● The F.A.S. worker had, for some time, helped an old lady who suffered from Parkinson's Disease. She frequently went up to her flat to light the stove, to see that she ate properly, write letters for her and, at one time, arranged for a 'Good Neighbour' to be assigned to her by the health department. When this came to the attention of a senior official of the welfare department she told the worker that the care of the old lady was her own agency's concern and that the F.A.S. worker had exceeded her functions. A meeting was arranged in order to discuss the issues involved. After the F.A.S. worker had explained the reasons for her intervention, the welfare department official agreed that welfare officers carried very large case loads and were often only able to make home visits at long intervals. While pointing out that old people should be encouraged to do as much as possible for themselves, the official agreed that this particular old lady would benefit from the services offered by the F.A.S. worker.

One of the characteristics of the 'G' project setting was the presence of a substantial number of families who became involved with many different social workers and officials either simultaneously or in rapid succession. The policies and services of the different workers were rarely co-ordinated to any significant degree and this led, in a number of instances, to all kinds of confusions, contradictions and misunderstandings among workers, officials and clients. This state of affairs also reinforced the already pronounced tendencies for manipulation, a method of coping with problem situations which was not only time-wasting and annoying to the professionals, but all too often detrimental to the interests of the clients. The F.A.S. worker was able in some cases to initiate the appointment of a 'key worker' or to assume this 'key' responsibility herself. It did, in fact, prove rather difficult for the F.A.S. worker, and absorbed much of her time and energy, to convince some of her colleagues that her specific functions, her on-the-spot availability and her relationship to the community provided the various agencies with a useful trouble-shooter-cum-co-ordinator and that it was in everyone's interest to avail themselves of the opportunities for co-operation provided by the detached family advice centre. In the case of some agencies and/or officials the marked distrust of the new service was never entirely overcome.

● The F.A.S. worker's many attempts to act as mediator between a confused and harassed client and a busy official or professional sometimes put the worker in a somewhat embarrassing situation. On one occasion, for instance, a distraught mother told the worker that her six-year-old son had wet himself at school. The headmistress had informed her of this, saying that she would not tolerate this behaviour and that she would have to punish the child physically if it happened again. Now the frightened little boy did not want to go to school. His mother said: 'Betty, like a fool I told the headmistress to go ahead and smack him. But my husband told me off and he's right. We don't want the kid beaten for something he can't help.' The F.A.S. worker knew that the child was somewhat retarded and had a speech defect, but his mother insisted that he did not usually wet himself at home. As the boy had to go to school the following morning, the worker felt that she had to intervene right away. She telephoned the school, explained to the headmistress who she was and what she was calling about and asked her to please refrain from physical punishment in case the boy should wet himself again in school. The headmistress asked, somewhat sharply, by what right the worker sought to interfere in matters which did not concern her. The F.A.S. worker said that she had merely drawn the attention of the headmistress to a situation which had aroused the anxiety of parents, and that she was fully entitled to do so as a child care officer. She tried to add some further explanations about the problems facing the boy, but the head- mistress informed her that she was 'very busy' and hung up. At this the worker as well as the boy's mother were rather upset and feared that the worker's intervention might have made matters worse. The F.A.S. worker contacted the project supervisor and the latter reassured her somewhat, saying that while it was doubtful that child care officers had a right to tell a headmistress not to smack a child, the fact that the F.A.S. worker had explained the situation and shown her interest in the matter would most probably cause the headmistress to give the issues involved some more thought. The child's mother gave the F.A.S. worker some idea of how her boy 'got on' at school. There was no physical punishment of the child and, after a few weeks, he had appar- ently made a good adjustment in school.

The F.A.S. worker also had to face the fact that a substantial number of her clients had acquired a certain notoriety in the borough and had a reputation for aggressive and manipulative behaviour which caused at least some officials and social workers to confront them with a degree of distrust and resentment. The F.A.S. worker had to invest a large pro- portion of her time and energy in breaching some of the barriers erected by harassed officials on the one hand, while trying to convince some of her clients of the unreasonable, self-defeating nature of their own attitudes and behaviour patterns on the other hand. This meant, in practice, that a large proportion of her time was taken up by liaison and mediation work between her clients and other agencies, and that her success in helping an individual, a family or the community as a whole was greatly dependent upon her skill and patience in carrying out this function. There is no doubt as to the F.A.S. worker's skill and resourcefulness in this area of her work. No one who has closely observed the numerous obstacles she had to overcome, put in her way by the people she sought to help, as well as by some of the colleagues and officials with whom she negotiated on her clients' behalf, will be astonished to note that her patience sometimes wore a bit thin.

Some attention should be drawn to the special problems posed by carrying out the liaison/mediation function with regard to the housing departments. In all the areas served by the family advice centres housing problems were acute and a very significant number of clients sought help with regard to such problems, and often needed advice concerning their negotiations with the housing departments. In the areas served by the 'G' project and the 'F' project centres housing problems were especially severe and the situation was exacerbated by the tensions and anxieties of slum clearance and the processes of rehousing or, in the term used by one of the housing authorities, 'decantation'. As some of the examples we cited will have shown, mediating between clients and housing departments did, at times, lead to some degree of tension between the family advice centres and housing departments staff. But, as we have also shown, there were cases in which housing department officials welcomed the F.A.S. workers' intervention and extended their full co-operation. The Seebohm Report pointed out that 'there is a great need for advice and guidance on housing matters . . .' (para 391), and proposed the setting up of housing advice centres. Our observations showed that family advice centres could be regarded as the appropriate agencies to furnish such advice. The 'F' project centre demonstrated that this type of advice can be provided in co-operation with the housing departments. There is no doubt that this area of service is beset with problems and obstacles and will, on occasions, lead to some manifestations of conflict of interests between the F.A.S. worker, intervening on behalf of his clients, and the housing authorities, overwhelmed by requests, chronically short of resources and in duty bound to enforce official policies. A recent American investigation underlines the inherent difficulties:

Findings obtained in the current study suggest the influence of social handicap or stigma on the relationship of the lower-status tenant to the public housing system, a relationship not unlike that between disadvantaged groups and

service bureaucracy generally. Socially handicapped tenants were less know-
ledgable about bureaucratic power structure and apparently were neglected
in favour of their unhandicapped counterparts (Levin and Taube, 1970).

A British writer asks 'how local authorities identify their poorest
tenants', and suggests that:

There seems a reasonable possibility that many do not; that rebates are not
received by some of the poorest families largely because income is measured in
crude terms and little attention is paid to income per head. Just as some of the
poorest families tend not to be in council houses, so those who are stand in some
danger of not receiving the benefits which differential rent schemes appear to
offer (Parker, 1962).

These findings reflect a situation which resembles that which we
observed in the council estate served by the 'G' project centre. Housing
departments can benefit from the on-the-spot availability of a family
advice centre and we found that, in some instances, the departments
acknowledged this and availed themselves of the mediation/liaison
function of the F.A.S. staff.

The high incidence of mediation on behalf of clients in need of
supplementary benefits and other forms of officially provided financial
assistance also demands attention. In many instances clients sought the
help of the F.A.S. workers in cases of financial need, where the client
did not know that he was entitled to official provisions, or where the
client had not been able to obtain the benefits to which he was entitled.
As Robert Holman (1970) pointed out:

Application would be easier if the attitudes of officials were always encouraging
and accepting. The Supplementary Benefits Commission has endeavoured to
improve the attitudes of its officers; none the less it is still claimed that some are
overbearing or off-hand, so deterring the questioning of the amount of benefit
awarded, or the appealing to a higher body (p. 189).

Another writer observes that 'little is known about the availability,
utilisation and effectiveness of advice for those contemplating appeals'
(Bell, 1969, p. 85), and Professor Abel-Smith (1968) emphasised that:

Before an applicant can be expected to apply for any benefit he must know how
to apply, when to apply and where to apply. Without expert help from a social
worker or Citizen's Advice Bureau or local information centre, the citizen
cannot be expected to have this knowledge. Centres where he can obtain this
help do not exist in every area and not all of them that do exist are equipped
with even this minimum of information. For many of the existing selective
benefits, eligibility requirements are a closely kept secret: the scales, disregards
and allowances are not published. This makes it impossible for the citizen to
know if he has been refused benefit simply because of an arithmetic error made
by a clerk or because of an error in his employer's accounts department. It
also makes it impossible for him to appeal against an adverse decision (p. 113).

Our observations showed that the family advice centre can and does fulfil an important function in providing clients with guidance with regard to financial assistance and in intervening on their behalf when necessary. Department of Health and Social Security officials and other agencies involved in this process sometimes co-operated willingly and regarded the F.A.S. worker as a colleague and ally. In some cases, however, the officials regarded the worker as an irritant and his attempts at mediation as unwarranted interference.

One of the measures of success of the liaison/mediation function seems to present itself in the frequency and validity of referrals to the family advice centre by other agencies. In practice, however, this supposition remained unproven and, in some instances, seemed to be contradicted by the fact. In all the centres referrals from the statutory agencies were recorded, but there were also referrals from voluntary agencies, the police, doctors, solicitors, clergymen, borough councillors, teachers etc. Some marked differences between the different F.A.S. settings deserve some attention:

In the 'C' project centre there were 66 referrals, out of a total of 293 from the legal advice centre. As the L.A.C. was located next door to the centre in the same agency, this is understandable enough. There were also 22 referrals from the local Citizens' Advice Bureau. This is of some interest because the question of a possible duplication of functions between the family advice service and the C.A.B. had been raised on several occasions (Leissner, 1967, pp. 62–4). We found the explanation for the relatively high incidence of C.A.B. referrals, which did not occur in the other centres, in the fact that the local Bureau participated in the initial discussion which preceded the setting up of the 'C' project centre. Apparently the possibility of setting up a combined centre staff by both agencies had been considered at one point. The fact that only two referrals by the children's departments appear on the records may be regarded as an indication of the lack of integration of the voluntary setting with the sponsoring statutory department.

In the detached setting of the 'D' project centre the number of 59 out of a total of 335 referrals from health visitors shows both the influence of the physical proximity of the health clinic, and the good working relationships which were established between F.A.S. staff and health visitors.

The most noteworthy fact that emerged from the observation of the community-based centres was that the incidence of referrals from other agencies was very low, and that the great majority of clients were self-referrals, referrals by friends and neighbours or were referred by community organisations which, in most cases, had been initiated by the F.A.S. staff.

A few examples may serve to show the kind and the validity of the referrals made by other agencies:

Referrals from Citizens' Advice Bureaux included a father who sought advice on how to react to the discovery that his sixteen-year-old daughter was pregnant, and a middle-class lady who wanted to discuss her pending divorce and her fear that her husband would 'kidnap' her baby.

Health visitors referred a mother of four children whose husband was in jail, and who was worried about her steadily increasing debts, the wife of a physically disabled man and mother of a small baby who suffered from the dampness and the extremely inadequate sanitary conditions of her home, and another mother who lived in one room without running water or toilet facilities with her five children.

A mother of three children at first sought the help of the police when her husband deserted her. She was sent to the welfare department where an official directed her to the family advice centre.

Another mother was sent to the family advice centre by the police when she reported to the latter that her fourteen-year-old son was stealing.

Before we conclude the discussion on co-ordination, mediation and liaison, some remarks about the case conference are in order in this context. Forder (1966) tells us:

Case conferences are useful where a number of workers are engaged in helping the same individual or family. The view has been expressed that the main purpose of these meetings is not to help the client but to help the worker. There is some truth in this (p. 190).

It would seem that there is nothing wrong with devising methods, such as the case conference, which help the workers, provided that this is to the benefit, not the detriment of the client. However, the same author raises a more important issue when he relates the pros and cons of the case conference to the question of confidentiality and the client's rights. He suggests that: 'There is a good deal to be said for someone who knows the family well discussing with the family beforehand any proposal to hold a case conference (p. 190). This does, indeed, touch upon one of the problems raised by the case conference in the F.A.S. setting. Our observations showed that, in some instances, the participation in case conferences furthered co-ordination of services and helped the different workers to exchange information and to gain better understanding not only of the client's, but of their own problems. There were, however, occasions when the F.A.S. workers felt uneasy about participating in case conferences in which clients were discussed without their knowledge and consent. There was also one case in which an angry client confronted the F.A.S. worker with a grossly distorted version of what the worker was supposed to have said about the client in a case conference. The client insisted that the statement which had upset her was reported to her by another statutory official who had attended the meeting.

We are convinced that the potential benefits of case conferences outweigh the possibilities of misuse. We feel, however, that F.A.S. staff should *not* participate in case conferences without the knowledge and consent of the client, and that every effort should be made to persuade all the social workers and officials concerned that, in most instances, it is possible and desirable to ask the client himself to be present at a case conference in order to hear what the people whose appointed task it is to help him have to say, and in order to express his own needs, wishes and opinions. It seems to us that, in most cases, there is no acceptable reason why a client should not be invited to discuss his own 'case' with the people who are seeking to help him resolve his problems, and that, on the whole, anything which cannot be said in the presence of the client, should not be said at all.

We were led to conclude that the family advice centres demonstrated clearly that they provide a valuable and badly needed service in assuming the responsibilities for sorting out who does what, when, where and why in the complex social service system. In doing so they assumed a role, that of liaison person and mediator, which perhaps more than any other demands great tact and professional sophistication. Quite understandably, the unavoidable feelings of impatience and frustration sometimes rose to the surface. However, we are well reminded that: 'Social workers as well as clients and administrators, are influenced by their feelings and by their need to feel secure in their working relationships' (Forder, 1966, p. 183). The F.A.S. worker's success in carrying out the liaison/mediation function therefore depends to a high degree upon his ability to bear this dictum in mind at all times and this, in turn, depends very often upon the support and encouragement he receives from his own agency.

5 Community work

The Gulbenkian Report (1968) tells us: 'Community work is essentially about the interrelations between people and social change, how to help people and the providers of services to bring about a more comfortable "fit" between themselves and constant change, how to survive and grow as persons in relation with others' (pp. 28–9). This definition encompasses the generic goals of social work itself, as well as the specific functions of liaison and mediation. The relevance to the goals and functions of the family advice service is apparent. As the exploratory study showed, community work was already included in the pioneering work of one of the earlier family advice centres (Leissner, 1967, p. 43). What we learned about the role of community work in family advice work led us to further investigation of this aspect of the family advice service. Our observations showed that community work can not only make a very significant contribution to the scope and effectiveness of the service, but may also provide a frame of reference for the entire range of family advice service functions. We started out with the assumption that community work would grow out of the requirements of advice, guidance, assistance, mediation/liaison and referral functions. We found that, while this holds true initially, the family advice service staff's receptiveness to the community work approach inevitably results in a marked increase of the demand for the entire range of services to individuals and families offered by the family advice centres.

The community worker has been described as:

the front-line man whose task it is to address himself to the social problems where they arise and spread, namely where people live. His job is to enable the community either first of all to become one, or to become a better socially healthier one. In doing so, due to the priorities of need, the community worker will very often find that helping people to improve their lives as members of a community means to help them to organise themselves to bring about changes in situations which are at best inadequate or, at the worst, destructive of decent living and human dignity (Leissner, 1968, p. 2408).

In observing the detached, community-based family advice centres we found that the F.A.S. worker in this setting gradually assumes the role and characteristics of the community worker, without, however, relinquishing the specific role of the family advice service worker.

Any discussion of community work immediately raises the question of what we mean by the term 'community'. Definitions of 'community' have been vague[1] and the term is often used in its widest sense to describe the whole of society. This kind of definition is obviously irrelevant to our purpose. More suitable is the description of a community as 'a living-together unit within society consisting of a grouping of individuals and families who live in close geographic proximity and, to varying degrees, share cultural traditions and socio-economic conditions' (Leissner, 1969a, p. 42). A textbook of sociology states: 'Wherever the members of any group, small or large, live together in such a way that they share not this or that particular interest, but the basic conditions of a common life, we can call that group a community' (MacIver and Page, 1962, p. 15). These two definitions appear to be complementary and can be applied to the areas served by the family advice centres including a 'mixed' neighbourhood of privately owned housing and council housing estates, a single medium-sized housing estate and an old-established urban neighbourhood in the process of dispersal through slum-clearance.

In our attempts at evaluating the effectiveness and the implications of community work in the F.A.S. setting we were, of course, influenced by our own belief that the warmth and security of community life is greatly preferable to living in isolation, regimentation or social chaos. We therefore tended to measure the success of community work by the degree to which it succeeded in stimulating, maintaining and strengthening all positive aspects of community life. However, some of the communities served by the family advice centres presented the F.A.S. workers with realities which were very far from ideal. These communities afforded their members little protection from the severe pressures and conflicts to which they were exposed. Where one could say that the community was the setting in which society in all its complicity became tangible, this tangibility was, all too often, experienced by the community as an amorphous, alien, and confusing threat, a cause of deprivation and a source of 'trouble'. Nor did we expect or find a rational consciousness of community relationships, identity, potentialities and limitations. It was the task of community work to try to introduce or re-awaken some of this consciousness.

[1] See, for instance, Stacey (June 1969b).

Community work (or 'community organisation' in the American usage) has been defined as

a process by which a community identifies its needs or objectives, orders (or ranks) these needs or objectives, develops the confidence and will to work at these needs or objectives, finds the resources (internal and/or external) to deal with these needs or objectives, takes action in respect to them, and in so doing extends and develops co-operative and collaborative attitudes and practices in the community (Ross, 1955, p. 39).

It has been described as:

The process of bringing about and maintaining a progressively more effective adjustment between social welfare resources and social welfare needs within a geographic area or functional field. Its goals are consistent with the social work goals in that its primary focus is upon needs of people and provision of means of meeting these needs in a manner consistent with the precepts of democratic living (McNeil, 1951, p. 123).

In the following pages we shall try to show how the goals and functions of community work grew out of the initial F.A.S. functions, how they helped to supplement the other F.A.S. functions and make them more effective, and by what methods and approaches the F.A.S. workers met the tasks and challenges of community work.

In the descriptive account of community work in four of the seven F.A.S. settings we shall distinguish between (1) *community action*, and (2) *services to the community*. These are distinctions of emphasis rather than precise differences of methods and goals.

Under the heading of community action, we shall include those community work processes which consisted of organisational activities within the community aimed at articulating the community's needs and demands, bringing about specific changes and at making services and resources available. For example, the initiation or the revitalisation of community groups aimed at improving housing conditions, obtaining information with regard to social services and planning policies and/or the introduction of certain provisions and services. This might take the form of a tenants' association which gives expression to the community's anxieties about redevelopment and rehousing policies, demands information with regard to these policies and represents the interests of individual members or groups in the community. Or else it may be a parents' group whose primary interest is the safety and the improvement of play facilities for the community's children.

Under the heading of services to the community we shall describe those processes and events which led to the provision of specific services, such as play facilities, youth clubs, mothers' groups, legal advice, which benefit the community as a whole. At least initially, these services to the community were provided by the family advice centres and the community was the recipient of the service. Here community participation and involvement was, at least in the beginning stages, less pronounced than in those processes we define as community action. However, in most cases, the family advice centre's objective in initiating the services was not only to meet specific needs, but also to bring about community involvement and participation in planning and execution.

It should be emphasised, and our description will show this, that the two kinds of community work often overlapped. Community action resulted in the provision of services to the community, and the provision of such services stimulated the emergence of community groups which engaged in community action with regard to issues which were either directly related to the need for specific services, or else were one of the effects of a greater degree of community cohesion resulting from the shared experience of helping to obtain and operate a community service. In fact, the various types of community work in any one of the areas often became integral parts of an overall community-oriented approach in which all the other functions of the family advice service, such as advice, guidance, assistance, referral and liaison/mediation played a major role.

The F.A.S. workers acted as initiators, consultants, resource persons and mediators in all the community work processes we observed. The intensity and frequency of their direct involvement, whether they exerted their influence and leadership openly or remained in the background, whether they themselves assumed responsibilities and carried out some of the work of community groups, or whether they restricted themselves to a supporting advisory role, whether they tended to keep the reins in their own hands or focused upon activating members of the community and urging them to assume responsibilities—all this depended on such factors as the demands and the potentialities of the situation, adequate or inadequate staffing of the centres, the characteristics of the communities and last but not least, the F.A.S. workers' own knowledge, skills and personalities.

For obvious reasons community work was most intensive in the detached, community-based centres, but the other settings were by no means unaware of the potentialities of community involvement.

In the 'A' project family advice centre, which was beset by many problems from its initiation and which, in fact, never really developed into an effective family advice service, a working party initiated by the child care officers assigned to F.A.S. duties stated in its findings the need for community involvement.

When the children's department decided to appoint one full time
F.A.S. worker, rather than continue the rotation system of five child
care officers which had been proved impractical, the job description
drawn up by the area officer in consultation with the staff stated:

Because of liaison with various social work agencies and involvement with the
community both in work and play, the Advice Worker will become aware of the
inadequacies of the social framework and the needs of the community. This will
give the worker the opportunity of helping to originate and develop groups and
project work such as play groups within certain areas.

In the 'B' project the possibilities of community work were first
raised with regard to the 'transient' families of military personnel in a
nearby army base. While most of the child care and welfare officers did
not feel that there was a need for 'reaching out' work in this area, the
opinion was expressed that there might be some need to help the camp
families in their relations with the local community whose members had,
on occasion, expressed resentment about the behaviour of these families
and had voiced concern that the camp children were lowering the community's educational standards. For a variety of reasons inherent in the
structure of this centre the possibility of community work with regard to
this kind of need was not put to the test. Another opportunity for taking
the first steps in community work presented itself when a local emergency
disrupted the life of the small town in which the centre was located,
affecting the poorest section of the town specially severely. The staff
discussed the possibility of going out of the agency to offer help and advice
directly to the afflicted families, but it was decided that statutory duties
obliged the workers to remain available for requests for help in the
agency. On one occasion the discussion turned to the possibility of
'detached' family advice centres, a possibility which had already been
hinted at previously. The disproportionate number of problems in a
large, privately owned, old country house on the outskirts of the town
which had been converted into flatlets was mentioned in this context.
It was felt that an on-the-spot family advice worker might alleviate
the situation there. Two supervised sites for gypsies which had just been
approved by the county council could also benefit from a 'detached'
or visiting worker. Someone said: 'Perhaps we don't know what service
people want because we don't try hard enough to find out by going out
and asking them.'

The settlement house in which the 'C' project family advice centre
was located had a long tradition of community involvement which had
become more clearly defined and more receptive to the application of
professional skills and methods in recent years. Recognition of the

potentialities of the F.A.S. setting for community work was given in the settlement's 1968 Annual Report in which we read:

We have been conscious for some time of the need for the case worker to go out into the community, rather than to wait for clients to come to the office. The relationship between case worker and community worker has yet to be worked out but it is a territory we are exploring, in the belief that incipient family problems can be prevented from deteriorating by the worker being known and available within the community, helping to mobilise neighbours, tenants' associations and the social services to meet the needs as they arise. We are in an area of rapid change and redevelopment, and there is a great scope for this sort of work on our doorstep. In practice and immediately, this has involved us in a play scheme for school children in the summer holidays, and in trying to meet the urgent need for playgroups for the tenants of the new blocks of flats, for which we hope to get the cooperation of the Housing Department for the use of their premises.

The head of the settlement house compared the local situation with that of an earlier detached centre located in a council housing estate and wrote:

The question relevant to the advice service is whether or not a similar approach can work in an area with similar problems but without the same sense of neighbourhood or quite so acute a concentration of difficulties; where main roads with plenty of buses exist but where social problems are still rampant; where redevelopment has scattered people or is scattering them and tearing up long established roots, making people's lives more anxious and difficult and giving the social worker extra, more diffuse problems, and less of a network of community relationships to work on.

During the period of this study the F.A.S. workers continued to discuss and explore the possibilities of integrating community work with the established functions of the family advice centre. The workers felt (a) that by mobilising community resources the centre would be in a better position to do preventive work, and (b) that increased availability of the F.A.S. workers within the community would enable them to identify hitherto unreached needs and initiate referrals to the centre. The F.A.S. workers helped to organise and maintain a two-week summer play scheme on one of the housing estates. In the course of this activity the workers co-operated with the settlement house community worker in meeting with the tenants' association of the estate and in establishing direct contact with the tenant families. One of the F.A.S. workers supervised a group of student volunteers who helped to run the play scheme.

While a beginning was made, it became apparent that the fundamental change in the concepts and methods of the centre which must be regarded as essential for a significant shift to community work did not come about.

In the 'E' project centre the F.A.S. worker invested considerable skill and energy in initiating services to the community, either on the correct assumption of need, or in response to expressions of need by clients or a combination of both. The youth clubs, the adventure playground, the arts and crafts play group, the mothers and children group and the legal advice service (which was initiated by the F.A.S. worker in the summer of 1969 but did not become operative until after the termination of the research period) were all services to the community. There is no question as to the need for and the value of these services, but all of them suffered to some degree from the lack of roots within the community. All these services brought about a fair amount of *community contacts*, but there were no significant indications of community *participation* and involvement. In this context it should be noted that the management committee which undoubtedly made a significant contribution to the services for children and youth provided by the centre, could not be regarded as a grass roots community organisation representative of the inhabitants of the area, and potentially able to enlist the support and stimulate the involvement of the community.

The Gulbenkian Report (1968) observed that:

It is precisely at the gap between result and purpose that community work comes to interpret to the local authorities how the services appear to the consumer, what is lacking in the services themselves and the way they are provided, and thus to facilitate a mutual adaptation between people and the services.

The 'E' project centre had a wide range of opportunities to carry out these tasks of interpretation, and to involve the inhabitants of the neighbourhood more closely and creatively in the provision of services to the area. The centre made skilful use of some of these opportunities, but it did *not* succeed in drawing any significant representative community groups into this decisively important process. One of the reasons for this was the fact that the target area, and the adjacent streets which soon became part of the action radius of the centre, made it difficult to identify and define community structures and characteristics, more difficult than, for instance, a housing estate or a cohesive, geographically well-defined and long-established neighbourhood.

The question as to whether the area served by the 'E' project family advice centre could or could not be defined as a community or possibly contained a number of different community groups, what discernible community structures existed in the area, or whether a marked absence of community cohesion did or did not indicate the need for fostering community activities, could not be fully answered. The answering of these basic questions should, however, be regarded as an integral part of a 'detached' community oriented family advice centre.

6

It should be stressed that the range of services the 'E' project centre provided must be regarded as a very valid contribution to meeting the needs of the area, and that these services did constitute a sound basis for the further development of community participation after the termination of the two-year study period.

The staff of the 'D' project family advice centre has been engaged in a variety of community work activities in the area for some time before the beginning of our study. During the eighteen months study period the centre broadened and deepened the scope and intensity of its community work. The 'E' project and 'F' project centres also engaged in a wide range of community activities, each centre responding to the specific needs and conditions presented by its client population. In these three detached family advice centres the staff achieved an impressive measure of success in integrating community work with the other F.A.S. functions. The community work carried out by these centres was very much concerned with social change and the interrelations between people. In carrying out the functions of advice, guidance and assistance, the F.A.S. workers were, at times, confronted with people whose relations with each other appeared to consist of a state of perpetual crisis in which acts of neighbourliness and community solidarity, which had once been much in evidence, had become exceptions which seemed to prove the rule of anomie and the lack of common concern. The workers' first task often was simply to use the relationships they established with the fast growing number of people who sought their help, to re-awaken the vestiges of community spirit still existing, to revive remnants of group solidarity and to help people get along better with their neighbours. In some instances this had to be done under ever-mounting pressures of deprivation and insecurity to which the people were subjected. There is no doubt that the family advice centres had some noteworthy successes in stimulating community spirit, in improving living conditions, and relations between neighbours.

Let us now take a closer look at the range of community work activities in the four detached family advice centres:

Tenants' associations and other community action groups

A British writer remarked:

At the preventive level, it seems to me that we often fail to make use of the local community and its constituent groups . . . Local groups can be pepped up to do a more effective job. Furthermore, new kinds of groups can be injected into the locality to pep up the whole neighbourhood (Mays, 1965, p. 74).

Our observations showed that community groups existed in the areas served by several of the detached centres. In most cases these groups, chiefly tenants' associations, had become ineffectual and needed new stimuli and professional guidance. The F.A.S. workers very soon realised the potentialities of such groups. They made skilful use of many of the opportunities presented by even the faintest traces of community structure and organisation, and also acted as the initiators and supporters of newly created community groups.

Community groups in the area served by the 'D' project centre

As already pointed out, the 'D' project family advice centre was involved in community work before the start of the F.A.S. study. It should also be mentioned here that the centre's community work was aided significantly by the availability of an ancillary worker.

In April 1968 a client referred by her health visitor complained about the lack of play facilities for children at the S Estate. A subsequent investigation by the ancillary worker in block A of the estate resulted in a meeting at the family advice centre of eighteen mothers from three blocks. It was decided that there was a need for supervised play facilities and an adventure playground, that a nearby street should be closed to traffic and turned into a play street, and that an open space behind a brewery could be put to use as a play area.

About the same time complaints from residents of a fourth block in the estate regarding the loitering of 'tramps' led the ancillary and the F.A.S. workers to visit this block. On this occasion residents expressed their wish to form a tenants' association.

During May 1968 the two workers investigated the possibilities of obtaining play facilities for the S Estate. The F.A.S. worker contacted the appropriate agencies but received negative replies. The residents rejected this response and urged the forming of a tenants' committee to pursue the matter.

While exploring the possibilities of providing play facilities for the S Estate, the F.A.S. workers helped a group of tenants to organise a general meeting in a local church hall. During this and two further meetings a tenants' association was formed, a committee and officers were elected and a wide range of community problems was discussed. The F.A.S. worker acted as consultant and liaison person to the association. The first success came when permission was obtained to use an open space between the blocks of the estate as a playground. The tenants themselves cleaned the playground area, the committee appointed a playleader and applied to several charitable trusts for financial assistance. About two months after its formation the tenants' association decided to join the Association of London Housing Estates and to take part in the fight against G.L.C. rent increases.

During the following months the tenants' association took part in a 'Happiness March' to open a local 'Summer Project' in which the ancillary and the F.A.S. worker participated with parents and about fifty children. A special subcommittee was formed to supervise the S Estate playground. The ancillary worker was instructed to canvass another block on the estate and, as a result, the tenants of that block joined the tenants' association.

The tenants' association was active in the following ways:

(a) As a result of a meeting with the area housing manager of the G.L.C., which involved official recognition of the S Estate tenants' association, better service on the estate re repairs and maintenance was achieved.

(b) Representatives of the tenants' association attended a meeting of the borough's residents' association to protest about rent increases.

(c) The secretary, on instructions from the tenants' association—and with guidance from the F.A.S. worker—wrote to London Transport to try to get a bus stop moved to a more suitable place.

(d) The association worked out a system for housing complaints: the tenants to notify the rent collector and, if nothing is done within a week, the matter to be referred to the committee of the tenants' association.

(e) Members of the association visited all the old age pensioners in the area and made them honorary members of the association.

The F.A.S. worker became minutes secretary on the committee, and acted in an advisory capacity when discussing the constitution and form of meetings. We gave advice on how to approach other agencies; how to write letters etc., and generally advised the association in such matters as requests for funds from voluntary trusts.

As the winter approached some conflict developed between the tenants' association and the playground management committee, and the latter eventually separated from the association and from then on constituted an independent body in which the tenants' association was represented. The F.A.S. worker attended meetings of both groups and acted as an intermediary. A local vicar acted as arbitrator in cases of disagreements between the two groups. There was also considerable friction between a group of mothers and a number of old age pensioners living nearby who objected to the noise made by the children.

The F.A.S. worker provided advice, guidance and assistance to the tenants' association in a number of ways. For example, when the tenants' association was still struggling with devising organisational procedures which would enable them to function efficiently, the F.A.S. worker drew up a model constitution and showed it to the group. This model was eventually used as a basis for the association's own constitution.

When a well-meaning local vicar was invited to participate in the committee meetings, it became apparent that the less articulate and experienced local residents who were present became somewhat overwhelmed by the vicar's decisive and voluble approach to the discussion. The F.A.S. worker, who usually kept his own participation at a minimum, intervened repeatedly and made certain that the local residents were able to express their views freely and fully. The vicar was tactfully guided to assume a somewhat more reticent role.

In his role as a 'resource person', the worker did, for instance, contact the area housing officer with regard to a complaint about heating cost and arrangement which had been raised by tenants. He also obtained information regarding redevelopment plans from County Hall and was told that no temporary open space for playgrounds would be available. He enlisted the help of the Association of London Housing Estates in some technical and legal matters and provided examples of summer holiday programmes, playground planning and community action methods regarding play space in other areas. All the items of information and instances of assistance were reported by the worker in a letter to the chairman of the tenants' association.

In November 1968, Mr S, a resident of the B estate, approached the secretary of the S estate tenants' association with a request for assistance in setting up a similar organisation on the B estate. He was referred to the worker, who agreed to help. Shortly after this the F.A.S. worker attended a meeting called by Mr S, the secretary of the S estate tenants' association, and the B estate tenants' association was formed. (The worker was told that such an association had existed some years before, but then had lapsed after the treasurer absconded with the funds.) In subsequent discussions it became clear that maintenance and repairs on the estate had been badly neglected, and that this was the first problem which would have to be dealt with. There was also an accumulation of derelict cars in an adjacent street, dumped there by a scrap dealer, which were not only an eyesore, but also endangered the children of the neighbourhood. A recent renovation of one of the blocks of flats was regarded as unsatisfactory. There was general concern about a rent increase due the following April. The washing machines on the estate were defective and there was no place to dry the laundry. The tenants of one block complained that the people from a nearby street were dumping rubbish into their courtyard. There were no play facilities for pre-school children and there was a need for an adventure playground. The Gas Board had instituted a method of payment which did not allow for a cash rebate to which tenants felt they were entitled.

The F.A.S. worker began to deal with the wide range of needs and demands immediately. He introduced the ancillary worker assigned to the family advice centre to the tenants. The ancillary worker was given the task of visiting the flats and obtaining the opinions of the residents, and some of the women were interviewed in the laundry room.

During the following months a mothers' group was formed and discussed the need for play space and the hazards to children from lorries using the adjacent streets. The tenants' association also discussed the needs of a number of elderly people living on the estate and a leaflet to draw the attention of tenants to this problem was distributed after it was discovered that an old lady had remained undiscovered for several days after she had been murdered in her flat. In the spring of 1969 a group of 'tough' boys who had come to the F.A.S. worker's attention when they caused trouble on the S estate playground came to the centre and demanded the use of an empty space near the B estate as a playground. The matter was discussed with the mothers' group and the F.A.S. worker obtained permission from the G.L.C. and the Parks Department to turn the empty plot into a playground. The mothers' group and several of the fathers began to engage in planning and fund raising activities in consultation with the F.A.S. worker and the 'tough' boys helped to clean the area. The mothers' group organised itself as an independent playground committee and it became the F.A.S. worker's task to ensure co-operation between this group and the tenants' association. The worker also acted as treasurer to the mothers' group and applied for a grant from the youth committee.

The opening of the B estate adventure playground took place in the streaming rain, but was nevertheless attended by a substantial number of youngsters who asked the soaking wet F.A.S. worker innumerable questions. Despite the rain, the work of clearing away the accumulated rubbish started. On the following day the sun was out and well over a hundred children worked diligently during that day. There were some scuffles between various groups of youngsters, but no serious clashes. The worker observed that groups of coloured youngsters tended to withdraw when white youngsters arrived and vice versa. Senior officials of the G.L.C. visited the playground on the following day and seemed satisfied with what they heard and saw.

During the summer of 1969 the F.A.S. worker himself shouldered most of the burden of supervising the playground. The number of youngsters attending varied from twenty to sixty per day. Despite the fact that the relatively short time of preparation had not mobilised adequate parent participation and community support, and even though resources were very limited (the entire budget consisted of £30), many children enjoyed the experience and quite a few formed relationships with the worker. One group of youngsters visited the family advice centre every week to chat and discuss matters of interest to them.

Having to cope with a wide range of commitments, the F.A.S. worker was not able to allocate as much of his time to the B estate as he felt was needed. Understandably, he became somewhat discouraged and perhaps a little more impatient than the situation warranted. The worker's records reflect this state of mind, though there was no evidence of any pessimism or impatience in his work with the parents and young-sters. There is no doubt that the people of this neighbourhood needed help in solving their many problems and in improving their situation as a community. There is equally no doubt that the family advice centre provided a good measure of direct help and somewhat less direct guidance in a range of problem situations. The worker's feeling that more could have been done is certainly justified, but this means only the obvious, namely that more could have been done if more staff could have been assigned to the task.

In May 1969 a health visitor consulted the F.A.S. worker with regard to the concern of a group of mothers about the safety of their children who played close to a narrow street which lorries and other vehicles used as a short cut through the estate. The worker advised the health visitor to refer the people involved to the family advice centre. The following morning the story of this group's concern appeared in a local newspaper, based on an interview with one of the mothers, who visited the family advice centre that same morning. She told the worker that the reporter who had interviewed her had advised her to organise a march of the parents to the Town Hall to deliver a petition to the town clerk. She and the other parents had doubts about the wisdom of this kind of demonstration. The worker said that he shared these doubts and that it might be wiser and more effective to use the proper channels first of all. He helped to draft a letter, and discussed the contents and form of the letter with a group of mothers. The letter was sent to the Town Clerk who replied the following day, promising an investigation.

During the following weeks the mothers' group enlisted the support of the other tenants of the estate and the ancillary worker recorded the volume of traffic in the 'problem street' and reported to the group.

A complaint to the police was ignored and the F.A.S. worker helped the group to compose a letter to the chief superintendent. Police officers visited the estate to investigate the complaints. When there were no further results the group contacted the local M.P. with the F.A.S. worker's help. At the termination of the research period the parents were still trying to persuade the authorities to close the street to traffic.

The 'G' project estate tenants' association

In comparison to the area served by the 'D' project centre, the geographical area and the number of clients served by the 'G' project centre were relatively small. The problems confronting the centre were, however, almost overwhelming in their immediacy and intensity.

It was clear from the very beginning that the target community which had been selected was beset by tensions, conflicts and various forms of social inadequacies and deprivations. It soon became apparent that most of the tenants regarded the very fact of living on the estate as the cause of all their problems and frustrations. Living in the G estate seemed to be a major subject of discussion, a cause for nearly everyone's concern, a source of bitterness and distrust and a cause of generally prevailing tension, periodically resulting in violent quarrels between neighbours or angry outbursts against outsiders who were regarded as representing some vague aspects of callous, malevolent authority which included each and every statutory official and social worker, with the staff of the housing department heading the list.

From the very moment of the opening of the family advice centre the worker was swamped with complaints about the bad state of the flats, dampness, filth, noisy neighbours, unruly teenagers, frequent thefts, delays or unfair treatment with regard to rehousing and disquieting rumours that everyone would be moved out of the estate, but no one knew when and where.

It was against this background that the F.A.S. worker took the first hesitant steps towards helping the community to embark upon some rational discussions of their common situation and to find some ways of helping one another to solve their common problems.

The worker had been aware of the existence of a tenants' association on the estate, and there was an elderly man still known to everyone as the chairman of this organisation. However, the tenants' association had been inactive for some time and no one showed any interest in reviving it. The first opportunity for community activity offered itself almost by accident, and in an unforeseen manner.

The need for clothing of all kinds was an acute problem for many of the family advice centre's client families. When a lady donated two boxes of secondhand clothing and shoes to the centre the F.A.S. worker, rather than distribute the things herself, discussed the distribution with several of the tenants. Her suggestion to open a clothing exchange was welcomed. Mrs T, a young woman who ran a play group in the area, offered to collect secondhand clothes from some of her better-off parents, and a pram shed was allocated for storage space. Within a month seventeen families had bought items from the clothing exchange for a nominal sum and three of the families had themselves donated secondhand clothes for the use of others. One family offered their services, and the use of their flat for sorting and cleaning.

An article in three local newspapers, which appeared shortly after this, included an item on how the clothing exchange had helped to arouse the interest of wider groups of the community. The local newspapers continued to play a significant role in raising the issue of community action. In December 1967, for instance, an article quoted a spokesman of an area 'United Tenants' Association' as stating with regard to the 'G' estate: 'The block is a slum, I fear the tenants may take most strong action if nothing is done.' However, there was, as yet, little sign of the tenants' readiness to engage in any community action. The increasing pressure which the centre's clients exerted on the F.A.S. worker was aimed exclusively at being rehoused or at getting badly needed repairs and renovations made.

That same month the F.A.S. worker was told that the housing department was planning to renovate and modernise the estate. Lifts, central heating and other amenities would be installed and play facilities would be provided. All the present tenants would be moved out. It was stated that it was not the policy of the housing department to move former tenants of the estate back into modernised flats.

Towards the end of the month the contact of several of the more enterprising tenants with their local councillors served to stimulate some community activity. A petition was drawn up and circulated which protested against deplorable living conditions and high rents. This petition was discussed with the F.A.S. worker and she offered some advice about the style and form of the document. The petition was presented to the local council. It resulted in a full scale council discussion and was reported in the local press. The chairman of the housing committee announced that modernisation of the flats would be speeded up.

Meanwhile, the clothing exchange prospered and provided opportunities for bringing neighbours together and for informal, impromptu discussions about community problems. Many tenants were reluctant to pay their rents, regarding this as a means of bringing pressure to bear on the authorities to rehouse them. The F.A.S. worker heard that a representative of the children's department had been asked to attend a housing department meeting in order to discuss the increase in rent arrears. The estate's tenants' association began to show signs of becoming re-activated and the F.A.S. worker encouraged this development. However, the association's chairman expressed rather pessimistic views of any possibility of bringing about some of the needed changes.

In February 1968 several F.A.S. clients raised the possibility of another petition with the F.A.S. worker. This brought about the first formal group discussion held at the F.A.S. worker's suggestion. After the worker explained the possible uses and consequences of the petition the tenants decided to go ahead and asked the worker to help them to formulate their opinions and demands in writing. Over a hundred tenants signed the document which was also reported in the local papers and brought a reply from the local council.

The people became increasingly concerned about the spate of rumours flying about the estate and the lack of reliable information about what plans the authorities had for them. As client after client came to the centre to express anxiety about the future and anger about being left in the dark, the worker pointed out repeatedly that the tenants' association would be the most appropriate forum for a discussion which would give all the tenants a chance to air their feelings. Finally a meeting was held at the family advice centre which resulted in the drawing up of a letter to the housing manager signed by seventy tenants. The letter expressed the anxiety of the tenants about their future and requested information about the timing and the conditions of the department's rehousing plans.

The housing manager replied three weeks later, stating clearly that, while a limited number of tenants would be offered alternative accommodation when the renovation of the estate began, the others would be moved internally into modernised sections. This letter, which was photocopied with the F.A.S. worker's help and distributed among the tenants, seemed to assure the tenants of a fair and constructive alternative to the dispersal of the community. The letter clearly implied that the modernisation of the estate would be carried out for the benefit of the very people who for so long had to bear the disadvantages of inadequate conditions in the same buildings. Somewhat surprisingly, the tenants seemed to take no notice of this authoritative statement. In fact, it soon became apparent that intentionally or not, the letter was misleading. All subsequent efforts of the housing department and other social service agencies were directed towards moving all tenants out of the estate reserving the modernised flats for people from other areas. The F.A.S. worker also failed to realise the potentialities of the housing manager's statement with regard to the preservation of the community and continued to direct her own efforts towards helping individual tenants and the tenants' association to speed up rehousing.

Meanwhile, the F.A.S. worker took advantage of an opportunity to involve members of the tenants' association in other relevant issues when the Child Poverty Action Group set up a study group on the school meals services and clothing maintenance which had been objects of concern to many of the parents. At the worker's suggestion two members of the tenants' association attended a C.P.A.G. meeting and both subsequently visited local schools to observe the conditions under which school meals were served.

During the summer of that year the F.A.S. worker discussed with the tenants an advertisement by a subcommittee on council housing set up by the Ministry of Housing and Local Government and asking for written evidence on council housing conditions. Many of the people were interested and during the following weeks a document summarising the views of the tenants was drawn up and sent to the Ministry of Housing and Local Government subcommittee. Copies of the fairly long and detailed statement were given to the housing department, borough councillors and the newspapers.

The situation had now become a matter of considerable interest to the local newspapers and a party political issue in the borough. Whatever the argument for or against publicity and political controversy in such situations, it tends greatly to increase the difficulties of a social worker employed by the local authority who finds herself inextricably involved. Having to attend to the increasing pressure of requests for help from her client families, which by now included nearly every family living on the estate and a few from the adjoining area, the F.A.S. worker sought to advise the tenants' association, maintain and further develop self-help activities such as the clothing exchange, and to assert and reconcile her own role as family advice service worker and local authority employee in her relations with her clients and her agency in the face of inquisitive journalists, local party politics, and the wary eye of local authority officials.

In September 1968 the activities of the tenants' association became more structured and meetings more frequent under the workers' guidance. The worker was asked to become a member of a subcommittee and a local councillor informed her that he planned to conduct 'tours' of members of the housing committee to impress them with the inadequate

conditions of the flats. Further articles about the estate appeared in the
local press.

One of the tenants carried out a flat to flat survey and registered
complaints about inadequate living conditions. A new secretary to the
association was appointed, an energetic woman with strong middle-class
aspirations who provided some badly needed leadership. She tended at
first to regard the F.A.S. worker as a rival, but overcame her distrust
after a series of discussions. It was especially interesting to note that
Mrs H, the tenants' association secretary, initially expressed the view
that the worker was a champion of the estate's down-and-outers and
did not show enough interest for the people who 'tried to cope'. However,
when Mrs H was invited to address a Council meeting and someone
made disparaging remarks about 'the welfare cases', she objected
strongly, speaking of the need for respect for those who needed help, and
that people with problems were people not cases. She used the F.A.S.
worker's own often repeated words, and later asked the worker whether
she had noted the contents of her speech.

A somewhat delayed consequence of the evidence to the subcommittee
on council housing was a reprimand from the children's officer. The
latter said that the F.A.S. worker had put him in a difficult position by
sending copies of the report to councillors and instructed her that in
future there should be no such communication with councillors without
prior consultation with him.

Local newspaper articles continued to draw attention to the G estate
situation. One article carried a picture of Mrs H, who had by now
replaced the chairman of the tenants' association in all but formal title.
This article also reported that tenants were being refused hire purchase
agreements by local firms because of the bad reputation of the estate.
Mrs H was able to gain direct access to the housing manager and
compiled a list of 'priority medical cases' whose rehousing should be
speeded up.

About this time the family advice centre had exchanged its cramped
little office for a fairly large flat provided by the housing department.
In agreement with the department the F.A.S. worker offered to share the
flat with the tenants' association, thereby alleviating the lack of a suitable
meeting place and office facilities. However, this did not solve all the
problems of the association. Mrs H's successful bid for leadership
aroused the resentment of other active members of the association and
the F.A.S. worker spent much of her time in trying to bring about a
conciliation between the warring factions.

In November the decision to go ahead with the modernisation plans
for the estate was officially announced and reported in the local press.

The tenants invited the F.A.S. worker to a 'victory celebration' at the local pub, apparently quite unaware of the fact that the modernisation would not be carried out for them, but for other people who would move into the renovated estate after they had departed. An article telling the life story and discussing the tenants' association work of Mrs H appeared in a local newspaper in November. Mrs H repeated some of the F.A.S. worker's remarks on the purposes of community work, self-help and the principles of 'helping others to help themselves' almost verbatim, while she also stated her opinion that the welfare state fostered dependence and was overly concerned with the 'shiftless'.

In December the tenants' association invited the F.A.S. worker to a meeting with the housing committee in which details of the planned modernisation of the estate, such as larger bathrooms, better laundry drying facilities, additional kitchen space, central heating, lifts, storage space on each floor, improved rubbish disposal and the planting of trees in the courtyard, were provided. Again no one seemed to be aware of the fact that all these benefits were not being provided for the present tenants. The difficulties which continued to arise with regard to rehousing were discussed and cases cited in which tenants had encountered delays and unco-operative attitudes on the part of housing department officials. Although the family advice centre was involved in almost all rehousing cases and constantly negotiated with the housing department on behalf of families, the department's representative did not mention the centre, but advised tenants to seek the help of the Citizens' Advice Bureau and the housing welfare officer. The housing department also announced the opening of their own housing advice centre.

Christmas came and an 'open house' all-day party was held at the family advice centre. The enthusiastic participation of the tenants in the preparations and the activities illustrated vividly the progress that had been made in forging the tenants of the estate into a community.

At the beginning of the new year a Dutch graduate student seconded to the centre by the research team conducted a series of home visits and discussions in order to survey the needs of the elderly tenants of the estate. As a result of this the tenants' association drew up a letter to the housing department in consultation with the F.A.S. worker and a group of the old people, spelling out the problems and fears of the latter and asking for specific information about the plans for their rehousing.

As more and more tenants moved out, the conditions of the estate deteriorated sharply and the morale of the remaining families became very low. The F.A.S. worker raised spirits somewhat by arranging with the Child Poverty Action Group to provide community lunches on the estate during the school holidays which were prepared and supervised by the centre and several of the tenants. The housing welfare officer now attended the meetings of the tenants' association at which people were able to direct their questions to him. Despite this most of the tenants still asked for the F.A.S. worker's intervention when difficulties arose. In May 1969 the F.A.S. worker sent the following memorandum to the Deputy Children's Officer:

I refer to our conversation today regarding the allowances which are made to families who are compulsorily removed by the GLC. This is done under the GLC's latest ruling on removal expenses (a committee decision dated 11 July 1968). Families who are decanted are entitled to disconnection and reconnection charges in respect of gas, electricity, telephone, refrigerators and other appliances. *In addition* to this they are allowed removal expenses plus a further allowance to include such items as curtains and floor covering to a total of £30. In exceptional circumstances the grant may exceed £30. Tenants are also allowed the first week's rent free. I think it might be useful to point out to the housing department that even the DHSS minimum grant allows 6/- to 8/- a yard for floor covering and curtaining, plus removal expenses and disconnection and reconnection fees. As far as I know, no one at the G Estate has received any money in excess of the £10 removal allowance and this is given as a discretionary grant, not as a right. Some tenants have even been told that they are not entitled to this £10. These additional strains place families at risk. It should also be pointed out that the GLC grants seem to be given as a right and the borough grants are not.

Rats, vandalism and pilfering by children became a growing concern and kept the F.A.S. worker busy. Many of the families who had moved to other areas continued to come to the centre for advice. The clothing exchange continued to operate until the last tenant had moved out. The tenants' association discussed a letter from the housing manager which asked for their co-operation in controlling vandalism and which suggested that tenants should be ready to accept provisional accommodation even if they found it unsatisfactory, upon the promise that they would be considered for better accommodation at a later date. The tenants' association decided to advise tenants *not* to accept any unsuitable offers.

By the end of July 1969 the G estate was empty and the family advice centre closed.

The 'F' project centre parents' group

Similar to the 'D' and 'E' project centres, the 'F' project family advice centre engaged in community work as a logical extension of the advice, guidance and assistance function of its service. The centre served a community which was beset by many severe problems, but which also had some hidden potentialities. The F.A.S. worker's achievement was that he was able to identify the community's areas of strength and that he enabled the community to revitalise their own fragmented and dormant traditions of community spirit and to apply their own potentialities to actions which fostered self-confidence and which met specific needs in practical, effective ways.

At least partly due to the redevelopment scheme which was in process when the family advice centre opened, all the inhabitants lived in a state of impermanence and anxious anticipation. The dominant attitudes were those of diffuse anger, apathy and fear of the future. In a great number of cases the physical conditions in which people lived could only be described as deplorable and many families lived in poverty.

Some of the positive factors should be noted. These were, first and foremost, the vestiges of community spirit and tradition still existing in the area and recollections of spontaneous social action which had become part of the lore of the neighbourhood. Three years before the opening of the centre the local inhabitants had launched a protest against the housing department, and the present chairman of the parents' association had his photograph in the local papers. Only three months before the opening of the centre one hundred signatures had been collected for a protest against rat infestation. Letters had been sent to the Prime Minister and to the housing department. People said that the Prime Minister's secretary had replied, but there was no response from the housing department. But perhaps most important of all there was, amidst apathy and petty quarrelling, the readiness to help one another which, perhaps imposed by the force of circumstances, is so often found in slum areas.

About three weeks after the opening of the 'F' project family advice centre a group of parents who had established contact with the centre formed a parents' association under the guidance of the F.A.S. worker. At the end of the first three-month period the association consisted of thirty members and had held nine meetings at the family advice centre.

The parents' association elected a chairman and a secretary, both members of the community. The F.A.S. worker functioned as consultant and resource person. The association functioned mainly as a forum for discussion of general and specific issues and problems affecting the community. Its goals were the improvement of neighbourly relations in the community, the improvement of the community's social, cultural and physical conditions, the fostering of a spirit of mutual aid and the care of the community's children.

Activities leading to the achievement of these goals were carried out by a self-help subcommittee, a working party and the management committee of the arts and crafts centre. A 'Friday Club' was formed and invitations sent to all members of the community to come and listen to talks by invited speakers on subjects relevant to the interests and concerns of the community.

Members of the parents' association supervised Guy Fawkes Day festivities in the autumn of 1968. A working party led by the group's chairman made minor repairs for people in the neighbourhood. The group discussed the setting up of an arts centre and play space for children, requested the securing of an abandoned factory which constituted a danger to children and drew up a list of traffic accidents involving children in the area. One of the members maintained a detailed record of weekly budgeting to be used as resource material in negotiations with the Department of Health and Social Security. The elderly people of the neighbourhood were contacted and brought together to discuss their special problems. The senior child care officer was invited to speak to the group on the functions and policies of the children's department. A family which had aroused the concern of the community was visited by the P.A. chairman and given material assistance. In November an arts centre management committee was formed.

In December the parents' association asked the housing department to permit the use of an empty corner store for the setting up of an arts centre. A local councillor was invited to attend the meetings of the group, and a re-housing officer addressed a P.A. meeting on the departments policies of redevelopment and rehousing. A Christmas Party attended by about 120 local children was organised in co-operation with a charitable organisation and a nearby school. Another Christmas Party for elderly people was given at the family advice centre.

In January 1969 a meeting between the divisional welfare officer and the chairman of the parents' association took place at the centre and a number of local welfare problems were discussed. Four P.A. members were deputised to meet with a police sergeant at the centre to discuss the high incidence of road accidents in the area. As a result of this meeting three local women were appointed as school-crossing attendants and luminous armbands were distributed to the children of the neighbourhood.

In February the parents' association appointed a 'contact-secretary' with the task of keeping in touch with the increasing number of people who were leaving the neighbourhood after rehousing. The group decided to compile a collection of essays, impressions and reports by members of the community on the history of the neighbourhood and the life experiences of people living in the area. It was decided that the clothing exchange, which had been established by the family advice centre some months before and had been conducted on a request basis, would hold regular sales once a week at an appointed time. The P.A. organised a theatre trip for fifty children, nine parents and three grandparents. The chairman of the self-help subcommittee reported to the group on the work of the subcommittee and the F.A.S. worker reported on the situation of delinquent and homeless youth in the area which was causing increasing concern. A case of theft by a local resident who had recently been released from gaol was discussed in a special meeting and it was decided not to involve the police but to settle the matter within the community.

In March the parents' association organised a bingo evening at the arts and crafts centre. An invitation by the parents' association brought six child care officers of the staff of the children's department area office to the centre for a discussion meeting with the group.

During the following months a group of lecturers and students from a local College of Arts met with the parents' association to discuss their participation in the arts centre. A letter was sent to the children's housing and health departments to express the community's concern about insanitary conditions and increasing vandalism in the area. Negotiations with the British Waterways Board for obtaining a canal barge for holiday trips were opened. The housing department lettings officer was invited to come to the family advice centre once a week to discuss housing matters with the people of the neighbourhood.

At the beginning of the summer an 'adventure weekend' for thirty-five children was organised with the help of a voluntary organisation and the children's department. A group of students helped the P.A. to conduct a survey of living conditions in the area and the Association provided funds to pay local teenagers who did repair work at the arts centre. The arts centre was registered as a charity.

Comments

The, of necessity, greatly summarised description of what we call the community action groups in three of the detached F.A.S. settings will have shown the reader some of the similarities in the three settings, as well as some of the characteristic differences.

Broadly speaking, the similarities and differences were that (1) vestiges of community organisation existed in all three areas; (2) the revitalisation of community organisation traditions and the creation of new community groups in all three areas occurred in response to strongly felt needs and tensions in the community; (3) in all three settings the success or failure and the degree of intensity of any one facet of community organisation was determined by the existing traditions of community cohesion or the degree to which the community presented a picture of apathy and disruption *and* the attitudes of the local authority bodies towards community organisation efforts.

In the 'G' project setting, where the problems were most severe and the obstacles to community work posed by the client population most formidable, the attitudes of the local authority were, with some notable exceptions, least supportive of the F.A.S. worker's community work efforts. In the 'F' project setting the local authority organisations offered the F.A.S. worker a noteworthy degree of support and cooperation. In both settings, the same challenges and difficulties were presented by the redevelopment process in which the problems of rehousing and the demoralising effects of community dispersal overshadowed all other matters of interest or concern.

In carrying out their community work functions in the combined roles of enablers, advisers, and resource persons to the indigenous groups, all the F.A.S. workers faced the problems which are so thoroughly familiar to anyone engaged in community work. These are aptly described by Goetschius (1969) in a list which reads like the account of an obstacle race:

Lack of knowledge of simple committee procedure.
Unfamiliarity with the duties of a chairman, secretary, treasurer.
Attempting to do too many things at once, so that the committee becomes overworked and discouraged.
Too much control of the organisation centred in a small 'friendship group'.
Inability to resolve tensions in the committee or on the estate.
Lack of specific skills, for example in working with children.
Inability to spread out the work among the committee and to involve the members.
The nature of the employment of many of the committee members—shift workers, long-distance drivers, workers in public transport and the post office, which makes it difficult for them to have regular commitments.
Lack of information on where to go for advice.
Aggressive attitudes towards authorities.
Lack of co-operation from authorities.
Inability to learn from other organisations of a different nature from their own.
Leadership . . . which brings personal problems to the fore in the group, blocking the accomplishment of its tasks (p. 3).

One should hasten to add to this awesome list that while the communities served by the detached family advice centres lacked experience in most, if not all, these matters, they often showed an impressive ability to learn and to grow, to gain confidence and self-awareness. Moreover, although the F.A.S. workers had considerable practical experience in community work, none of them was formally trained in this social work method. As a result workers and clients often learned and experimented together, a process which seemed to serve to draw them together in a shared experience of growth, sometimes frustrating and painful, but often rewarding.

Community self-help groups and neighbourly assistance

Self-help groups have long since been part of the British social welfare tradition. On the whole they have tended to be transitory, serving their initial purpose and then gradually or rapidly running out of steam. In most cases such groups have also been more likely to be initiated and run by small elites of well-motivated, erudite and resourceful people *for* the less articulate, socially and economically deprived population groups, rather than *with* these people. Only fairly recently, with the advent of community work as a social work method, has there been some awareness of the potentialities of self-help groups for fostering community cohesion, self-confidence and self-assertion. At the same time the decisive importance of strengthening the grass-roots, indigenous character of community self-help groups in deprived areas and of preventing or counteracting any domination by elitist groups, however benevolent, has begun to be recognised. A recent article on the subject asked: 'What is a community self-help group in the context of social welfare?' and answered as follows:

There are various types of groups, but the one which is of particular interest in the context of grass-roots community development, rural or urban, is the group of individual citizens, local people, who get together, firstly on an informal basis, in order to take action and to meet social welfare needs as they themselves perceive them. The important point about such groups is that the impetus for their formation and current activities has come from the individual members themselves, though note, this does not preclude some outside agent from acting as catalyst for the formation of the group. The members work on their own behalf, for though by their actions they may benefit other members of their community, primarily they are self-interested. They may not necessarily be original in their aims, they may well be imitating and possibly refining the methods of others: occasionally they may be real innovators, in which case, if successful, they may well be imitated (Groves, 1969, p. 124).

Our observations showed that, in the detached family advice centres, the advice, guidance and assistance functions lead logically to the F.A.S.

workers acting as the outside agents who help to stimulate and support a wide range of indigenous self-help organisations and activities. We were also led to conclude that this process *can* and *should* occur in other F.A.S. settings provided that the F.A.S. staff were receptive to the dynamics and potentialities of areas they serve, although the study did not provide concrete evidence of this.

The processes which lead to self-help activities are relatively simple: for instance, a number of individual clients or client families seek the centre's advice regarding the same type of need or problem. This might consist of the need for a play group, the difficulties of including adequate clothing for all members of the family in hard-pressed budgets, or the lack of organised, creative and entertaining social activities which are needed to ease prevailing tensions and to relieve an atmosphere of depression and frustration. It is a commonsense response for the F.A.S. worker to react to half a dozen or more such expressions of need by different clients living in the same area by suggesting a group discussion of the common needs and problems by the people concerned, to point out possibilities of self-help activities to alleviate the need, and to take some practical steps, such as providing a suitable meeting place, to help the group 'get started'.

The experience of the detached family advice centres showed that community self-help groups are sometimes the first steps in stimulating community interest and in mobilising community resources, setting in motion processes which lead to activities geared to representing the communities' needs and demands in a wider context through organisations such as tenants' associations. On the other hand, such functional representative organisations arising in the community often result in the emergence of self-help groups. As far as the relevance of these processes to the goals and functions of the family advice services is concerned, one might say that, as one of the major goals is to enable people to help themselves, the creation of self-help groups is one of the most significant measures of the family advice centre's effectiveness.

Some of the self-help activities in the detached family advice centres have already been mentioned in the discussion of community action groups. In the following pages we shall briefly reiterate some of these and describe others, not previously mentioned.

Self-help groups in the area served by the 'D' project centre

Self-help activities in the area served by the 'D' project family advice centre had their beginnings in the request for advice by a client and were, initially, directed towards helping the community to meet a specific common need and, in one instance, combined the interests of two different community groups, namely the parents of young children and the elderly.

In April 1968 one of the mothers from the S estate was referred to the family advice centre by a health visitor. She was worried about the safety of her children who had no suitable play space and were endangered by the heavy traffic in the nearby streets. As the matter seemed a cause of concern to all the parents in the estate the ancillary worker was assigned to visiting the flats to discuss the matter. Shortly after this a meeting took place at the centre which was attended by fifteen mothers with sixty-three children between them and one old age pensioner who represented the interests of a group of old people who suffered from the noise of the children who played in front of their windows. A series of further meetings followed. A mothers' group was formed and the F.A.S. worker opened negotiations with the appropriate authorities on the group's behalf. The result was the opening of an adventure playground on an empty plot near the S estate. The playground was prepared, equipped, staffed and financed by the parents' group in consultation with the F.A.S. worker and in co-operation with the Youth Committee, voluntary organisations and the children's department. In the summer of 1968 an average of 150 children per day attended the playground. The 1969 Easter holidays saw an even more numerous attendance.

During the following summer a group of adolescent boys from an adjacent estate caused serious disturbances in the playground. Equipment was destroyed, a child was injured and one of the S estate fathers slapped one of the boys. The F.A.S. worker persuaded the housing area officer not to involve the police. With the help of the playground youth worker, a young teacher, camping trips for the boys were organised and the F.A.S. staff discussed the situation and the need for recreational facilities with the parents. A coach trip to Brighton was organised by a newly formed parents' group and went off well, although there was some trouble when several of the teenage girls slipped into the boys' tent at night. A satisfying measure of co-operation between the parents' groups in the two estates was achieved in the following months. There were five three-day camping trips, football tournaments and drama activities. Over 400 youngsters between the ages of seven and fifteen made use of the playground and participated in a series of recreational and cultural activities which included barbecues, fancy dress competitions, swimming, bowling, music and dancing.

The success of the adventure playground and recreational programme aroused the interest of the tenants of the B estate tenants' association who were also concerned about the lack of play facilities. After a series of meetings a playground was opened in the vicinity of this estate with the help of the F.A.S. staff.

The 'D' project pre-school play group

The services described above came about as the result of community action processes in which the staff of the family advice centre functioned as initiators, resource persons and consultants, as well as participating directly in carrying out the necessary work. The 'D' project play group, to which we shall now turn, was the result of discussions of the need for such a group in the immediate vicinity of the family advice centre between the minister of a Methodist church and the health visitors of the local clinic, both institutions neighbours of the centre.

The minister offered the use of his church hall and the pre-school play group began to function as a project in May 1968. The church also provided a play group leader who had teaching experience but had not previously worked with the under-five age group. The six mothers who were referred to the group by the family advice centre and the health visitors agreed to help supervise the group on a rota system, but they were at first somewhat uncertain of their roles and it became apparent that they had not been sufficiently involved in the early discussions and planning. Most of the families were relatively stable and were not known to any of the social service agencies. This selection of families had come about upon the advice of the F.A.S. worker who felt that, while there was no doubt of the priorities of need in the area, the play group would have more of a chance to get started if it was not burdened with multi-problem families from the outset.

Difficulties arose when it became apparent that the church was exerting a considerable measure of control over the group, although this was counteracted to some degree by the close involvement of the F.A.S. worker. In the summer of 1968 two of the mothers volunteered to run the group when the play leader left. They were assisted by a part-time church volunteer and child care students assigned by the children's department. Fund-raising for the group was in the hands of the minister.

The two mothers, who had eight children of their own between them, had no training or professional experience whatever, but showed quite remarkable understanding of the needs of small children. Their effectiveness was, however, somewhat curtailed by the turnover of student assistants, which they felt was unsettling for the children, and by the church volunteer who had a tendency to assert her authority over the group. The two mothers felt that they were well able to run the group and discussed the possibility of being given this responsibility with the F.A.S. worker. The latter agreed and explored the possibilities of a training course for the two mothers with the Inner London Pre-School Playgroups Association. The health visitors were quite enthusiastic about the idea, but the minister showed some signs of anxiety.

The two mothers were enabled to attend a course in the Autumn of 1968. This served gradually to improve their professional standards and they became more aware of what they were doing. They were paid 17s 6d per session, with the understanding that this sum would be increased when they became qualified. The F.A.S. worker was closely involved with the group, discussing behaviour difficulties and the children's backgrounds with the two workers, providing equipment and giving support to the two mothers in some of the difficulties which arose in their relationships with the parents. The F.A.S. worker served as secretary to the management committee which was chaired by the minister and consisted of the two mothers, the two workers and the health visitors. The F.A.S. worker also attempted to bring similar groups in the borough together. She and the two workers attended monthly meetings of the pre-school playgroups association where they became the advocates of indigenous leadership in pre-school play-groups, a concept which had so far not been considered in any of the other groups, all of which, with one exception, were administered and staffed by voluntary organisations.

By the end of the year over twenty children attended the play group and there was a waiting list. Two more local mothers agreed to work with the group and were enabled to attend a training course in the spring of 1969. Afternoon sessions were now added to the initial morning sessions. As the four indigenous workers became more confident and experienced, the F.A.S. worker limited her own role more and more to that of con-sultant and resource person. At the same time the relationship with the minister became more problematic and his suggestion to bring the group more firmly under the authority of the Church Mission caused concern. The F.A.S. worker advised against this step and the management com-mittee decided to register the group as a charity. As the financial situation began to be somewhat precarious, the committee ceased to rely entirely upon the financial support of the church and started a series of fund-raising activities, such as raffles and jumble sales, but had to do so clandestinely, as the church did not permit such activities. Although this led to some further deterioration of the group's relations with the minister, the group continued to gain self-confidence and stability and became more effective in its work with the children which, by now, included a significant proportion of children from problem families.

The mothers' group at the 'E' project centre

The mothers' group was initially set up by the children's department sector of the 'E' project area on the premises of the family advice centre. It was supervised by the senior child care officer supervising the sector and the family advice centre, one of the centre's youth workers and several child care officers. The group, consisting of seven mothers and their small children, all of them referred by the children's department and the nearby infant welfare clinic, started in May 1969. In July the group held a fund-raising jumble sale at the centre, attended by about 150 people. The children's department made sizeable contributions to the financing of the group.

The group met once a week for lunch (cooked by the mothers) and an afternoon session of informal discussion, sewing and recreational activities. Excursion trips were organised from time to time.

The 'G' project clothing exchange

As already mentioned the clothing exchange provided a much needed service to the 'G' project estate tenants for nearly two years. Many families were provided with secondhand clothing in exchange for other items, or for nominal payments. For many of the mothers it became a stimulating social activity and gradually a number of tenants assumed responsibility for the service. There were also flare-ups of jealous quarrelling over the exchange from time to time, highlighting the tensions and conflicts which beset the community. After the exchange had become well established, the tenants themselves decided to use the funds which accumulated through cash sales for small emergency loans to members of the community. In all cases the money was repaid promptly.

The 'F' project secondhand clothes and furniture exchange

The community served by the 'F' project family advice centre also operated a thriving business not only in secondhand clothes, but also in furniture, most of it rescued from the vacant buildings of the redevelopment area. The sorting and trading went on in the family advice centre, but the responsibility for running the sales and for deciding on the use of the profits was that of the self-help committee and the parents' association. While the sales were a source of inexpensive clothing and furniture for the people of the neighbourhood, they were, from the outset, regarded as part of the fund raising activities of the community and helped to finance the arts and crafts centre and other community activities.

The 'F' project self-help committee

The most effective example of community self-help activities was provided by the experiences of the 'F' project family advice centre. As already mentioned, the parents' association which came into being shortly after the opening of the family advice centre, formed a self-help committee as one of its first steps to bring about changes in the community, and as an expression of the community's wish to participate in the work of the family advice centre. The committee originally consisted of six members, but eventually twenty-two members of the community were directly involved in discussing and carrying out the activities of the committee. All but seven of the members were also clients of the family advice centre. About a year after its inception, the goals and functions of the S.H. Committee were recorded in writing by the parents' association as follows:

1. To assist families in special need and this why Mrs K is employed as a part-time community based home help. She has been employed for three months. Mrs K makes special arrangements to keep in close contact with any Child Care Officers involved with a family that she visits. The families concerned know about this contact as permission is always requested before any contact is made with the Children's Department. The same procedure applies to any clients interviewed at the Family Advice Service.
2. The second function is to have secondhand clothes sales regularly. This provides families in special need with clothes and furniture at reduced prices. In certain cases, where there is an emergency situation, we provide clothes and/or furniture free of charge. All the proceeds are given to the art centre, i.e. 'to keep our children off the streets'. All who buy from these sales or contribute know that the money is used for this purpose.
3. The third function is to provide outings and make holiday arrangements for children who are in special need. Forty questionnaries that have recently been completed by members of the community show how necessary it is for children, and later possibly parents,

to be able to go away on regular outings and holidays together. During the last holiday period, nearly 80 children were taken on day trips to Sutton Park and 40 children have been on weekend holidays, and 10 boys and girls were provided with a whole week's holiday.

'All the functions, particularly in regard to this community, are to prevent family break-up.'

In order to show the range and type of activities carried out by the self-help committee we shall list them briefly, including those already mentioned in other contexts:

Concerned over reports about lonely elderly people frightened by the upheavals of the redevelopment process, the S.H. Committee assigned two members to seek out such people, inquire after their needs, visit them from time to time and try to establish contact between them and the F.A.S. worker.

The S.H. Committee participated in the organisation and supervision of a Christmas party for the neighbourhood's children in a local school and a party of elderly neighbours at the family advice centre.

Reports of the maltreatment of the children of a local family led to the assignment of a member of the committee to visit that family, report on her findings and to refer the family to the F.A.S. worker. Discussion of this case led to the decision to meet once a week at the centre with the specific purpose of discussing families in the community who had caused concern and/or needed help. Members of the committee were given specific assignments to visit a number of families in the community. One member was assigned to offer help to a family where the father had been arrested and jailed, another member to visit a woman who had been taken ill. Material aid and neighbourly support was offered to other families.

Members of the committee participated in, and helped to supervise, a theatre trip for children, parents and grandparents. The chairman of the committee drew up a list of equipment and goods needed by five families which the children's department was asked to supply.

The chairman of the committee was appointed community home help, to be paid from the petty cash fund of the family advice centre. Her first assignment was a family where the mother was going to hospital for her confinement, and where the children would otherwise have to be taken into care.

The committee, with the help of the F.A.S. worker, arranged a camping weekend for thirty-five children. The committee chairman reported to the parents' association on the current situation, means of collection and distribution, etc. of the clothing and furniture exchange. The housing department authorised the committee to remove all usable items and materials from the vacated houses in the area. A jumble sale was held at the arts and crafts centre. The committee discussed the acquisition and the uses of a canal barge for holiday trips, and a second camping trip was organised.

The committee planned and organised an evening's 'entertainment', including a strip show in a nightclub, in order to raise money for the arts and crafts centre. One of the members was appointed community children's help on a part-time basis with the task of looking after the needs of pre-school children. Another member was given the task of keeping the centre's notice board up to date. The committee discussed the planning of camping trips for teenagers with a local volunteer with youth work experience. Another camping trip in which fifty-three children, supervised by three members of the community, took part, was organised. Shortly after this a mothers' outing took place.

A member of the committee assumed the responsibility for providing storing and cleaning dressing-up clothes for the children of the arts and crafts centre.

A discussion meeting about the contents of an article about the community and the family advice centre which appeared in the *Sunday Times* was held, and the committee discussed the effects of the noisy activities of children who wandered into the family advice centre while clients discussed their problems with the F.A.S. worker. Another meeting discussed the problems facing the community with a local councillor and three members of a voluntary association engaged in community work in another part of the city. The committee help organised a children's party at the arts and crafts centre and, in consultation with local councillors and the F.A.S. worker, the committee organised a 'broom drive' to clean up the area in which sanitary conditions had sharply deteriorated, mainly due to the demolition process. Three local councillors and twenty-five parents participated and the event was reported in the newspapers.

The Seebohm Report pointed out that: 'Getting citizens involved in the services provides an invaluable source of information about "real" needs and at the same time can be a creative and fulfilling activity in its own right' (para. 493). The self-help committee of the 'F' project area provided a good example of the truth of this observation.

The 'F' project arts centre

Although the F.A.S. worker was not aware of it at the time, the arts and crafts centre was conceived on the first day of the opening of the family advice centre when the neighbourhood children watched the worker put the F.A.S. sign on the door. The first 'customers' were two eight-year-old boys who had wandered in and were handed paper and crayons to keep them out of mischief for the moment. This advance party was soon followed by other boys and girls. Two days after the opening of the centre, over a dozen children were busily drawing and painting in the front room of the centre. The youngsters were delighted when the worker pinned the results of their artistic endeavour to the walls. Soon, the worker was kept busy giving 'advice, guidance and assistance' to a growing number of striving young artists. Every available space on desks, tables and floors was occupied. Gradually the mothers began to look in and were encouraged to stay. 'That's my Alan's picture,' a mother said, and another lady pointed admiringly: 'Look what my Janice has done.' 'Gawd, what's that supposed to be, then?' another mother asked her five-year-old who had proudly presented her with a large red blob on a sheet of paper. One of the women wanted to know: 'What's this place, Mister? Is it for children only?' The F.A.S. worker explained what the family advice centre was for. 'Why don't you come in for a chat?' he asked, 'We'll have some chairs after the weekend and there's going to be electric light and a telephone.'

Responding to the children's demands, the centre reserved one hour on Tuesday afternoons, Friday lunchtime and another hour between 4 and 5 p.m. on Fridays for the youngsters. About forty children crowded into the centre each time. Drawing paper was donated by a local firm of printers and the children's department provided eight easels.

A few weeks after the opening of the centre the arts and crafts activities had become an integral part of the family advice service. The children formed a committee to help to keep order and clean up, voluntary organisations were asked for cash donations to buy more equipment and the teachers of a local school visited the centre to observe the activities. The newly formed parents' association expressed full support for the arts centre.

In October 1968 the F.A.S. worker enlisted the help of students and staff from a local College of Art and the parents' association formed an arts centre management committee. The following months negotiations started for setting up the arts centre in a large corner store a few steps away from the family advice centre. The art college students who had become closely involved in the activities wrote a report in which they stated:

We believe it to be at present an almost unique situation. Rather than an authority or a foundation creating an arts centre and then inviting people to attend, the 'F' project centre has arisen in a purely organic way from the interest and activity of the people, adults and children who live in the neighbourhood. The eagerness of the children to take part in the activities is matched by the willingness of the parents to help.

The children's department made Section 1 funds available to help to defray the costs and additional funds were provided through the sale of secondhand clothes and furniture by the parents' association, greatly helped by one of the fathers who made his lorry available to collect saleable items. An art college lecturer, a student and the children's department supervisor of the centre joined the management committee as members, while the F.A.S. worker and the principal of the art college were appointed as consultants.

By the end of the year an average of fifty children attended the arts centre three times a week. In January 1969 the corner shop was made available by the housing department and renovation began with the help of members of the community, among them several teenagers. In February the parents' association applied for the registration of the arts centre as a charity organisation, a bank account was opened and an honorary auditor was appointed. Shortly after this collection boxes for the arts centre were set up in two local pubs.

In April 1969 the arts centre opened in the corner shop on five days and three evenings a week. A slide and a rocking horse provided some fun for the smaller children. Four mothers volunteered to help to supervise the activities and a bingo evening was held at the centre. In August two mothers found a piano in an abandoned building and pushed and pulled it to the arts centre. A student volunteer provided music activities. In September an article on the centre appeared in one of the national newspapers. Books and materials arrived from a writer of children's books living in France. The F.A.S. worker and members of the community constructed a sand pit for the smaller children in the backyard of the family advice centre. A group of students who volunteered to help to maintain an intensive summer programme of recreational activities, trips and events wrote in their report:

Until the arrival of the F.A.S. there was nowhere for the children to play except in the streets, and their response to the Arts Centre would make an outsider think that they had been given a million pound purpose-built fun place, instead of the use of a small shop with only a swing, a slide, a piano and drawing materials for equipment. But they arrive before opening time in the morning, leave only after the greatest persuasion in the evening, and have been known to force their way in again at night. Most of the children are cheerful and enthusiastic, some to the point of aggressiveness in their need for attention, but a few are clearly in need of intense support and care, which they are obviously missing in the normal conditions of their home and neighbourhood.

Indigenous workers in the community

The term 'indigenous worker' has aroused much interest and has found many applications in the social welfare field in the United States. An American writer tells us:

Within the past decade a different type of non-professional, the indigenous worker, has emerged on the social welfare scene. This new worker must not be confused with the traditional non-professional worker; unlike the latter, the indigenous worker is recruited from the target neighbourhood and the risk population served by the employing agency (Loewenberg, 1968, p. 65).

The Seebohm Report seems to indicate that the possibilities of employing indigenous workers are now also being considered in this country. It states:

Implicit in the idea of a community-oriented family service is a belief in the importance of the maximum participation of individuals and groups in the community in the planning, organisation and provision of the social services. This view rests not only upon the working out of democratic ideas at the local level, but relates to the identification of need, the exposure of defects in the services and the mobilisation of new resources (para. 491).

The reader will note that the views expressed in this passage are entirely compatible with the objectives and the methods of the community-oriented family advice service. At this point we wish to emphasise the implication that community participation should include participation in the *provision* of services, because the community work carried out in the detached family advice centres showed that it is not only possible to involve community groups in community organisation and self-help activities, but also to draw members of the community into the process of directly providing some of the needed services.

We have already described the valuable work done by local mothers who were employed in supervising the 'D' project play group, and who were given opportunities for training. We have also mentioned the employment of indigenous workers by the 'F' project family advice centre and shall now give some further account of this interesting development of the F.A.S. approach.

During the year of study the 'F' project centre employed a number of people for a variety of tasks. These can be divided into two categories:

(a) Indigenous workers employed as 'community home helpers' and 'children's attendants'. These were four women who lived in the neighbourhood, all of them mothers of several children. All four had initially become involved in the activities of the parents' association and the self-help subcommittee and had done voluntary work for the centre. These workers were paid for four hours per day by the children's department.

(b) One adult and several teenagers, all living in the target area, who did occasional part-time repair work and other 'odd jobs' for the centre. These workers were paid partly by the children's department, partly from arts centre funds raised by the parents' association.

The community home helpers and children's attendants can be said to have functioned as 'expediters' of the centre's service to the community, and as 'mediators' between neighbourhood families and the centre. Increased community participation was an important factor in the employment of all the indigenous workers. While the indigenous workers made a very real and valuable contribution to the work of the centre and to the community, the work they did was also a source of satisfaction and support to them personally. The 'employment' motivation played a major role mainly in the utilisation of 'local talent' for repair and other occasional work, but also had some relevance to the employment of community home helpers and children's attendants. In employing teenagers to do 'odd jobs' in the centre and the neighbourhood for a few hours a week, the F.A.S. worker was also motivated by the youngsters' need for pocket money, the wish to channel their energies into constructive activities as an alternative to delinquent ones, and the assumption that 'unemployable' boys could be made more employable by work experience in a sheltered, permissive setting.

The variety of the tasks of the indigenous workers can be shown by a brief listing of the duties carried out and recorded by one of the community home helpers over a three-month period:

Home visits to a young mother just returned from hospital, a bedridden elderly lady, an emotionally upset mother, a father looking after several children after his wife left him, two families whose children would benefit from attending the arts centre. There were visits to eleven families to discuss the need for clothing and furniture. One family was visited when the mother had to go to hospital and the community home helper arranged for someone to look after the children. One mother was visited when neighbours reported that her children were left unattended in her absence, and a meeting with the F.A.S. worker was arranged. There was a series of visits to a woman who suffered from depressions. When a teenage boy had to stay away from work because he had to cook for the family, the home helper took over the cooking and sent him to work. The home helper cooked meals for two other families and bathed the children. There was an early morning visit to get a truant boy out of bed, washed and to school. A child was taken to hospital after a minor accident. A woman who had been assaulted by her husband was visited and calmed down. With the help of a teenage volunteer the home of one large family was given a thorough cleaning. A young woman who had given birth to an illegitimate child was visited and given some moral support.

During this three months period the community home helper contacted the housing department, the Department of Health and Social Security, the Electricity Board several times on behalf of about a dozen neighbourhood families. The home helper had several 'chats' with clients who came to the centre. She rounded up the people who wished to see the housing department official who was available for interviews at the centre, helped to supervise a jumble sale and helped to prepare and supervise a children's party at the Arts Centre.

While there is no doubt about the benefits to the centre and to the community derived from the work of the home helpers and children's attendants, there were, of course, also some problems. One of these was the issue of confidentiality. For obvious reasons the indigenous workers had access to all sorts of information about the personal affairs of members of the community and the workers themselves, the F.A.S. worker and members of the community were, at times, somewhat uneasy about this but no serious difficulties arose. There was also a tendency to adopt middle-class attitudes with regard to the standards of living and the behaviour of some of the clients. There were occasions when this made it difficult for the workers to be wholly accepting and, in a few instances, clients became aware of this. The F.A.S. worker guided and supervised the indigenous workers in all their duties, and it is one of his significant achievements that these problems caused no major friction.

Finally, it should be pointed out that the clerical assistant and the centre's domestic help both became part of the centre's service to the community and helped people through simple advice, visiting, a supportive chat at the centre etc. in many instances. Both were familiar with the problems of the neighbourhood through their own life experience and could well be regarded as indigenous workers.

The role of the ancillary worker

In May 1969 a report by the Home Office Research Unit described the results of

An experiment carried out in six local authorities at the request of the Home Office Children's Department after consultation with the former Advisory Council on Child Care. This experiment was designed to establish whether there was scope for the employment of ancillary staff engaged on work which is necessary to support social case work, but which need not be performed by case workers and which is not clerical in nature (Lowry, 1969).

The report concludes that: 'The chief advantage of ancillary workers lies in their flexibility, both of time and commitment.' The report lists the functions of ancillaries as escort duties, transportation of clients, debt collection (especially rent collection), switchboard duties, helping with records, studying local papers for employment and accommodation advertisements, gathering and summarising information on various matters, supportive home visiting, helping out with the care of children and housekeeping, distribution of clothes and furniture etc. to needy clients.

In view of the still experimental nature of the employment of this latest addition to the staff of children's departments in a number of local authorities, the use made of ancillary workers in the 'D' project family advice centre is of some interest.

● Mr D, a young man who had formerly been employed by the Department of Health and Social Security, was given a part-time assignment with the 'D' project family advice centre in February 1968. During his work with the project he carried out the following tasks:

Mr D gathered information about the uses made by children of a neighbourhood park in support of a community campaign to obtain adequate play and recreational facilities. He interviewed park department staff and approximately 200 adults and children living in the area and reported his findings to the family advice centre and the tenants' association. About a month later Mr D canvassed the residents of two housing blocks in order to obtain their views on the priority needs of the estate and to gauge their attitudes regarding the formation of a tenants' association. He helped to organise group meetings at the family advice centre and visited another borough in order to observe and report the organisation of play groups in that area.

In the summer of 1968 Mr D assisted a local volunteer to organise play activities and interviewed the mothers of a housing estate about their anxieties regarding traffic hazards in the neighbourhood. Shortly after this he obtained the co-operation of some of the parents in observing and recording the incidence of traffic in the hazard area. A few weeks later Mr D conducted a door-to-door survey of a tower block in the 'D' project area with the aim of providing some insights of the community problems in this relatively new type of accommodation.

7

Mr D visited the flats of a number of parents to discuss the uses and the need for participation in a new adventure playground and to determine their readiness to support a tenants' association.

In September Mr D completed his survey of the tower block and drew up a detailed and highly informative report with the help of the F.A.S. staff. Interviews with about 100 residents, the porter and the playground attendant pinpointed a number of immediate problems, such as a general atmosphere of tension and frustration on the eleventh floor where there were twenty-two children under five, lack of play facilities in the immediate area, a somewhat rigid attitude towards children by the playground attendant, insufficient protection from traffic noise, an isolated, bed-ridden ninety-year-old pensioner who caused concern to the neighbours but refused help, and friction between the tower block tenants and the inhabitants of adjacent maisonettes.

Some time after the completion of this survey Mr D expressed the wish to be released from his other children's department duties and to be permitted to focus on the kind of community work in which he had become engaged as a part-time member of the F.A.S. team. When his request was turned down he left in order to attend a course.

● In December 1968 another ancillary worker was given a part-time assignment with the family advice centre. Mr C had formerly worked in a children's home and applied his experience to helping in the organisation and supervision of play and recreational activities in the area. He assisted in the centre's work with the tenants' association and interviewed twenty-three tenants in one of the blocks in order to obtain their views regarding their association. Soon after this he undertook another survey of this kind in another block of the estate. He helped a group of mothers to form a group which set itself the task of planning a summer programme for the block's children. During the following months Mr C helped the F.A.S. staff and a group of parents to develop and supervise a new playground. His availability became especially useful when conflict developed between a mothers' group and the tenants' association of the estate. Mr C gave support and guidance to the mothers' group, while the F.A.S. worker was able to continue to advise the tenants' association.

Both F.A.S. workers felt that the two ancillaries made a significant contribution to the work of the centre. Our own observation confirms this view. The guidance and supervision provided by the F.A.S. staff enabled these untrained workers to acquire considerable skill in community work, enabling them to assume an impressive range of responsibilities within a relatively short period of time.

6 Services to the community—I

Aside from the family advice service itself, the detached centres also initiated and supported a range of services to the community with varying degrees of community participation. Among these were attempts to relieve material needs, services for the elderly, efforts to improve race relations and legal advice.

The 'G' project school holidays lunch service

As already mentioned in the preceding pages, the free lunch service was provided by the 'G' project family advice centre for the one-week Easter holiday in the Spring of 1969. This service was financed by the Child Poverty Action Group for children who received free school meals during the school term and initiated and organised by the F.A.S. worker. The latter was helped by a young Dutch student and two of the tenants in preparing and serving the food. Forty lunches were served each day and the children greatly enjoyed the party atmosphere of the daily event.

Services for the elderly

The physical and emotional needs of the elderly and their all-too-frequent isolation in the community aroused the concern of the F.A.S. workers in a number of cases. We have already described those instances in which the community work carried out by the 'D', 'G', and 'F' project family advice centres served the needs of elderly people in the neighbourhood and even involved them directly in community activities. Some of the issues highlighted by this aspect of community work are important enough to bear description. The 'G' project F.A.S. worker observed in her records:

● In my role as F.A.S. worker in a community I had to give help
to old people from time to time when other services for various reasons,
were unable to respond. When a crisis situation arose, it became apparent
that the existing welfare services were sometimes overburdened,
understaffed, or too rigidly structured to provide the kind of immediate
and flexible service that the elderly need. The Good Neighbour Service
went some way towards providing neighbourly help and, at its best,
provided skilled daily help which enabled old people to remain in their
homes. However, there seemed to be over reliance on voluntary services.
Less than £1 is paid, no matter how frequent and intensive the care
required. Skilled supervision is limited and the people who work as
'good neighbours' do not receive the guidance and support which
they need.

Loneliness and social isolation were among the main causes of distress
to the elderly in the G estate. After a number of individual contacts with
elderly people in the community, and after discussing some of the needs
of the old people with the tenants' association, the F.A.S. worker
organised a Christmas Party for elderly tenants at the centre with the
help of the caretaker's wife. An application to the mayor of the borough
resulted in a grant of £24 which was distributed to twenty-four elderly
tenants shortly before Christmas. Many of the old people attended the
party and greatly enjoyed themselves. At the same time coffee and cake
was taken to the flats of a few bedridden old people who could not attend
the party. A direct result of the party was the development of a much
closer relationship between the centre and the old people, as well as more
direct involvement of other members of the community in helping their
elderly neighbours.

A few weeks after the Christmas party a group of old people met for a
discussion of their needs and problems at the family advice centre.
Shortly after that the secretary of the tenants' association asked the
worker to provide information about the difficulties encountered by the
elderly tenants with regard to rehousing. A flat-to-flat survey was
organised by the F.A.S. worker with the help of a Dutch student assigned
to the centre and a lecturer in sociology who volunteered her services.
The worker recorded the following observations:

● At a supervision meeting in January I expressed my concern that
other social workers in the area with responsibility for old people would
feel that I was encroaching upon their territory. I formally obtained
the permission of the children's officer to do this work. The senior
research officer pointed out that I was working in response to a need
expressed by the community, as the tenants' association had asked

me to find out about the old people. At this time I was becoming very aware of the social networks in the neighbourhood and of the importance of mutual help within the community, e.g. the family of three generations living on the same estate giving support to each other—the grandmother keeping an eye on the children and acting in a 'wise-old-authoritarian' way. I was also becoming more aware that often the wrong type of service is provided for old people without first consulting the old people themselves. For example, the Meals on Wheels Service assumes that old people want a hot meal delivered to them and served up for them when they would often rather take time in deciding what to have for lunch, going to the shops to buy the food, and then enjoy cooking it themselves. They are also concerned that they have to pay £3 for reconnection and 17s 6d for disconnection of their gas supplies. They feel that as they are being moved compulsorily, the housing department should meet these charges. I explained to them about social security grants and how they work. I told them how to apply for special grants and issued them with forms on which to do so. I got a book *Arrangements for Old Age* from the Consumers' Association. Now the older people often come to me and say, 'It says in the book that . . .'

Miss J, the Dutch student, completed all the interviews by the middle of February. Two schedules were drawn up to tabulate the information. Every one of the elderly people were visited and interviewed except for an old lady who had recently been robbed by two men posing as council officials and who now refuses to open her door to strangers.

As a result of the discussion with the elderly tenants and the tenants' association a letter stating the anxieties of a group of thirty-six elderly tenants was drawn up and sent to the housing manager. A favourable reply was received from the housing manager and a series of acceptable rehousing offers were made. The F.A.S. workers' records continue:

● During the interviews with the old people, Miss J discovered some rather more urgent needs. These were followed up at the end of the survey. For example, we called on Mrs N and explained the process of making a chiropody appointment; we called on Mrs O who required a new mattress; we visited Mr and Mrs P, who are being visited by a welfare officer already—they gave us permission to send a memo to the welfare officer regarding their needs; we wrote letters to the Department of Health and Social Security on behalf of Mrs Q and Mr and Mrs R.

The main object of the survey as far as I was concerned was to find out how the family advice service could be an effective referral service after the old people are moved. However, it was not quite clear to me that I was making an unfounded assumption. No one wanted referral to the personal social services, some even strongly resisted the idea. The older people were proud of their independence and anxious to retain it. 'As long as I can crawl up to the shop, I'd rather manage myself' said a frail and infirm elderly widow. I tend to think that resistance is due to the fact that social workers and geriatric social workers especially, visit intensively at point of breakdown, when the geriatric visitor or social worker often invokes transfer arrangements to institutions. There is a real fear of this among people.

Shortly after the completion of the survey a 'social evening' for the elderly tenants was held at the family advice centre. There was lively discussion of such matters as special benefits grants and rehousing preferences. There was some resistance to the worker's suggestion of closer co-operation between the elderly tenants and the tenants' association which ceased when the worker read out a letter to her from the secretary of the tenants' association expressing concern about the situation of the old people on the estate and asking the worker to liaise with the association in providing all possible help. Two old people, a man and a woman, were elected as representatives of the old people's group and the chairman of the tenants' association was called in to talk to the group. The latter invited the group to attend the next meeting of the association. A further meeting of the old people's group at the centre was arranged.

While the concern for the elderly resulted in some noteworthy instances of much-needed community involvement of this section of the population, the F.A.S. worker never lost sight of the need for straightforward practical help. The workers showed full awareness of the down-to-earth fact emphasised in the statement: 'No increase in the quantum of community care for the old can compensate for inadequate income and inadequate housing. We may gain satisfaction from being busy as community carers but the old will lose in self respect (Titmus, 1968, p. 92).

Helping the community to accept strangers in their midst

A report of the Youth Service Development Council (1967) on *Immigrants and the Youth Service* states: 'The presence of an immigrant population has become one of the major social issues in Britain today'. The report points out that this country

has often shown towards the immigrants a somewhat ambivalent attitude in which a traditional liberalism and tolerance, in welcoming those whom religious, political or economic circumstances brought to this country, was accompanied by resentment and suspicion as the presence of the newcomers made itself felt in the midst of the host society.

It was inevitable that the community-based family advice centres should have to face the dynamics and effects of these attitudes of resentment and suspicion in the areas they served. It is perhaps unfortunate that our study did not have the opportunity to observe a family advice centre in an area containing sizeable minority groups or immigrant communities. Such an area would have enabled us to examine whether a detached family advice centre can make a significant contribution to solving the immigrant adjustment and race relations problems in such areas.[1] We may, however, be able to provide some insight into the problems encountered by the community work approach in the widely present situations in which individual immigrant families and/or small groups of ethnically different people are subject to the invidious processes of social isolation and scapegoating with results which are as destructive to the victims as to the perpetrators of discrimination.

A recent article discusses the problems this type of situation poses for social workers and others in the social services:

Situations will inevitably arise where an individual or community decide to discriminate against a particular group, such as coloured immigrants, or to be self-destructive, by the use of drugs, alcohol, etc. How can prejudiced or self-destructive attitudes be combated? There are no easy answers. On the one hand the worker must make it clear that he disapproves of the decision or action of the group or individual, but on the other hand, he must avoid doing what society has always done and continues to do, namely to reject not only the deed but also the doer. This means making clear the thin, yet very real, dividing line between disapproval of certain attitudes or actions while continuing to accept the individual or the community concerned.

Nor does acceptance mean excusing or condoning. Rather it implies the recognition that if changes are to be brought about, they will come in the main through the . . . client's . . . trust and ability to see the relevance, and often advantages, of different ways of behaviour. Of course, outward conformity can be more or less readily enforced. But no one, not even the youngest child, can ever be made to conform when 'authority' is not watching unless he does so of his own free will (Kellmer Pringle, 1970, p. 15).

This passage is important not only because it raises the issue of the possible conflict between the worker's own values and the attitudes and behaviour of his clients, but also because it approaches discrimination as a social problem which must be seen in the same context as others' self-destructive behaviour. Both issues were highly significant in the

[1] For a description of a situation of this type see, for instance, Rex and Moore (1967), *Race Community and Conflict*.

experience of one of the detached family advice centres as our description of the work process will show.

Ethnic problems were present in the areas of all four detached family advice centres, but did not seem to have any significant impact upon the work of the centres in the 'F' and 'G' project areas. As will become apparent in a later section of this report, racial tension had far reaching effects in the youth work carried out by the 'E' centre. However, the problems of isolated immigrant families raised special concern in the tense atmosphere of the 'G' project and we shall describe the ways and means in which the F.A.S. worker in that setting tried to deal with the problem in the following pages.

Immigrant problems in the 'G' project

Among the inhabitants of the G estate there were a few immigrant families from Cyprus, the West Indies and Africa. These people faced the problems usually faced by immigrants and members of ethnic minorities, as well as the same deprivations and frustrations experienced by many of their English neighbours. From time to time they became objects of the kind of hostility that was rampant in the community, and that often turned the diffuse anger of the inhabitants against each other. The immigrant families did, at times, find this hostility more painful, less easy to shrug off or to return in kind, because they felt that their neighbours resented them because of their origin, the colour of their skins, their language, in fact because they were different.

The virulence of some of the racist feelings often subjected the F.A.S. worker's own feelings and patience to severe tests. In September 1967, for instance, the worker recorded:

● Mrs S and Mrs K standing at her front door: 'We're just talking about some of your bleeding black friends up there. It's bleeding murder here. Throwing their shit and muck over the balcony. This used to be a decent place before the blacks got in. There was that bleeding boy climbing up a tree the other day. Not that they aren't bleeding monkeys and shouldn't live up the bleeding trees. All you get is bleeding abuse if you say anything. These people up the Town Hall, you can talk and talk and they never listen!' She struck the wall—'You might as well talk to that bleeding wall.' I said perhaps she thought I wasn't listening either. What did she expect me to do? She thought the blacks should be shifted out of here. I said I was quite sure that people wouldn't be shifted out because they were black, or brown-haired or blue-eyed or had any other category of colours.

'By the way, Mrs S—is *that* some of the excrement that's been thrown over the balcony?'—I pointed to a large brown pile on the courtyard in front of us. 'No,' said Mrs S, 'that's my dog's shit—and I clean it up myself.'

Mrs S said she was a diabetic, and although she wouldn't say these bleeding people had given her diabetes—she would say that she might go into a coma on account of them. I said that she could have a coma on account of diabetes, as far as I knew, and that I realised that upsets didn't help. Why didn't she speak to Mrs A, she'd find her a rational person—she's a trained nurse. Mrs K broke in to say that speaking wouldn't help anybody here, they were all past it. Nothing you could do for them would change them. I said this was definitely not my impression—I found that many of the residents here were pleasant people, certainly not 'beyond' anything.

There were also encouraging signs that many people understood the difficulties facing the strangers in their midst and tried to show them kindness:

● In the second week in November, two tenants, Mrs W and Mrs L, complained to me about the noise from Mrs J in flat 74. There is a constant and regular banging which seems to come from a machine of some sort. It goes on until late at night and starts again in the morning. The J's happen to be coloured, but Mrs W assured me that her complaint had nothing to do with this. It was agreed that we'd ask Mrs J to join us for a cup of tea. The following day we met in the centre. Mrs W talked to Mrs J very pleasantly. At one time she laid a hand on Mrs J and told her: 'You're scared that we are getting at you because you are coloured. We are not, dear, it's just the noise.'

Like all other community problems, the F.A.S. worker regarded the difficulties experienced by the immigrant families as part of the daily tasks with which she had to cope in order to help the people concerned, and in order to help the community improve their living conditions and their relations with each other. She always felt that she could have done much more if her many other duties had left her more time and if she could have delegated some of her work to an assistant.

● Soon after this the F.A.S. worker visited the flat of Mrs L, a young African mother of five children, after neighbours had complained that the children were left unattended. After discussing the matter with Mrs L the worker arranged for the provision of a baby sitter from Task Force. A close relationship between the F.A.S. worker and Mrs L grew out of a series of talks and requests for help. As Mrs L was a very intelligent young woman the worker was able to discuss her strong feelings of being the victim of the community's prejudice with her in a rational manner. She encouraged Mrs L to pursue her interest in writing and put her in touch with one of the editors of a local newspaper. Soon after this an article by Mrs L about her life as an immigrant in a council estate was published. This aroused the interest of many of the neighbours and enhanced Mrs L's status in the community. With some guidance by the F.A.S. worker Mrs L began to take interest in the problems of other immigrant families on the estate, visited them in their homes and helped them to deal with some of their problems and their feelings of isolation. She was eventually contacted by the tenants' association and asked to work with them towards establishing better neighbourly relations between the immigrant families and the other tenants. Mrs L was especially pleased when one of the white families gladly accepted her help in providing and altering second-hand clothes for their children.

The F.A.S. worker arranged for Mrs L to do part-time work as a home helper and to attend meetings of the local branch of the Child Poverty Action Group where she made a much appreciated contribution to an analysis of the free school meals service in the area. Soon after this Mrs L was asked to join a group of tenants who were drawing up a report for the Ministry of Housing and Local Government on living conditions in the G estate. A month after this Mrs L was invited to give a talk on the socio-cultural background of African immigrants to a sector staff meeting at the children's department.

Mrs L continued to require advice and assistance with her own problems and, while her relations with her neighbours improved greatly, there were occasional setbacks. For instance, when the F.A.S. worker enlisted Mrs L's help in providing free school holiday lunches for the children of the community Mrs L withdrew after three days because she could not cope with the insulting remarks of some of the more aggressive youngsters. Shortly before the closing of the centre the F.A.S. worker obtained an educational grant for Mrs L which enabled her to enroll for a course in higher education and she was referred to a child care officer for further support when she was rehoused and moved to another area of the borough.

Complaints and accusations by several of the tenants drew the F.A.S. worker's attention to the Cypriot families of the G estate. She discussed one of the families with the housing welfare officer and established a long-term supportive relationship with the fourteen-year-old son of another family. Eventually there was also consultation with the N.S.P.C.C. inspector and the health visitor about the many problems of the Cypriots in the community. Gradually, in spite of the language problems, the F.A.S. worker gained some insight into the traditions and living patterns of these families. She enlisted the help of a young Greek Cypriot socio-logist who explained to her that most of the Cypriots in the borough were engaged in the catering and tailoring trades, and that many of the women did sewing work at home on piece rates. Visiting the flats with the volun-teer interpreter the F.A.S. worker heard bitter complaints about prob-lems ranging from stopped-up sinks to incidents in which Cypriot children had been abused and beaten up by the neighbours.

Soon after this the F.A.S. worker was able to obtain the help of a Greek Cypriot social worker employed by the Council of Social Services. Mr E took a personal interest in the Cypriot families of the G estate. He visited them repeatedly, sometimes accompanied by the F.A.S. worker, and helped in many different ways. In the spring of 1968 Mr E organised a 'Cyprus Week' with the support of the libraries and arts committee of the borough and under the patronage of the high commis-sioner of Cyprus. He tried to involve the G estate Cypriots in this event, but they did not show much interest. Together with the F.A.S. worker Mr E organised English lessons at the family advice centre, but atten-dance was only sporadic. When 'Cyprus Week' opened in May of that year the F.A.S. worker took several of the Cypriots and some of the English parents and children to see the exhibits and watch a theatre performance.

At the end of the summer Mr E drew up a letter to Archbishop Makarios which stressed the cultural and economic deprivation of the Greek Cypriots in the borough and made serious accusations of discrimi-nation against this immigrant group by the authorities. Mr E asked the F.A.S. worker to co-sign the letter. As the accusations were not substantiated in the document, and as there was a strong possibility that the letter would reach the Press, the F.A.S. worker was advised that she could not sign as a statutory officer employed by the borough.

The F.A.S. worker and Mr E continued to visit the Cypriot families and the F.A.S. worker provided advice, guidance and assistance with a wide range of problems. At the end of the year she referred three of the families to the local Citizens' Advice Bureau which appointed a Greek speaking social worker.

Legal advice

The need for legal advice with regard to matters of law and litigation in general, and with regard to the law as it pertains to social conditions,

welfare provisions and individual rights in particular, has been a subject
of discussion in Britain, the United States and many other countries for
some time. Lawyers as well as social workers have been involved in this
discussion. A recent article by an American author, for instance, notes
that in the U.S.A. 'The rapid development of programs—largely under
the Office of Economic Opportunity—making legal services more widely
available to social work clients . . . has increased the need for social
workers' understanding the legal nature of their case load content and
the institutions and practitioners to whom they must turn for help'
(Fogelson, 1970). A British lawyer has given a detailed listing of some of
the prevailing conditions which point at the need for legal advice for
large segments of the population. The writer tells us:

Not only do local authorities vary in their interpretation and use of their many
discretionary powers: they vary in the extent to which they are prepared to give
information to the public. One large housing authority does not inform tenants
being moved from slum-clearance property that they can obtain a small grant
towards furnishing their new house—areas with the longest waiting lists do
not inform those anxious to put their names down that their chances of receiving
a council house for many years to come, are very meagre. Nor do some housing
authorities publish how council houses are allocated or what point system exists.
It is probable that coloured immigrants, in effect, are discriminated against
by not being granted a council house because some authorities will not rehouse
in advance of slum clearance which is likely to include areas where they live in
multiple-occupied houses. It is not known to what extent some local authorities
make only two or three offers of accommodation, sometimes one offer at least
of unacceptable 'improved' housing, so that then the tenant can be labelled as
uncooperative and placed at the bottom of the list, without discovering the
reasons for refusal. With rent rebate schemes local authorities appear to have
made not only their means test, but their own practice rules. One housing authority refers inquiries about rent rebates to the M.S.S. omitting to tell them that
supplementary benefit rent allowances are based on a different means test
which may be less generous (rent rebates prevent them from making a wise
choice about the 'best buy', and incidentally the housing authority's accounts
are less likely to go into the red). Similarly, lack of information or explanation
about the functions of rent tribunals and rent officers may lead somebody
to make the wrong choice and as a result he may lose the home.
    The social services in some areas appear to have evolved separate procedures,
to the extent of establishing a more favoured position for themselves in the legal
system. Some major housing authorities may be dilatory, if not reluctant, to
carry out repairs on their own property. The public health inspector cannot take
his own authority to court as he could a private landlord. Housing authorities
sometimes obtain eviction orders against tenants and then hold them over
their heads like a sword of Damocles—sometimes for years. It is most unsatisfactory for tenants that they should have to be given a formal notice to quit
before their rent can be raised. Some councils will refuse to have the wife as the
tenant or to have the husband and wife as joint tenants, so if the family breaks
up the housing authority may well not grant the tenancy to the wife until she has

gone to court and got a separation order or a divorce (yet the tenancy was probably granted to the family because there were children). The 1967 matrimonial homes act does not apply to council tenancies (Brooke, 1969, p. 93).

At the 1968 International Conference on Social Welfare and Human Rights the question was asked: 'To what extent do adults have access to adequate legal aid and appeal regardless of their economic, educational or social status when their human rights are in question? What can be done to improve the availability of legal services?' (Turner, 1968, p. 17). A well-known British lawyer answered the first of these questions by stating that: 'Quite clearly the vast majority of people with legal problems never get anywhere near a solicitor' (Zanders, 1968, p. 188).

A well-established legal advice service was available only in one of the seven areas served by the family advice centres, namely the area served by the 'C' project centre. It was not integrated with the family advice service, although, as we have pointed out, there existed a close and effective referral relationship between the two services. We are by no means maintaining that a legal advice service could not be provided outside the F.A.S. setting. We do, however, find that the provision of a legal advice service within the community, and close co-operation between social workers engaged in community work and lawyers, may be one of the important contributions of the detached family advice centres. The most interesting work in this type of service was done in the area served by the 'D' project family advice centre.

A short paper drawn up by one of the two 'D' project F.A.S. workers describes the reasons for, and the processes of, introducing a legal advice service to the area. We reproduce this document in full as we cannot hope to improve upon the clear concise way in which it states the case and describes the problems.

● Discussions on the inadequacies of the existing legal service in the area began in January 1968. Taking part in these were local Tenants' Leaders, a teacher and a neighbourhood social worker [the F.A.S. worker]. At first the problem was seen as a result of lack of resources as with other services such as housing and education where a 'poor' service was provided for 'the poor'. A closer analysis of the situation revealed that the problem was more fundamental than just a matter of resources and that merely providing more solicitors would not answer the need. A different service from that of the traditional law firm seemed called for.

The present difficulties which led to this point of view were:

(a) *Poor image of solicitors.* They were viewed by local people as only being concerned with clients where fee payments were guaranteed. They were not easily accessible owing to the limited number of lawyers in the district. They operated a rigid appointments system ill suited to the needs of local people. Communication was difficult owing to the different use of language by the solicitors from that of their clients with a different educational background.

(*b*) *Discrimination of substantive law against working people.* This results from the tendency of the law to have few remedies for the grievances of working people. Thus, for example, a tenant is not allowed to withhold rent whether or not the landlord is fulfilling his responsibilities. This tendency reinforces the poor image held of lawyers as they appear to be aligned with authority (e.g. police and local authority) and those with money (e.g. landlords, hire purchase companies, etc.). This view, coupled with the resulting apathy and ignorance, leads to a widespread neglect in this area of the rights and benefits which do exist. Thus people allow themselves to be evicted without question, do not apply for rate rebates and welfare benefits for which they qualify etc.

From the discussion it emerged that a legal advice service was needed which:

(*a*) Was appropriate to the needs of the working-class population of the area, i.e. was accessible to individuals and able if necessary to take on litigation as well as advice, thus avoiding the misunderstandings and lack of confidence in existing 'poor man's legal services which were hampered by legal etiquette'.

(*b*) In addition if it were to operate an effective service it would need to have a built-in educative function. This is almost a pre-condition of operating the service if the already existing bias against lawyers and legal remedies was to be overcome.

How to set up this service then became the main theme of the continuing discussion. A local solicitor was consulted about the problem in general terms. This proved unproductive, apart from the fact that it gave the group an appreciation of the problems which they would have to face in achieving a legal service adapted to local needs. The solicitor who was working in one of the few local firms was already too overburdened to take on any further work. Thus, whilst illustrating the problems, also confirmed the need for a new approach.

Following this failure, attention was turned to finding lawyers who were prepared to give time to considering the needs of this 'grass roots' project. Through personal contacts in November 1968 the help of an American law research student and a barrister were enlisted. At this stage it was decided to set up a consultative service to deal with the legal problems which came to the notice of the group members in their respective roles in the neighbourhood. It was felt that with the limited resource of only one qualified lawyer it was not possible to set up a more comprehensive service. This avoided the danger of producing an inferior duplication of existing 'Poor Man's Lawyer' organisations. In this way the skills of the barrister would be available in consultation and those of the research student could be used to investigate the referred problems at ground level. Owing to his experience in the 'neighbourhood law firms' in the States, he was well suited to developing a neighbourhood-oriented rather than a pseudo-professional service.

The period from December to May 1969 showed the potential of the original ideas but also exposed the limitations of a service which was operating without more qualified lawyers. As might be expected the most successful cases dealt with were in the field of administrative law which was, in any case, outside the field where legal aid could be used. In one case it was possible to fight both the landlord and a cautious Rent Officer with the result that the premises were classified by the Rent tribunal as unfurnished and referred back to the Rent Officer for a fair rent to be registered with Security of Tenure. In cases where clients were reluctant to risk opposing a landlord, the support of legal argument to the advice of the social worker, helped boost the morale of the client.

One of the major problems which was revealed could not be tackled. This related to those council tenants who were living in what amounted to sub-standard accommodation caused by water penetration and/or faulty workmanship. The barrister discovered that the Local Housing Authority were in the main excluded from those statutes which set out the responsibilities of landlords. Thus to initiate litigation was likely to prove expensive owing to the need to provide expert evidence from surveyors and there appeared little likelihood that legal aid would be granted for this type of case.

Another problem which arose was that it was not possible to take on individual cases which could be followed through the full legal process, if necessary, because of the lack of a solicitor. In cases where it was deemed that referral was necessary all the inadequacies of the existing services were apparent. These were that either the client did not keep his appointment or else the solicitor was reluctant to take on a case as the client could not meet the fees in advance.

Thus to evolve an effective service more groundwork had to be done in seeking allies within the legal profession. Fortunately, through personal contacts, we were able to discuss our needs with the Attorney General Sir Elwyn Jones. He was able to direct us to the appropriate section of the Law Society where we were able both to contact interested solicitors and to obtain official sanction for the project.

This preliminary work was completed by 20 August 1969, when a meeting of the full group decided that the lawyers should have a

once-weekly session at ———[1] open to the public. The organisation was
to be known as the ——— Neighbourhood Law Centre.

The setting up of the Neighbourhood Law Centre was discussed in a
series of meetings with the tenants' association of a nearby council estate
during the autumn of 1969. At the request of the tenants' association a
barrister visited one of the flats and ascertained that the lack of repairs
over a long period of time warranted legal action. He recommended that
a surveyor's report be obtained. Before taking any legal steps the F.A.S.
worker wrote to the housing department describing the state of the flat
and pointing out the legal rights of the tenant.

Some time after the termination of the research project in October
1969, one evening per week legal advice sessions were introduced at the
family advice centre. Although the new service was not publicised, thirty
clients made use of the service by the end of the year, seeking advice
on problems ranging from hire-purchase debts, industrial and rent
tribunal cases, and criminal and juvenile court proceedings to a variety
of housing problems.

Throughout the two-year study period of the 'E' project centre there
were cases in which adults or young people presented problems requiring
legal advice and representation. In a number of such cases the centre was
able to refer to a solicitor. This experience led to a growing awareness of
the need for making legal advice available to the people of the area.

In the summer of 1969 the F.A.S. worker took the initiative in
raising the possibility of a legal advice service at the centre with Michael
Zanders, Professor of Law at the London School of Economics. Professor
Zanders's response was favourable.

Early in August an advertisement was inserted in the *New Law Journal*
asking for a volunteer solicitor to provide legal advice at the centre
one evening per week. An appointment was made in September. The
centre distributed posters in local launderettes, libraries, restaurants,
stores, schools etc. The posters read:

FREE LEGAL ADVICE

AVAILABLE AT THE FAMILY ADVICE CENTRE

Call or ring for appointment

Social workers also available daily to offer
advice to persons of all ages, on a wide range
of personal and community problems.

Almost immediately the Town Clerk objected, pointing out that the
centre had not received permission for publicising a legal advice service.

1 The building in which the family advice centre is located.

Some of the posters were removed upon the instruction of the children's officer. Nevertheless one evening a week legal advice service was established sometime after the termination of the research period.

In September 1968 an M.P. stated in an article which discussed the need for legal advice services: 'Our present Legal Aid system in Britain does not deal with the needs of those whose social problems are worst.' The writer pointed out that: 'The people who are least able to cope with life, and do not find their way to a Citizens' Advice Bureau, M.P. or lawyer, are the same ones who are most in need of the Rent Act's protection or of their full social security.' He added: 'A solicitor's client is almost invariably already in trouble; what is wanted is a preventive service, reaching those who are frightened and fatalistic about the law— even when they are able to reach a lawyer' (Whitaker, 1968).

A review of a report by the Society of Labour Lawyers (1968) was summarised as follows:

The report assembles massive evidence that the present legal aid scheme leaves a large volume of unmet need for professional legal services. It calls for expansion of the existing schemes by all possible means . . . [the report recommends the setting up of local legal centres which] . . . would draw its clients only from its own area but would not operate a means test. It would tackle most legal work except those things which the private practitioner now did adequately such as divorce, conveyancing and personal injury cases (*The Guardian*, 2 December 1968).

The same paper reviews *Rough Justice*, a report issued by the Conservative Political Centre:

One serious gap in our social services, says the report, is the failure of the present legal service to reach a multitude of people who need little more than legal advice to settle their problems. There were three main reasons. One was the shortage of solicitors in the poorer areas; secondly for many people the idea of consulting a solicitor was alien, even repugnant; and thirdly the whole system of legal aid was heavily geared towards litigation.

A variety of attempts have recently been made to provide legal advice in areas where this type of service seems most needed. There is a growing body of opinion which holds that this is an essential preventive service.

7 Services to the community—II

All four of the detached family advice centres were more or less intensively engaged in the provision of services for children and teenagers. The needs for such services were obvious, the problems of meeting the needs demanded imagination, skill and perseverance. The reasons for the preponderance of unmet needs in this decisively important area are well-known and have been stated again and again. To cite only a few of the many informed opinions: Joan Cooper (1965) observed that: 'Cultural poverty is a marked feature of many children received into the public care. Lack of cultural aspirations is a marked feature of multi-problem families. Communication tends to be by way of a hug or a cuff and the value of constructive play is not understood' (p. 100). M. L. Kellmer Pringle (1965b) pointed out that 'the great majority of children in this country from under-privileged homes also attend "under-privileged" schools' (p. 139). A recent study on housing conditions cites the Plowden committee report as indicating:

Some of the physical conditions of the home which have an adverse influence upon children's development: overcrowding, lack of play space and of variety of stimulation, insecure tenancies and lack of, or sharing of basic amenities. The children of manual working class fathers were worst off in having no play area attached to the dwelling (Spencer, 1970, p. 108).

D. M. Downes (1966) wrote:

Instead of regarding the working-class delinquent as a deviant in a conformity-promoting society, it is possible to regard the working-class boy as born into a pre-ordained delinquency-promoting situation. Our task can only then be to change that situation, so that the bulk of working-class youth is freed from pressures to deviancy and heavy personal costs (p. 260).

The unmet needs have their origin in the social milieu and the physical environment, and in trying to respond to these needs the family advice centres had to seek to bring about at least partial changes in these factors. The means and realistic possibilities of doing so were limited.

It is all the more remarkable to observe the range of services which could be provided.

Services for children and youth in the 'G' project

With regard to the 'G' project centre it may be said that the most valuable services for children of all ages were provided by the centre itself through its advice, guidance and assistance functions and largely due to its almost unlimited accessibility.

The F.A.S. worker aroused the curiosity of the children from the very first day. Within a few weeks of the opening of the centre it became apparent that the centre and its worker attracted children of all ages like a magnet. When the centre closed at the end of the two-year period, there remained no doubt in anyone's mind that the family advice service worker had become an important source of support for many of the community's children, an educational and cultural influence, a restraining, watchful, often critical, but always accepting friend, a source of comfort and help in times of crisis.

For a fifteen-month period, between August 1967 and November 1968, the F.A.S. worker's records of her daily contacts with the children were so detailed and consistent that we were able to tabulate the number of these contacts during that period. (After this period the pressure of work became so great that the research staff agreed with the worker that a more summarised form of recording would have to be accepted.) The data regarding the F.A.S. worker's contacts with children during this fifteen-month period may provide the reader with some impression of the intensity of this aspect of the centre's service to the community, and give some indication of the time and attention the children demanded and received.

In the following table we define 'contact' as any formal interview or casual meeting between a youngster and the F.A.S. worker, either individually or in groups, inside the family advice centre or in the courtyard of the estate. Contacts with children during home visits are *not* included. A 'contact' may have taken a few minutes or stretched over several hours. In the latter case it usually meant that the worker took care of a number of other matters (such as recording, correspondence or discussion with adult clients) while one or several youngsters were 'hanging about'.

As the figures below show, contact with the girls was more sustained than with the boys. This is probably due to the fact that the F.A.S. worker is a woman. There were, indeed, strong indications that a

Contacts with children: 3 August 1967 to 3 November 1968

Number of contacts	Girls	Boys	Boys and Girls
80 and above	1	0	1
50 and above	1	0	1
40 and above	2	0	2
30 and above	3	0	3
20 and above	6	2	8
10 and above	7	9	16
5 and above	9	11	20
Less than 5	34	40	74
Total number of children	63	62	125

male youth worker was needed in order to reach the boys, especially the
teenagers, of the community. The 125 children were members of 65
families. Exclusive of the numerous times the F.A.S. worker saw children
in their homes or in the company of their parents in a wide range of
helping situations, the worker had a total of 1,007 individual and
group contacts with children during the fifteen-month period. These
contacts did not, of course, decrease during the subsequent nine months.
On the contrary, the work with children increased and, in a number of
cases, became more intensive.

A detailed, chronological review of the family advice centre's services
to children and youth would require a fair sized volume. We can only
afford the reader some glimpses of this work, the approaches used and
the atmosphere in which it took place, by describing some characteristic
occurrences and incidents and citing some of the children's own reactions
and excerpts from the F.A.S. worker's records. But first let us look at
the F.A.S. worker's relationship with one of the girls in order to illustrate
the complexities and demands, the setbacks and the rewards of the work.
The worker recorded:

● I met Jean and her friend Elaine the week I opened the centre
when the two girls came to tell me that some boys had pulled the
F.A.S. sign off the door and they offered to wash my car. There was some
rumour that they were in trouble with the police because of shop-lifting;
when I spoke to them they were close-mouthed and suspicious. The next
day they came to the centre: 'Hello! Who are you? Are you the lady who
puts children away in homes, or a probation officer or something,
in this office with all those white walls?' I told them about the family
advice service. They asked me whether I could arrange a holiday for

them. I asked them what they had been up to the previous day. Jean
went red: 'Well! It's these flats that make you nick things. In any case
it wasn't us—it was Margaret (a five-year-old)—she's ever so naughty.'
I said they needn't tell me anything—anyway perhaps it was better to
say nothing as they did not know who I was and they did not know if
I would keep it to myself. 'Oh! we've done a lot of nicking. Tons of things.
The policeman has told our Mums not to hit us. The man decided not to
take us to court but we weren't half frightened!'

This was the beginning of a relationship that lasted for two years.
The F.A.S. worker allowed Jean and her friends to accompany her on
errands in other areas of the city and put Jean in contact with a theatre
group. Jean wrote down her comments:

> 'Down the Dramer Senta there are people who do plays and poetry
> and sometimes I go down there and do some acting too and it is
> very good because they let you dress up. They had a childrens play
> but I couldnt go and see it because I was feeling sick so my Mum
> said I can stay in for a little while.'

The worker arranged for a holiday for Jean and Elaine and they sat in
the centre writing down stories of their exploits. The stories showed that
Jean had talent and imagination and that she had never learned to spell
even the simplest words. The stories also threw some light on the girls'
behaviour:

> 'me and elaine and margaret and Debra went knicking every think
> we could get hold of. First of all we went in Fine Fare and we thought
> we were having a great time till we got calld [caught]. We got a
> basket from Fine Fare and got half a pound of lame jobs [lamb chops]
> and we knicked three tins of coke cole 2 tins of sliced orange 4 packets
> of bicicts 2 bottles of milk 1 tin of nescafe coffe 2 jellys 3 packs chrisps.
> Then we went in woolworths and I took 1 purse and that was all.
> Then we went in the LCS and I knicked 1 pare of baby pants 2 packets
> of baby food 1 pare of boys shorts packet of bath bubles and two tins
> of baby cream and as we was going out of the door we was caled by
> some police woman and they grambed hold of us and they took us
> in a room and they took all are thinks out of are bag and they took us
> to the police station and they let us go but they brought are mums
> up and the police man said dont'it [hit] them and do not do it again
> Rosie [Mrs C, another tenant] came in and said you have no write
> to hold these children so elaine's mum to her to shut her mouth
> because you haven't got no children hear.'

Jean's mother came to the centre to talk about the trouble she had with her daughter and Jean spent many hours chatting and discussing her adventures in school. Jean and her friends washed the worker's car and told the worker about her father who died in hospital, told of how her mother took him to court because he wouldn't give her any money, of how he was often in prison and that her mother hit him once with a poker.

Jean went off on the holiday which the F.A.S. worker had arranged for her, but was back the next day, claiming that 'a dirty old man' had interfered with her. During the following months the worker learned that Jean and her mother seemed to have very frequent encounters with 'dirty old men'. Then there were complaints by other tenants that Jean and her friends were screaming in the courtyard. Jean's comment was: 'We'll scream some more. That woman who told you screamed at us we shouldn't go with wogs. When my Dad was dying my mother had to put up with it.'

During the school holidays Jean and her friends made up a play, wrote it down in the centre and performed it. The play was about mothers and daughters and about quarrelling over money. At other times Jean asked interminable questions about the worker's activities and her private life. She made tea for the worker and for her friends and rolled on the floor with laughter when she found out that the worker didn't know what a 'jolly bag' meant. Talk about sex was a favourite subject, and Jean spread a story about a love affair between the worker and the caretaker. Jean and her friends listened in rapt attention when the worker told them about the processes of conception and birth. Laughter and affection changed quickly to anger, screaming and kicking when the worker asked the children to leave because she had to talk to an adult client. Jean slipped a note under the door:

> 'The FAS is alright to old people—they come in the office and tell their business—but when children come in they are told to go. She can be nice when she gives things but when she doent give she's disgusting.'

The complaints by tenants about Jean's behaviour, especially her 'filthy language' multiplied. Her mother vacillated between claiming that people 'picked' on her daughter, to asking the worker to 'have her put away'. One afternoon fifteen children were crowded into the small F.A.C. office drawing pictures and a small boy's fingers were jammed in the door. His mother came and accused Jean of having hurt the child and there was screaming and crying. The worker established the fact that another girl had hurt the boy and Jean found out that there was someone who was ready to defend her. The next day a crying, hysterical woman told the worker that she was going to kill Jean because she couldn't take any more abuse from her.

The F.A.S. worker discussed Jean with the children's department, a health department official and the headmaster of her school. By now the girl had become a habitual truant and her behaviour was quite uncontrollable. The possibility of referring Jean to a psychiatrist was explored. The worker recorded:

● During one of the late afternoon sessions just before Christmas, Jean and her friend Marion, were being particularly difficult, trying to manipulate me to agree to additional concessions. When I refused they began to shout and swear: 'You are filthy, you don't wash, you need a bath, you dirty Jew.' They were being so disruptive that I took them by the shoulders and shoved them outside. They crashed and smashed on the door. Marion's older brother and a friend of his came along and to my surprise said they were sorry for the way in which the girls were behaving. That evening, Mrs S, Marion's mother came along after her son had reported the incident to her. I told her that they had behaved badly, but that I didn't like running to the mothers about this sort of thing. Mrs S went outside and called Marion and gave her such a bashing that I ran over and asked her to stop. I then thought this might be a good time to have a few words with Jean's mother so I went over to see her. Mrs L went on in her complaining way that everyone talked about Jean all the time just because she has not got a father. I said: 'Not at all. Jean does get blamed unjustly on occasions, but the majority of complaints have substance and one of these days you will have to face the fact that we are not blaming your daughter just because she has not got a father. In fact, you're quite sensible enough to know that this is nonsense. Jean is your daughter—why don't you control her?' Mrs L, who had been siding with Jean, said in a contemptuous way: 'Control her? I wouldn't soil my hands on her. I'd sooner send her to a Home. She can go away.' I said that that would be one way, but another way might be for her to give Jean the control she needs. The discussion ended there. As I was going home, Jean and Marion ran after me and said: 'Betty, will you take us out so that we can talk things over with you?' I said that I had found that 'talking things over' didn't work out so well with them, and that I would see them the following day.

A few days after this Jean and her friends gave a Christmas party at the centre attended by ten girls. The F.A.S. worker was invited. At the start of the new year Jean and Elaine discovered where the F.A.S. worker lived and visited her one Sunday afternoon. The worker told them that they could come again if they attended school and if there were no complaints about them from the neighbours for one entire week. They didn't quite make it with the neighbours, but school attendance improved. It was just in time, because that week the F.A.S. worker was informed that legal action would be taken if Jean missed any more school. Her attendance was recorded as 43 out of 108.

A few weeks later Jean and another girl stole money from a neighbour's flat. When the worker had a long talk with her Jean broke down and cried. It was the first time the girl had shown any real feelings about her behaviour. Even her mother was amazed. Jean had stopped going to school again and the F.A.S. worker spoke to her class teacher about it. Jean had to appear in court on a shoplifting charge and the F.A.S. worker took her to the children's department and introduced her to the court officer. The court ordered a psychiatric examination and the F.A.S. worker took a reluctant Jean to the guidance clinic. She also saw an educational psychologist and was very proud when he said that she was 'quite brainy'. The psychiatrist wrote in his report:

● Lastly, I would stress that the work that Mrs D, the Family Advice Service worker is doing from her office in the buildings where Jean lives is giving the best possible support to Mrs L and I would hope that it would enable her to get on better with Jean and to help her daughter with her difficulties.

The following weekend Jean telephoned the worker at her flat twelve times, saying that she would run away from home. On Monday she apologised and was very pleased when the worker let her 'mind the office' during her home visits. Then Jean did run away and the F.A.S. worker toured the neighbourhood in her car and found her strolling along with a friend and a dog.

Jean's older sister had an illegitimate child in the spring of 1968. Jean's behaviour continued to arouse the wrath of her neighbours. She went to school only sporadically and started to break into the family advice centre in the worker's absence. The Juvenile Court made a supervision order and a child care officer was assigned to Jean. The child care officer arranged for tutoring sessions, but Jean refused to attend. In the autumn Jean and three other youngsters stole £15 from a flat. There were long and heated discussions about this with Jean, her mother and the victim of the theft. Jean demanded more and more attention. Not only did she constantly come to the centre and insisted on speaking to the worker, but she also came to the worker's home. From time to time the worker invited her for lunch. Sometimes she dressed up in the worker's hat, shoes and jewellery and strutted about pretending to be 'the welfare woman'. She told the worker that she loved her and began to write her letters:

'To betty this is my third letter and I am going to go to school on monday and make a start and I mean that and I hope you will write some letters to me because I am writing them to you and this is the truth betty. I love writing letters to you because I no the words that I write down in my letters you believe them and understand them and betty why dont you let us come in to the office and then we will be much happy and we will think of you moor and betty you know when I swear and tell you of I dont mean it I am just in a bad temper but betty I think we should get some work done in the new office and then we can all go in their. Thats all thank you for lisening. p.s. dont forget to write the letter betty and I want it to be a long one. If you dont I will be wild. good by betty.'

One evening in November Jean referred a client to the F.A.S. worker, a girl who had been sleeping 'rough' and was pregnant. Together she and the worker went through the procedure of finding accommodation for the girl. Although she continued to be truant, there were comments in the community that her behaviour had improved. However, at the beginning of 1969 Jean and one of her friends went shoplifting again. The F.A.S. worker went looking for them and cornered them one morning and made them go to school. The following weekend Jean broke into the centre, invited a group of other children in. Jean served soup and sandwiches and wrote notes to the mothers of the youngsters saying that they were not behaving themselves. Soon after this Jean was expelled from school. The F.A.S. worker informed Jean's child care officer who arranged for an interview with the psychiatrist. Jean began to come to the centre to ask the worker to give her 'lessons' and worked diligently. A week later she brought five pages of writing she had done. The F.A.S. worker and the child care officer accompanied Jean and her mother to the interview with the psychiatrist.

The L family were rehoused in March 1969. Jean continued to come to the centre and the F.A.S. worker visited her in her new flat. Soon after this the worker took Jean and two other girls for a weekend in Wales. Jean's behaviour was beyond reproach. She continued to write letters to the worker and the latter replied. Once a letter with two poems came:

'dear betty, just a note because i wrote some poems. I hope you like them. I all ways seem to make them rime, i probley be a poet when i get older and do you think you can write another letter i hope you

got my other one about shoes i now its a cheek but i do need them
any way dont forget write keep yourself fit and do plenty of execises
goodby betty do write me a letter i love having them.'

The Miserable Day

1.

The sky is miserable
people are irritable
and babys are skreaming like mad
the dogs are barking
I am laughing as well I think wear mad.

2.

The wind is blowing like flipping mad
made my head turn flipping round—
my coat is nearly of my back
my feet are like flipping sacks.

3.

The Record players bursting like mad
I can feel my head go bank bank—
I feel so sleepey could fall into bed
　　without undressing.
I feel like I am dead.

The Days are Long

1.

The days are long,
the hours short,
I don't no about seconds I
　　think their neat.

2.

The days are boring without anythink
　　to do—pick some sweets and sit down
and chew.

3.

Look at the walls around wear you
　　live large small never tall

4.

The walls seem strange when you
　　look around laugh about and
make funny sounds.

The F.A.S. worker continued to visit her, provided some furnishings for the new flat and arranged for a domiciliary teacher to see her. Jean was able to form a very good relationship with the teacher.

A few days after the opening of the centre in the summer of 1967 a group of girls became regular visitors at the centre and a number of boys, most of them under twelve and among them two West Indian youngsters, began to drift in and out at all hours of the day.

The estate's older boys kept their distance at first, though a few youngsters met the F.A.S. worker during the latter's contacts with their families. Eventually a few sixteen- to eighteen-year-old boys came to the centre. They stopped the smaller children from making too much noise and told the F.A.S. worker that they had nowhere to go because they were turned out everywhere. The worker asked whether they couldn't go to the nearby adventure playground. They shook their heads: no, they had already been there and had been told not to come back. Eventually a group of six teenagers came to the centre from time to time to play cards. Although the worker had not laid down any conditions, the boys tried to hide the fact that they were playing for money and usually stopped when an adult came in. Sometimes the worker made tea for the boys and they talked about their aspirations and about how bored they were. Once they asked the worker to lend them her car, but when she refused they accepted this with a shrug. Peter, a fourteen-year-old fat boy came frequently to talk about his troubles in school and discuss dieting. In exchange for giving up sweets the worker helped him to collect stamps. A local clergyman struck him off his holiday-camp list because he had caused trouble and the F.A.S. worker pleaded for him, so that he was reinstated.

In the autumn of 1967 the worker started to keep the centre open for two evenings a week at the request of the youngsters. There were discussions, stories were told and the younger children drew pictures. Sometimes the older children were left in charge when the worker had to go out. Some of the mothers told the worker how glad they were that their children had a place to go. Watching the worker write her records some of the youngsters began to write stories for her. The children also came during the days and sometimes there were tears and temper tantrums when the worker had to ask them to leave because she had to interview a client. Mr E, who had been very helpful in establishing relations with the Cypriot families of the estate, formed a drama group and twenty children took part. There was an attempt to introduce the children to the library service. This was not successful. A children's librarian came once, read stories to the children in the centre, was appalled by their unruliness and did not return. Several attempts to introduce some of the older children to youth clubs in the area also failed.

The 'rough' language and behaviour of the youngsters put severe restrictions upon the range of activities in which the F.A.S. worker could involve them. When the worker took eight of the girls to a theatre performance the girls engaged in so lively a form of audience participation that people became very annoyed and the worker had to take the group home. On another occasion the worker took a group of girls to an exhibition at a local arts centre. The exhibition held the girls' interest for only a short time. They became rather noisy and the worker had to think of something else. The girls themselves suggested going to a nearby park and were delighted with the squirrels. Then this palled on them and the worker took them to her flat where they had a cup of tea and consumed mountains of toast and cake for which treat they were, as Jean loudly proclaimed, 'very grateful to Betty'. Some time later the F.A.S. worker took sixteen children on a barge trip. The youngsters greatly enjoyed themselves, but the master of the barge did not. He objected to the running about and was very upset when one of the girls whom he had reprimanded put her tongue out. Finally the trip had to be interrupted and the worker took the group to the boating lake to save the day.

Planned organised activities seemed to be quite beyond the capacities of the children. This was often difficult for people who offered the worker their help to accept. For instance, when an artists' council offered to provide art classes for a group of children, provided the youngsters 'sit down and do it properly, not just play around' and attend regularly, the worker had to explain that these children needed a more informal, casual atmosphere. The council decided that they could not provide this type of setting.

During the summer the F.A.S. worker took a group of children swimming twice a week. In August 1969 the children's department granted a sum of money from Section 1 funds for a country holiday with the F.A.S. worker for a group of children.

The 'G' project estate pre-school play group

The tenants of the estate repeatedly expressed their concern about the lack of supervised play activities for the smaller children of the community. Trying to find some solutions to this problem the worker explored the existing facilities in the area. She found that, while there were a substantial number of nursery and play groups in the borough, there was a long waiting list and a fairly large gap between the needs and the available services.

A few weeks after the opening of the centre the F.A.S. worker found a trained nursery school teacher who was ready to expand her small pre-school play group to include G estate children. As most of the tenants could not pay the full fee of £1 5s per week, the worker applied for supplementary payments granted by the health department under a special scheme. After a promise of these payments was given Mrs T, the nursery school teacher, began to accept G estate children and ran the play group at a loss. For the next eighteen months the F.A.S. worker provided supportive guidance to the mothers who were sending their children to the play group, and to Mrs T, who could not make ends meet. She obtained a small grant from a voluntary organisation and reasoned, pleaded and argued with the health department month after month for the money promised to Mrs T. Although there was room for fifteen children only ten attended the group regularly.

The play group moved from its former premises in a church hall into an empty flat in the estate. The tenants' association sponsored the application for supplementary payments after they were assured that this would not put them under any financial obligation. When in March 1969 Mrs T still had not received any payments for her work she gave up and the play group closed down, but Mrs T continued to spend a few hours each week with the children of one multi-problem family. She was finally paid in May 1969, shortly before the last tenants of the estate moved out.

The need for a detached youth worker on the 'G' project estate

While the F.A.S. worker was relatively successful in reaching a group of the most disturbed and delinquent girls, the adolescent boys were, as could be predicted, less accessible to the influence of a woman worker. Nevertheless the worker established relations with quite a number of teenage boys during the two-year study period. Whether boys or girls, the teenagers demanded much of the worker's time and attention, quite often to the detriment of the needs of adult clients. While the worker learned a great deal about the adolescent youngsters, their needs and activities, there was much that remained hidden from her and her numerous other tasks did not leave time or energy for an in-depth investigation of this important aspect of the community. As the weeks and months passed, the need for a youth worker became more and more apparent.

The need for a youth worker was discussed with the youth officer. The latter submitted the request to his committee after the children's department ruled that Section 1 funds could not be made available for this purpose. Meanwhile, there were several incidents between a group of adolescent boys and adults in the estate which resulted in a simmering feud between the boys and one of the tenants. Several attempts by the worker to get the boys to make use of some of the available youth club facilities and an area adventure playground failed. One of the estate's youngsters set up a youth club in a nearby church hall, but after a few weeks the club closed down because of a series of incidents with aggressive youngsters. The need for a youth worker became even more urgent when a number of the community's adolescent girls became involved with a group of highly delinquent teenagers outside the estate. The summer brought complaints about young men who raced motorbikes through the courtyard. One couple in their late teens were injured in a motorbike accident. The F.A.S. worker visited them in hospital, arranged for legal aid and later helped the boy to obtain an apprenticeship. When a group of teenagers asked the worker for her help in organising a football team she had to side with the tenants who objected to the youngsters kicking a ball around in the yard.

The children's officer continued to pursue the need for a youth worker with the youth officer, and in August there were a number of discussions with the latter, a representative of the borough's Council of Social Service, at consultative committee and supervision meetings. Before the primary issue of the financing of this appointment was even nearing a solution, difference of opinion regarding the manner in which the hypothetical youth worker would be employed arose between the F.A.S. worker and the Council of Social Service representative. The former felt that the worker should be responsible to a management committee consisting of local tenants, while the latter felt that the management committee should also include representatives of the C.S.S. and the statutory agencies, as the local tenants could not be expected to have the necessary experience and background to 'manage' a youth worker.

A newly appointed caretaker proved very co-operative and interested in helping the F.A.S. worker to help to improve relations between some of the older teenagers and the rest of the community. He took a special interest in one eighteen-year-old boy, induced him to paint his parents' flat and helped him to search for employment. The worker initiated a series of group discussions about the need for and the functions of a detached youth worker in which twenty-three tenants and a local councillor participated.

In September 1968 the F.A.S. worker submitted a detailed proposal for the employment of a detached youth worker accountable to a community management committee. During a discussion of the proposal by the consultative committee the housing department representative expressed the view that the G estate tenants were not capable of assuming this responsibility. That week a thirteen-year-old boy led a group of youngsters in burgling the family advice centre. All the toys the worker had collected for the pre-school playgroup were stolen. The worker found the culprits and they became regular and friendly visitors at the centre. The negotiations for the appointment of a youth worker seemed to make good progress when, in November 1968, the children's officer informed the youth officer that in view of the planned rehousing of all the G estate tenants there was no further need for a youth worker. The F.A.S. worker's argument that the need for such a worker was greater than ever during the rehousing period was not taken into account.

In December one of the tenants sought the F.A.S. worker's advice when her son was charged with 'robbery with violence'. It seemed that the boy had attacked homosexuals with a gang of other youngsters. The boy was put on two years' probation. Some weeks later the worker arranged for guitar lessons for one of the teenage boys who had begun to bring his guitar to the centre.

At the beginning of March, Jean, who had been on a shoplifting spree with a group of other girls recently, asked the F.A.S. worker to permit her to run a club in the family advice centre. After some discussion with the girls and several of the mothers, and after two mothers had agreed to share in the supervision of the club activities, the worker gave the permission. The club met, twelve to fourteen youngsters attending, but Jean's need to dominate the other children was a cause of friction from the outset. After a few meetings the club meetings ceased, mainly because of the mothers, who had to cope with some hostility from Jean, withdrew their offer to help with supervision. Shortly after this the wife of the chairman of the tenants' association agreed to run an afternoon club at the centre which proved fairly successful. About that time a boy who had been referred to Inter-Action for guitar lessons was accused of stealing a sum of money there. The F.A.S. worker had sufficient grounds to believe the boy's protestations of his innocence, but the very desirable association with the Inter-Action group ceased.

In April the F.A.S. worker received an inquiry from the Juvenile Liaison Bureau of the police with regard to the fourteen-year-old son of a client.

The teenagers in the 'F' project area

The needs and problems of the teenagers of the area were every bit as urgent as those of the younger children, but were less easy to meet in constructive ways.

Articles published in the local press in January and March 1969 reported the concern of a local councillor and of a Church Army chaplain over the effects of the derelict buildings and the general atmosphere of decay and chaos ruling in the city's slum clearance areas upon youth. The articles spoke of vandalism and violence, school age procurers and of vacant buildings being turned into brothels for thirteen- and fourteen-year-old girls. The newspapers may have exaggerated the situation, but our experience at the 'F' project family advice centre shows that there was certainly reason for serious concern. Two weeks after the opening of the centre, the F.A.S. worker learned that there had been a gang fight involving about twenty teenagers in the area in which one boy was hit with the blunt end of an axe. Several of the boys were charged and appeared in court.

Soon after the opening of the centre in September 1968 a group of nine fourteen- to sixteen-year-old boys began to come to the centre. Three of them were in trouble with the law, one of them accused of a post office burglary. They 'hung out' in a café in an adjacent area but said that they were not comfortable there because it was usually overcrowded. After a while they started to use the centre as a regular meeting place at lunch time and on two evenings a week. A member of the parents' association volunteered to 'keep an eye on them' and to lock up after they left. The F.A.S. worker's application to a local school for the use of the gym was refused. The centre donated a football to the group which they kicked about in the street. The F.A.S. worker spent a considerable amount of time discussing their delinquent involvements with the boys and helping them to obtain employment. After some time several of the youngsters began to help out at the centre, and later at the arts centre, painting furniture and doing repair work. One boy made paper hats with the smaller children, some of the boys helped to clean up and they made coffee at meetings of the parents' association. The probation officer of one of the youngsters visited the centre.

Meanwhile another group of older teenagers had begun to come to the centre. They asked for help in finding jobs. There were five boys and two fifteen-year-old girls. They were involved in delinquent activities and some of them were 'sleeping rough'. They helped with small chores, talked about other youngsters in their 'gang' and brought some of them to the centre.

One afternoon the boys brought Nellie, an eighteen-year-old Irish girl who looked much younger, to see the F.A.S. worker. They said that they were worried about her, that she was 'sleeping rough' and would become a prostitute if she didn't find a job and a place to stay. The matter was discussed with the self-help committee and the girl was provided with lodgings with a member of the committee. The children's department paid £3 a week for her upkeep.

The group came to the centre regularly and held meetings there in the evenings. There were talks with the worker about their delinquent activities and about the girls' exposure to prostitution. Legal aid was arranged for one of the boys after he had thrown a brick through a window.

The youngsters came into the centre frequently, sometimes two or three times a day. They felt safe and welcome there and, although their presence sometimes annoyed the adults who came to the centre to see the F.A.S. worker, the latter made every effort to avoid anything that would chase the group away. On one occasion, Lenny and Eddy seemed so exhausted that the worker allowed them to take an hour's nap on the settee. They sometimes made coffee for themselves and anyone who happened to be in the centre, and showed their appreciation by fetching coal from the cellar, doing some shopping for the staff or delivering second-hand clothes to neighbourhood families.

The community, while often critical and suspicious of the youngsters, were responsive to the F.A.S. worker's requests for help. After Nelly had been provided with a room by one of the members of the self-help subcommittee, other families offered weekend accommodation for Lenny, Eddy and Bob from time to time. One family offered to provide lodgings for Margaret and Dorothy, but the girls refused. The youngsters were permitted to use the office telephone to contact relatives, friends and potential employers. The chairman of the parents' association found jobs for Eddy and Lenny, but the boys did not take advantage of the opportunity.

Despite the lack of privacy which sometimes interrupted discussions at a crucial point, and although there was occasional friction between the youngsters and other clients, the family advice centre was of some benefit to the group. Nelly's situation was greatly improved and she began to work full time; Dorothy returned to live with her family; Bert met a neighbourhood girl and came to tell the worker that he was getting married. However, the centre alone could not prevent the boys from seeking adventure and satisfactions in their accustomed ways. Towards the end of the year of study, Eddy, Lenny and Bob stole a car and were arrested. The F.A.S. worker could not visit them, but he wrote to them at the remand home to which they had been sent and they answered his letters.

From time to time the F.A.S. worker heard about other groups of boys and girls 'operating' in the area. At one time eight youngsters were arrested and charged. None of these youngsters came to the centre and the F.A.S. worker's many other tasks made it impossible for him to seek them out. The need for a youth worker became more and more urgent as the neighbourhood was gradually vacated by its inhabitants and more and more derelict buildings provided shelter and opportunities for mischief.

The West Indian youth club at the 'E' project centre

The story of the West Indian youth club began with the referral of Dorinda, a fourteen-year-old West Indian girl, to the family advice centre. Dorinda's mother and the headmaster of her school had expressed concern over her behaviour. The F.A.S. worker visited Dorinda's rather strict mother and talked to her about the difficulties and conflicts facing first-generation immigrant children. The worker tried to arrange for Dorinda's attendance at one of the youth centres of the borough, but after the first attempt Dorinda told him that she and her friends found the youth club too restricting, its programme not interesting enough to hold their attention. What she and her friends, all of them West Indian girls, really wanted was a place where they could meet without too much adult interference, where they could listen to music, dance, chat and make a cup of coffee for themselves. The implication was that this would become a West Indian club and that white youngsters would not be welcome. After consultation with the children's department supervisor and the research team a room in the family advice centre was made available one evening a week and Dorinda and her friends held their first club evening. Soon after this the headmaster of Dorinda's school called and thanked the F.A.S. worker for his help, saying that the girl's association with the centre already showed some beneficial effects.

Club attendance was very sporadic during the first few weeks and the F.A.S. worker visited Dorinda's flat and discussed the club with her. A record player was provided and the worker explained that he would be available at the centre on club evenings, but that the youngsters would be free to run the club themselves. Dorinda drew up a list of eleven girls and three boys who wanted to become members of the new club. Dorinda's headmaster, who continued to show interest in the girl's relationship with the family advice centre, again said that Dorinda seemed to show marked improvement, but expressed some concern about the formation of an 'all-coloured clique'.

Dorinda and four of her friends decorated the club room, put up posters and curtains. Several of the girls asked the worker to visit their flats and explain the new club to their mothers, some of whom seemed to fear that their daughters might 'get in trouble' there. The mother of one of the girls said that 'clubs always bring trouble' and that she had recently forbidden her daughter to go to a 'Black Power' club in the neighbourhood. The discussions with the girls and their mothers enabled the F.A.S. worker to gain some understanding of the attitudes and fears of the West Indians in the area, their distrust of, and their isolation from their white neighbours.

The official opening of the club was something of a let-down, although Dorinda and her friends had prepared for the occasion with great enthusiasm, providing sandwiches, soft drinks and blue-beat records. Only six girls turned up for the occasion. However, at the following meeting the girls went out and brought a dozen West Indian boys to the centre and the evening was a great success. That night some of the girls stopped calling the F.A.S. worker 'hey Mister' and started to use his first name. Shortly before the centre closed a police constable arrived, wanted to know what was going on and said that he had seen 'a coloured fellow messing about on the balcony'. He left after the worker explained the functions of the family advice centre and the club. The worker talked about this with the boys. He found out that they knew the girls from a café in another borough where Dorinda and her friends used to spend their evenings before they came to the centre.

During the following weeks the club meetings were well attended. There were some sullen looks when the F.A.S. worker discovered one evening that the lights had been switched off and insisted that they be turned on again, and there was some arguing about closing down at 10 p.m. That night the youngsters also decided on a name for the club.

The question of whether the lights should be on or off continued to be argued and brought up the issue of the F.A.S. worker's right to 'interfere' and to impose rules. The latter pointed out that some basic rules would have to be imposed because the centre was council property, and that these rules were also necessary to prevent the club from 'getting a bad name'. The matter of the lights was resolved by wrapping the light bulbs in red crêpe paper to give the place 'atmosphere'. Gradually the youngsters began to feel more at ease with the worker, and he with them. Several of the girls and a few of the boys had an occasional chat with the worker and some of them asked for his advice with employment problems. A real breakthrough came one evening when the girls asked the worker to come into the club room and invited him to dance. By the end of the year there was a regular attendance of about twenty youngsters and, although the girls had founded the club and Dorinda continued to dominate it, there were more boys than girls there on most occasions.

In March 1968 Dorinda introduced her twenty-year-old cousin Eddie to the worker. Eddie proposed turning the club into a commercial enterprise, a West Indian club with a sound system and a bar which would also attract adults. The worker explained that this could not be done in the centre, but Eddie continued to visit and offer some useful help and advice. It also became apparent that the boys who came to the club evenings belonged to two different 'gangs'. There was some tension between the two groups, but there were no serious incidents. The attention of the F.A.S. worker was drawn to one boy who came regularly but always withdrew to a corner, reading in the dim light and complaining about a variety of ailments. Gradually this boy was able to participate in the activities and finally began to dance with the others.

A minor crisis occurred when Dorinda became threatened by the presence of a growing number of youngsters whom she did not know and who challenged her leadership. At one point she tried to declare the club closed, but this was ignored by the others and she soon adjusted to the new situation. As the number of club members grew the language became less inhibited. Four-letter words were used frequently and there was some sexually provocative behaviour. The worker also suspected that the boy who acted as disc jockey was smoking hashish on the premises. The centre's neighbours also began to show some hostility. One morning when the F.A.S. worker picked up copies of *West Africa* for the club from the newspaper store across the street the store owner threw them at him saying: 'Here, take them for your wogs.' Soon after this incident there was an angry scene when the girls put up posters of nudes and the worker objected. There was some discussion of the effects the posters might have upon parents who visited the centre and the matter was resolved when the F.A.S. worker brought an armful of pop posters and magazine cut-outs to replace the 'nudies'.

In May 1968 the club held a dance. The event was described in a report by the centre's supervisor:

● The dance was held in a hut belonging to another adventure playground, as there were fears that the floor in the centre would collapse if too many danced on it. The playground leader had taken an interest since the 'E' project adventure playground first opened and was very willing to lend us the hut, although there were feelings that his senior boys might be jealous.

The West Indian youngsters themselves made most of the plans. They had tickets printed, the usual method of controlling admission to West Indian parties, so that no one they didn't like would get in. They wanted refreshments—West Indian cola and crisps—and advised on where these could be bought. They also found someone with a sound system, complete with flashing lights, who would do the evening for £5. The staff at the centre and at the children's department had misgivings about the whole thing and some fears of race riots, pot-smoking and drunkenness were generated. The children's officer was somewhat concerned and came himself at 10 p.m. to see how things were going.

Adult helpers present were the F.A.S. worker, myself, and a West Indian child care officer. A club member was stationed at the entrance to examine tickets and one of the men was usually there with him. Although it had been thought that 200 might arrive, the numbers were about 40—the club members, plus some of their friends. It had the same qualities as a good club night—the kids were very smart in bright colours and had obviously taken extra trouble with dressing. The music was Blue Beat played very, very loud. It was a good-tempered cheerful evening with the usual lively and sexy dancing. It began at 8.00, warmed up slowly and finally had to be stopped at 12.30 because we had promised to take the girls home. It ended in a very funny van-ride. When we reached the flat of the boy who had organised the sound system we were invited in, and the atmosphere was very friendly and informal.

We ran at a loss (charging 2s per head) and the cost of the drinks etc. came out of Section 1 funds. The remaining crates of drink and boxes of crisps were stolen from the F.A.C. the following week by a group of young white boys.

During the summer the club used the 'E' project adventure playground in addition to their club room. A group of white youngsters from a nearby estate demanded their own club at the centre and this worried the West Indian youngsters who expressed concern about possible 'race trouble' and also because the white group was suspected of stealing from the centre. Club attendance fell for a while, but in June there were twenty-eight boys and six girls at the club meetings. The centre was now teeming with youngsters and friendly, though still somewhat distant, relations between the West Indian and the white youngsters developed. Even when the club room decorations were torn down by white children this was shrugged off. Some of the white girls were admitted and the West Indian girls taught them to dance.

In August attendance of the West Indian club evenings had risen to forty-five and the room had been redecorated. The centre was offered the use of an adjacent building and the possibility of moving the club to the new building was discussed. The relationship between the F.A.S. worker and the West Indian youngsters had grown much closer. The club members regarded him as 'their worker' and resented having to share him with the white children. Some of the boys discussed their views on racial discrimination and 'Black Power' with him. The mothers of several of the girls continued to express concern and distrust. One mother complained that she had seen a boy walk down the street with his arm around the waist of her daughter, another mother said that the club should be 'mixed' and not for coloured youth only.

In the autumn there was a growing feeling among the club members that they were being neglected and 'pushed out'. There were the first signs of friction between the West Indian and the white teenagers.

In February 1969 Mr G, an immigrant from Trinidad, was introduced to the club as a part-time youth worker for a one month trial period. This was a chance to test the youngsters' reaction to an indigenous worker of their own cultural background. The group was very reserved in their reaction to Mr G. None of them came to the first two meetings at which he was present. He subsequently made some contact with the club, but found the permissive, unstructured atmosphere uncomfortable. He had worked in conventional youth clubs and was personally convinced that West Indian youngsters needed, and expected, a more authoritarian and directive attitude. Attendance of meetings was quite good during the next weeks and the youngsters were polite and friendly to Mr G, but he felt that they did not show much interest in his suggestions of creative activities. He also expressed the opinion that the F.A.S. worker's continued involvement with the club and his physical presence at the meetings made it difficult for him to establish himself as the 'new worker'.

Carmen, a seventeen-year-old girl who had been one of the 'founder members' of the club, ran away from home in March, but returned after four days. Dorinda's mother forbade her to come to the club as punishment for some misbehaviour and the girl tried to persuade the F.A.S. worker to tell her mother that she was going to night school, so that she could come to the club. The worker explained to her that he could not be used that way. The worker also spoke with Carmen about her wish to leave home. He offered his help in finding employment and, if she wished, to find a place in a hostel for her. The child care officer, assigned to

Carmen's younger sister Linda stated that she was opposed to such an arrangement. In May Carmen left home to live with a young man. She continued to come to the centre.

Mr G's attempts to 'reach' the club members remained unsuccessful, and his fundamental disagreement with the F.A.S. worker regarding his attitude towards the youngsters became more and more apparent. The F.A.S. worker maintained that the youngsters should be permitted to make their own rules at the club, and be assured of a permissive, relaxed atmosphere. Mr G felt that it was his duty to get the club to take an interest in more constructive activities than dancing and listening to music, and that he should be able to ask them to conform to certain standards. He felt strongly about his own, and the youngsters', cultural origin and was determined to uphold West Indian traditions rather than to give way to the laissez-faire attitudes which he felt dominated the British scene. He also felt that the F.A.S. worker's 'possessiveness' with regard to the club defeated his own attempts to establish a relationship. At the time, the senior research officer suggested that Mr G should be given a chance to test his own approach with the youngsters, who were well able to reject him if his methods or his attitudes were not acceptable. The F.A.S. worker, however, was convinced that this kind of experiment would drive the youngsters away from the centre. He also felt that Mr G's autocratic attitudes were incompatible with the values of social work. The other members of the centre staff concurred with the views of the F.A.S. worker and Mr G resigned. The reaction of the youngsters seemed to be one of indifference. Some of them had not even been aware of the fact that Mr G had been appointed as a youth worker and thought that he had just been a visitor.

In April one of the boys printed invitation cards to 'swinging evenings' at the club and these were distributed to West Indian youth in the area.

The issue of 'integration' continued to be a matter of concern to the centre. In this context it is interesting to note that two West Indian boys, who were referred to the centre by a child care officer, spent an evening towards the end of April at a club meeting of white teenagers and encountered no hostility. Youngsters from the white and the West Indian clubs told the worker that they wanted a 'mixed club', but for the moment the matter was not pursued. Mr J, the youth worker, thought that one reason for the hesitant attitude of the white youngsters might be the fact that they were afraid of being 'taken over' by the West Indian boys, many of whom were older and more mature. Meanwhile the invitation cards and a new sound system had resulted in a significant increase in the number of West Indian youngsters who came to the club meetings. On Wednesday nights they practically took over the whole of the centre: some of the boys played cards in the office, and there was a discussion group in the front room, some necking went on in the kitchen and on the stairs and there was dancing in the upstairs room.

During the first week of June the F.A.S. worker mentioned the issue of the 'mixed' club to a group of white youngsters who were milling about in the office. They seemed entirely opposed to the idea, but one of the girls spoke up for integration and told the boys that they were 'prejudiced'. At that point, Lee of the West Indian youngsters appeared at the door and there was an embarrassed silence. One of the white boys asked: 'Do you want us to come upstairs?' Lee said: 'Sure, come on up.' Several of the white youngsters then went upstairs and met with a friendly reception. Some other white boys and girls stayed downstairs in the office, but were soon joined by a few of the West Indian youngsters who had come down to see what was happening. The evening went well; however, the harmony didn't last. The club members showed no eagerness to mix and held themselves aloof. The white youngsters remained distrustful and on their guard. Some of them stopped coming to the centre. The two groups continued to share the upstairs room and danced to the same records, but they kept some distance between each other.

There had been rumours about the 'Main Road Gang' looking for trouble for some time. The centre had no contacts with this gang and little was known about them. One night during the last week in July, when about ninety West Indians and white youngsters were dancing, roaming through the building and spilling over into the street, a van load of 'Main Road' gang boys drove up 'looking for a coloured fellow'. At the time the entire building was supervised only by Mrs C, the arts and crafts play leader, who could not be expected to deal with a situation of this kind on her own. West Indian as well as white club members melted away in the face of the threatening violence. The 'Main Road' boys drove off, yelling that they would be back for the next club meeting with 'a hundred' of their boys.

During the next week there were many rumours about a threatening outbreak of racial violence and the atmosphere at the centre was tense. The F.A.S. worker and the youth worker discussed the situation with the police and were promised that patrolmen would be alerted to the danger.

On the night of the next meeting, the F.A.S. drove the van to Roy's house to pick up Roy and his sound system as usual. Neither Roy nor any of his friends were there. The F.A.S. worker drove around in the neighbourhood and finally saw one of the West Indian youngsters. The boy told him that Roy wasn't coming that night as it was known that there would be a fight at the centre. The F.A.S. worker advised the youngster to stay away as well. Sometime later, the worker saw a group of white teenagers outside the local pub, noting that they muttered racist epithets whenever a coloured man or woman passed. He stopped to talk to the boys and one of them told him that they were looking for a coloured boy who had knifed his brother last Sunday. These boys claimed to belong to the 'Main Road' gang and the worker was surprised to see one of the boys who came to the centre with them. Some of the boys said that they would get *any* coloured boy that night and were not looking for a particular one. One boy said something about throwing a petrol bomb into the club and the worker pointed out that they would probably hit some of their own brothers, sisters and friends who attended the centre. They replied that they didn't care. After a while, however, several of the boys walked away, saying that they wanted nothing to do with this. The F.A.S. worker informed the remaining gang boys that he would close the club down for the night.

That evening the centre remained closed. There was general tension in the neighbourhood. Groups of youngsters could be seen clustering at street corners and messengers went back and forth between them. Early in the evening two plainclothes policemen drove up, quickly searched two West Indian boys who were there and took them away without a word to the youth worker. Mrs C said that a boy had told her that he and his friends 'had to put the niggers down', and some of the white teenagers who attended the centre indicated that they would turn against the West Indian club if a fight developed. About 10 p.m. Mrs C, on her way home, saw a group of white teenagers chase some coloured boys down the street in the direction of the centre. A group of West Indian youngsters came down a side street and another group of white teenagers approached the centre where a group of white and coloured boys, who attended the club at the centre, were gathered. Stones and bottles were thrown and the police arrived in force and rounded up the youngsters. They permitted the F.A.S. worker and the youth worker to talk with the boys, then took their names and let them go. Later the F.A.S. worker found that a police officer had been attacked and that one white and one coloured boy had been arrested. Some of the boys claimed that they had been 'roughed up' by the police. Later the police went to a nearby estate, questioned youngsters and collected a variety of weapons.

The staff of the centre discussed the situation at some length. All seemed to regard the situation as rather serious and there was a tendency to seek a solution in accommodating the white youngsters and to make sure that the West Indian teenagers would not, in future, be seen to have 'special' privileges. The youth worker said that he had not been able to establish a satisfactory relationship with the West Indian youth club and found it difficult to understand their background or even their language. There was also some indication that the youth worker was deterred from seeking a closer relationship with the club because of the F.A.S. worker's continued involvement. It was pointed out that the supervision of the youngsters, who had greatly increased in numbers lately, was inadequate. Often there were only Mr J and Mrs C on the premises. The view was also expressed that the incident was *not* specifically caused by the activities at the centre, but was one incident in a general atmosphere of racial tension which had in recent weeks been felt in the area.

The week after the incident the club was closed, apparently due to a misunderstanding between the youth worker and the F.A.S. worker. The children's officer, who had been informed of the recent events, stated that he did not agree with the closing of the club, as this meant colluding with the youngsters who had threatened the West Indian group. The F.A.S. worker had spoken to Roy that morning and the boy said that he was ready to bring his sound system as usual, and that he saw no reason for closing the club, but he agreed with the youth worker's decision when he came to the centre in the evening. He was later overheard to discuss the matter with other West Indian boys, saying: 'We'll have to do the "Main Road" gang to settle this.' He also said that he was worried about what would happen if other coloured gangs became involved and the adult coloured clubs in the area heard about the situation.

The following week the club was open and there were no incidents, though reports of fighting between groups of youngsters in the area continued to come in for some time. A sizeable number of West Indian youngsters who usually came to the club did not attend. Shortly after this the F.A.S. worker and the youth worker went on leave and the club remained closed again for two weeks.

After the two workers returned from vacation, in September 1969, the club was open again, but most of the West Indians did not show up. Six West Indian boys, including Roy, did attend. No attempt was made to contact the other youngsters.

After the termination of the study period contact with West Indian youth remained infrequent and sporadic for several months. The West Indian youth club had ceased to exist. It should, however, be emphasised that this period of experimentation had taught the centre many valuable lessons, and in the summer of 1970, while this report is being written, a number of West Indian teenagers have once more begun to attend club activities at the family advice centre in its new location.

The story of the West Indian Youth Club is one of trials and tribula-
tions, but it also tells of the considerable achievement of providing
recreational and social activities for a significant number of immigrant
youths. The club is perhaps most interesting and instructive as an
example of a family advice centre's response to the request of immigrant
youth for 'separate provisions'. This matter of 'separate provisions'
has become a subject for debate in this country in recent years. A Youth
Service Development Council (1967) report on services to immigrant
youth states the cases for and against and points out some of the dangers:

> It is one thing to state that integration is our aim, and to propose this as a goal
> to be worked for by such agencies as the Youth Service. But no one can be forced
> to integrate, any more than mutual tolerance and respect can be legislated into
> existence. What can be done is to try to put our aim into practice, by finding
> appropriate institutions and arrangements which will facilitate contact, and
> encouraging and supporting mutual tolerance and respect. We can try so to
> formulate our ways of meeting and the needs of young people—young immi-
> grants among others—as to create the opportunities for integration on an equal
> footing (para. 49).

We believe that the 'E' project family advice centre demonstrated
one of the ways in which separate provision in a setting which provides
opportunities for establishing relationships between different ethnic
groups can make a positive contribution. It did so in an area in which
there were indications of prejudice and discrimination[1] and this did,
predictably, lead to a certain amount of conflict.

Stating the cases of the proponents of separate provision the above
cited report notes that 'the coloured immigrant is obliged to feel and
confirm his national identity, because the door to integration has been,
or appears to him to have been, closed in his face' (para. 52). The club
constituted a positive response to this need for confirmation of national,
or perhaps more aptly, cultural identity. The report goes on to state:

> Arguments in favour of separate provision have been advanced from other
> stronger positions. There are even those who favour it as a necessary but
> transitional measure. This seems to us a more realistic argument, and has a good
> deal to commend it. Our doubts are less about the proposal itself than about how
> long the transition is supposed to last. Establishments which are set up for
> interim periods often gain an institutional life of their own, and become per-
> manent. Unless transitional provision of the separated variety have behind them
> the pressure to become more fully integrated, and unless the routes from the
> separate to the integrated situation are mapped out in advance, we are likely

[1] The following may serve to define our terms: 'By *prejudice* we mean essentially a hostile
attitude towards an ethnic group, or a member thereof, as such. . . . By *discrimination*
is meant disadvantageous treatment of an ethnic group' (Berelson and Steiner, 1964,
p. 495).

to be led to take steps, for reasons of expediency, which run counter to our long-term aims (para. 54).

This is a very relevant cautioning. But we must point out that any pressure to integrate, as for instance the insistence on ethnically mixed groups maintained by many conventional youth clubs, would have been met with hostility by the white youngsters and led to the withdrawal of the West Indian youth in the 'E' project setting. Nor are we convinced that advance planning for integration in situations of this kind is realistic. We believe that the 'E' project centre was right to adopt a wait-and-see attitude, while remaining alert to the opportunities for establishing relationships between the different ethnic groups which might present themselves.

Miscellaneous club activities at the 'E' project centre

Shortly after the opening of the family advice centre the F.A.S. worker noted in his records:

● I had parked my car and was walking towards the centre, when I saw about twelve boys (all between nine and twelve) in the front gardens of the house next to the centre. One of the boys had a long iron bar and was beginning to smash the windows of the vacant building. When a woman came out of the adjacent house and chased them, they ran away jeering and crossed the road to congregate outside a tobacconist's shop. I followed them and as I did the shopkeeper came out to chase them as they were crowding his doorway and generally causing a commotion. As they moved away from the shopkeeper I approached them and asked them 'What's happening?' and one of the older boys said, 'Ah, that feller said we was gonna break his window.' 'And were you?' I asked. 'No, we wouldn't break his bloody window, would we?' I told them I thought they might as they had a long iron bar which one of the boys kept waving about. 'Anyway,' I went on, 'I just saw one of you break a window up the road, its a good job the police didn't see you, isn't it?' They became agitated at my remark and all began talking at once. I told them to 'shut up' and to let the boy with the iron bar speak, but he didn't. The boy who had already spoken to me appeared to be the leader. 'Well, what do you want to know?' he said. 'What are you doing? Where are you going?' I asked. Another boy answered this time: 'Well we went to the park, but we got chucked out 'cos they won't let us do what we want to do.' 'What's that?' I asked. 'Aw you know, just play.' I asked them if they had anywhere to play other than the park where they wouldn't get into trouble. Again they all began talking at once and the 'leader' eventually said, 'Well, we once had our own club but they closed it down.' A younger boy said, 'They use it for weddings, but they don't invite us.'

Gradually we talked easier as they crowded round me and they told me they lived in the nearby block of flats. When I asked if they wanted to have the club in the flats reopened again they said 'yes' in chorus. I asked them if they knew where the Family Advice Centre was and one of them said, 'Yes, the place with the notices on the wall.' I suggested they discussed the need for a club with other boys (they had indicated there were more) who wanted a club and then come along and see me. Immediately the leader said 'When? What time?' I told him tomorrow and he answered 'O.K. 4 o'clock.' As they began to move off I said to the boy with the long iron bar, 'You should be careful with that—you know what it is, don't you?' Again the 'leader' replied 'It's an offensive weapon' and the boy holding it hurried across the road and put it behind a wall.

The boys did not keep their appointment, but a few of them showed up that evening. The worker talked about the possibility of club activities at the centre with them. The following day he discussed the boys with a neighbour who had witnessed the incident described above, and she suggested that the vacant house next to the centre could be used to provide club facilities for the youngsters. However, when the worker raised the matter with the housing department he was told that the building was not available for this purpose. Soon after this the worker encountered another group of boys smashing windows in the estate. He talked to the boys and later discussed them with one of the tenants and a local shopkeeper. He was told that there was a considerable amount of vandalism and other delinquent behaviour in the area. About that time an F.S.U. worker contacted the family advice centre to ask whether club facilities for a dozen teenagers could be made available at the centre.

During the following months a few boys and girls came to the centre from time to time, but no organised activities were provided and there was no attempt to find out more about the youngsters from the estate. However, in May 1968, shortly after the 'work camp' weekend that initiated the adventure playground, a dozen boys, three of them from the estate, told the F.A.S. worker that they wanted to have a club at the centre and stayed to paint the basement. With the coming of the school holidays a sizeable group of eleven- to fourteen-year-old boys and girls began to drift in and out, using the playground and demanding much of the staff's time and attention, Among these the youngsters from the estate were the most delinquent and while the younger children mixed freely with each other, regardless of their origin, the older ones refused to associate with immigrant youngsters, which they described as 'niggers', whether they were West Indian or Cypriot. The appointment of Mr J provided a focus of attraction for the early adolescent group who liked his easy going manner and his many creative skills, and the interest in organised club activities was given new impetus.

Meanwhile there had been several thefts at the centre and Mick, a very disturbed sixteen-year-old boy broke into the adjacent building which had now been made available to the centre. He and a group of other youngsters built a fire, roasted potatoes and spent the night in the building. Soon after this there was a heated discussion about their behaviour with a group of boys. The youngsters admitted that they were stealing regularly and had also broken into the centre to take what they could find. After the discussion these boys worked diligently, if not very efficiently, in making repairs and in securing windows and doors. Mick was especially helpful, but had to be watched closely because he had a tendency to 'procure' things for the centre, for instance light bulbs, which he had stolen from the stairways of a nearby estate.

In November the adjacent building was officially opened. A great number of boys and girls arrived and helped to clean, carry in furniture, make minor repairs and paint the walls. The girls brought a variety of kitchen utensils and someone painted CAFÉ over the door of the kitchen. From then on about twenty youngsters came in the evenings and formed little groups in different rooms, some of them playing table tennis, others listening to stories or chasing each other about. Two of the girls stole the F.A.S. worker's cigarettes from his desk and both the newly acquired electric heaters disappeared. Mick returned one of them when he was confronted by the F.A.S. worker and admitted that he had sold the other one. Behaviour was loud and rowdy, the language obscene. Miss L, a newly appointed youth worker, resigned because she found the unstructured situation too threatening. A fire broke out and after some attempts to put it out Mick suddenly went wild and smashed walls, light switches and windows with a hammer.

Repairs were made and, as December drew near, preparation for a Christmas party began amid continuous tensions and eruptions of aggressive behaviour, interrupted by brief periods of peace and harmony. Shortly before Christmas Mick, who had been very well-behaved for a while, threw a chair at the F.A.S. worker. The worker ignored the incident and that night Mick broke in, apparently with some other youngsters. The telephone was ripped out, files scattered and the record player was stolen. The following day Mick returned the record player

and contacted the telephone company to have the telephone reconnected. The scattering of the files aroused the interest of some of the
youngsters. The need for keeping records was discussed with them and
they were allowed to read some of the files.

Two days after the burglary Mick was arrested for stealing a motor-
cycle. He was sentenced to three months' detention the following day
without prior consultation with his probation officer, his child care
officer or the F.A.S. worker. To the staff's surprise almost all the other
boys were very upset about Mick's fate. There were heated discussions
about the affair and finally some of the boys proposed a petition on
his behalf. This document, demanding a reconsideration of the sentence,
was signed by eighty-one youngsters. A committee was appointed to
present the petition for publication to a local newspaper and it was
decided to meet the F.A.S. worker at the offices of the newspaper
for this purpose. When the worker arrived at the appointed hour the
youngsters had failed to show up. Acting as their spokesman, he
presented their case to a newspaper reporter and an article appeared in
the paper.

Despite all anxieties and upheavals the preparations for the Christmas
party proceeded until the big event arrived on December 21st. Miss J,
the children's department supervisor described the evening:

● Between 6.30 and 7.45 we prepared the upstairs room for the
party, transferring decorations because they had destroyed their own
the night before. Preparations were interspersed with arguments
through the door with various groups demanding early admittance.
The kitchen was turned into a canteen with a counter for serving hot
dogs and Pepsis.

Just before 8 p.m. large numbers of kids began to arrive. There were
about 40–50 in the course of the evening, ranging from a small group
of ten-year-old girls, to the estate crowd, the 'Greeks' and other older
teenagers. More boys than girls. They brought some records and took
charge of the gramophone. Soon after we started, bottles of beer began
to appear and at least one bottle of wine. The F.A.S. worker took charge
of several full and a number of empty bottles of alcoholic beverages
locking them in the office. A lot of the older boys quickly got 'high' on
what they had consumed on or off the premises. At about 9.40 when
further bottles appeared we decided on serving an ultimatum and said
they could either stop drinking or close the party and drink elsewhere.
They decided to stop drinking.

The younger kids made a lot of effort to get everyone to dance but
there was no sustained interest in this and on the whole boys and girls

danced separately. Quite a lot of sexual horseplay came from Ken sticking a frankfurter in his fly and exhibiting this to female helpers.

At 10.00 it was discovered that the office had been broken into, handbags rifled and a volunteer helper's purse stolen. The F.A.S. worker was very angry and stopped the party. He told the kids what had happened. Older boys grabbed Geoff and Alan, told them 'You're the biggest thieves in the neighbourhood—where is it?' As usual they acted injured innocence, and although they were searched—and the kitchen, where Geoffrey had just been—nothing was found. The party then broke up. The estate kids stayed behind, demanding full bottles of Pepsi to take with them. All the older boys and the helpers congregated downstairs in the office. They were very fed up and dispirited—one boy even refused to take back his beer. Finally they organised a whip-round and collected £2 8s which they gave to the victim of the theft. Staff and boys then parted very amicably after discussing arrangements for a theatre trip.

Helpers for this party were the supervisor, the youth worker, the voluntary helpers, a child care student and I. Mick's child care officer and his wife also looked in and stayed a while.

At the beginning of the new year the financial situation had greatly deteriorated and there were rumours among the youngsters that the club might have to be closed down. This aroused much anxiety and several boys and girls asked whether they could help in any way. A trip to a theatre performance organised by the F.A.S. worker eased the tension somewhat. The youngsters enjoyed themselves greatly. On the way home two of the boys talked to the worker about stealing and burglaries and speculated on 'whether it's worth it'. Another boy talked about his father, the ways he avoided beatings, his aggressive behaviour in school and his fear that the centre would be closed down and he would 'end up in Borstal'.

The aggressive testing behaviour phase seemed to have abated. The youngsters now seemed to be eager to become closely involved with the staff and expressed a need for a more firm setting of limits. Some of the boys attached themselves to Mrs C, volunteered to baby-sit with her small daughter and discussed plans for the centre with her. There were, however, no signs of any lessening of delinquent behaviour. Three flats in the area were burgled and some of the youngsters of the centre were suspected. The children's officer and the borough architect offered paint, timber, lino and furniture and several of the boys helped to clean and repair the building. Several of the youngsters had to be told that they could not bring stolen goods into the centre, and the youth worker had to go to court with two boys who had been charged with burglary. A sixteen-year-old boy who had run away from home and was 'sleeping rough' was permitted to stay in the youth worker's flat for a few nights and then returned to his family. A rather disturbed and usually very withdrawn ten-year-old girl began to pursue the worker with uninhibited outbursts of physical affection, and a mother gave him 'a piece of her mind' for permitting the youngsters to smoke in the club.

At the beginning of March the F.A.S. worker heard rumours that a group of five youngsters had been involved in a burglary at the local offices of the family service unit. He investigated the matter and found that F.S.U. could identify several of the boys. Five typewriters, a record player and £15 from a social worker's handbag had been stolen. While F.A.S. worker and F.S.U. agreed not to inform the police, the worker felt that he was obliged to bring the incident to the attention of the boys' parents and ask the youngsters to make restitution. There were a series of heated discussions with the boys and their parents. Some of the boys were angry that the worker had 'grassed' on them, others were glad that he had not told the police.

One mother blamed the influence of the centre for her son's delinquent activities, one father gave his boy a severe beating, another father had to be dissuaded from locking his son up at night to prevent him from stealing. A fraction of the money was recovered. Although this was the first time a member of the centre's staff had been the cause of youngsters being punished, the boys continued to come to the centre. There was some anger about the worker's actions, but the relationship between him and the youngsters apparently survived the crisis.

The staff had, for some time, been concerned about the slot machines in the café across the road from the centre. It was felt that the children spent considerable amounts of money on the machines and that this might be a further inducement to stealing. However, it seemed that there was nothing to be done other than try to offer constructive alternative activities at the centre. The availability of games and other equipment was essential.

The older youngsters seemed to become more aware of their identity as a group. They tended to separate themselves more from the under-twelves, showed more interest in records and dancing and formed a committee which submitted a written request for equipment to the Management Committee. Inspired by Mrs C's and Mr J's artistic talents, a group of girls went off one evening to take rubbings of manhole covers in the neighbourhood. Although there were still periodic flare-ups, the aggressive and destructive behaviour of earlier days had stopped almost completely.

Encouraged by the F.A.S. worker a group of boys began to form a football team with another group in the estate. They were given permission to use a local school playing field. There was another break-in and, to the staff's surprise, the youngsters insisted on calling the police. Sometime later the Juvenile Liaison Bureau approached the centre and asked for information on certain boys. The matter was discussed among the staff. It was felt that, while enquiry as to whether a youngster was known to or attending the centre had to be answered truthfully, every instance of giving more detailed information about the children had to be considered carefully and presupposed the agreement of the children and the parents concerned. In most cases the staff would refuse to give information to the police.

There was some racial friction in April when a small group of West Indian youngsters arrived at the club. The white children abused them and called them names, but relented and invited them to take part in their activities when reproached by the F.A.S. worker. An irate father came to the centre one evening and yelled at one of the boys who had pulled his young son's trousers down. The parents of two youngsters forbade them to attend the club because of the swearing and the permissive atmosphere. The staff were faced with a problem when one of the girls continued to come to the club secretly.

About that time a gang fight in the area in which the two local gangs were said to have been involved, and which resulted in the death of a boy who had been stabbed, aroused some concern. The incident was reported in the papers. Four boys were charged with murder and nineteen others with 'using threatening behaviour with intent to provoke a breach of the peace'. The incident was discussed at the centre, but apparently none of the youngsters attending the club were involved.

A group of boys who were thought to be members of the 'Main Road Gang' turned up one evening and, rather meekly, asked for permission to come in. One of the girls said that they were 'troublemakers' and they were left hanging about outside for a while before the club members agreed to let them in. Although they were older, tough-looking boys and the staff felt somewhat threatened by their presence, they themselves seemed very cautious and when it was suggested that they go upstairs they asked the youth worker to accompany them. When the incident was discussed the staff remembered with some amusement how worried they had been about 'tough' Bob when he first showed up. This boy was now a loyal and fairly well-behaved member of the group.

There was some discussion about camping trips and 'Outward Bound' was suggested. Bob said that they were 'effing sergeant-majors' there and he would prefer to go with the F.A.S. worker and the youth leader because: 'You don't push us around and we respect you.'

An increase in sexually provocative behaviour between boys and girls became the object of some concern. This was discussed among the staff and it was felt that the problem should be 'worked out' in the sheltered setting of the centre, rather than being pushed out into the street. The centre's ability to offer interesting alternative activities was the best solution. The staff also were becoming aware that many delinquent youngsters in the area were not being 'reached' by the centre. It was suggested that a 'detached' youth worker could do some useful work in the neighbourhood, but that the realistic limits of the centre must be accepted. There was neither space nor staff enough to accommodate *all* the young people of the area who needed help.

In May two members of Inter-Action came to the club and provided the youngsters with a fascinating two hours of learning the mysteries of drama. A few days later Mr J and Mrs C took a group of youngsters to see a musical documentary about young people trapped in situations which lead to trouble with the law.

The number of youngsters coming to the centre continued to grow steadily. The possibility of participating in a 'Community Action Union' sponsored charity walk was discussed with the older teenagers. When this led to a discussion of poverty, the boys cited the centre as an example of a place that is 'poverty-struck'. Shortage of space had become a serious problem and the older youngsters complained that the 'little ones' were constantly in their way.

Mike, a student who worked in the club one evening a week, had become very popular. He was nicknamed 'Jesus' because of his beard. Unfortunately it became apparent that one of the reasons the youngsters were interested in him was because they enjoyed seeing him lose his temper.

In mid-May the F.A.S. worker, Mr J, and two volunteers took seven fifteen- to sixteen-year-old boys on a camping weekend. The boys behaved very well, enjoyed themselves hugely and there was a general clamour for more such trips. Mr J had taken a film of the camping activities and this was shown at the centre. The management committee provided £70 for football equipment. Geoff's father agreed to manage the team and the first game was scheduled for the weekend. Although everyone had by now heard that the centre would soon be transferred to another building nearby and that the two buildings now used would be demolished, there was a sudden spate of decorating and repairing initiated by the youngsters.

Three seventeen-year-old boys who had recently begun to come to the centre were rumoured to be involved with drugs, and this aroused some anxieties among the staff. It soon became apparent that Graham, one of the 'regulars', had begun to take pills of some kind. A girl who worked in a chemist's shop said that she had been asked to supply drugs by some of the boys. There was a full-scale discussion. It was decided that all staff members would be alert to any opportunity to discuss drug use with the youngsters, but that no one would be barred from the centre because of it. 'Better here, where we can work on it, than in the street, where no one knows or cares until it is too late' was the general attitude. A meeting with the police to discuss the situation was suggested, but there was also some fear that the word 'drugs' would alarm the police and the centre would become the object of surveillance, raids and searches. The workers' task would be to warn the youngsters again and again about the physical, emotional effects and the legal consequences of drug use.

The youngsters' interest in narcotics soon flagged, but stealing and vandalism continued to cause trouble in the neighbourhood. However, the relationship between the centre staff and the delinquent boys and girls had now become much more stable and almost everything was discussed openly. In July 1969 the F.A.S. worker attended a court hearing with three boys accused of stealing. In court the worker spoke to police officers about the use of drugs in the area. The officers expressed the opinion that coloured boys (to whom they referred in abusive terms) were responsible for the spread of narcotics. The youth worker discussed the drugs problem with Barry, one of the older boys. Barry said that many teenagers smoked 'pot' in preference to drinking, and that they found the behaviour of their parents in the pubs 'disgusting'. He thought that all teenagers used 'soft' drugs from time to time. It was just 'part of the scene'. Smoking pot was all right for the boys, but not for the girls. The boys wouldn't stand for their girl friends using the stuff.

There was the outbreak of gang fighting and 'racial trouble' described in the discussion of the West Indian youth club. The attitude of the white youngsters toward the West Indian boys was ambiguous and evasive. Most of them seemed to wish to avoid trouble, a few muttered threats against them, a few said that they had 'nothing against them'.

Despite the stealing, the threats of fighting in the neighbourhood, the concern about drugs, the atmosphere at the centre was surprisingly free of tension. A chief inspector of the Juvenile Liaison Bureau visited the club and impressed the staff with his understanding, co-operative attitude. Two mothers visited to see how their daughters were getting along. A sixteen-year-old girl wrote a long, sad poem on one of the walls of the club room.

After the episode of racial violence the club was closed for some time. When it reopened it was apparent that relations betwen black and white teenagers, which had been gradually improving, were once more uneasy and distant. Mr J organised another camping trip and activities gradually returned to normal. On some evenings there were about ninety youngsters in the building and the staff became utterly exhausted trying to supervise the activities. The need for an additional worker was clearly indicated. Mr J was invited to the flat of a family by one of the boys who attended the centre. He found a group of five brothers who were notorious and feared in the neighbourhood, all of them involved in delinquent activities. Walking through the neighbourhood one weekend he observed the boredom and frustration of groups of youngsters who attended the club during the week. One of the older boys was arrested on a narcotics charge and another boy was arrested for stealing from his parents.

A group of about a dozen thirteen- to fifteen-year-old boys who had been very active, and often disruptive, during the past year, held a meeting to discuss their situation in the centre. They said that they sometimes felt 'out-of-place' or 'a nuisance', that they enjoyed music or dancing for a while, but then 'had to go wild'. They said that they needed a room where they could go wild and another room where they could calm down afterwards.

One evening there was a sixteen-year-old Greek boy hanging around outside the centre who had not been seen before. He looked tired and miserable. Freddie (14) claimed that the boy had 'pinched' Mr J's coat. An older boy ran out and dragged the boy in roughly. A group of youngsters pushed the frightened boy into the kitchen and pummelled him until Mr J arrived, rescued him, took him to the new family advice centre (which had recently been opened) and gave him a cup of tea. At first he said that he could not accept anything from the worker because he had tried to steal his coat, but after a while he relaxed and told his story. He lived in a town outside London and had stolen £35 from a market stall there. He spent the money and when the police started to look for him he ran away and had been on the run for the last three months. Mr J brought the boy to the F.A.S. worker and the F.A.S. worker spoke to him, assuring him first that he was not a policeman. Some of the boys who had gathered around explained the functions of the centre to him. The F.A.S. worker urged him to return home, but the boy said that he could not face his father whom he had 'dishonoured'. He said that he would have to stay away for at least six months to 'prove that he was a man'.

The F.A.S. worker arranged with the children's department for a

bed for the night at a hostel. The next morning at 10 a.m. the F.A.S.
worker went to the hostel with a travel voucher to his home town for the
boy. He was told that the youngster had waited for him since the early
hours, but had finally run off. Some of the boys came to the centre to
ask what had happened to the Greek boy. After their initial hostility
they had shown a kind of fatherly concern for him and now were worried
about his fate.

Later that week a fourteen-year-old girl ran away with one of the club
boys. A few days later two boys were arrested for housebreaking. The
F.A.S. worker went to the police station where the boys were held for
an identity parade, but he was told not to interfere. On another evening
the mother of a boy and a girl who attended the club appeared outside
the centre with a police constable and was heard telling the officer
that the club should be closed down, because drugs and alcohol were
used there. The F.A.S. worker asked them both to come in. Mrs P
entered, but the police officer walked away. She listened to the F.A.S.
worker's explanations about the centre and, although she seemed to
remain unconvinced, promised to come to a parents' meeting which was
being planned at the time.

By now the building in which the club activities took place had
literally begun to fall apart and staff and youngsters were trying to
shore it up until new accommodation became available. The staff
submitted a memorandum to the children's officer, asking for urgent
repairs and pointing out that vagrants and rats had begun to inhabit
the building and that the morale of youngsters and staff was low because
of the growing fear that the work of two years would be abandoned.
By the middle of September the family advice centre had to be closed.
The staff maintained contact with many of the youngsters. Club
activities were resumed in the new premises of the family advice centre
after the termination of the study period. A good proportion of the
youngsters who had attended the old centre continued to come, and
many new boys and girls joined.

During the two-year study period the 'E' project family advice
centre provided advice and assistance for many of the boys and girls
who attended the club activities. Supportive guidance, as defined in this
report, was given to fifteen youngsters, helping them to cope with a
variety of personal problems. The process of guidance (or counselling)
was a more subtle, informal one than with adult clients. It may be called
an 'opportunist' approach, in the sense that the workers usually could
not proceed according to any defined treatment plan in the framework of
a series of scheduled meetings between the worker and client, but had
to make use of the opportunities which presented themselves during a

game, after a fight, on a trip, during a court appearance, etc., each time attempting to use the immediate situation to help the youngster to increase his self-awareness, examine his attitudes and to explore alternative responses to his problems. In some instances a youngster 'presented' a problem in the same way in which an adult client might ask for help. In most cases, however, the youngsters drew attention to their need for help through their behaviour, for instance by aggressive, destructive conduct in the club, delinquent activities in the street or through markedly withdrawn, apathetic attitudes. As far as we could ascertain, 'guidance cases' did *not* include any of the West Indian teenagers of the youth club. It is possible that this was due to the lack of need for such personal attention among this group, but it may be a reflection of difficulties encountered by the staff in establishing a close relationship with these young people.

The 'E' project adventure playgound

The idea of making use of a large piece of overgrown land in the back of the 'E' project family advice centre had arisen as early as November 1967. The F.A.S. worker's first enquiries as to whether this land could be made available for play space received negative responses, although it was obvious that the ground was already being used by numerous 'trespassing' youngsters in the neighbourhood for all kinds of harmless fun and some not so harmless activities.

The F.A.S. worker discussed the need for an adventure playground during the following months with teachers and child care officers working in the target area. The children's officer gave his support to the proposal and obtained the agreement of the chairman of the borough's housing committee. Shortly after this the town clerk gave his permission for the use of the land at the back of the centre as an adventure playground. In April 1968 the proposed playground was discussed with two of the centre's clients who confirmed the need for play facilities. A suggestion made at the time to canvass the neighbourhood in order to enlist the support of the local population was not pursued.

In May a weekend 'work camp' was organised to clean and fence in the overgrown and rubbish strewn ground. Private firms, borough departments and voluntary organisations promised their support. Approximately forty adults and fifty children participated in the work camp. Among the adult participants were local teachers and child care officers, members of voluntary organisations and several of the people living in the vicinity. The playground was declared open the following day and, while cleaning and other work continued, children of all ages, the centre's club members and a few parents with small children began to use the new facilities. The youth officer and the vice-chairman of the children's committee visited the centre and promised their support. With the advent of the school holidays an increasing number of children arrived. In mid-June Mr S joined the staff of the centre as a youth worker with the task of supervising the playground.

As the number of youngsters making use of the playground increased, so did the tensions and problems. A significant number of the youngsters were aggressive and destructive. They spilled over into every room of the family advice centre and Mr S found it difficult to control the situation. He and the F.A.S. worker disagreed on the degree of controls which should be imposed and on the division of tasks between them. There was further cause for concern when complaints from neighbours about pilfering came in and a shopkeeper near the centre asserted that she had been abused by some of the coloured children who came to the playground. A neighbourhood woman, one of six people who were approached by the F.A.S. worker with regard to the setting up of a management committee, said that her participation might turn her neighbours against her. She said that she had stopped going into the newspaper store across the road from the centre because of the owner's angry remarks about the playground and about the coloured youngsters who came to the centre.

By the end of June an estimated 150 children, most of them five to thirteen years old, had come to the playground. A group of youngsters from the S estate seemed to cause most of the problems, causing damage to property, stealing and putting considerable strain on the staff's nerves. Administrative and maintenance problems and the search for materials, equipment and money made increasingly heavy demands on the F.A.S. worker's time.

The need to establish relations with the police was demonstrated by an incident early in July. One evening two policemen in plain clothes came into the centre and said that they were looking for 'a fair-haired bastard' who had thrown a bottle at a bus. An adult who was in the centre at the time objected to their language. Children crowded around while the children's department supervisor and the F.A.S. worker spoke to the two policemen. The officers were told that they could not search the centre. They were angry and said that they were being obstructed in carrying out their duties.

An interesting event, which became the subject of a considerable amount of discussion between staff and children, occurred when a handbag containing £15 belonging to a teacher who had visited the centre, was stolen. An hour later, the children returned the bag and the money, saying that they realised that this was the teacher's housekeeping money and that she needed it.

In July a group of students held an international work camp at the centre. They constructed a sandpit in the playground, painted the walls of the centre and generally added to the excitement by speaking Italian and German with the youngsters. The F.A.S. worker was on vacation and several volunteers and child care officers of the area sector helped Mr S and the centre supervisor. At that time the police received a complaint about noise and vandalism from one of the centre's next door neighbours and passed it on to the education officer and the chief nursing officer. The latter contacted the F.A.S. worker, but was understanding and encouraging. A local police constable came to the centre from time to time and usually showed a sympathetic attitude.

Towards the end of the month a playground management committee was formed. A housewife living in the neighbourhood was elected chairman of the committee; another local housewife acted as secretary. A lecturer in social work studies served as treasurer: other members were: a borough councillor and vice-chairman of the children's committee; the headmistress of a local school; a general practitioner; a former borough councillor; a former teacher; a member of the board of governors of the above-mentioned school; a housewife living two doors away from the family advice centre; the West Indian parents of children attending the centre, living in the neighbourhood; a West Indian housewife whose daughter attended the centre and who lived in the neighbourhood; a West Indian living in the area; and a housewife who worked as a cleaner at the centre. Five of the members of the committee had themselves made use of the services of the family advice centre. Eight of the fourteen members of the committee attended less than three of the eight meetings. One member resigned from the committee because she did not approve of the activities of the centre. Miss J, the senior child care officer supervising the local sector of the children's department and the 'E' project family advice centre, and the F.A.S. worker, functioned as consultants to the management committee.

At the beginning of August Mr J joined the staff of the centre as a youth worker and Mr S resigned at the end of the month. Parent participation remained very low and sporadic, although ten mothers and one father had come to the playground during the past two months. At the end of August there was a sudden influx of new children and some of the 'old-timers', especially a group of girls, became very aggressive towards the newcomers.

By the second week in September most of the children had returned
to school and the staff could sit back for a moment and take account of
the events of the summer holidays. An estimated 200 children, ranging
in age from five to fifteen, had come to the playground since its opening.
A group of about forty regular attenders used the playground every day
during the vacation period. The younger children came more often than
the teenagers. The F.A.S. worker felt that he and the youth worker had
not been able to give all the children the attention they needed, and
that more staff were needed. On the whole it seemed that the children,
especially the young and pre-adolescent ones, did not find it difficult
to establish relationships with each other and with the workers. It
took them about three days to 'settle down'. Usually they talked
freely about themselves, their parents, the police, sex, etc. The teenagers were somewhat more difficult to reach and needed more time
to learn to trust the staff.

A number of parents, mainly mothers of the younger children, came
to the playground from time to time and met the workers. Some of them
were clients of the family advice centre and had clearly benefited from
the availability and the experience of the playground. Mrs T, for
instance, a client who had been referred to the centre by a mental
health social worker, at first expressed the fear that the playground
might be dangerous for her children. Obsessively protective of her
three youngsters, she was gradually persuaded to let them come to the
playground and soon came there herself, sometimes twice a day.
Eventually she asked the headmaster of the school her children attended
to send them to the playground after school. A few days before the end
of the school holidays, Mrs T told the worker that, observing her
children in the playground, she had begun to understand that she may
have been too strict with them at home, and that this may have been the
reason for their destructive behaviour in the flat. She felt now that
there might be something to be said for being more permissive. The
children now seemed to be happier and less aggressive.

By the middle of September the financial situation had become
critical and the management committee made every effort to raise funds.

In October there were a number of critical reactions: the youth
officer expressed concern that the fact that the centre was open during
the day might result in youngsters truanting from school. There had
been a high rate of truancy in the area for some time, and it was reasonable to assume that truant youngsters were better off being accepted in a
supervised setting where a social worker could keep them out of mischief
and discuss the causes and effects of their truancy with them, than
running wild in the streets. There were also complaints about the

centre from neighbours. A local councillor called at the centre in this connection and asked Mr J to 'control' the youngsters.

The great event of the November half-term school holiday was a bonfire night, described in a report by the centre supervisor:

● The idea of having a bonfire in the playground came from the kids in the club and the workers thought it would be better to organise a properly supervised event than to leave them all to let off fireworks and light fires in the street. The kids produced a leaflet with drawings of a bonfire, fireworks, etc., which I had duplicated in the department. They delivered these—about 200 of them—round the neighbourhood, inviting people to come and bring their own fireworks. They also built a huge bonfire round one of the existing structures in the playground. We laid on hot dogs and tea in the back room and sold them—just about covering costs, although quite a lot of food was stolen. I ran this stall with a couple of friends.

Families came in from all over the neighbourhood and let off their own fireworks in little groups. They all said it was nice to have somewhere safe to come, where they wouldn't bother anyone.

There were quite a lot of adult staff present as we all felt a bit appre-hensive about what could happen given the combination of fire, explosives and our kids. In fact, there was very little trouble, apart from a few bangers let off in the house. When the children's officer tried to take a strong line on this, one of the boys splashed him with tea.

Children's department staff present included the children's officer, who lit the bonfire, most of the C.C.O.s from the sector—many of whom brought children with them; the F.A.S. worker, the youth workers and myself. There were also three or four of our volunteers present, some of whom brought their friends.

It was a very good evening and although it got a little over-excited towards the end, there were no serious incidents and no casualties.

In the middle of November the Youth Service agreed to grant 75 per cent of the youth worker's salary. The youth officer also recommended the centre to Y.M.C.A. youth workers who had enquired about club facilities with a permissive atmosphere. Two students were accepted on field placements at the centre, to attend six evenings each between November 1968 and February 1969.

On 25 November Mrs C was appointed as youth worker. She immedi-ately applied her considerable skill and experience in arts and crafts and quickly encouraged most of the younger children and a few of the older ones to express their interests in painting, modelling, paper folding, etc. Mr J commented that the fact that the younger children were occupied and supervised made it much easier for him to focus his attention on his work with the teenagers.

With the onset of winter playground activities waned until snow brought new attractions. There were Christmas parties at the centre which raised everyone's spirits, but in January another financial crisis caused general depression. In February the F.A.S. worker became concerned about the rising number of truant school children who came to the centre. He invited the area education officer to discuss the matter. It was suggested that a tutoring service, possibly enlisting the help of student placements and other volunteers, be provided at the centre, but this was not followed through.

In the beginning of April 1969 there was a disturbing incident when a group of children who had attended the playground the previous summer and had not been seen since then, came to the centre. There were four coloured children among them. These children were bullied by the white children and there was chanting of 'go home wogs'. One little coloured girl started to sob and said that this had never happened to her before. The F.A.S. worker showed his concern and spoke sternly to the ringleaders of the white group. His reprimands made an impression and after a few minutes the white youngsters apologised, put their arms around the immigrant children and drew them into their own circle of activities.

The second week in April the borough cleansing department cleared glass and other litter from the playground. Preparations for the school holidays began, but they were somewhat frustrated by the lack of equipment and materials. The children's department permitted the centre the use of a dormobile van to be driven by Mr J. A piano was donated to the centre by one of Mrs C's friends, and fell apart after three days of enthusiastic use by the children.

In May the evenings became lighter and the number of children attending the playground in the evenings increased. In June Mrs C's purse containing £5 and her keys was stolen when she supervised activities in the playground, and when she returned home that day she found that her flat had been burgled and £53 which she put aside for the rent was taken. The management committee made a grant of £20 to recompense Mrs C, but the rest of the money could not be replaced. Although it was fairly certain that the youngsters who attended the centre had committed the theft, the culprits were never identified.

At the beginning of July, a budgerigar was found in the playground and became the focus of interest. For a while the bird's welfare was discussed and argued about among all the children and the workers were constantly admonished to feed the budgie, clean his cage and make sure that he was happy. Mr J was highly praised for his ingenuity in constructing a large cage for the bird.

The F.A.S. worker made renewed attempts to obtain equipment and materials for the adventure playground in preparation for the summer school holidays. A swing was erected with rope donated by a commercial firm, and Mr J erected a kennel for a puppy which had been 'taken into care'. One of the boys brought a goldfish. At the end of July the family advice centre offices moved. A demolition firm donated some timber to the playground, some structures were erected and the sandpit was completed. During the school holidays a number of children who had been referred by teachers and by an educational psychologist came to the playground. The centre staff felt that the special needs of these children could not be met adequately because there were not enough youth workers available.

During the first week in August there was an outbreak of gang fighting with strong racist undertones which affected all activities at the centre. Police patrolled the area and an inspector, who was also a member of the local committee of the Race Relations Board visited the centre, looked at the playground and expressed his sympathy with the goals and methods of the centre.

Another budgerigar and another goldfish were added to the centre's collection of pets and the playground continued to be well attended, but there was a marked deterioration in the behaviour of the youngsters in the centre and increased worries about drugs, thefts and destructive behaviour. The F.A.S. worker and the youth worker both showed signs of strain and when both took a two-week vacation it was decided to suspend all the centre's activities, as Mrs C could not be expected to supervise these by herself. However, the centre's supervisor intervened and she and several child care students attached to the sector ran the playground. Some teenagers expressed anger that the 'little children' had their playground while the club facilities were closed, but there were no incidents. The children made good use of a lean-to shed and a stage constructed by Mr J and used old clothes left over from the jumble sale to 'dress up'. A group of the younger children put on a play for the students who had helped to run the playground.

By the time the research period came to an end the 'E' project adventure playground, beset by difficulties and faced by a multitude of problems, had provided a valuable service for a very substantial number of children and parents in the area served by the centre, much had been learned and everyone concerned, from the children's officer to the F.A.S. staff, was determined to improve the playground and to keep it open for the neighbourhood's children.

The 'E' project arts and crafts play group

Like so many other things at the 'E' project centre, the play group for the younger children was neither planned nor organised, but just grew out of the needs of the children and was kept going because someone with talent and imagination was available. This someone was Mrs C, who was appointed in November 1968.

The need for creative play activities for the 'little ones' became apparent as soon as the adventure playground opened and children of all ages began to come to the centre. The playground itself took care of some of these needs, but sometimes the weather was bad, or the children were tired of chasing about outside, or the playground was closed, and then keeping the children occupied and entertained became something of a problem. Often any one of the adults who was at the centre sat down with a group of children and involved them in some activity. In July 1968, for instance, we observed two school teachers who had volunteered for the afternoon supervising a group of youngsters drawing and painting in the kitchen.

When Mrs C joined the staff things became more organised and consistent, though the feeling of spontaneity and the readiness for improvisation were never lost. The children 'took' to her from the very first moment. Not only the toddlers, and the six-, seven-, eight- and nine-year-olds were soon clustered around her, enthralled by her many ideas and skills, but some of the teenagers came to watch and often stayed to participate, give one of the children a hand with a bit of difficult cutting or pasting, or just to talk to her. One of the older girls observed the new worker for a while, then commented: 'You've done this before, haven't you?' A teenage boy asked how one could make 'a frieze around the walls', listened to the explanations and looked after the little ones while Mrs C went out to get some materials. Pictures were drawn, stories written, book covers designed. The younger children felt comfortable and safe, Mrs C's own five-year-old daughter often among them. The older ones liked the way they were listened to and the simple, straightforward way the new worker talked to them. 'We got respect,' one of them said.

In December Mrs C had everyone busy making masks and puppets. A nativity play was put on by the little ones and when they sang carols Derek, a fifteen-year-old boy, joined in. On 20 December there was an afternoon Christmas party for the toddlers supervised by Mrs C, with intermittent help from Miss J, the F.A.S. worker, two volunteers, the youth worker and several members of the management committee. There was an abundance of food and sweets and a large cake with the sugary legend: '"E" Project Playground' on it was donated by the management committee's secretary. Mrs C's daughter was there and a member of the committee brought two children. Two girls brought their puppies which, as became all too obvious, had not been house-trained. The children sang, put on a little performance (the F.A.S. worker called it a 'mini-play') and over two hours passed in great enjoyment, interrupted only once by a group of boys from the estate who pretended to 'crash the party', but didn't really mean it and soon left again.

The management committee provided a £5 weekly grant for materials. For a while building fires in the playground vied with clay modelling inside the centre as a favoured activity.

After the first few months the increasing number of children made it necessary to impose more structure. A downstairs room was reserved for the play group and all the arts and crafts activities took place there. The children became quite possessive of 'their room' and chairs were labelled 'Mum's chair' and 'Dad's chair'. Many of the teenagers, especially the girls, continued to show an interest in the activities of the younger ones and sometimes participated.

During the summer of 1969 the number of children who needed Mrs C's special attention increased. The worker began to meet some of the mothers, many of whom emphasised the need for pre-school play groups in the area. Mrs C took some of the children swimming and to visit museums. She began to feel that the increasing demands made on her by the teenagers made it more and more difficult for her to give the younger children the attention they needed. The research team discovered that Mrs C had paid for some of the activities from her own very limited resources. It was pointed out that this should not be allowed to continue. There was only a very little recorded material on Mrs C's work with the younger children. There is, however, no doubt that this work made a major contribution to the overall services of the centre. At the end of the research period everyone was thoroughly convinced that this worker's specialised services should be fully applied in the future.

8 Community work in the F.A.S. setting: comments and discussion

Neither community work nor family advice services can be regarded as a panacea for ensuring adequate services or as a cure-all for social malfunctions. Both can make an important contribution to the improvement of unsatisfactory social conditions in certain areas and under certain conditions.

The areas in which community work in the family advice service setting appears to be effective are those neighbourhoods usually described as 'underprivileged', 'high-need' and 'multi-problem' areas. These are neighbourhoods in which there are inordinately high percentages of bad housing conditions, of people who earn low wages or who are irregularly employed, of large families and fatherless families, neighbourhoods where there is a high incidence of social inadequacy and/or isolation, mental and physical disability, delinquency and children in care, neighbourhoods in which problems of immigrant adjustment and community conflict abound and in which there is a marked lack of cultural and educational opportunities.[1] This is not to say that other types of areas could not benefit from professional guidance in community organisation and advice with individual and family problems. Our emphasis is on the need to assign priority of service to the underprivileged areas at present and, we fear, for some time to come. These are areas in which, in the words of Professor Kaim-Caudle (1968), the institutions which govern this country 'have failed to bridge the ever widening gap between us (the ones who are pushed about) and them (the ones who do the pushing)' (p. 28). One of the main reasons for the need of a special, imaginative and intensive effort of 'reaching' these communities is given by Professor Titmuss (1968) when he points out that:

High rates of staff turnover and shortages of professional skills are most apparent in poorly housed, working-class areas and in districts which contain substantial

[1] For a more extensive discussion of social deprivation see Holman (1970a), pp. 144–58.

COMMUNITY WORK IN THE F.A.S. SETTING 245

proportions of immigrants. This particular factor, which in large measure determines continuity of care, makes co-ordination and collaboration much more difficult, if not impossible. Yet in these areas, the slums of modern society, high quality services are most needed if levels of living and opportunity are to be improved for the poorer sections of the population, and if the new immigrants from overseas are to be peacefully and tolerantly absorbed into society (p. 76).

In such areas not only the inhabitants need help in overcoming their difficulties, but so do the social service agencies whose mandate is to provide services and resources to meet the needs. Our observation of the experimental work carried out by the detached family advice centres leads us to conclude that these centres may be one of the most effective approaches to providing this help.

The best conditions for effective community work in the F.A.S. setting are: (1) a community which is aware of its needs and willing to act together to improve its conditions; (2) a local authority system of statutory services which is ready to co-operate with the family advice centre in its efforts to help the community to help itself, which welcomes constructive criticism, which is willing to adapt its policies to the needs of deprived areas and which can tolerate a certain amount of conflict. These are ideal conditions which rarely are found to exist in reality. At best they are provided in part: a client community may be aware of some of its needs, while ignoring or evading others. The inhabitants of a high-need area may waste their energies in internal conflict and diffuse anger against their environment, but there may be vestiges of community feeling and dormant traditions of community organisation.

In every local authority there will be some agencies and officials who are more accessible to constructive suggestions and co-operation than others. In all cases it is the F.A.S. workers' task to try to create the conditions within which effective community work can take place. We have sought to describe the processes and dynamics of this task in the preceding pages.

The basic concepts of the family advice service, the focus on prevention and accessibility, are as essential to the community work tasks, as they are to all other F.A.S. functions. The community work role of the detached F.A.S. worker is determined by the functions of the family advice service. In his role of enabler, mediator, consultant and resource person, the F.A.S. worker offers advice, guidance and assistance to the community, as he offers these services to individuals and families in the community. The worker who offers 'simple advice and information' to an individual client who wants to know where he can complain about an item of shoddy merchandise he bought, may also advise a group of tenants where to go in order to get their overspilling dustbins emptied

9

more promptly. A young couple may receive guidance with regard to their marriage difficulties at the centre, and a feud between neighbours may be settled through patient guidance work in which other members of the community become involved in a conflict-solving process. Assistance may take the form of providing a secondhand cot for a family, or of helping a group of parents to set up a clothing exchange. A family may be referred to a case work agency for help with a severe child-rearing problem, while a tenants' association may be referred to a voluntary organisation for help in providing a service for the children of the community. Perhaps most important of all is the application of the F.A.S. worker's mediation/liaison function to the community as a whole, especially when, as so often happens, the channels of communications between the community and the statutory agencies (housing departments, Department of Health and Social Security, police, etc.) are very inadequate. As an American writer pointed out:

Communication alone is not going to make all the difference, but it is one of the things that has to take place. There are vested interests on the scene; there are real conflicts that aren't going to be wished or talked away. There are also extensive marginal areas of common interest that are not recognised as such either because people in different groups are not talking to each other or because these areas are considered to be in conflict when in reality they may not be (Hunter, 1970, p. 227).

Our observation of the detached family advice centres showed that community work is not only compatible with the concepts and the functions of the family advice service, it is, in these settings, essential as a frame of reference which enables the F.A.S. worker to evaluate the services to individuals, families and certain groups in the target area in view of what can be learned about the needs, attitudes and expectations of the community. The integration of community work with the other F.A.S. functions not only raises the level of effectiveness of the services to the individuals and families and to the community as a whole, but it brings about a balance between the different goals and functions, serving to prevent an overemphasis on any one objective or approach which may be brought about by such factors as the demands of specially articulate and persistent clients or groups of community members, by pressures exerted by one or another local authority agency, or by the workers' own interests, and inclinations. This integration of community work and other F.A.S. functions requires a continued revaluation of the goals and perspectives of the family advice service in each one of the particular settings. If this need for the revaluation of goals and perspectives was sometimes displaced by the overwhelming demands of daily practice and if a satisfactory balance between community work and other F.A.S.

functions was not always maintained in the detached centres, we must remember that the F.A.S. workers were engaged in an experimental process in which much learning had to occur by trial and error. The descriptions of the community work activities presented in the preceding pages will have given the reader some insight into this trial and error process. Let us now briefly examine some of the most significant lessons we learned:

The possibility of role conflict

On the whole, the detached family advice centres most intensively involved in community work also were most successful in integrating this aspect of their service with their other functions.

There were, however, instances in which clients were not able to separate the staff's different roles and functions. On several occasions a client, who was also a member of a community organisation group guided by one of the F.A.S. workers, approached the worker during or immediately after a group meeting and asked for advice regarding a personal problem. This was sometimes frustrating and distracting to the worker, whose time and attention was needed to deal with often complex community and group problems. Perhaps more important, it raised the question of whether it is always good professional practice to mix the tasks of community work and the special requirements of the more intimate one-to-one relationship needed to deal with personal problems. Undesirable side effects may for instance arise in a situation in which a local leader who has assumed a key role in a tenants' association to which the F.A.S. worker acts as resource person and consultant, has also sought the worker's advice and support with his own marital problems, about an accumulation of debts or the delinquency of his children. Although assured of complete confidentiality, this client might become embarrassed and inhibited by the worker's presence in a group situation in which he has to assert his leadership and use his influence.

This sort of situation was usually handled flexibly and intelligently by the F.A.S. staff and did not pose a major problem. Nevertheless, it should not be ignored. It may be advisable to bring about a more clearcut definition of roles by dividing or alternating the tasks of advice, guidance and assistance on the one hand, and the community work activities on the other. This does not contradict the finding that F.A.S. and community work can and should be integral parts of the overall service, each complementing and reinforcing the other. It does mean

that the integration of the various aspects of the services is brought
about by a team approach in which each member of the team, either
permanently or alternately, assumes specific roles. The range of intensity
of the centre's work may necessitate the addition of another worker to
make the team approach viable. The appointment of an F.A.S. assistant
at the 'E' project centre proved helpful in this respect.

Community participation

The initiation of, and the support for, community participation in
the identification and meeting of community needs and the solving
of community problems must be regarded as the foremost objective of
community work. For the detached family advice centres, as for all
community work settings, the first essential step towards achieving this
goal is to get to know, and to become known and accepted in the community. It was easiest to take this first step, in fact it became almost
unnecessary to do so, in the community-based settings of the 'E' and 'F'
projects. The very location of the centre brought about a process of
involvement between the centre and the community. In the other two
detached settings it became necessary to do what another report on
community work describes as 'spending time walking around the area
both absorbing and being absorbed by the community' (Fitzwilliams,
1969). The staff of the 'D' project centre approached this task with skill
and enthusiasm. The 'E' project centre, on the other hand, did *not* make
a sustained effort of reaching the people of the neighbourhood and
the consequent lack of community involvement became apparent in
the services to the community offered by this centre.

This lack of grass-roots community participation was, perhaps,
most clearly demonstrated by the composition and the characteristics
of the 'E' project adventure playground management committee.
As we have pointed out, the committee was well motivated and made
important contribution to the services for children and youth, especially
in the area of fund raising. However, the committee was dominated by
a small group of middle-class professionals who could not provide the
kind of neighbourhood support which becomes especially important
when the attempt to provide a permissive service for hard-to-reach
youngsters brings undercurrents of conflict and tension to the surface
and arouses controversy.

We may learn from the experience of another experiment in setting up
an adventure playground in a deprived area in Birmingham. A report on
this venture states:

There was common agreement that the condition of the deprived was due not just to inadequate social services but to their lack of power over the decisions which determined their lives. It followed that one objective was to promote their control over their environment. Two practical policy implications were deduced from this analysis: firstly, the committee should consist only of persons directly involved in the playground, namely parents whose children attended, and workers. Secondly, it should be free to adopt any techniques or strategies which might promote its objectives (Holman, 1970b, p. 37).

That this policy can be implemented was shown by the experience of the 'F' project family advice centre. The difficulties of bringing about community participation should not be underestimated. In areas such as the one served by the 'E' project centre, where cohesive community patterns are difficult to identify, and geographic demarcations hard to define, it will not be easy to bring together a group of people who are truly representative of the area's population. Even when this has been achieved, it may be found that a non-representative, but more resourceful elitist body would be more successful in obtaining and administering the necessary financial support for a range of services. It may also become apparent that a 'grass-roots' group is, in fact, more conservative, less ready to experiment, less broadminded in its attitudes than a middle-class group would be. In such cases we feel that the development of community participation should take precedence over other, more immediate goals. Where it becomes necessary to meet existing needs immediately, services should be provided directly by the family advice centre and co-operating voluntary and/or statutory bodies. Such services should be clearly identified as being offered under the auspices of a social service agency initially, but every effort should be made to involve the community through the recruitment of volunteers, the formation of auxiliary groups, social events to which the community is invited, and the employment of indigenous workers. As soon as possible, the centre should seek the co-operation of parents and other members of the community in planning and running the services, with the goal of eventually handing over the responsibility of managing them to a representative community organisation.

It is our view that the setting up of management organisations which consist mainly of professionals and middle-class volunteers should *not* be considered even as an interim step. Experience shows that such bodies not only tend to develop their own momentum and become permanent arrangements, but that their very success (and they often are more quickly successful than grass-roots groups) reinforces the tendency to rely on elitist groups, to let 'them' do it, which perpetuates apathy in the community and a deceptive sense of comfort and achievement among social workers.

Short and McCulloch (1968), reporting on a pilot experiment in setting up a family advice centre, conclude that 'it will be extremely interesting to ascertain whether it is feasible to develop active community participation in an area which is at present regarded as socially incompetent' (p. 108). It is our view that the detached family advice centres showed that community participation in such areas can indeed be developed. The successes as well as the failures experienced by these centres provided us with theoretical insights and practical guide lines for the future.

The problems posed by community dispersal

The problems posed by the dispersal of communities have been subjects of discussion and controversy in this and other countries for some time without, apparently, bringing the issue any closer to rational solution. Cloward and Ohlin (1960) wrote over ten years ago of:

the demoralising effect of the massive slum clearance programs which have recently been undertaken in many large urban areas. Most low-income housing programs destroy whatever vestiges of social organisation remain in the slum community, in part because they fail to give priority in reoccupancy to site tenants. As a result, traditional residents are displaced and dispersed to other areas of the city, while persons who are strangers to one another are assembled in the housing project. Thus the residents of the housing project find themselves in a community that is not only new and alien but lacking in patterns of social organisation to which they may link themselves and through which they might develop a stake in community life (p. 209).

We encountered the destructive effects of community dispersal in two of the areas served by detached family advice centres. In one of these, the 'F' project area, the decision for redevelopment and dispersal of the local population had been taken some time before the opening of the family advice centre and was irreversible. The family advice centre accepted the task of helping this community to face the upheavals and tensions of the redevelopment process in a constructive manner, geared to improving existing conditions and to provide the community with opportunities to assert their own rights and express their own needs and views with regard to the detrimental effects of the situation. We believe that the families of the 'F' project area gained some important benefits in personal help and in self-confidence through the experience of community action and self-help activities. There was *no* realistic possibility for the centre to halt or reverse the process of community dispersal. The family advice centre entered a situation which had already gained its own momentum and helped the community to make the best of a bad situation.

The role of the 'G' project family advice centre was different in some significant aspects. Almost from the first day of her appointment the F.A.S. worker had endeavoured, and in some instances succeeded, in guiding the community towards acting together to improve their conditions of daily living. We have described some of these efforts in a previous section of this report. With the onset of 'decantation' the F.A.S. worker found herself in the position of having to allocate most of her time and effort to helping people to obtain information regarding their future accommodation and to depart from G estate as quickly and advantageously as possible. In fact, the F.A.S. worker had to use her relationships, her influence, her resources and professional skill to assist in the dispersal, not in the preservation, of a community. This is a sad and frustrating task for a community worker. It was carried out competently and persistently, and the situation seemed to show that there was no other alternative. We must, however, ask whether the F.A.S. worker's efforts, while no doubt determined by the given circumstances, served acceptable professional goals, or whether they were mainly dictated by expediency.

Our observations showed clearly that the majority of the G estate tenants, with a few notable exceptions, *wanted* to leave the estate and their neighbours. However, we also know that many of the tenants wanted to take advantage of each other and the authorities whenever possible, they wanted to get rid of the 'blacks', put the Greeks in their place, let their dogs defecate in the courtyard, beat some sense into the noisy teenagers who felt that they had a right to kick a ball, and so on. It is certainly a misconception to regard the community worker as merely someone who uses his skills and experience to help people to do what they want. Like all other social workers, community workers work within the frame of reference of a value system and according to certain sociological precepts and professional principles. It is this value system and those principles which determine the goals of the community worker and, as far as possible, these goals are chosen in accordance with their compatibility with the wishes of the client group and the requirements of the official structure of society. In the case of the 'G' project estate we are not convinced that this compatibility between professionally acceptable community work goals and goals imposed by the local authority and, admittedly, accepted by the client population, did indeed exist. The facts as we see them are these:

A community in an advanced stage of deterioration, largely due to the concentration of a large number of 'bad tenants' and 'multi-problem families' living in inadequate housing conditions, is beginning to take the first hesitant steps towards becoming a viable community which could learn to mobilise their combined resources to express their legitimate needs and to improve their living conditions. The local authority, represented by the housing department, acknowledges the highly unsatisfactory physical conditions of the estate and decide to modernise and renovate it.

It could have been expected that the renovation and modernisation of the estate would have been carried out for the benefit of the community which had for several years lived in officially acknowledged inadequate conditions, and that the authorities would have found ways and means to carry out the necessary alterations and improvements which would allow the tenants of the estate to weather the renovation period with a minimum of discomfort and return to their flats within the shortest possible period of time.

These expectations not having been met, it would have been logical to set the goal for all social workers concerned in providing services for this community, and especially for the F.A.S. worker in her community work role, to make every possible effort in helping the G estate tenants to understand that it would be to their benefit to express their collective wish to remain a community, to benefit directly from the long overdue improvements of their living conditions, and make use of the opportunity to continue to create a better, healthier, happier community in a decent, safe physical environment.

This alternative to the proposed plans for the G estate was, to the best of our knowledge, not given any consideration. All social workers involved in trying to alleviate the intensive needs of the G estate people, among them the F.A.S. worker, appeared to take it for granted that the community must be dispersed and that other people, from other dispersed communities, would be moved into the renovated building.

We understand the position of the F.A.S. worker and are fully aware of the prevailing pressures on her and the community. We also know how difficult it is to gain perspective and to see all the implications of official policies in the midst of upheaval and when the pressing needs of a great number of people have to be met. The F.A.S. worker cannot be held responsible for having preferred to attend to the immediate needs of her clients rather than to engage in the quite hopeless task, in the given circumstances, of helping the community to adopt more constructive long-term goals. The F.A.S. worker would have had to attempt this task in almost complete isolation and with a community which was most probably not yet ready to support her.

But our own task is to learn and draw conclusions. We must, therefore, state our view that the goals imposed on the family advice centre by external circumstances (e.g. the 'decantation' and the dispersal of the client community), made it impossible for the F.A.S. worker to carry out the community work which is a key function in this type of F.A.S. setting, in accordance with the goals and principles of such work. Our observations lead us to conclude that the community work goals of the detached, community-based family advice centre cannot be realised in a situation such as the one described in this report, unless the children's department, which is the responsible agency, is able to persuade the relevant local authority planning and financing bodies to take all necessary steps to ensure that the client community is preserved as a community.

Having accepted the inevitability of dispersal, the G project family advice centre provided effective advice, guidance and assistance to the community as a whole, and to a great number of individuals and families in particular, thereby considerably easing the strains and stresses of the dispersal and relocation processes. This phase of the centre's work demonstrated the value of the services of the detached family advice centre as a source of practical help, guidance and emotional support in the crisis-prone 'decantation' and rehousing situation. This experience may provide guidelines for the uses of temporary detached community-based family advice centres in situations in which dispersal and relocation of a neighbourhood have been found to be inevitable or advisable. It is well known that such situations arise with increasing frequency in most of the cities and towns of this and many other countries. The community work experience of the 'G' project also demonstrated the need for careful critical examination of each and every case of community dispersal, and of the role of social work in all its functions with regard to local authority policies.

It also became apparent that there is a marked need for advice, guidance and assistance for families *after* they have been relocated and are faced with a wide range of adjustment problems in their new neighbourhood. In the 'F' and 'G' project areas a number of clients maintained contact with the F.A.S. worker after they left the estate. In many cases the workers would have wished to continue to make their services available to relocated members of the community in a more consistent and sustained manner, but were prevented from doing so because of other pressing demands on their time and, finally, by the closing of the centres and their assignment to other duties.

It seems that a case for planned follow-up procedures can be made in view of these observations. In other words, in those situations in which a detached family advice centre is given the task of helping a community to mobilise its own resources to cope with the crisis situation of redevelopment and dispersal, the employing agency should, from the outset, include provisions and adequate staff for extending the help of the centre to the rehoused families in their new neighbourhoods. The setting up of detached community-work oriented family advice centres in new housing estates or in areas where an influx of new tenants has occurred should also be considered. Such centres would have the specific task of helping a community to become one. It will hardly be necessary to point out that it would be more constructive and economical in terms of social potential and service resources, to prevail upon planning authorities to consider on-site rehousing wherever possible.

9 The image of the service

The word 'image' is rich in cultural, philosophical, psychological and social connotations. It is closely associated with the infinitely wide scope of imagination and with the narrow confines of the stereotype. The images we form of individuals, groups, organisations and institutions in our environment have roots in our past, are influenced by the dictates of our present situation and effect our future. The images we form of others are reflections of our self-image and may determine how others see and experience us. More often than not the images we form of others or which we ourselves project have more to do with feeling and emotion than with fact. We may do well to keep all of this in mind and relate it to our goals, functions and methods in social work practice. One social worker reminds us that 'everything we do or do not do communicates to the client some attitude, and may also become the focus for a great deal of fantasy. In fact, we have to remember that the clients are studying us and interpreting our behaviour quite as carefully as we are doing to them' (Irvine, 1967, p. 106). We may add that it is equally well known, though not always given recognition in practice, that other social workers, professionals and officials with whom a social work practitioner comes into contact, scrutinise his behaviour, interpret and evaluate his action and attitudes, and form certain images which influence their own attitudes towards him and his functions and may determine their own actions and reactions.

The image of a service may be the result of a conscious creative effort, like any work of art. We believe that this would be appropriate and compatible with a thoroughly professional approach in any profession which is concerned with the entire spectrum of human relationships, social patterns of interaction and cultural norms, traditions and aspirations. One might even say that this conscious creative effort is as essential to providing a good service as it is to writing a good novel. In both cases even the very best tools and the most conscientious application of technical skill and factual knowledge are not enough.

There has to be that intangible something that inspires and involves the audience. However, the most impelling creative drive cannot produce valid and lasting results if it is not structured and disciplined by skill and method. It seemed to us that the conscious, creative effort to fashion the image of the service was most clearly discernible in the 'F' project centre. The 'P' project centre, on the other hand, tended to play down any overt appeal and favoured an approach in which the centre did its work unobtrusively, in the background. One result of this attitude was that the staff of the centre objected to interviewing of clients and workers from other agencies because they felt that it would change the character of their approach and might distort the image of the service as they saw it. The high opinion we formed of this centre's work, and our confidence in the soundness of their judgment, made us respect their wishes.

In most cases the image of the family advice centres, or rather the different images held by different people, emerged more or less accidentally. In some cases the workers were only marginally aware of the need for concern about the image of the service. In other cases the different ways in which people formed impressions and opinions about the centres were determined by chance encounters which left some vague, sketchy picture, or by a dramatic or controversial incident which imprinted a partial, and sometimes misleading, view of the centre.

The degree to which a family advice centre succeeds in establishing the image of an easily accessible, no-strings-attached, confidence-inspiring service is the key to its success or failure and largely determines its effectiveness. The image of the service may also determine the degree of success in meeting the implicit goal of bridging the gap between 'us' and 'them' which still prevails and which obstructs the relationships between the consumers and the providers of social services. Our observations showed that the image of the family advice centres also determines the relationship with the wide range of other agencies, services, professionals and officials whose understanding and co-operation may promote or hinder the centres' work. In the following pages we shall attempt to supplement our own impressions of the images the family advice centres succeeded or failed to establish by reporting on a series of interviews with the F.A.S. workers' clients and colleagues. For reasons discussed in the introductory chapter, we were not able to conduct these interviews in all seven projects. The picture that emerges therefore cannot be regarded as conclusive, but it may serve to provide the reader with some specific insights and overall impressions.

The interviews were conducted in an informal manner aimed at enabling people to express their views freely and in their own way.

The results we obtained differed fairly widely. Some of the people we approached found it difficult to express their feelings and opinions, others were carried away by their own rhetoric. Some were clearly influenced by the problems of the moment. We found that a harassed member of the community known to have had the most friendly relations with the F.A.S. worker included the centre in his angry rejection of all of 'them' under the impact of a recent frustrating experience with a social worker from another agency. Conversely, a person who had just had a pleasant chat with the F.A.S. worker was full of exaggerated praise for the centre. Some of the people we interviewed, clients as well as professionals, were guarded and defensive for reasons which were not always discernible. Others seemed eager to be 'positive', to say nice things about the centre without giving much thought to objective facts. There were some who tried to analyse their own experience with, and their own reactions to, the centre carefully and conscientiously. Many of the people we approached regarded the interview as an opportunity to talk about their own problems and to express their own views about a wide range of issues which were not connected with the family advice service.

Adrian Sinfield (1969), giving a series of examples of negative views expressed by social work clients about the help and advice they received, or rather failed to receive, points at the need for more accurate and systematic assessment when he says:

What we need to know in undertaking a re-ordering of existing programmes is how representative and accurate these accounts are. There are admittedly two sides to what happens in any encounter. But the client's recollection and definition of the situation is important in determining both the effectiveness of services and the extent to which she [the client] is likely to make further use of them, or recommend others to do so (p. 16).

The need for more systematic research into consumer opinion in the social service field remains. What we present here can only be regarded as part of the descriptive process. Whatever the failings and inadequacies of this type of reporting, we learned enough to contradict with some certainty the kind of supercilious dismissal of community workers in detached F.A.S. settings as people who 'stand at the door and appeal in a highbrow voice for people to participate' after having previously 'chatted up' local clergy and professionals (Holman, 1969).

Clients express their views

Interviews with six clients of the 'E' project family advice centre
1.   *Mrs S*, mother of two children, works as a part-time secretary. Her husband is a cutter in a clothing factory. She first met 'that nice

man' when she noticed the sign outside the centre shortly after it opened. Initially she enquired about a club for her thirteen-year-old son. The worker explained the functions of the centre to her and said that, if a sufficient number of youngsters wanted a club, the centre could provide the facilities. After receiving a leaflet about the centre, Mrs S visited the worker with her husband and asked for help with the payment of a debt. Mr and Mrs S were very pleased with the way in which he helped them, commenting: 'He caused us no anxiety and his advice didn't cost us anything. He was very helpful and understanding.' Mrs S said she would use the centre again if she needed help and she presumed that it was financed 'from the rates' like the other welfare services. She did not know of any other place where she could get advice. She knew about the Citizens' Advice Bureau, but did not know where its offices were located. In some cases she had consulted her solicitor. Despite her initial interest, her children had not joined the club activities and were unaware that these were available. She said that it would be good if the centre were open at weekends, as this was the time when her children were 'at a loose end, and watched TV all day'.

2.   *Mrs T* was not at home, but her seventeen-year-old daughter Joan agreed to discuss the centre. Joan said that her mother had consulted the F.A.S. worker about her wish to divorce her husband in April 1968. Mrs T had heard about the centre from a neighbour who told her how helpful the worker had been in her case. Joan accompanied her mother when she visited the centre. She said that the worker was 'great'. 'He is the type of person who has a lot of patience and can listen to what you have to say, without you thinking that he was doing you a favour.' She thought that the F.A.S. worker was 'doing all he can' and that starting the club was 'a good idea', although no one in her family attended the club. Joan had helped the worker by occasionally visiting an old lady nearby, at his suggestion. Joan said that the centre was financed by the council and her mother had recently advised a friend to go there for advice with regard to a divorce.

3.   *Mrs U* is the mother of ten children; four are in care. Her husband is a nightwatchman. She met the F.A.S. worker in the summer when her child care officer told her about the playground and suggested that she take her children there. She remembered him from her contact with F.S.U. where he was previously employed. She did not know who employed him now, but felt that it was 'handy' to have him nearby 'in case you wanted a chat'.

In August 1969 Mrs U talked to the play group leader when she collected her children from the playground and told her about her debts.

At her suggestion she spoke to the F.A.S. worker and told him that her gas and electricity had been turned off. The worker contacted the Department of Health and Social Security, but they said that they could not help, neither were the children's department able to help this family. The F.A.S. worker then contacted the moral welfare officer who knew the family well. The latter tried very hard to get the debts cleared and services reconnected, but did not succeed. The F.A.S. worker was still trying to help her but Mrs U was still without gas and electricity at the time of the interview in March 1970. Mrs U thought that the best thing the centre had done was to provide a playground and a club because there was nowhere for the children to play and it was important to keep them off the streets. She liked the workers at the centre and therefore felt that it was a 'good place'.

4. *Mrs V*, mother of three children, works as a part-time clerk. Her husband is a lorry driver. She first met the F.A.S. worker in the summer of 1968 after the head mistress of the school her children attended told her about the adventure playground.

The worker helped Mrs V in July 1969 when her fourteen-year-old son 'got into a little spot of trouble'; he and some other boys committed a theft and had to appear in court. The worker visited Mrs V at home, accompanied her to court and submitted a report there. Mrs V felt that the worker's statement had carried more weight than anything she could have said, and she was 'very grateful' for his help. She also felt that the playground had been of some benefit to her nine-year-old daughter. The worker had been 'very understanding' with the girl who had been receiving treatment at a child guidance clinic.

Mrs V attended two meetings of the mothers and children group and met the youth worker and play group leader on this occasion. She felt that there was not enough discipline at the club: 'the bad boys influence the others'. Her son had been 'led into trouble' by some boys there and she had forbidden him to go to the club. Nevertheless Mrs V felt that providing the playground and the club had been the best thing the F.A.S. worker had done. There was 'nothing to do' for children in the neighbourhood, and 'the kids were at a dead end when the club closed down'.

Mrs V thought that the Citizens' Advice Bureau offered a service similar to that of the centre. She thought the worker was paid by the council.

5. *Mrs W*, a young West Indian immigrant, is separated from her husband, has four children and works as a nurse. She called at the

centre to ask for help in finding a nursery or play group for her four-year-old daughter; the worker contacted several other agencies and was able to help her.

Mrs W thought that the centre was there for people who needed advice and that it was a 'good idea' to have someone like the F.A.S. worker in the area. She felt that better provisions for the care of pre-school children, whose mothers had to work, were needed, and would have liked to have seen a nursery provided by the centre. She did not know of any other agency in the neighbourhood which she could go to for advice. She assumed the centre was financed 'out of the rates'.

6. *Bob*, a young man who attended the club activities at the centre, is seventeen years old and has a sister aged twelve. His father is a porter in the market; Bob works locally as a van driver and delivery boy. The family have lived on a housing estate in the area for three years.

Bob first met the F.A.S. worker when he and his mates went along to the playground in summer 1968. He knew that the worker was there to give advice to families with problems but could not say much about this. He had been a regular member of the club and thought that it had been 'a really good place' and he had 'lots of laughs' there. His mother had also met the worker on one occasion at the club. Once, when he had been out of work, he had a long chat with the F.A.S. worker about his dislike of work and he felt that the worker had helped him just by being there 'to sound off to', as well as assisting him to find a job as an electrician's mate.

So far as Bob was concerned, the most important thing the F.A.S. worker had done was to start the playground and club, which he thought was a great place for kids of all ages. He had particularly enjoyed a weekend camping trip which the F.A.S. worker, youth worker and two volunteers had organised. The youth workers 'had put up with a lot from us' in the club and had a pretty tough time; however, he said, the important thing was 'to have a few laughs, and all be friends'. His criticism of the club was that there should be more youth workers there as each group wanted someone to keep an eye on them. He had been to the new club on the first night it opened, and was disappointed. Although it was a better building and more attractively decorated (he had helped the youth worker to decorate the basement), it lacked the atmosphere of the previous club; the small rooms caused groups of teenagers to stick together rather than all join in. He said the club was a good place for 'the little villains; the ones who are always nicking because there's nothing else to do'. He had talked to a couple of policemen whom he knew and they had told him to stay away from the club because it had a bad reputation and drugs were taken there, but Bob said this was not true.

Bob is keen on football and explained in great detail how he thought this could really attract a lot of boys to the club. He and a group of others had explained to the F.A.S. worker that they wanted to enter the local football league last season. He had gone as far as to get a team together and the father of one of the boys had offered to coach them. Bob had encouraged the boys to pay five shillings each towards equipment and was pleased that the F.A.S. worker had got £100-worth of equipment from 'some committee' (the voluntary playground management committee). They had sent for application forms to the football league but unfortunately the F.A.S. worker had not filled them in and sent them off on time, and they had therefore been unable to join the league. Bob said he had been angry about this at the time. He had to give the money back to the boys who had been interested, and explain to them what had happened. He wanted to try again this year but did not want the same thing to happen.

Bob felt that the F.A.S. worker was more concerned about families and their problems than about the youth club. He was very much in favour of help given to the boys who had got into trouble with the law, 'going to court with them and that', and thought this was very important for the lads who had no one to support them 'when they went down'.

When there had been some fear of the club closing down because the youth workers were in doubt about their wages and where they were coming from, Bob had asked the F.A.S. worker if he and the teenagers could do something to help. The F.A.S. worker had given them the name and telephone number of 'the head geezer' of the committee and had suggested he try to speak to him about the fears which the children and teenagers had should the club be closed. Apparently, Bob had tried to contact 'the head geezer' (the children's officer), but had not been able to get through to him on the telephone.

Bob said he didn't think he often needed advice, and didn't know of anywhere he could go other than to the F.A.S. worker, should he need help with a problem. He no longer goes to the club, he prefers to go for a drink in the pub rather than to the club, but still 'keeps in touch'.

Interviews with twelve clients of the 'F' project family advice centre
1. *Mrs A*, a widow who works as a cleaner, is mother of two school age sons and one married daughter. She first contacted the centre to seek advice about rent arrears. She saw the worker as 'a friend in need' and someone to go to for help, and said that he had helped people to 'get some action' from other social services. Life had been made easier for

people in the neighbourhood because of the centre, everyone was welcome there and nobody was turned away. Her sons had been on a weekend trip arranged by the worker. Mrs A knew of no other place to go for advice in the area, and did not know who paid the worker's salary. She hoped that there would be a family advice centre in the neighbourhood she would move to after rehousing.

2.   *Mrs B*, a housewife, is the mother of four children under five years. Her husband is unemployed. She heard about the centre from neighbours and her children who attended the arts centre daily. She thought it was 'a great place for kids'. She had tried to get her children into three different nursery schools, but all of them were full up, and she felt that the arts centre helped to prepare children for school. She had seen a housing department official at the centre and had obtained some second-hand clothing for her children from the parents' association.

3.   *Mrs C* is a divorced woman doing part-time factory work, mother of a married daughter and twelve-year-old girl twins. She is physically disabled. She first asked the centre's help with regard to a rehousing problem and is a frequent visitor at the centre. She helps with cleaning and the clothing exchange and is an active member of the parents' association. She has visited a number of old people in the neighbourhood and put them in touch with the centre. She thinks that the centre is 'a good place', and praised the arts centre highly. Since she was rehoused in another area Mrs C tried to get help from a Citizens' Advice Bureau, but 'they didn't help you any'.

4.   *Mrs D*, separated from her husband, is mother of four children. She heard about the centre from a neighbour. She had not asked for any specific help, but had obtained second-hand clothing from the parents' association. She felt that the arts centre had provided a good service for her children and the two younger ones had taken part in a weekend trip organised by the centre. Mrs D felt lonely in her new neighbourhood and had visited the centre more frequently since being rehoused.

5.   *Mrs E* is a housewife, mother of six children. She thought at first that the centre was a 'welfare place' where children were weighed and examined, but later learned that it was run by the children's department. The F.A.S. worker helped her effectively with a rent arrears problem and her children attended the arts centre regularly: 'It's very good for them because they have nowhere to play.' Her two eldest children had taken part in a weekend trip organised by the centre. She knew of no other place where she could get advice, but had greatly benefited from other services provided by the children's department. She would like to

have a family advice centre available in her neighbourhood after rehousing.

6. *Mrs F*, a housewife and mother of four children, is married to an invalid husband who has been unemployed for the last six years. She heard about the centre from her son and asked for advice about a rent arrears problem. She said the worker lends money to people to pay their rent and bills, and looks after the neighbourhood children, he has made it easier for people in the neighbourhood to get some of their difficulties sorted out without having to travel into the town.

Mrs F goes to the centre to chat to the clerical assistant when she feels depressed, 'to get away from my problems' for a while. She knows of no other place where she could get help and advice; a district nurse used to help her but she has left the area. She supposed that 'the welfare' paid the worker's salary.

7. *Mr G*, an unemployed elderly bachelor, used to visit the centre daily after being introduced to the worker by a neighbour and was helped with a number of problems. He regarded the F.A.S. worker as a 'good man' and said that it was a good thing that the worker kept the children off the streets because of the many accidents. The F.A.S. worker visited Mr G at home on several occasions, especially after he had undergone an eye operation. Mr G knew of no other place where he could get advice, except for the 'lady almoner' at the hospital. The clerical assistant had been specially kind to him. He felt that 'the council' should continue the family advice centre in another area because it had 'proved itself'.

8. *Mrs H*, a housewife and mother of eleven children, first heard about the family advice centre from a neighbour, and asked for the centre's help in getting her house repaired, after she failed to get any response from the housing department. She voiced jealousy of neighbours who had been helped more than herself because they had done some work at the centre. Mrs H said she could get information and advice from the local councillor, she thought that the latter 'had something to do' with getting her rehoused. Her children had attended the arts centre and taken part in a weekend trip.

9. *Mrs I*, a West Indian immigrant, is separated from her husband and the mother of five children aged six to fourteen. She first visited the centre at the suggestion of a neighbour to see the F.A.S. worker and the housing department official who interviewed people there. Mrs I thought that the F.A.S. worker's job was to help people. She knew that many people asked him for money and other help, but she preferred

to look after herself. 'I'm not one to get involved.' Her children did not attend the arts centre because they preferred to play in the yard.

Mrs I knew of no other place where she could go for advice and help. If she were in trouble and there was no F.A.S. worker, she would see a solicitor. She would not see her local councillor, because she had tried that and had not received any help. She herself did not need any help at the moment, but her children were reaching adolescence and might need someone like the F.A.S. worker who would 'show them some authority and warn them about not getting into trouble'.

10.   *Mrs J*, a young housewife, is mother of two young children. Her first request for help concerned the need for repairs in her home. The F.A.S. worker had also intervened successfully with the Department of Health and Social Security when her husband was ill and she ran into difficulties in obtaining his 'sick money'. The worker also enabled her to receive some benefits she did not know she was entitled to.

Mrs J felt that the centre was 'a very good thing', because people often didn't know who to turn to. She visited frequently and had done some typing for the centre. She thought that the weekend holidays the centre had arranged were the best thing they had done, because so many children in the area never had a holiday. She knew that the centre was part of the children's department and that it was 'only a trial run' which would show how other centres of this kind should be operated. She very much wanted to see a family advice centre in her new neighbourhood.

11.   *Mrs K*, a mentally handicapped housewife, mother of two children, one nine years old, the second a two-year-old, said that she often visited the centre because 'she liked the company there and it was nice to sit and listen to what was going on'. The F.A.S. worker had 'done a lot' for the children and her nine-year-old daughter was 'very fond of him'. Mrs K said that the F.A.S. worker and clerical assistant sometimes helped her to fill in forms she didn't understand.

12.   *Mr L*, a factory worker, is the father of three children and chairman of the parents' association. His children attended the arts centre regularly and his wife helped supervise the children there. He had become interested in the centre through his wife and agreed to become chairman after the first chairman left the neighbourhood.

Mr L said that it was difficult to define the functions of the centre. He thought that the most important task of the centre was to protect the children and keep them off the streets. He was enthusiastic about some of the activities of the parents' association, like the bonfire night, although he would like more fathers to participate. He praised the volunteer work of the art college students and had himself helped with repair work at the centre.

Interviews with eight clients of the 'G' project family advice centre
One of the council estate tenants was overheard saying that the F.A.S. worker had 'put the tallymen and moneylenders on the run'. The F.A.S. worker had soon become fully aware of the disruptive influence of the tallymen and moneylenders when she had had to arbitrate in violent quarrels between neighbours and within families, or had to raise funds for emergency loans. But the worker had never taken direct action against the legitimate creditors or local usurers, although one of her clients lent money at a stiff rate and made threats when payments were tardy. Still, at least one member of the community felt that the worker had forced the tallymen and moneylenders to retreat.

1. *Mrs A*, an unsupported mother with five children, said that she first went to see the F.A.S. worker when she got behind with her rent; the F.A.S. worker helped her make a successful social security application. Then she 'had words' with the worker about the clothing exchange. She felt at the time that the F.A.S. worker 'wasn't fair' about the distribution of second-hand clothing, that she 'had favourites'. She felt that the F.A.S. worker should have 'gone around to everyone to find out what they need, not just sit in her office and wait for people to come to her'. She had been delighted when she was offered a flat on the estate, because they had lived in one room before, but now she was glad to have left: the people and the language they used were 'shocking'. She had withheld her rent to make them rehouse her, and had since paid up.

2. *Mrs B* is the mother of four children. She and her family were given a flat on the estate through a 'welfare lady' because her daughter, at the age of fifteen, had tried to commit suicide. Whilst they lived on the estate, Mr B worked as a painter and decorator. Mrs B did not work, but has done so since her husband left just before moving to the new flat.
Mrs B first met the F.A.S. worker 'properly' through the clothing exchange, but had seen her around in the courtyard. However, Mrs B 'didn't really have problems and so didn't really use the worker for advice. The only thing was that she got me curtains from the social security when I moved into my new flat.' Mrs B described how helpful the worker was to other people on the estate. 'She had such a domineering way that if you asked her to do something she would make sure that it was done. I knew that if I ever wanted help I could go to her. . . . I think the most important thing she did was to organise lunches for the children during the school holidays . . . The worker made me laugh at Christmas

time when she made lots of mince pies and had sherry and invited us all
down to her flat—she is such a jolly kind of woman. . . . I got angry
with her when she got some clothes from Canada, but wouldn't give my
daughter a cardigan—she said she didn't need it. I went down and
tore a strip off her. It was all right though—she'd never bear you
spite and she'd talk to you the next minute. . . . I saw her every day
walking across the courtyard or something. She was always ready to
give a hand. . . . She came to my flat once when she was organising
the lunches. She came to ask me if I wanted to join in.

'Where I live now there is nothing like the family advice centre. I
don't know where I'd go if there was something troubling me—they
could certainly do with someone like her here. I don't really like living
here. Everyone is so stuck-up and toffee-nosed and they don't talk to you.
They even have their make-up on to empty the rubbish. It was a pity
they scattered everyone from the estate—we would be inside each other's
flats and there was always a kettle on the boil. I'm very lonely here. I
often have a cry—I miss the old crowd. I didn't want to move from there
—it was a good laugh—those balconies, you could have a good giggle on
them, and somebody would be always bringing you a cup of tea—you'd
be out chattering all day and then we'd all rush in when the men were
due in from work. There's nobody here—I've got to know the woman
next door a bit but if you died in here no one would ever know. I don't
really like this flat either. I'd got my old flat looking great.

'I couldn't tell you who paid the worker—that was a private affair. . . .
If someone asked me what she did I would say she had this office where
you could go if you wanted help with something. She'd have the kids in
drawing with pencils and papers—mind you she'd chase them out as
anybody would. She took all the children away for a day once and they
didn't half play her up. There's some kids—if you give them the moon
they won't be happy. We used to call her all the names under the sun,
but she wouldn't take offence—she'd laugh. She helped lots of people.'

Mrs B was very anxious to know how the F.A.S. worker was 'getting
on'—how she was and what she was doing now that everyone had moved
out of the estate. She asked the interviewer to pass on her regards.

3.   *Mrs C*, mother of four, has a partially blind husband. She said
that her children had had more to do with the worker than she had.
Her husband had been working as a gardener for the council and the
family were given the council flat when he became disabled.

Mrs C had only asked for the F.A.S. worker's help when she was about
to move; the worker explained to her 'how to go about the removal'. She
liked her new flat, but there was nowhere for the children to play and the

children missed the old courtyard. She and the children find it lonely in
their new neighbourhood and miss their old friends. She is visited by
'welfare people' and talks to them about any problems she has. She
supposed that the F.A.S. worker was employed 'by the council'.

4.   *Mrs D*, mother of eight children, first met the F.A.S. worker in the
courtyard. She had a vague idea that 'she had something to do with
families'. She first sought the worker's help when her second eldest
daughter had been in trouble with the police. The worker had also
helped her to claim from the Department of Health and Social Security.

Mrs D found it difficult to remember any specific occasion on which
the F.A.S. worker had given her useful advice. 'I used to see her every
day and treated her as a friend. We enjoyed a chat together.'

Mrs D had helped the worker to confront some of the tenants more
confidently and assertively. 'Some of the mothers, the noisy and rowing
ones, hung around the centre and were always effing and blinding at her
—something terrible. I told her to answer them back and give as good as
they gave her. It was sometimes difficult to talk to her in private and
I didn't like to ask her to turn the others out. . . . She did so much—
she helped everybody—she was always in and out of the flats. She got
money for different people—she set up the clothing exchange—she
arranged dinners for the kids during the school holidays, and gave them
parties. . . . I wouldn't know who to call on for help now—perhaps the
health visitor. A man, from the children's department I suppose, looks in
occassionally to ask if he can help in any way.'

Mrs D couldn't describe the F.A.S. worker's job—'family advice,
family planning, something like that'. She assumed the local authority
paid the worker's wages. 'Life seems that much easier to run these days.
I can manage better. Perhaps it's because the children are growing up.
I've got five bedrooms here where I had only three before. There are
more places for the children to play here—they can use the garden at
the back. There isn't so much noise and there are fewer footballs flying
about.'

5.   *Helen*, a fourteen-year-old, met the F.A.S. worker 'the day she moved
into the rent hut'. She was then twelve years old. 'We played her up,
pulled faces and asked her who she was. She got fed up with us and swore
at us to clear off. I think she had something to do with helping families
and keeping the children out of trouble. People came into her office to
talk to her and she would try to turn us out. We didn't think much of this,
and sometimes we would get her to let us stay.'

Helen had enjoyed the outings that the worker arranged. 'She was
always joking with us—if she was mad with us one minute, she was

happy the next. We used to see her every day. We called to see her when
we came home to dinner, from school, and we would see her again in the
evening. She was good to everybody.

'I don't really know what her job was—perhaps to help people on the
estate. She was paid by the rent officer. I wouldn't visit a family advice
centre if there was one here because the people are snooty and high and
mighty. They are less willing to chat and have a laugh.'

Helen's mother hopes to be able to move back when the renovations
are completed. She misses the activity and lively atmosphere even though
the present flat was more pleasant and spacious.

6.   *Mrs E*, mother of four, had lived in a four-roomed flat on the estate
for eight years. They moved in when their own house was acquired by
the local council for demolition. When they moved in the housing
department said that it would be for about six weeks: 'We wouldn't
have moved into the estate if we'd have known otherwise.

'There was a woman next door to me, Mrs T, who had problems. The
health visitor went to see her but was told to eff off because she had sent
some shoes for the oldest daughter which weren't even a pair—they were
different sizes. Anyway, the health visitor knew me quite well because I
do daily child-minding so she called in to me to ask me to go in to see
Mrs T once in a while. Her daughter, I think, was neglected, so I used to
go in to help her out. However, she began to take advantage of me so I
went to the family advice centre to ask what I should do. The worker
said that I should stop trying to help because it was the health visitor's
responsibility. Then the next thing was when the woman upstairs
started driving us nuts. She lived above Mrs T and she was a bit backward. She used to knock on the floor all night long. I told the worker
about this and I think she used some pressure at the housing department
to get this woman rehoused away from us.

'Mrs J used to come up to me to talk about her husband who was
playing her around. I said to her once that I wasn't much good to her
and that she should go down to the F.A.C. She did so and got to know
the worker very well, and through her I kept in touch with the worker.
I used to see her go in to see Mrs J and I'd go down because I knew
there would be a cup of tea going—the worker would say to me: "You
smell the teapot".

'She helped us with the petition we sent to the housing department and
it was because of this that we were told a definite date for the rehousing.
Before that it was terrible. We never knew what was happening. For two
years we waited for rehousing—we couldn't go on holidays—we couldn't
decorate our flats.

'She was always there to drop in for a chat. I saw her almost every day that she was there. Some people would spend hours with her. She used to help with all sorts of things: taking people to hospital, sorting out bills. If someone came down ranting about their husband, she would make them sit down and would say "sleep on it and you'll feel better in the morning". I know of two families where the husband has left and I'm sure these families would still be together if she was still around. There's another family—the husband was put away for seven years last week for trying to stab his wife. I'm sure this wouldn't have happened if she'd still been around. Mrs T who lived next door to me—her husband left her two weeks after the F.A.C. closed. This wouldn't have happened. The worker used to go up to them and talk things over with them and they would calm down.

'The children loved her, but used to play her up—after an outing she would say it would be the last one, but the next week she would be out with them again. I said to her: "Why do you do it?" She'd say:"Anything to get them out of here."

'The people used to play her up too. They were a very difficult lot—you could never do right—swearing and shouting at her. One day she went home very upset. She said to me afterwards: "Mrs E, I'm not going to make myself miserable by them—I'm going to give them as good as I get." And one day in the centre—I was in there to use the phone—someone came in an started effing and bleedin'. She just sat there and said "Stop your effin' swearing" and she really said the word—and in that accent of hers. I nearly dropped the phone.

'But she had the patience of a saint. I don't know how she put up with it. We thought that the children's department had something to do with her, but that was her business and we didn't ask. I now live next door to the clinic and know them quite well in there, but its not the sort of place where you can drop in for a chat and a cup of tea. They're all toffee-nosed in there. The health visitor was, I think, jealous of the worker because she thought she was taking away her babies, which was ridiculous. She used to go round the estate asking what the F.A.C. was for, but we didn't know so we couldn't tell her. I think she was jealous because she couldn't understand what the worker was doing.'

7. *Mrs F*, mother of three, said: 'I'm not the sort of person who would bother the worker. I never asked for her help, but used to meet her in the courtyard and around the estate. I used to mention how I was getting on, and the next thing I would find that she was helping me without my asking her to.

'One evening, it was pouring with rain; I left my pushchair outside a shop and when I returned it had gone. Together we looked for it for about an hour; we eventually found it. Another time she helped me when I happened to say to her that my father was ill in Ireland and that I'd like to see him. Without my asking for anything she got me the fare from the Society of St Patrick. She was very good like that. When I moved here she got me money for the new curtains and carpets, I think from the Society of St Patrick. She made me laugh; she'd say: "We'll try St Patrick again—he's been good to us before."

'We need somebody like her around here. I have had a few difficulties —my husband was out of work but the health visitor came and was very helpful. And there was one time when the gas was to be cut off because I owed £2 but I managed to borrow this from a friend—I don't like borrowing from friends, though.

'The worker took a lot; the people didn't appreciate her and she was very good to them. She was very good to the children too.'

8. *Margie*, a fourteen-year-old: 'I didn't have much to do with her, but she was a good person—how is she? My mother and sisters had a lot to do with her. She helped me when I wasn't going to school. I didn't go for a week because one of the girls there told me that my blouse looked like rags—it was, too. I'd had it for two years and then it was secondhand. The school inspector wrote three notes. I managed to hide the first two but my Mum saw the third. She went down to the F.A.C. and told the worker that I wasn't going to school because I didn't have a blouse to wear. The worker came up straight away and together we went round the shops and she bought me a white blouse. I must say I was secretly hoping I wouldn't find one, but now I realise it was for the best. I'm doing my "O" levels this year.

'She was very good to the families and helped people to get together. The children got together in the family advice centre and I think she had something to do with the tenants' association. I went to one of their meetings once—it was more like a social evening than anything.

'I didn't like living there; I hardly ever went out, but Mum would prefer to go back; she misses the people.'

When the family advice centre was about to close down, a group of tenants sent a petition to the children's department, asking that the services of the family advice centre be made available to them in their new neighbourhood:

● Mrs D copes with us beautifully. She throws her weight on our problems; her unofficial office is a place to go for a cuppa, when the

M.S.S. money can't stretch to the end of the week, when Billy's shoes have holes in them, when the National Health doctor would not call, when the clerks from the M.S.S. become difficult, when help is needed from the Task Force, when a husband decides to take the law into his own hands, when warm vests are needed urgently for the kids. Every child had a new toy last Xmas.

But the point is she successfully reaches us in a way which the official social officer can never do. The child officers are very good, kind polite ladies, but they are so distant. Mrs D pops in on us uninvited, sits anywhere, we shout at her and she thunders back. A lady recently said: 'I'll tell them cold officers what I think they want to know, but Nosey Mrs D will find out.'

The opinions of social workers, officials, professionals and volunteers

The 'A' project family advice service
A health visitor had learned about the family advice service at the 'open day' held at the area office, but was not able to distinguish between the latter and the F.A.S. functions. However, a referral she had made to the area office had been handled promptly and efficiently by an F.A.S. worker. While she had no contact with F.A.S. workers in the area, she sometimes met child care officers at social worker's luncheon meetings.

The health visitor felt that all social services were concerned with prevention and saw no reason why child care officers and not other social workers should staff family advice centres, especially as child care officers tended to feel superior to their colleagues. While it was difficult to think of any functions of the family advice service not already performed by the existing services, there was an unmet need in services to adolescents and children, especially in areas with high delinquency rates. Work with youngsters could lead to preventive work with their parents and F.A.S. workers could do this while attached to community centres or any other social agency. In a unified social service department F.A.S. workers could function as referring agents, co-ordinate services and prevent overlap.

A nursery school headmistress found it difficult to distinguish between the family advice service and the children's department area office, although she had heard the children's officer lecture on preventive services and understood the functions of family advice centres. She had made referrals to the area office, but had not been aware that these referrals were directed to an F.A.S. worker. Nearly all the children who attended her school came from families who needed some type of social work support and she thought it would be very useful to have a child care officer attached to the schools in the area.

The headmistress defined the F.A.S. functions as providing help and advice with regard to marital problems, family planning, child rearing problems, psychological support and economic assistance. While there were a number of agencies which provided this kind of help, people needed guidance and information about the various services available. Prevention could be regarded as the most unique F.A.S. objective, the worker acting as a 'catalyst' in the community. This service should be part of a unified social service department and should provide one single, known address to which people could turn for help and direction.

The headmistress had heard about the arts and crafts centre initiated by the 'F' project detached family advice centre and was interested to meet the F.A.S. worker there.

An after-care social worker could not distinguish between the child care and F.A.S. functions at the area office, but was well informed about the work of the 'F' project detached family advice centre. She felt that her own duties as after-care worker were very similar to those of the F.A.S. worker: casework involving the whole family. The family advice service should aim at convincing clients that it offered more than material assistance and the emphasis should be on 'helping people to help themselves'.

A Department of Health and Social Security official did not know about this family advice service. He defined the functions of the family advice service as working with the family as a whole, and helping families to co-ordinate help with their various problems with the 'welfare jigsaw'. They should focus on preventive work and serve as an 'early warning system' as the people in greatest need of help were often the ones least able to make contact with a social worker, and he mentioned fatherless families in this respect.

Police officials had gained some insights into the F.A.S. functions from what they had heard about the detached family advice centre serving the 'F' project area, but found it difficult to distinguish between F.A.S. and children's department functions at the area office, adding that a community based family advice centre would be more useful.

Liaison between agencies, encouraging field-level co-operation and helping the public to use the appropriate services were the main functions of F.A.S. The F.A.S. worker should have less specialised knowledge than the child care officer and should be trained in community work with particular emphasis on the severe problems posed by teenage delinquency as there was a scarcity of youth workers with the special talents needed to work with young delinquents.

A *clergyman* was not aware of any distinction between the family advice service and the child care functions of the area office. He thought that the functions of a family advice centre might be similar to his own; to offer 'intelligent advice to people whose own background made it difficult for them to cope with their problems or to find the appropriate help'. In its present form F.A.S. seemed to be too narrow a concept, perhaps because of its location in a statutory bureaucratic organisation rather than being community-based, well known, personal and trusted.

The 'B' project family advice centre

A *housing official* said that he referred a range of problems to the centre and also received referrals. He felt that co-operation between his agency and the centre was most useful, but seemed confused between the work of the centre's welfare and child care staff and of the health visitors. He thought that the centre was not easily accessible; that it should publicise its services; that, in giving an advice service, it should not be tied to statutory rules and regulations. Informal work was needed in this relatively small community.

A *health department official* was in frequent contact with the centre but saw its functions as those of the children's and welfare departments. 'It is highly desirable to have a community-based, easily accessible service to which people can go with any kind of problem. I all too often see people battered between so many departments.'

Health visitors regarded the centre as a combined area office of the children's and welfare departments and referrals to the centre involved 'going through channels': their own senior officer, the medical officer of health and the children's officer or the chief welfare officer. They felt that the preventive approach had not been developed sufficiently, and as a result some of the preventive work was passed on to the health visitors. Contacts with the centre were inadequate and there was little opportunity for exchange of views and discussions.

Child guidance psychiatric social workers had frequent contact with the centre and made and received referrals. They saw the role of F.A.S. worker as that of a 'free-floating case worker' not bound to administrative structures and, therefore, able to serve people who 'fall through the net of social services'. A family advice service should be more community-based, 'rather like the old settlement houses', and seek to mobilise community resources and local volunteers.

A *mental health social worker* knew the centre as the area office of the children's and welfare departments. He was reluctant to refer to the centre because of the time taken to process applications, particularly with regard to homelessness. He suggested that the advice, guidance and assistance functions could be assumed by the health centres, and that an F.A.S. worker could be appointed as receptionist.

A home help organiser regarded the centre mainly as the area office of the welfare department. She did, however, feel that the centre should be ready to deal with any kind of problem and provide an open door to anyone seeking advice.

An education welfare officer made several referrals to the centre, but was not always satisfied with the response. He had, on occasion, been told that the client should contact the centre directly to ask for help. This put too much of the burden on the client, and child care officers should be ready to take the initiative by visiting the family to offer their services.

The education welfare officer did not think the centre could be regarded as a family advice service. He was not convinced that a service of this type was needed in such a relatively small community.

A probation officer regarded the centre as an area office of the two statutory departments. He felt that a family advice centre should be community-based and act mainly as a referral agency, but suggested it might overlap with the Citizens' Advice Bureau. He thought the centre should do more to publicise its services. The word 'family' in the name should be omitted as it might prevent those without families from seeking advice.

Employment officers remarked that the centre should concern itself with some of the current community problems which affected the town. A local factory, for instance, to be transferred to another location, will have some impact on employment, housing etc. Employment problems emerge when the local industries employ women at lower wages, leaving the men without work. 'People use the employment offices to seek advice with regard to financial problems, the filling out of official forms, social security benefits etc., so there is undoubtedly a need for such a place and even we find it difficult to keep up with the ever-changing regulations.'

Department of Health and Social Security officials said that people in the area refer to the centre as 'the welfare'. 'I referred a woman, by telephone, who was under great emotional stress and threatened with eviction, and whose children were obviously suffering from the crisis situation and was told by a member of the centre's staff that no help could be given until an actual accommodation problem had developed. This seemed to indicate that the centre does not function as a family advice service, but is restricted to the statutory functions of the two departments.'

The officials were often called upon to give advice on a wide range of problems, but could not always satisfy such requests. They gave all possible information regarding clients' rights to benefits, appeals, etc., but changes in the regulations and provisions were so frequent, that they themselves were sometimes unable to sort them out. An advisory service in the area would certainly be useful.

Town clerk's department officials had more contact with the welfare staff of the centre than with child care officers. They had discussed community problems with the welfare officers, as, for instance, a new factory that is coming to the area which will result in demands upon the social services and housing facilities.

The officials felt that a family advice service 'to which people can go with any kind of problem and which will help people sort out all the many different services available' would benefit the community. Such a service would alleviate the frustration of having to go from one department to another. Social workers do not 'go to the people' often enough and there is a feeling that some of the severe problems are referred for help when it is too late. A senior official said: 'The more community spirit can be developed, the more accessible people with problems become.'

The headmaster of a secondary school felt that there was need for more co-operation between the schools and the centre, and it might be useful to have a social worker attached to the school. The functions of the family advice service did not seem to be very different from those of teachers. His own school planned to include information on the social services and on people's rights to these services in a community education programme.

A police officer said that they regarded the centre as an agency to which all types of problems could be referred, although their contacts were solely with the child care officers at the centre. Closer consultation between social workers and the police was needed and might lead to more effective delinquency prevention.

A Council of Social Service official established good co-operation with the centre. She felt that the centre should limit its services to the statutory functions of the two departments. 'It is important not only to help people with their problems, but to give them the opportunity to help others. The centre doesn't really have time to do this.' She added that her own functions included those of a family advice service.

The 'C' project family advice centre

A senior child care officer regarded the family advice centre as an unnecessary duplication of services and suggested that the work could be carried out by the children's department if sufficient staff were made available as the F.A.S. functions required no special expertise or setting. Referrals from the family advice centre constituted a needless shifting of clients from one worker to another.

A welfare officer did not seem to be aware of the family advice centre though she had received clients referred from it. She assumed that the centre's functions were the same as those of the Family Welfare Association. The officer said that her own agency does not deal with people who do not fall within the prescribed statutory categories, and such people can neither be helped nor referred.

A mental health social worker did not know anything about the family advice centre, although his department had received a referral from it. There were rumours that 'detached' family advice centres were to be set up on some of the estates in the area. While the functions of such centres, and of community work in general, seemed 'a bit woolly', such centres could be of considerable advantage in providing on-the-spot support for people with mental health problems.

Housing department officials differed in their opinions. One officer had received several referrals from the centre and regarded it as an agency mainly dealing with problems involving children—its functions resembling those of the children's and welfare departments, though more informal. Another official thought the family advice and the legal advice centres were one and the same. He knew nothing of the functions of the family advice service and had no use whatever for community work.

A health visitor did not understand the functions of the family advice centre and said that referrals would be more appropriately directed to the children's department. The F.A.S. function of serving people 'with any kind of problem' would be made superfluous by the setting up of the unified social service departments. Some forms of community work were already carried out by health visitors. Family advice centres might do well to focus upon the special problems existing in redevelopment areas.

A school care organiser felt that the family advice centre had not publicised its services sufficiently. He had made referrals to the centre in cases when the Citizens' Advice Bureau could not be reached. As the centre is financed by the children's department it would make more sense to refer the appropriate cases directly to the department. Anyway, school care did not like to make referrals to voluntary agencies as these could then apply for I.L.E.A. grants.

A Department of Health and Social Security official had had little contact with the centre and thought that it dealt mainly with problems not handled by the statutory services, such as legal advice.

A clergyman expressed the view that of all the services offered by the settlement house, the family advice service was the least needed. He regarded community work as one of the most essential services in the area, but did not feel that the F.A.S. workers have a significant role in community work. If the family advice service is to become more effective, the workers should be more 'outgoing', more involved with the community.

A Family Welfare Association social worker said that his agency referred clients to the centre who needed short term help, while the centre referred people who needed intensive case work to the F.W.A. Both agencies 'share' cases who might benefit from having a place 'to drop in for a chat', in addition to attending regular case work sessions. The family advice service could be described as a short-term case work and referral agency. The family advice centre filled a gap, partly because it operated outside the statutory system.

A Family Service Unit social worker referred cases to the family advice centre not suitable for the kind of intensive case work offered by F.S.U. On some occasions a family referred to F.S.U. was sent to the family advice centre for a preliminary diagnosis. The centre has referred cases, especially complex marital problems, to F.S.U. Co-operation between the two services is fairly close. 'The family advice centre provides a service for the general public in a more easily accessible and informal place than the children's department, a place where people have the opportunity to discuss family problems and can be referred to the appropriate agencies. The centre could do more by engaging in community work, and by inducing the existing agencies to deal more effectively with social problems.'

A Citizens' Advice Bureau social worker said that the centre had shown a tendency to duplicate the C.A.B. functions, instead of providing the preventive and long-term case work services most needed in the area. The C.A.B. refer clients who need intensive case work to the Family Welfare Association, and those who need short-term help to the family advice centre because of the latter's connection with the children's department. Co-operation between the centre and the Citizens' Advice Bureau was not satisfactory. More intensive home visiting by the F.A.S. workers could serve to detect problems and the centre would be more effective located on an estate or a block of flats. In this type of setting the family advice centre could complement the work of the C.A.B. through intensive help and information.

The organiser of a settlement house family counselling project felt that the centre had been adversely affected by 'too many boundaries' set by the differentiation between legal, general and simple advice. What is

10

particularly needed in the area is a service which meets the material needs of the clients. It would have been better to locate the centre in a specific community so that it could concentrate on community problems and provide a 'sifting' and information service. The family advice centre seems to have many similarities with the Citizens' Advice Bureau and should develop closer relations with the latter.

The settlement house community worker knew the F.A.S. workers as colleagues employed by the same agency. He felt that his own frame of reference differed from that of the 'case work orientation' of the centre, but thought that the family advice centre could become more closely involved with community work. While the centre seemed to meet an existing need in the area, it could complement his own work more consistently if the staff would leave their desks more often and go out into the community. There was an advantage of having a family advice centre outside the statutory system, but even the settlement house setting intimidated some of the would-be clients. The workers could do more home visiting and community work. The worker felt that the functions of the family advice centre were similar to those of the Citizens' Advice Bureaux.

The 'E' project family advice centre

A group of child care officers who all had a variety of contacts with the family advice centre, the F.A.S. worker being a member of their group in the children's department, were interviewed. They found it difficult to understand exactly what the centre was doing, but thought its functions were wider than those of the department, and it provided a more readily available service in one area. The services to children and youth, the centre's accessibility to people with any kind of problem and the availability of legal advice were all valuable provisions. The group felt there should be more contact between the centre and the neighbourhood and that perhaps the location of the centre, in an exposed position between two communities, was a deterrent in this respect.

Several of the workers thought that the advent of the unified social service departments would make family advice centres superfluous. Others thought that the detached centres would have a function in the unified departments, such as providing an alternative to the authoritarian image of the statutory services, discovering undetected needs and providing services in high-need communities.

A welfare clinic superintendent said that her agency had established close co-operation with the family advice centre and there was frequent consultation between herself and the F.A.S. worker with regard to families they both knew.

The worker saw the functions of the centre as helping and advising people who 'do not know where to start' when they are in difficulties and need help. The centre seemed to concentrate on services to adolescents and had done a great deal to help these youngsters 'for whom the social services provide very little', but she was unsure where the family advice service ended and youth work began.

The worker said that it was good that the centre was part of the children's department and that child care officers felt welcome there. It might be a good idea to attach F.A.S. workers to the new unified social service area offices, or else have F.A.S. workers available at large health centres.

A mental health social worker had received one referral from the family advice centre and felt that F.A.S. worker's on-the-spot availability was very useful. Although the centre was 'nearer to the ground' than other services, it had perhaps 'jumped to conclusions' too easily in deciding that the greatest need in the neighbourhood was for services for young people as she was concerned about the many isolated people who had not made themselves known to the centre. She thought that the 'outgoing function' of the centre had been overlooked and the needs of the community should have been surveyed before services were provided. Nevertheless the contacts the centre had established with children and youth in the area were a valuable part of the child care service.

A geriatric visitor 'shared' three clients with the F.A.S. worker. The latter had visited these elderly people at her suggestion and they had visited the centre. The value of the centre lay in the fact that it was open sometimes in the evenings and that the F.A.S. worker had more time to spend with his clients than other social workers. She felt that the worker should have a closer look at the problems of old people in the area as an Old People's Club at the centre would be useful.

A school psychologist had referred immature, acting-out adolescents to the centre which had shown itself able to accept such youngsters and the F.A.S. worker had demonstrated his understanding of this particular adolescent problem. The referral of a family with regard to a disturbed six-year-old West Indian boy had also been helpful. The F.A.S. worker visited the family and discussed the case with the school psychologist at the child guidance clinic.

He said that the centre responded to the needs of the area as they became identified and talked of the need for 'therapeutic structuring of the neighbourhood', e.g. enlisting the aid of older children to look after small children left unsupervised. Unlike most other social workers the F.A.S. worker not only helps individual families but also tries to get the community to help itself, an important preventive service as the problems of one family may be expressing those of the entire community. The centre needs the backing of the children's department, which is the key agency in child care. In a unified social service department family advice centres should be detached to smaller areas than those covered by the area offices and should liaise with the department with regard to community problems.

A youth officer agreed with the centre's permissive approach to the very difficult children who attended the centre. He thought the staff had done a good job with the youngsters after weathering the 'testing period'. He was impressed with the F.A.S. worker's caring for disturbed children and felt that the use of the dilapidated building had the advantage of permitting a certain amount of destructive behaviour which could not be tolerated in a more valuable accommodation. He thought it was unfortunate that people equated the effectiveness of a club like the one run by the centre with its physical appearance. The centre's youth work should be given more recognition and better resources, but it should be physically separated to some extent from the family advice service.

The youth officer thought that because of the complexity of the social services there should be more family advice centres; they could provide the same services to people who need help as travel agencies give to people who wish to travel.

Two I.L.E.A. play centre organisers said that, while they had several contacts with the centre, they did not know enough about it to attempt a definition of its functions. The F.A.S. worker was a 'very sincere and likeable chap', but playgrounds should not be part of a family advice centre's functions. However, there was no reason why such centres should not initiate play facilities, provided there was consultation with other agencies.

They felt that the centre was making a valuable contribution by providing an 'area of safety' (the playgound), by keeping children off the streets and helping them to make constructive use of their leisure time. Both disapproved of the bad physical conditions they had seen at the club, which could have had a detrimental effect upon the image of playgrounds in general.

A local authority statutory officer who asked that his agency should not be identified regarded the family advice centre and the playground as one and the same thing. He said that the use to which the youngsters had put the two buildings and the wear and tear they had caused were an indication of the need for such facilities in the area. He felt that a family advice centre of this type was needed in an area which had the lowest standards of housing in the borough. He saw the functions of the family advice service as trying to keep families together and preventing children from coming into care.

The youth programme was the most valuable part of the centre's service, as youngsters needed a permanent place of their own where they could 'let off steam' and he would like to see a sturdy, purpose-built building for the centre and club. He thought that the simple, friendly atmosphere of the family advice centre made it easier for many people to ask for help with their problems than the large, impersonal setting of the statutory departments.

A Department of Health and Social Security official had found his contacts with the family advice centre useful and informative, and thought that this service filled certain gaps; he cited the prevalence of old people who were not adequately served by the existing agencies. He said that the worker was a 'practical chap who talked sense', but that there should have been more publicity and information about the centre. He saw such centres as an important future link between the community and the unified social service departments.

The headmistress of an infants school, member of the adventure playground management committee, said that she had made two referrals to the centre and had found that the centre's services had been very helpful. She saw the F.A.S. worker's role as that of a liaison person for parents, children and other agencies, such as schools. The great advantage of the centre is that it is not an official-looking office and it is 'on the spot'. While play areas are scarce in the borough, and are usually the responsibility of the parks department, the family advice centre provided a play area for children, something which had not been done previously by a social work agency. The playground filled a need in the area and this and the non-exclusive youth club were most valuable.

The headmistress would welcome more contact between the centre and parents in the neighbourhood and suggested that one room in the centre could be used for 'social gatherings' by parents. She felt that it was good that the centre was part of the children's department because of its strong links with children and teenagers in the area and thought there would always be a need for this type of family advice centre as it could provide a service for people who are reluctant to contact officials.

A senior police community liaison officer felt that the centre was of benefit only to the youngsters in the centre's immediate vicinity; the club had a 'free-and-easy' atmosphere and relied on the youngsters to develop self-discipline, rather than impose discipline upon them. He and the F.A.S. worker had discussed various boys, but the latter had been very careful not to identify the youngsters or to divulge information about them. Other members of the force had called at the centre, and the new patrolman in the area had been informed of the functions of the centre and had been asked to be co-operative. He thought perhaps an increase of youngsters who attended the clubs coming to the attention of the police may indicate the centre's failure; so far only a few boys who attended the club were known to the police. While he agreed that experimentation with a permissive approach may eventually 'prove something about working with these youngsters', he himself felt that the teenagers wanted and needed controls. He added that the decrepit state of the building may have prevented adult clients from visiting the centre.

A solicitor had accepted a number of referrals concerning matrimonial and criminal cases at the request of the family advice centre. He had no clear idea of the functions of the family advice centre, and thought it resembled F.S.U. and C.A.B. to some degree. He felt that people are frightened of officials and it would be a disadvantage for the centre to become known as an official agency connected with the borough council.

The treasurer and the secretary of the adventure playground management committee said that the management committee regarded itself mainly as a fund raising organisation. The treasurer regarded the task of the F.A.S. worker to identify the needs of a neighbourhood and attempt to meet these needs. He had found that leisure time activities for children and teenagers represented the most pressing need and he acted upon this, providing a permissive atmosphere in which the youngsters 'could work things through and let off steam' prevailed.

Both thought the centre should be more involved with community groups and it was difficult to say whether the management committee could be regarded as representative of the community, as the latter was so mixed. However, the majority of the people in the area were working-class, while the committee consisted mainly of middle-class people. The committee had been 'set up in a rush' and the people who joined were mainly those who wanted to be involved for personal reasons, rather than as representatives of any group. It would have been useful to establish contact with some of the resentful people in the neighbourhood, even trying to get them to join the committee, but no one had done so.

The children's department provided as good a setting as any other statutory agency, but could have done more to support the centre financially, and the management committee had felt that the department was not fully aware of the amount of money the committee had spent on the centre.

The 'G' project family advice centre
Child care officers expressed a variety of opinions about the family advice centre. One said that one of her clients felt threatened by the centre and

thought that anything said in the centre would 'go all around the estate'. Another C.C.O. avoided visiting the centre because she did not wish clients to identify children's department and F.A.S. functions. One C.C.O. said that she would not make referrals to the centre, because it was the latter's task to reach 'unreached' families, not to work with those families already known to the department. A C.C.O felt that families had tended to 'play off' child care officers and F.A.S. staff.

Child care officers who shared clients with the F.A.S. worker said that the referral relationship was fairly good, certainly better than it would be with staff of other services. Referring to the case of a delinquent girl, one C.C.O. said: 'We [child care officer and F.A.S. worker] both had the same interests at heart.' Another said that the children of one of her families would have been received into care if it were not for the F.A.S. worker.

Several child care officers thought the distinction between their own functions and those of the F.A.S. worker were not clearly enough defined. Contacts between them and the F.A.S. worker were fairly frequent, but the confidentiality factor prevented the latter from detailed discussion of her work. One C.C.O. said that the F.A.S. worker had given the child care officers 'a new dimension' to their work. They described the functions of the family advice centre as those of referral, provision of recreational facilities for children, providing 'a place where people can let off steam, a safety valve'. Someone remarked that the F.A.S. worker had to 'take a lot of aggression' from her clients. Some felt that the worker, as a local authority employee, could not really function as a community worker. The child care officers wondered if a detached family advice centre as part of the statutory framework led to some conflict, especially when housing was the predominant problem. 'The centre fills a gap because it is on the spot and covers a much wider spectrum than any of the other agencies. Being on the spot means that the worker cannot refuse to see clients, as one can at the department offices. The centre encouraged mutual aid in the community and recently there were signs of strong community identity on the estate, and many of the families were sorry to leave.'

A housing department official referred a number of cases during the early days of the family advice centre, mainly concerning debts and quarrels between neighbours. Soon, however, the F.A.S. worker knew the tenants so well that this was no longer necessary: 'She saved us a lot of work.' The F.A.S. worker consulted the housing department official with regard to tenants' problems and discussed the 'decantation' with him. The F.A.S. worker 'fought for her clients' when necessary and relations deteriorated when the worker 'started to back up the tenants against the housing department'. She said some uncomplimentary things about the department in the local press and became 'too involved with her clients'. The F.A.S. worker was 'very backward' about seeking the advice of the housing department; she was 'aggressive towards all other social workers' and was 'fighting for the tenants all the time and often not knowing whether she could keep it up'.

The official described the functions of the family advice centre as the offering of advice and practical help to families. Her advice on such matters as delinquent children, debts, budgeting, etc. was very useful, but her work could not be regarded as a success. The community had deteriorated, families breaking up, people going to jail, rent arrears increasing. 'Mind you, the type of families she had to deal with, it's a wonder she got anywhere—a shocking crowd.'

Nevertheless, the family advice centre was a good idea. The F.A.S. worker shouldered a lot of responsibility and took a lot of trouble from the tenants and from other social workers. There was definite improvement in the children up to the age of twelve, the F.A.S. worker gave them the home life they lacked and the children talked to the worker when their own parents couldn't be bothered. There did not seem to be any positive results with the parents.

Through being on the spot and her attitude in working as one of them and becoming one of them, the F.A.S. worker gained the confidence of the tenants and could pass on valuable information to other agencies. The tenants were very anti-authority and the worker helped them to 'get over this block'. However, she tended to side with the tenants and to withhold valuable information, she associated herself with the tenants' association which really had nothing to do with the family advice centre. The families would not take advice from other officials and needed someone to work among them. In this sense the centre was valuable, but it must be stressed that working with tenants' associations cannot be regarded as an F.A.S. function: 'It is a dangerous game to play.' The F.A.S. worker could have provided valuable liaison between the tenants and the council, but this had not worked out because the worker sided with the tenants.

The housing department official felt that the estate was full of problem families and, therefore, not a 'fair example'. A family advice centre could be set up in 'one of our prize blocks' and prevent problems from starting.

The official felt that it was right to operate family advice centres under the auspices of the children's department because this gave the centres the backing of the financial and legal powers of the department.

Health visitors expressed a range of views: one of them said that there was 'a lot of community feeling and community unrest' on the estate. One thought that the main functions of the family advice centre were to be in the area of need, to be available to the public, to hear what they are worried about, to clarify their worries, and to refer or to bring in other services that may be appropriate.

'The most important thing about a family advice centre is that it is community-based. I think a family advice centre could be a moveable feast, for example, it could go into an estate for six months whilst rehousing is taking place. It is feasible for health, welfare and children's department staff to work together, and the centre could be a multi-disciplinary team. I am not sure of the difference between a C.A.B. and F.A.C.'

A health visitor attached to a G.P.'s surgery commented: 'I find it difficult to distinguish the work of the F.A.S. worker from *my* work. It is false to separate social problems from health problems. I cannot talk to a family about their health problems without reference to social implications. I could not talk about the family's health problems if their electricity is cut off; the first thing is to try to alleviate the financial situation and get the electricity reconnected. I suppose I might have referred to the F.A.S. worker to get this done, but I would more probably have done it myself in the course of my duties.'

The health visitor thought that it was very useful to have someone in the area to whom one could turn: the centre had been an 'in-between' for the people and the agencies. Nevertheless, the centre did not fill a gap because there were no gaps: the services in the area were adequate and the health clinic was near enough to the estate to fill the 'someone to turn to' need.

'I don't think that one worker in the F.A.C. is the answer. In my view there are too many people visiting one family and what we need is more co-operation in the field between say the child care officer, the H.V.s, the G.P. It is often forgotten that the H.V. knows the mother during her antenatal period and when the baby is first born. During this time the H.V. can win the trust of the mother. And then, after this, other workers go into the family without the knowledge of the H.V. Maybe the F.A.C. should have included all the local workers.'

A third health visitor said that she had been sceptical about the family advice centre from the outset. Having worked on the estate for three years she had formed good relations and was worried about another social worker moving in. 'I went to the F.A.S. worker's office on only three occasions. I did not, and would not, refer anyone to her. The work I do as a health visitor is comprehensive and encompasses all and I am trained to do this work. I have complete control of the 139 families on the estate and when the F.A.C. was set up I was at the stage where I never had any trouble with the families.' The health visitor said that she felt that the estate was her own responsibility. She had trained the families to see her at fixed hours, three times a week, at the health clinic. She had found it difficult to talk to the F.A.S. worker because the centre was always full of people.

The health visitor described the functions of the F.A.S. worker as being 'an extra person who has provided secondhand clothes cheap or free of charge and who has taken children out'. She did not think that the family advice centre provided any service not already available through the existing agencies. 'A lot of what the centre did, the other agencies do as a matter of routine; for instance, writing letters to the Department of Health and Social Security, approaching charities for grants and providing secondhand clothes and toys at Christmas. The F.A.S. has caused a lot of trouble in the community. It has caused jealousies and friction because the worker does not make any attempt at confidentiality. I found that the people could not understand the difference between what I did and what the worker did and tended to play one off against the other. For instance: I have a family of Irish tinkers. We give them W.V.S. vouchers once every six months and when the mother went along to W.V.S. she took advantage of a new clerk there and took far more clothing than she was entitled to and arranged to call back the next day for more. When we heard of this, we got on to the W.V.S. to tell them not to supply clothing the next day. They did refuse it to her, but the following day she turned up with a letter from the F.A.S. worker asking for more clothing. The mothers come to the clinic and show me letters the worker has written to the social security on their behalf. They open and read them, you know.' The H.V. did not know that the F.A.S. worker writes the letters with the clients present and asks the client to approve the letter. She was convinced that the worker was obtaining additional grants for clients who received adequate social security benefits. The health visitor also disapproved of the centre's connection with the tenants' association which had 'put nasty letters about the housing department in the papers'. She felt that the borough's housing department was 'the best in the country'.

A mental health social worker said that there was no need to refer clients to the family advice centre as the people there 'knew themselves that the centre was the place to go if you wanted your problems sorted out'. The children especially knew all about the centre. She felt that the F.A.S. worker had not been very efficient in her referrals to the mental health department and was sometimes rejected because she did not use the appropriate referral channels through the local general practitioners. The worker could have made more of an effort to encourage families to accept community care; one of the clients benefited from the centre's availability as a place for children because it 'took a great load off the mother'.

The social worker saw the main function of the family advice centre as that of on-the-spot availability for people with problems and as a referral service. She saw the worker as a community worker, but not as one who activated community self-help. 'Apart from the convenience angle and from the point of view of making advice more easily accessible, the centre does not provide any service that is not available elsewhere. Advice, guidance and assistance were available at the central offices of the statutory departments and at the health clinics.' However, the centre was valuable in that it had been able to 'take the edge off people's anxieties during the crisis situation of rehousing'.

The social worker thought that family advice centres should be staffed by a group of workers from different agencies. One social worker could become isolated and, if attached to a particular statutory department, could become narrow and paranoid with regard to other departments.

A good neighbour service organiser received several valid referrals from the family advice centre, although one or two might not have been relevant. She was 'very happy' about the functions of the family advice centre, but thought that it was there to advise tenants in any sort of difficulty and refer them to the appropriate agencies. It was good to have the centre because of the many problem families on the estate, though she didn't know how economical it was. The functions of the family advice centre probably overlapped with those of the Citizens' Advice Bureaux: 'There are always clients who will try every agency and waste people's time.'

A Department of Health and Social Security manager said: 'I only come into the picture when there is an argument between a claimant (or, in the case of claimants from the estate, the F.A.S. worker) and the local territorial officer. For example, two weeks ago the F.A.S. worker claimed £15 for a mattress for an old lady. Personally, I thought this was quite reasonable, but my officer assessed the price of the mattress as 10 guineas. The matter was referred to me, but of course, I had to support my officer.

'I don't think there is anything that cannot be sorted out by personal contact. Sometimes when the F.A.S. worker is on the phone she is fighting mad—she doesn't seem to understand that we are tied by rules and regulations as to what grants we can give. I think social workers think we are mean and that we are not using our discretion in the proper way.'

The manager had frequent contact with the F.A.S. worker. He described the functions of the F.A.S. worker as follows: 'She is there to try to put individual claimants on the right lines—to be a guide to them—to explain other agencies to them. The main thing is that even though she was employed by the children's department she covered all aspects of life —she co-ordinated the services. The claimants tended to use the F.A.S. worker to let off steam. Also they used her as a liaison between them and the other agencies. The only disadvantage was that the tenants tended to use her as a lever—to get grants they are not really entitled to. However, in an area like this we in the social security have many untrained officers (no employee has been here for more than two years) so it is useful to have someone like her to protect the rights of the clients. This would presumably be the case in all high need areas where the turnover of staff at the social security office is very high. I think it might have been better and more logical for her to have been employed by the council rather than by a particular department.'

A *local councillor* had received several referrals from the family advice centre; one concerning housing and another about a danger to children from spikes and barbed wire. He had 'learned a lot' from discussions with the F.A.S. worker. He said: 'I would rather put another label on the F.A.S. worker, that of community worker.' The estate really was sick. It was a design fault, everything was inward-looking, there was a feeling of being different from the outside world. Because of the design of the place, noise reverberated around the flats. A proportion of the families, say one in ten, could be classified as socially inadequate. The housing department came out of this lousily, especially with regard to maintenance of flats. What happened was that a family would move in from homeless families' accommodation and would be expected to live in a dark, damp flat with broken windows, and every time they went out of the estate they would look onto modern, well-kept flats all around.

'Because the tenants were constantly moving in and out, it was difficult to get them to function as a community. However, it was a community in that it was cut off from the surrounding areas. The F.A.S. got the community onto its feet and at war with the local authority. The worker revived the tenants' association and got them to know what they wanted, until in the end there were impassioned speeches from both sides about the rehousing. She was really a local ombudsman, working with the tenants to sort out their grievances with the local authority. I think this is valuable so long as the local authority itself can see it as a useful process. It would be a failure, if, for example, the housing department were to say "the next referral we get from the F.A.S. worker will go into the wastepaper basket". It is feasible to have a community worker employed by a local authority so long as the authority sees it as valuable, and so long as she is backed up by her own department.

'Elected members like myself find it very difficult to get to know the difficulties of the people in the borough and especially the difficulties of tenants of the local authority. There is a certain paranoia on the part of chief officers—they do not like the idea that councillors are getting to know of difficulties between their departments and the general public. I very much appreciated the work the F.A.S. worker was doing in bringing the people and the councillors closer together. She was the eyes and ears in the community as well as the tutor to the community— she made them conscious of what they could do about their problems. I think it is very important that we decentralise the social services. The central office is very much a "them" place and as the housing department is there it has many unhappy associations for people.'

A headmaster said: 'The problem is that the family advice centre did seem to be exclusive to the tenants of the one estate. We have our own social workers in the schools [school care workers] and there are social workers in the children's department. Normally when we have a difficult child, or a child in trouble, we would work through these official channels.'

One of the headmaster's colleagues, the headmaster of the lower school, who was present at the interview, said that he had had personal contact with the F.A.S. worker twenty to thirty times during the two-year period; the year masters who are responsible for the general social welfare of their classes had also been in contact with the F.A.S. worker.

He added: 'I think she tried to solve the internal problems in a block of flats in a neighbourhood. I do not think that she did anything that the other social workers of the neighbourhood were not already doing. The family advice centre has been harmful in that it gave children a loophole: I am sure truancy was aggravated because of the F.A.C.; the children spent a lot of time in the centre during the day and this gave them an official reason for not being at school. The area is well served by social workers already and the parents are quite incapable of sorting out the various agencies. It is very difficult for us to say how and in what way the parents have been helped. There comes a time when you can do too much for the parents. Self-help is not encouraged by the multiplicity of agencies—to put a social worker on the spot does not help. There has been no change in the children who attend this school: it would need more than an F.A.S. worker to change that lot. When there are so many social workers around, it makes it easier for the parents to shed their responsibility. Parents are now *demanding* things like free school dinners as a *right*! I think the best thing to do would be to have a school-based social worker.'

A playground leader said that the F.A.S. worker never really referred a client to the playground. However, once or twice she brought children to the playground and discussed possibilities of play facilities for the young people of the estate. The leader described the functions of the F.A.S. worker as: 'To be a kind of punchbag for residents' complaints and to attempt to co-ordinate these complaints into a coherent statement to the local authority. This area is fairly fortunate in that it has one or two schools, residents' associations and other semi-statutory agencies which seem to be more than competent at their work. The grapevine works very well and the local authority is sympathetic when it can afford to be.'

The playground leader could not describe the work of the centre and said that he was not certain how much of a role the centre had played in rehousing of the tenants, or how far the tenants' association and the local authority had handled this. At this point the headmistress of a local school who had listened in said: 'They've practically blown up the estate and the F.A.S. worker did this single-handed.' The playground leader felt that the work of the family advice centre was important, but that more training and a more comprehensive picture 'of the scope of provisions' was needed. He thought that a community worker should be incorporated in the statutory framework, but should not be directly employed by the statutory authority.

A clergyman spoke warmly of the time the F.A.S. worker had brought a distressed woman to him: 'I cannot really tell you very much about what she did, but when I visited the F.A.C. for the first time I could immediately see that everyone knew and trusted her. I can see that it was not an easy job to do—she was at the disposal of everyone and there were lots of people who were not so pleasant to contact, and in whose homes one was not so welcome.'

A family service unit social worker first heard of the family advice centre when one of his clients mentioned 'that woman in the hut'. Shortly after this he had occasion to discuss two of his clients with the worker and she 'helped to relate these families to the community'. He co-operated with the F.A.S. worker with regard to several families. 'It was a block of problem families. It had been used as a dumping ground. Some of these families made a lot of use of the social services and part of the function of the F.A.C. was to find out how appropriate the social services were for the needs of the families. The centre was concerned with the whole neighbourhood. The worker had the opportunity to get to know the neighbourhood—to get to know the underlying pressures which only come to light very much later with the other social services. She gave the families support by allowing them to know their own strengths—particularly with regard to rehousing. The F.A.S. filled a gap in providing the advice-part of advice, guidance and assistance. For example, arranging hospital appointments, explaining the functions of the other agencies.'

A Citizens' Advice Bureau social worker who had worked closely with the family advice centre with regard to the Cypriot families said they benefited from the services of the centre. 'When I talk to these families now they are always very grateful and tell me how kind and helpful the F.A.S. worker had been.'

A journalist on the local newspaper heard about the family advice centre from the pre-school playgroup leader. She said: 'I thought this was something new—the mountain coming to Mohammed—to go out to the people and work amongst them. I went along to see it in action and indeed it was something new. The people who called in whilst I was there seemed to treat the worker as a friend.' She described the functions of the centre: 'To help people to help themselves and to bridge the gap between "us" [the tenants] and "them" [officialdom]. The gap is so great at the moment. The centre brings help to those who otherwise would be missed out. The clients see the "helper" in the F.A.S. as one of them and eventually get to know and trust the "helper". Also the centre has helped the tenants to stand on their own feet. I think they are conscious of their position in relation to society, as when I talked to them they said : "Ah! problem families." The local councillor has fought valiantly for them over rehousing, but it would not have happened without the tenants themselves making a stand—and this would not have happened without the F.A.S. It has encouraged neighbourliness— the tenants have been very helpful to one another. It has done a lot to keep children out of care, which the mothers obviously do not want, and the F.A.S. has made it possible, by giving and encouraging support.'

In December 1967 an article written by this journalist appeared in three local newspapers in which the following impressions of the family advice centre and the F.A.S. worker were given:

Adults and children call her by her first name and think of her as a friend, though perhaps as a rather remarkable friend who knows all the answers, from how to use a phone, to which ministry or social service agency to contact. And, often enough, which person to contact at these places.

This confidence has grown up gradually, as the tenants have got to know her. Now people arrive constantly; the knocker is banged every few minutes.

Sometimes it's a social call, sometimes a problem, sometimes it's ostensibly a social call with a problem finally broached in a casual 'oh, by the way . . .'

People arriving at the centre are frequently greeted with coffee. Children come pouring in, too, on their return from school, lured perhaps by the warmth and welcome, the hot chocolate or coffee, the serious attention, discussions and friendly atmosphere, or by the stock of paints and crayons for them to use. Dozens of their pictures adorn the walls.

One woman wants to get her gas meter cleared before she goes away. What is the phone number of the Gas Board? And now she's here, will the worker make a call for her? Here's the sixpence . . .

The 'F' project family advice centre

A group of child care officers were all aware of the activities of the family advice centre in their area, but only six out of eleven had visited the centre. The C.C.O.s who had referred clients to the centre said that these referrals had been useful, either because the client was reluctant to visit the area office, or because they took care of those aspects of the case which the child care officer was not able to attend to adequately due to lack of time, resources or personal attitudes towards the client.

One C.C.O. said that he and the F.A.S. worker were 'on the same wavelength' and their discussions and exchanges of information regarding clients and contacts with other agencies were very useful. There was mutual respect between child care officers and the F.A.S. worker and the latter provided useful insights into the patterns of the community which added to the understanding of the officers' clients.

Four of the C.C.O.s thought that the concepts and functions of the family advice centre were 'very hazy'. Others felt that the centre's purpose was to establish contact with community groups, and that the work with teenagers and the arts centre was especially significant. The centre's functions included the encouraging of community self-help activities and social action, to help other agencies to identify needs, to channel information between the community and the local authority and to involve fieldworkers of all agencies in community activities. One child care officer saw the F.A.S. worker as an interpreter who should be allowed to bring conflict out into the open.

The accessibility of the worker was a great advantage and the people of the community had begun to feel that they 'were somebody' through the presence of the centre. One C.C.O. said that the boundaries between community and case work were vague and the F.A.S. worker's role was not clearly defined; it was also said that the factor of the worker's personality must be distinguished from the results of the centre's work.

The child care officers suggested there should be a playground and a larger centre with more rooms. The view was also expressed that, while the F.A.S. worker should have local authority experience, he should be 'financially and politically independent'.

Several C.C.O.s felt that detached family advice centres should be set up throughout the country, they should be financed by children's departments, but be part of a voluntary setting. The F.A.S. workers should not be identified as child care officers as this would make people shun them, as most of the C.C.O.s felt that the department had a 'bad image'; only one officer denied this assertion. Someone said that the F.A.S. worker might have made an important contribution by improving the children's department's image and by modifying some of the people's misconceptions about the statutory services.

A welfare officer said that when the first of their clients asked the family advice centre for help, the staff of the welfare department had been 'puzzled and worried' as they had no information about the centre. He criticised the initial lack of publicity. However, as more clients began to make use of the centre it became clear that the F.A.S. worker was always ready to co-operate with the welfare department and did not interfere with their work in any way. The community support fostered by the centre was beneficial for elderly and handicapped people. Co-operation between welfare department staff and the centre had been very good and productive and the F.A.S. worker's initiative in holding pre-liminary discussions of referrals should be regarded as 'very sophisticated practice'.

The welfare officer felt that the F.A.S. worker saw himself mainly as a community worker and that his functions certainly seemed to be broader than the prevention of children being received into care. The F.A.S. worker is a 'community growth catalyst', using many skills, identifying with the community, but balancing loyalty to his clients with his obligations to the local authority. The amount of freedom the F.A.S. worker had been given showed remarkable progress in the thinking of the children's department and other statutory departments still lagged far behind. The welfare officer had some doubts about the role of family advice centres within the structure of a unified social service, and thought perhaps more scope could be given to voluntary community work agencies.

A housing department official had frequent contact with the centre, had referred many people to it and had, in turn, received many referrals. He himself interviewed clients at the centre once a week and was convinced that the centre's clients benefited from its services.

He saw the F.A.S. worker as 'someone on the spot who people can turn to', even if their problems seem trivial. By encouraging the housing department staff to see clients at the centre he has helped all concerned: 'The only way to learn about families and their real needs is to live among them as the F.A.S. worker is doing here.'

He felt that, in addition to the arts centre, the neighbourhood's children needed a well-equipped playground. He was certain that the children's department was the most suitable agency to maintain family advice centres and would like to see advice centres all over the city, visited regularly by a mobile housing liaison officer.

A mental welfare officer had found the referral relationship and the co-operation between himself and the family advice centre very useful. The F.A.S. worker's supportive home visiting had been helpful when he himself was prevented from carrying out these visits because of heavy commitments.

The officer described the functions of the F.A.S. worker as that of liaison between families and social workers. 'He is closer to the families in the area than we are, they understand him and he knows how to work with them. He makes contact with families a damn sight earlier than other social workers, giving advice on seemingly trivial problems which could accumulate to crisis level if not helped with.'

Detached family advice centres 'fill a gap' and there should be more such centres in areas scheduled for demolition, staffed, however, by people of the calibre of this worker. The health department's attempt to operate a family care service broke down because of the severe staff shortage, but the officer said he would like to see family advice centres attached to the mental health service.

A school welfare officer, also very active in voluntary organisations, had become closely associated with the centre with regard to services to children. He had discussed the behaviour problems of two children with the F.A.S. worker. He described the functions of the centre as liaison, support and advice for the families in the area. He sees the F.A.S. worker acting as referral agent and as someone who helps people to know their rights and as someone who tries to 'redress the wrongs' done to people who 'have been stamped on by the machinery of local government'. The worker does what a good voluntary association community worker would do, although he is part of the statutory system and represents local authority.

The biggest advantage of the service was its availability 'on the doorstep' of the people in need. Under the unified social service system the family advice centre should be part of the area teams, but there would still be need for family advice centres to help communities where there were particular stresses.

A probation officer first contacted the family advice centre in order to discuss two boys on probation. The centre had made valid referrals to his agency and he was impressed by the F.A.S. worker's co-operation.

The officer noted that the F.A.S. worker was able to get members of the community to extend practical help to a family he knew. He sees the functions of the centre as those of a 'miniature Citizens' Advice Bureau, a social surgery, a spur and a safety valve'. He feared that the centre was exposed to political pressures detrimental to its goals and wondered how far the F.A.S. worker was able to 'stir the consciences of the people in power'. The centre had been valuable in raising the morale of the community and of the area's social workers, providing a more effective way of dealing with community problems than previously available. He added that there was no better agency than the children's department as a setting for the family advice service, and there was a future for this service in the unified social service department.

An after-care social worker said that the F.A.S. worker was doing a 'tremendous amount of work' with families she knew whose husbands were in gaol, and good 'from the case work point of view' as it relieved these families of some of the pressures.

The worker thought that the functions of the F.A.S. worker might be more similar to those of her own than of child care; he carries out case work with the entire family and is 'a father figure, almost a father confessor, who is needed emotionally and who is working right in the thick of it'. He seems to be singularly free from red tape and had given some of her own clients a good deal more than just material and financial assistance. One of her client families made fewer demands on her since their contact with the centre; they continue to see the F.A.S. worker although they have now left the area and have to take a sixpenny bus ride to get to the centre. She hoped that the family advice service would never become like the F.S.U., which supported families for many years without helping them to help themselves. There should be more centres of the detached type, some of them in shopping centres on new estates.

A local councillor was involved in the policy decision regarding the setting-up of the family advice centre. He was in contact with the centre since its inception and invited the worker to address a meeting of the children's committee.

The councillor defined the functions of the F.A.S. worker as that of 'catalyst' in the community, to 'roam about' in the area, listen to people tell of their difficulties and suggest ways of improvement. The work carried out by the centre was much broader than was suggested originally in the 1963 Children's and Young Persons Act, the worker taking on any problem which comes to him 'on the spot'. He is a 'prototype of an all-purpose social worker, encouraging creative work in the community and is an educator in the widest sense'.

While the councillor was certain that the centre had reduced the number of children coming into care it was difficult to produce statistical evidence of this. However, the most valuable result was that people in the area were realising that there are things they can do for themselves, and the F.A.S. worker has reminded them of their responsibility for each other. The centre not only could relieve the problems of transition, but also was able to teach people organisational skills and self-help methods which would be applicable in their new neighbourhoods.

The councillor felt that, rather than expand one centre to the point of unwieldy bureaucracy, he would advocate making such centres available in several other areas. He saw the family advice service as an important preventive service of the children's department which would improve further with the advent of the unified social service department. Family advice centres could, for instance, act as catalysts for lower-income private housing associations. The smaller the population group served by the centre, the better, but the target areas would have to be carefully chosen on the basis of need and economic viability.

Two clergymen thought that the advent of the family advice centre had been a major, though not the sole factor in reducing the number of people who came 'begging' to the vicarage. The F.A.S. worker had shown idealism and commitment, but was not always wholly realistic and tended to 'eulogise about art therapy'. A leaflet describing the functions of the family advice centre should have been distributed. While the F.A.S. worker is a valuable person, it is difficult to define his functions precisely. The F.A.S. worker functioned as a catalyst and helped to articulate the needs of the people in the area.

While other social workers usually represent authority in a more tangible form, the people from this area came to accept the F.A.S. worker and regarded him as 'being on their side'. He did not seek out the problem families, but they came to him, and although the centre could not be described as 'an ever open door', it came close to being that.

A valuable contribution of the centre was its attempt to 'help people to help themselves'. When one of them visited a parishioner in the area, the woman talked about the centre in terms of 'what *we* are trying to do'.

The family advice centre should definitely come under the auspices of the children's department because it is one of the few services which meets problems 'at ground level'. This service was especially important because working class people were often 'lost in a world of officialdom' and used the centre as a 'place where they could earth their problems'. At first the F.A.S. worker did not clarify his position as a children's department employee. Perhaps the worker would be wise not to stress the connection, as people tend to see the children's department as an authoritarian agency. Both felt that family advice centres were needed in high-need areas, even under a unified social service.

Four voluntary workers, members of charitable organisations, saw the functions of the family advice centre as those of providing recreational facilities which prevented children from playing in the streets, and helping parents to help themselves for the benefit of the children. The F.A.S. worker 'bridges the gap' between the services and the people of the area and acts as 'go-between and neighbour to the people of the community'. Family advice centres should continue to be operated by children's departments, and more centres of this kind should be set up in problem areas.

The headmaster of an infant and junior school first heard about the family advice centre through the school attendance office, but had since been in repeated contact with the F.A.S. worker.

The headmaster described the functions of the family advice centre as helping with immediate problem situations in which so many families find themselves. Most of the help consists in alleviating the shocking physical conditions, and helping with domestic problems. He felt that the worker was in a better position than other social workers to cut through red tape. The best attributes of the centre were the worker's warm friendly and confidence-inspiring manner and the ease with which people could make contact with him; he posed no threat to people, unlike, for instance, the education welfare officer who had an authority role. He felt that the centre should have better accommodation. He had doubts about the children's department setting of such centres because of the bureaucratic structure of statutory services. The voluntary services have less red tape and are more co-operative.

The headmaster thought that a 'clearing house' type of family advice centre would be needed even under a unified social service. He added that his only conflict with the family advice centre had arisen when he discovered that a group of boys were late for school because they had been having a discussion at the centre.

10 Issues and conclusions

The selection of the target areas

What kind of areas are most likely to benefit from the availability of a family advice centre? Who are the people most in need of this type of service? The answers to these questions are related to a number of factors which must be taken into account in any future planning of family advice services.

We must have some factual knowledge of the socio-economic stratification and the socio-cultural differences of our society, and of the imbalance of aspirations and opportunities, the supply and demand of material needs; we must know something about the uneven distribution of the precipitating factors of frustration, aggression, apathy and isolation and of creative, compensatory, legitimate outlets and sources of satisfaction provided by different socio-economic and socio-cultural environments.

We must obtain some factual information about the resources available to different areas and population groups in the form of the wide range of services which have become indispensable for the adequate functioning of our society, services which range from public transport to public access to information, from shopping facilities to educational opportunities, employment, housing, personal social services, and leisure time provisions. Moreover, we must have some understanding of the intricacies of communication between the providers and the recipients or users of the range of services, including the obstacles to communication raised by geographic distance, local norms and traditions or unsuitable bureaucratic structures.

We must decide on our priorities. This is not a simple decision, because it is determined by our social philosophy and humanitarian values, as well as by financial and manpower resources, by the pressures of public opinion, as well as the professional obligation to provide a competent and efficient service which produces results.

Last, but not least, we must decide upon a clearcut definition of the service we wish to offer. In other words, we must define the concepts, goals, functions and methods of the family advice service as a whole, as well as the specific objectives and tasks of the different types of family advice centres in relation to the specific needs of the areas and population groups they serve.

The literature of the last decades is rich in description and analysis of those areas and population groups in our society which appear to be most in need of competent and imaginative professional services geared to prevent the perpetuation of social pathology, to detect and combat pathogenic factors and to help to bring about social change. The term used to describe these areas and population groups is that of 'poverty'. Professor Abel-Smith (1968), for instance, states:

The general acceptance of the existence of poverty in Britain represents a revelation in thinking compared with only three years ago. For far too long people on the left as well as on the right believed that the slogans of the Beveridge era were descriptions of facts. But there never has been 'cradle to grave' security in Britain. There never has been a 'safety net' beneath which none can fall. All the Beveridge benefits from family allowance to pensions have always been below the 'official' poverty level laid down by the National Assistance Board or the Supplementary Benefits Commission. Moreover, the Board and Commission have never helped families with heads in full time work, have always operated unreasonable rent, wage stop and cohabitation rules, and have never met capital payments on mortgages, only the interest. There has always been a large number of people who have not applied for means tested aid (p. 112).

These are what might be called the 'structured gaps' in the provisions of the Welfare State. The 'relative' disparities were spelled out at the Helsinki Conference on 'Social Welfare and Human Rights':

There are two groups of poor people. One suffers acute want and deprivation. The other endures what might be termed 'relative poverty'. This is particularly a problem in the developed countries where large numbers of persons, though provided with the actual necessities, cannot acquire the means for a full life with the meaningful work and recreational interests and the wide range of material benefits enjoyed by their neighbors. It is this group that the Swedish sociologist Bent Rolf Andersen referred to when he remarked:

The poor stand alone in the welfare society and can measure their own situation only by everybody else's prosperity. The sense of shortcoming is intensified and poverty is all the more humiliating for the poor and for society (Willard, 1968, p. 36).

This is the overall background against which we have to place our selection of target groups and against which we have to measure our priorities.

Our conclusion is that family advice centres should be used as special services for those areas and population groups which are commonly classified as 'lower-class' and 'poor', and we regard these areas and population groups as priority targets for the family advice service. The descriptive material offered in this report will have shown the relevance of the concepts, goals and functions of the service to this substantial part of the overall population. More specific criteria for the selected target areas and groups have been enumerated. Robert Holman (1969), for instance, included in the criteria of 'community stress' 'the amount of vandalism and illiteracy, the lack of essential shops, the non-use of services like free meals and rent officers, the number of children separated from parents (in private as well as public care), and the lack of immigrant women in proportion to the number of immigrant males' (p. 445). The same author summarised the criteria offered by the Plowden Report and the official circulars:[1]

Preponderance of unskilled and semi-skilled workers, large families, families receiving state supplements, overcrowding, sharing of homes by more than one family, poor school attendance and truancy, retarded, emotionally disturbed or handicapped children, fatherless families and children unable to speak English. This was summed up as evidence of 'multiple deprivation' because of the 'combination of several [of these disadvantages].' Added to this was '. . . a rapid turnover of teachers or difficulties in attracting them' in such areas. Also listed was: 'The general quality of the physical environment such as crowded, old, sub-standard and badly maintained houses.' Among the conditions for Urban Aid Programme grants was 'a serious degree of overcrowding or at least 6 per cent of immigrants on the school roll'.[2]

One additional factor, or combination of factors which must influence the selection of target areas for the setting up of family advice centres is the availability and suitability of the range of statutory social services, supplemented by voluntary agencies and organisations, in areas which meet the criteria listed above. The Seebohm Report makes the inadequacies of the existing services the very basis of its recommendations. The Report (paras. 73–86) speaks of the inadequacies in the amount, range and quality of existing provisions, or poor co-ordination, difficulty of access to, and insufficient adaptability of the services. We know all too well that these inadequacies affect the areas of the greatest concentration and complexity of need most of all.

Because of an apparent possibility of a duplication of services between family advice centres and Citizens' Advice Bureaux, special attention should be paid to the availability of C.A.B.s in an area considered for the provision of family advice services. Citizens' Advice Bureaux differ

1 Central Advisory Council for Education, *Children and Their Primary Schools* (Plowden Report), H.M.S.O., 1967; (2) Department of Education and Science, Circular 11/67; (3) The Local Government Grants (Social Need) Act 1968.
2 This paragraph is a summary of Holman (1970a), pp. 174–5.

widely in the range and depth of their services, mainly due to local policy variations and the availability of trained social work staff. Kahn *et al.* (1966) state: 'We could not determine whether the most disorganised among the poor and multiproblem families, who reach no service in the United States unless one reaches out to them, fare better with C.A.B. which leaves most initiative to the inquirers' (p. 28).[1]

Local authorities are often either unaware of any significant gaps in their services, or are reluctant to draw attention to such gaps, not only because this would throw aspersions upon their competence but because of the lack of resources or knowledge needed to fill them. This makes it difficult to get an official assessment of inadequacies and gaps in the services with regard to high-need areas which meet the criteria of selection for special services, such as family advice centres. Nevertheless, our observation showed that statutory agencies such as the children's departments, and, in some cases, the housing departments, can and will point out priority areas with great accuracy and acumen. In our study of detached family advice centres we relied entirely on the children's departments and, in one case, the housing department, to suggest target areas for the centres. In at least some cases it would, of course, be preferable to carry out a thorough preliminary survey of the suggested target area. On the whole, however, we feel that it is quite sufficient to rely on the judgment of experienced chief officers and their staff.[2]

One other issue relating to the selection of target areas and populations must be mentioned: the question as to whether the family advice service should be available to middle-class clients. The exploratory study found that:

In some departments staff stated the need for a concerted effort to make the advisory services more attractive and accessible to middle class clients. The reasons given were:

(*a*) that many middle-class families were not receiving preventive help because they regarded the social services as mainly intended for the lower socio-economic strata of society;

(*b*) that a significant proportion of middle-class people in the F.A.S. clientele would serve to remove the stigmatising image of the service as one used mainly by the failures and the destitute of society (Leissner, 1967, p. 29).

Attractiveness and accessibility should, of course, characterise the family advice service in any case. A family advice centre should be made more attractive in order to induce those in greatest need of the service to make use of it, regardless of their social class. In practice, our experience

[1] See also the discussion of C.A.B. functions in comparison to the family advice service in Leissner (1967), pp. 61–4.

[2] The definitions of 'unreached' population groups by children's department staff are summarised in the report on the exploratory study (Leissner, 1967, pp. 24–6).

showed that the issue is somewhat irrelevant, especially in the case of detached, community-based centres. The goal here is to make the client community feel that the centre is *their* centre, the F.A.S. worker *their* worker. It is very doubtful that any stigma could be removed by inducing middle-class clients, probably from outside the community, to use the centre. Another possibility is the setting up of family advice centres for middle-class communities. Our own view is that at present the priorities of needs and the scarcity of resources in money, staff and all too often in readiness to reach out to bring the needed services to the 'hard-to-reach', cannot justify the allocation of special services such as detached family advice centres to middle-class communities. This is not to deny that middle-class families and communities may have a need for preventive and other services. The choice is one between the frequency and urgency of need and, most important, the availability of alternate solutions. In the case of family advice services in settings that are *not* aimed at a specific high-need target population, but serve an area of 'mixed' population groups as intake and referral units of children's department central or area offices, or in the case of family advice services offered by voluntary agencies there would, of course, be no question of excluding or in any way avoiding middle class clients. We are, however, entirely persuaded that all efforts of the F.A.S. staff must be focused on making the service physically and psychologically accessible to those who find it most difficult to seek early preventive help with their problems, and to those for whom it is most difficult to establish relationships and to make constructive use of the available services.

The different settings

The word 'setting' has, like so many other social work terms, meant different things to different people.[1] We define 'setting' as a frame-of-reference term which describes as *one whole* a set of concepts, goals, functions and methods carried out by one or several workers in a specific physical location in relation to a group of people we call the client population. Thus defined, we can group the different types of F.A.S. settings into four main categories:

1.   *Family advice centres which are units in the wider settings of a children's department central or area office, or of the combined offices of two or more statutory agencies.* These centres could be regarded as sub-settings, similar to adoption or foster care sections.

[1] The reader may refer to a detailed discussion of the term in Timms (1968) pp. 45–57.

The concepts, goals, functions and methods of these sub-settings *can* be the same, and have the same scope, as other F.A.S. settings. In practice, however, the difficulties encountered in distinguishing F.A.S. functions in these settings from those of the agency as such, tend to lead to some confusion and needless duplications. The confusion is increased because this type of F.A.S. setting serves essentially the same client population as the parent agency. Things are even more confusing when the same workers alternate between assuming the roles of statutory officers, carrying out routine agency duties, and 'doing turns' as F.A.S. workers. In the form described here, this setting can *not* be regarded as viable. It could, however, make a valuable contribution to the parent agency by redefining its role in either one of two alternative ways:

(*a*) The F.A.S. unit restricts its role to that of intake or reception unit with the additional functions of simple advice and information, referral and follow-up. Staffed by suitably skilled and experienced workers this type of F.A.S. unit becomes the entrance door to the agency for all *new clients*, and/or all clients who have used the services of the agency in the past, but present a *new problem*. The F.A.S. workers conduct the initial diagnostic interviews and refer the client to the appropriate officers in the parent agency or else they prepare, carry out and follow through referrals to other agencies. The F.A.S. unit would also provide a service for anyone who seeks simple advice and/or information.

(*b*) The F.A.S. unit becomes the community work branch of the social work department. While based in the central or area office of the parent agency, the family advice service carries out its functions in specific areas in which a need for special services has become apparent. An agency based family advice centre of this type could, for instance, be open for advice, guidance, assistance, and referral services every Monday and Wednesday in the parent agency. Every Friday the F.A.S. worker could provide the same service in a suitable location for the people living in a remote corner of the area served by the department. Tuesday and Thursday would be reserved for community work in a multi-problem council estate in the area. It is also conceivable that a centre of this type could supervise one or several detached youth workers, as well as volunteers and indigenous workers, help to provide and support such services as mothers' groups, social clubs, play groups, adventure playgrounds, youth clubs, etc. possibly in co-operation with other statutory and voluntary agencies.

2. *Family advice centres in the wider setting of a voluntary agency, but financed
and supervised by the statutory children's department.* Unlike the F.A.S. unit
in a statutory department, this type of family advice service may very
well develop its own client group and its functions are more likely to be
distinct from those of the parent agency. The 'C' project family advice
centre complemented rather than duplicated the work provided by the
settlement house, and offered services to a substantial number of clients.
However, as Owens (1969) rightly emphasises: 'The voluntary organisations are not just gap-stoppers or alternative sources of help: they
should be partners with the statutory authorities in one of the most
important jobs in our nuclear age, the attempt to improve the quality of
life for all of us' (p. 135). In the case of the 'C' project centre this partnership did *not* materialise. This may have been due mainly to a lack of
joint planning, and the voluntary agency and the statutory service
may have to share the blame. But it is not at all certain that such a
partnership, in itself no doubt desirable, is indeed practicable or even
necessary in the context of a family advice centre which is a sub-setting
of a voluntary agency. While it is certainly useful to offer people an
alternative range of services through the voluntary organisations,
the definition of the voluntary service as an alternative may ignore
one of the most important objectives of the family advice service:
the objective of bridging the gap between 'us' and 'them', a gap which
runs counter to the goals of prevention. If we regard the family advice
service as an effective approach to changing the authoritarian, punitive
image of the statutory service, then it is reasonable to assume that
this can be done only by clearly identifying the family advice centre as
a service provided by the statutory agency. There is still much scope
for co-operation. A detached, community-based family advice centre,
for instance, would greatly benefit from close co-operation with voluntary organisations in the provision of such community services as play
groups, youth clubs and a wide range of educational, social and
recreational activities.

3. *Detached, community oriented family advice centres* differ from detached
community based centres in that they direct their service *at* a target
area which may consist of one identifiable community or several such
communities, rather than being located in, and focusing on, one specific
community. These settings could also be regarded as F.A.S. neighbourhood centres. Represented in our study by 'D' and 'E' projects, these
community oriented settings include the entire range of F.A.S. concepts,
goals, functions and methods. While they may start out initially by
providing services to the community, their objective should be a maxi-

mum degree of community involvement and participation. These types of family advice centres would be most useful in neighbourhoods some distance away from the central and area offices of the social work children's department.

4. *Detached, community-based family advice centres* serve a specific community and are located *within* that community. While including the entire range of F.A.S. functions, these centres focus from the outset on a community work approach which has the objective of community involvement and participation. These types of settings were represented by the 'F' and 'G' projects. While both these centres served communities in the process of dispersal, we feel that the experience of the two centres showed conclusively that community-based centres *can* and *should* also be set up to serve permanent communities, with the objective of strengthening and preserving these, as well as serving communities in transition. Furthermore, we were led to the conclusion that community-based family advice centres could provide a very useful and much-needed service to *new* communities, especially in cases where these new communities are formed of groups and families rehoused as the result of redevelopment or slum clearance schemes and originating from several different areas.

In recent years the social work profession in the United States, in Britain and in some other countries has become increasingly aware of the need for 'bringing services to people, whoever and wherever they are' (McCormick, 1970), through new types of social service settings in which new approaches and methods are applied. Neighbourhood service centres set up in deprived urban areas in the United States some years ago were examples of such settings. Such a centre was intended to be

physically and psychologically visible, accessible and comfortable. Its services must be integrated, relevant, comprehensive and coordinated . . . [and] consistent with the values and life styles of the neighbourhood. Its social action must be carefully planned and well executed, appropriate to local needs and related to the larger community; it must meaningfully involve neighborhood residents (O'Donnell, 1968, p. 12).

This description can be applied word for word to the community-oriented and the community-based family advice centres. While there is no doubt that the other types of F.A.S. settings we have described can make valuable contributions, our observations have convinced us that the community-oriented and the community-based family advice centres provide settings which can add a new dimension to the statutory services.

The staffing of family advice centres

Staffing, in the family advice service settings, involves the following factors:

1. *Personality*. We start with this because it has become almost a cherished tradition in social work to regard it as the most significant determining factor, a sort of 'force majeur' which provides the ultimate explanation for a wide range of questions pertaining to all aspects of the work process, the relationship between client and worker, between the worker and his colleagues, between worker and agency, and with regard to the effectiveness of the service. Before we go any further, let us say here while we are convinced of the great significance of the worker's personality, we also feel that this 'great intangible' is too often used as an excuse for a lack of precision in defining professional concepts, goals, functions and methods. Unless we deal with pathological traits, 'personality' includes a wide range of resources and potentialities which enable a person to grow and to adjust, provided the setting offers a frame of reference in which adjustment can take place, and scope for creative expression and self-realisation and the kinds of challenges that stimulate growth. Our observations have shown that the worker's personality is the dominant influence in the setting, but it is never the *only* determinant. While we have seen family advice centres reflect the personality of the F.A.S. worker, we have also seen workers change and adapt themselves to the structural and professional demands of the settings.

2. *Qualifications*. The F.A.S. workers who participated in the study brought with them a wide range of academic and other training qualifications and professional social work experience. Our observations indicate that the basic requirements for the job include:

(*a*) a training course in social work, preferably including at least some rudimentary training and/or practical experience in the three basic social work disciplines of case work, group work and community work;

(*b*) practical experience in at least one local authority statutory department. We regard children's department experience as most relevant, but additional experience in other statutory services and/or voluntary organisations can be very useful.

Diagnostic skills and a good basic knowledge of the structures and functions of local authority statutory services and a thorough understanding of social welfare provisions, such as social security benefits, are important assets in the F.A.S. settings. For community-oriented and community-based centres training and practical experience in group and community work is highly desirable. We also noted that certain types of training and experience, in themselves valuable and deserving of recognition, can lead to some degree of imbalance in the F.A.S. setting. For example, we were led to conclude that a worker's past commitment to psychoanalytical techniques, long-term case work or a special interest in marriage guidance *can*, in certain circumstances, lead to a narrowing of the scope of the family advice service and to a shifting of a disproportionate amount of time and energy to one specific need or one specific function.[1]

We also found that the personal background of the worker, his 'life experience' must be regarded as a very significant aspect of his or her overall qualifications. In another context this was described as:

the kind of life experience that makes for a large measure of self-assurance about one's own values and for personal integrity, while leaving ample room for respect for different beliefs and values and tolerance for nonconforming attitudes and behaviour. . . . The worker must also bring with him the ability to demand respect and to exert his leadership, as well as organisational skills, resourcefulness and considerable knowhow in dealing with the complexities of living in modern society (Leissner, 1969a, p. 138).

In selecting social workers for F.A.S. appointments we would also look for such qualities as flexibility, imagination, readiness to question and, if necessary, challenge established procedures and, last but not least, a sense of humour.

3. *Suitability.* By this term we mean to point at the importance of assigning the worker to the type of setting which is most suitable to his or her personality and qualifications. The suitability of the worker is not always easy to predict, but there are some obvious criteria. It would, for instance, be wasteful to assign a worker with training, experience and pronounced interest in community work to an F.A.S. setting which is intended to function mainly as the intake and referral unit of a children's department central office. On the other hand, a worker who is obviously most comfortable in a highly structured, 'protected' setting, or who states clearly that he would find it impossible to take the initiative in meeting

[1] It is interesting to note that the Citizens' Advice Bureaux may have the same problem. An American investigator reported: 'One CAB unit which is excellent on the Rents Act shows a very high incidence of rental inquiries. Another CAB effective in Hire Purchase matters, shows a higher than average number of inquiries in this area. Of course it can be argued that the number of inquiries produces the expertise and reputation of these particular CABs. But it might well be the other way around' (Kahn *et al.*, 1966, p. 41).

people informally outside the agency setting, would not be a suitable person for a detached centre but could do very well in one of the other F.A.S. settings. A worker who is seen to be ready to assume a wider range of responsibilities and who feels the need to realise his potentialities for leadership will not be happy in a one man setting restricted to advice, guidance, assistance and referral. On the other hand, a worker who is most comfortable in a situation where he does not have to use his own initiative too often may find himself in an untenable position as the leader of a team.

4. *Adequate staffing* is a prerequisite for effective service. It is therefore necessary to examine carefully the number and composition of the staff complement of a family advice centre before it opens its doors, as well as to be ready to re-assess the staffing periodically and to be ready to make changes and additions if the need arises.

In agency-based F.A.S. settings which do *not* carry out community work functions it would seem that one F.A.S. worker and one F.A.S. assistant, or two F.A.S. workers, are sufficient. If community work is included in the tasks of this type of setting, it may be necessary to appoint one F.A.S. worker and one F.A.S. assistant as well as one F.A.S. worker with a special community work assignment. A second worker, possibly an assistant, is always advisable, because this ensures the availability of a worker in the centre when duties of one of the F.A.S. workers make it necessary for him to leave the centre to accompany a client, make a home visit, attend group meetings, contact other agencies, etc. In all cases the centre should have at least a half-time clerical assistant. The lack of clerical staff always results in a disproportionate and wasteful use of a professional worker's time for paper work.

The detached F.A.S. settings clearly necessitate a team work approach. We know of some instances in other countries in which detached social service centres employed a very large number of workers. A centre of this type in Holland, for instance, consisted of a 'community organiser', a youth worker and three case workers. The centre served a housing estate of 10,000 tenants (see Rae Price, 1968b, p. 1805). Several neighbourhood centres maintained by Mobilization for Youth in New York, each serving a fairly large area, listed the following staff complements: one director, two supervisors, three social workers, five to seven untrained 'case aids', two to three untrained 'family aides', one receptionist. In addition there was a part-time nurse and several specialist consultants, including a psychiatrist (Perlman and Jones, 1967, p. 13). Such large teams seem more appropriate for the new area teams of the unified social service departments.

The detached family advice centres will serve smaller areas and will not need staff teams of this size. However, as we assume that the detached centres will serve areas and population groups with a wide range of intensive needs, a team work approach including several workers is required. On the basis of our observations we find that the following can be regarded as adequate staffing for community based family advice centres serving high need communities with a population not exceeding 350 families:

one F.A.S. worker who has the responsibility of leader of the team;
one F.A.S. assistant;
one clerical assistant;
one youth worker;
two to four part time community home helpers (indigenous workers).

In community-oriented settings the size of the team depends, of course, on the size and population of the area served by the centre. If we examine the example of the 'D' project centre, we find that the staffing by two F.A.S. workers, a part-time ancillary worker and a part time clerical assistant did not meet the need. In addition to the two F.A.S. workers this type of setting should employ an assistant F.A.S. worker, a youth worker, a full-time ancillary worker and a full-time clerical assistant. An especially high incidence of need in an area necessitates special staff adjustments. In the 'E' project centre, for instance, staffed by one F.A.S. worker, an F.A.S. assistant, a youth worker, a play group leader and a clerical assistant, there were indications that an additional youth worker was needed in order to meet the demands.

As already indicated, indigenous workers, volunteers and workers seconded by other co-operating agencies can and should be used whenever possible. There must, however, always be sufficient professional staff to provide guidance and supervision for untrained workers and to ensure a co-ordinated approach by all members of the team.

We learned a great deal about the recruiting and employment of indigenous workers through the action research of the 'F' project centre. There is no doubt that this experience could serve as a model for other centres of this type. The contributions made by indigenous workers in bringing about community participation, in providing services, fostering self-help activities and, last but not least, in reducing the need for professional intervention can be very significant indeed. However, success in this area demands clear role definition and skilful guidance. As the original proposal of Mobilization for Youth (1961) pointed out: 'The employment of these [indigenous] leaders by the project may

11

undermine their influence among group members. To the extent possible, therefore, indigenous leaders must be discouraged from attempting to remould themselves in the professional image' (p. 134). In other words, in deciding on the appointment of an indigenous worker one should ask: How representative is this man or woman of the people we serve? How is he or she regarded in the community? How similar are his or her norms, interests, socio-economic and socio-cultural standards to those of the people of the neighbourhood? How capable is this person of asserting himself in a team dominated by professionals, of telling the F.A.S. worker and other members of the team that something they are doing may be wrong and should be handled differently? The criteria for the appointment of indigenous workers should *not* be this worker's readiness to shape himself in the image of the professional social worker. The foremost objective in adding indigenous workers to the F.A.S. team is to provide one more way in which the community can take an active part in the planning and the carrying out of the service; it is *not* primarily to obtain allies for the professional F.A.S. staff. Working as a member of the F.A.S. team *should* become a source of personal growth and satisfaction for the indigenous worker. It *may* enhance self-confidence and have a therapeutic effect by providing constructive solutions to personal problems and needs. However, the appointment of an indigenous worker should *not* be determined by therapeutic goals only, but should be guided by the aim of making the service to the community more effective.

Some other problems arise in the use of volunteers, especially if these come from outside the community. Outside volunteers, no matter how well motivated, or how badly needed, must be used with the greatest care and circumspection. Over-reliance on such volunteers may, in the long run, diminish the chances of a lower-class community to become self-confident and self-reliant. When volunteers are used, this should be done in close consultation with the community and under the guidance and supervision of professional staff. As an experienced social worker has pointed out: 'If we can identify the professional role more clearly then we can also bring clarity to the role of the volunteer' (McInnes, 1970). To this we may add: the more clearly the enabling functions of community work are spelled out to the volunteer, the more constructive will be the volunteer's contribution to foster community participation and self-help, and the less likely it will be that the outside volunteer will unwittingly reinforce tendencies of dependency and apathy by doing things *for* people, rather than *with* them. It is our view that, while there can be no objection to using the services of outside volunteers, it is advisable to encourage volunteer work by members of the community whenever possible, and to integrate the outside volunteer in a team work approach with local volunteers, indigenous workers and the professional staff. This kind of integration took place in the 'F' project centre and proved to be both stimulating and efficient. In the 'E' project centre integration of local and outside volunteers was not effected and, while we do not have sufficient evidence to say that this prevented community participation, we tend to regard this as one of the missed opportunities for encouraging community involvement.

Finally, a word about the clerical staff. In those centres in which clerical assistants were not sufficiently available, this had a markedly bad effect on the efficiency of the service and put additional burdens on the workers. In contrast to this, clerical assistants in other centres proved to be a welcome addition to the staff. Beside relieving the F.A.S. worker of much of the routine paper work and looking after the filing and the telephone, clerical assistants could be relied on to make clients comfortable when they had to wait, sometimes gave simple advice, helped to supervise children who strayed into the office, made an occasional home visit and generally became part of the team. Our observations convinced us of the importance of the clerical staff and of the wisdom of choosing clerical assistants carefully and of making every effort to enable the clerical worker to regard herself as part of the team.

5. *The leadership responsibilities of the F.A.S. worker* are of the utmost significance in ensuring the adequacy of the team work approach in the detached F.A.S. settings. Personality, qualifications and suitability all become factors in the carrying out of this key task.

The great variety of tasks carried out by the detached, family advice centre, the constant need to improvise and to 'invent' new and imaginative approaches, the informal, permissive and accepting setting which is an essential prerequisite of this service, make it all the more important that a sense of security and competence be provided. This can only be done by a consistent, carefully planned and constantly re-assessed structuring of the tasks and the responsibilities of the professional staff, indigenous workers and volunteers. This is the job of the F.A.S. worker as the senior member of the team. The task consists of such relatively simple matters as drawing up duty rosters, providing for much-needed 'breaks', adjusting leaves of absence to the requirements of the work, and ensuring that no staff member feels that he is expected to carry out his assigned work without the necessary equipment or time, or is victimised in any way. It consists of making sure that no member of the staff who has made a mistake or has become involved in a controversial situation is left 'holding the can' without support of the team and the assumption of full responsibility by the team leader. It also means dealing with more subtle matters, such as learning to understand the areas of strength and weakness of every worker and his or her special interests and talents in order to assign the right task to the right man, and to integrate services offered by colleagues from other agencies. It means also making valid use of consultation and discussion without shirking the responsibility of making decisions.

As we have already pointed out, we tend to assign at least as much importance to professional competence as to personality factors in the selection of staff. Our experience shows, however, that the combination of professional know-how, organisational skill and those personality traits commonly described as 'leadership qualities' become a decisive factor in a setting in which the F.A.S. worker functions as a team leader. A report on experimental neighbourhood-centred social work in the United States speaks of staffing 'by highly trained professionals with creative and often charismatic leadership' (Bernard *et al.*, 1968, p. 78). We found this type of leadership in some of the F.A.S. workers of the detached settings and regard it as an invaluable asset, provided the inspiration it provides and the enthusiasm it engenders within the F.A.S. team, among colleagues from other agencies and in the community, are tempered by professional self-discipline and self-awareness.

The range of services provided by the family advice centres

The purpose of the advice, guidance and assistance functions can be summed up as: 'To help people get needed service at the time of acute need with a minimum of the administrative obstacles that tend to eliminate all but the most highly motivated or most chronically dependent' (Rapoport, 1961, p. 11). The purpose is to enable people to seek and to receive effective and immediate help before acute problems become chronic conditions, or before identifiable, manageable problems become immersed in a cataclysmic welter of crisis situations and panic reactions. This is one of the dimensions of the range of services provided by the family advice centre. In the functions of mediation/liaison, referral and follow-up it includes 'help with reference to bureaucratic structure, professional ritualism, unnecessarily restrictive guidelines, de facto discrimination, cultural chasms, problems in communication, practical obstacles which stood in the way of expression of one's needs or assertion of rights' (Kahn, 1969, p. 5).

Another dimension consists of the processes of community work and the wide range of services to the community. In both these approaches to community improvement the F.A.S. workers function as initiators and consultants, as advisers, resource persons, mediators and enablers. In order to meet existing needs, the family advice centre may have to make the services of a number of 'special task' workers available, such as youth club leaders, detached youth workers, playground supervisors, arts and crafts teachers, play group and nursery school staff, and community home helpers. These may be professionals, indigenous workers, volunteers or staff members of other voluntary or statutory agencies who co-operate with the family advice centre. The team they form will find that the concepts, goals, functions and methods of the family advice service may serve them as well as a basis and as a frame of reference for a co-ordinated structured approach. The family advice centre may also take the initiative in bringing otherwise somewhat remote services, such as legal advice or consultation with a housing department official, to the community by providing suitable accommodation within or outside the centre, and by acting as mediator between such community-based services and the people who would benefit from them.

The usefulness of the family advice centre to other services, organisations and professionals may be regarded as a third dimension of the service. The family advice service, especially in the community-oriented and the community-based settings, can offer a wide range of information, advice and practical co-operation to other agencies. As Joan Cooper (1965) pointed out, the 'fragmentation' of the social services has led to too many social workers from different settings trying to help those people commonly described as 'high-need', 'deprived' or 'multi-problem' families. This highly experienced social worker reminds us that: 'As these families have difficulties in personal and community relationships, it is unrealistic to expect them to relate to a series of social workers' (p. 97). It may also be said that social workers, statutory officials and various professionals whose work is related to the social services may find it difficult to relate to people in high-need areas, families beset by a multitude of problems and inadequacies and in some cases from different cultural backgrounds, especially when the problems these people bring to them do not fit any one specific statutory category or professional competence. Here the family advice centre provides a valuable service by helping to 'sort things out', by liaising between clients and workers, by helping colleagues from other agencies to gain more insight and perspective with regard to their clients and by doing some of the on-the-spot work, such as carrying out home visits or arranging for community help, thereby reducing a colleague's work load. In some cases this service has been welcomed and greatly appreciated. In other instances social workers, officials and other professionals have reacted with distrust and hostility. The lesson we learned was that the F.A.S. staff have to be fully aware of the need of making their services accessible and to establish the image of a 'no-strings-attached', accepting, confidence-inspiring service, not only with regard to their clients but also with regard to all those many agencies, organisations and individuals who carry out the tasks of the welfare state. A key function of the detached family advice centre serving a 'high-need' community is clearly implied in the lucid analysis presented to the 1966 Children's Officers' Conference:

(1) Problems and needs may not be properly diagnosed because each service looks at the situation from its own narrow agency function.

(2) Needs when properly diagnosed do not fit clearly into specific categories for which responsibilities are defined by legislation or agency constitution which might lead to—

(a) refusal by all services contacted to accept any responsibility at all,

(b) longstanding arguments as to which service [is] responsible or what degree of responsibility [is] to be accepted by each service and for what,

(c) grudging or partial acceptance of degrees of responsibility by different services which when aggregated do not adequately meet the total needs of the situation,

(d) free and full acceptance of responsibility by different services as defined by legislation but still leaving areas of unmet needs or still providing [an] overall service which does not meet [the] total needs of [the] situation.

(3) Needs may be interpreted or diagnosed in different ways by workers from different agencies with different functions, different training and different objectives. This will tend to make agreement on the most appropriate methods of meeting needs hard to achieve and in some cases almost impossible.

(4) The existence of several different categories of needs or problems for which a number of different agencies might be responsible may lead to doubt, confusion and delay in the calling of help by any other person aware of difficulties but uncertain as to which agency is actually responsible. Or a person seeking help may be passed from one agency to another and give up in the process.

(5) In going to or in being referred to a particular agency a client can never be sure how he will be received, how he will be dealt with or whether his total needs will be rationally and fully assessed and met. So many different factors will affect choice of agency or referral to a particular agency, especially when there are a variety of problems, that it may be largely a matter of chance as to where a client begins, where he ends up and the extent to which total needs have been met (Collis, 1966, pp. 70–1).

The prevalence of unmet needs in high-need areas was brought sharply into focus by the experience of the detached family advice centres and resulted in demands for a wide range of services to the community. As we have shown in the descriptive sections of the report, these demands were met with varying degrees of success. The range of services offered by the family advice centres, either by providing them directly, or else by initiating and supporting them, can be given as follows:

1. Cultural, recreational and educational services for children, teenagers and adults of all ages.
2. Material assistance and supportive social work services for all members of the community in need of such services.

The common denominator of this range of services was that they were community-based and aimed at fostering community participation, and that they were *not* aimed at replacing existing services, but at supplementing them, or at providing services where the relevant agencies had failed to do so. In some cases the family advice centres attempted to induce the relevant agencies to meet their obligations to provide the needed services before or while the centres themselves became engaged in providing these services. It is our view that this attempt to induce the authorities to provide the needed services should *always* be the first step, and that whenever possible the community should be involved in such attempts. In other words, the family advice centres should assign priority to community action aimed at obtaining services either before making its own provisions, or else while immediate needs are met through activities initiated and organised by the centre's staff.

Among the services for children the setting up of arts and crafts centres and adventure playgrounds proved most rewarding and led to a wide range of creative endeavour. As a report on a series of American projects stated: 'Art as a way of reaching the young, and art as a way of mobilizing a community are not new, but are at least becoming more visible to people who never thought of art in this light' (Grant *et al.*, 1968, p. 2). The promising results of some of the initial attempts to use various art forms to provide learning experiences, cultural enrichment and community involvement in the 'G' and 'F' project centres showed the potentialities of this approach. The considerable degree of community involvement and the interest and support obtained by the 'F' project arts centre seems to have proved its value.

Pre-school play groups and nursery school facilities also proved to be very much needed and not sufficiently available. Our experience showed that the provision of these services must play an important part in the preventive work of the family advice centres. The case was stated clearly by M. L. Kellmer Pringle when she pointed out that the pre-school years are

of fundamental importance to all later development. Not only does the child have to learn more during the first few years of life than during any other comparable time span, but because this learning provides the basis for all later progress, much greater attention—in terms of time, money and other resources—must be given to this early period of growth. How well he will get on with authority figures and contemporaries; whether he will come to regard new problems as a challenge or a threat; how successful he will be scholastically; these are just a few examples of the many tasks of childhood, the mastery or failure of which depends to a very considerable extent on the opportunities the child had available in the most formative early years (Kellmer Pringle, ed, 1969, p. 113).

Joan Cooper (1965) tells us: 'Social workers should be more concerned with and demanding of an enrichment programme for pre-school children whose learning and emotional development is inhibited by the cultural, as well as the emotional, poverty of many of the homes where social problems are most acute' (p. 100).

Arts centres and adventure playgrounds have the added advantage that they lend themselves especially well to serving older children and adolescents in addition to pre-school children, and to providing rich opportunities for community involvement and the employment of indigenous workers and volunteers, as well as providing common grounds for practical co-operation with workers from other agencies and professions, such as statutory and voluntary agency staff and school teachers. In this context Dr Kellmer Pringle's observation is especially relevant that, while 'exploration of the physical world, space for vigorous physical activities and opportunities to mix with other children are part of play which is essential for emotional, social and physical growth', it is equally essential to provide 'continuous and reliable adult supervision'.

The adventure playground has become an accepted approach for meeting the needs of children for imaginative and creative play facilities.[1] The need for supervised playgrounds as part of the range of services for children provided by the detached centres became especially pronounced in the re-development areas where the destruction wrought by the bull-dozer and the demolition workers had become a source of fear and insecurity, as well as an opportunity to daring exploits for the children of the neighbourhood. The worried remarks of the Vicar of such an area serve well to illustrate this: He tells us: 'The young, so starved of space, now had space in abundance. But all it encouraged was the smashing of anything left to smash—with ammunition provided free. Soon there was not a street-lamp left whole in the area. It was the best school of vandalism I have ever seen' (Power, 1965, p. 38). Our own observations showed that, in order to compete successfully with the attractions and dangers of refuse strewn empty plots, demolition sites and aban-doned buildings, the family advice centres have to engage in three

[1] For detailed discussion see Benjamin (1961).

simultaneous activities, each of them with a clearly defined objective, but all of them closely co-ordinated. The first is the provision of a programme of activities of great variety and imagination, offering the children and teenagers of the area creative outlets, new and exciting experiences and adventures, and wide leeway simply to have fun. Secondly, there must be adequate and suitable provision of staff, consisting of the type of workers who are able to establish the kind of relationship of mutual acceptance and trust which youngsters need. Thirdly, the family advice centre must gain the support and the participation of the community in the attempt to provide a range of services which will reach even the most withdrawn, the most vulnerable and the most distrustful of the young-sters. The support of the community becomes a decisive factor when reaching the 'hard-to-reach' youngster involves tolerating behaviour and providing activities which may disturb neighbours, shock some of the parents and become objects of concern and controversy in the area.

The range of services for school age children and youngsters also may include youth club facilities geared to reaching those youngsters who find it difficult or impossible to accept the limits and conditions of the more conventional clubs. A permissive, one might say a daringly accepting, approach is needed. But the focus should not be solely upon reaching the aggressive acting-out delinquent. As an eminent psychiatrist pointed out: 'There are just as many solitary, shy, unhappy members of big families under persistent social stress who do not draw attention to themselves at home or in school' (Gibbens, 1966, p. 33). For the delinquent as well as for the withdrawn youngster, and for their families, the family advice centre's potentialities for an integrated availability of recreational programming, advice, guidance and assistance and community work can provide a very valuable service. This type of service is in line with Joan Cooper's (1969) description of the intermediate treatment services recommended by the 1969 Children and Young Persons Act as 'a more general contribution towards enriching the lives of vigorous, restless, physically healthy, but under-occupied adolescents who, in our present pattern of urbanised living, have too few outlets for their creative energies and too few opportunities to carry responsibility and practice adult roles'.

The Research and Development Committee of the Advisory Com-mittee on Child Care, in assessing the needs of children likely to be in-troduced to intermediate treatment, suggests a constructive approach of offering support to children who lack it at home. They suggest that many will benefit by being introduced to experiences and activities designed to stimulate new interests: 'indeed for some children the enrichment of interests may be all that is needed'. It is stressed, however, that these interests and activities should be related to resources available in the local community, in an attempt to obtain the 'responsible involvement of children in their community' (Powley, 1970).

The need to include detached youth work (or street club work) in the range of F.A.S. services became apparent in all four detached family advice centres. This specialised social group work approach was developed

in response to the growing realisation that there existed in the urban poverty areas a large segment of the youth population which could not be 'reached' by the conventional methods of group work in the settlement house, community centre or youth club settings. These youngsters, mainly lower class adolescents congregating in street corner gangs or groups, adhered to delinquent values and norms which they expressed by unlawful, destructive and self-destructive behaviour.

The street club worker was charged with contacting these groups in their own environment and establishing a relationship with them which would permit him to identify the structure and norms of the groups, gain insight into the sources of the problems confronting these youngsters, their mode of reacting and their motivations, and to diagnose their needs, frustrations and expectations. The worker uses the insights gained through his relationship to the group to enable the youngsters to face and cope with the realities of their situation. He attempts to strengthen the positive potential of the group, helps the youngsters to improve their relations to the community, finds alternative sources of satisfaction precluding delinquent behaviour, and helps them channel their energies into socially acceptable activities (Leissner, 1969a, p. 115).

Finally it should be pointed out that in those areas in which there are marked problems of immigrant adjustment and ethnic conflict, the detached family advice centre must be ready to provide services for the youngsters or immigrant groups, and that these services must be so designed as to further the goals of integration, as well as to afford opportunities for cultural self-expression and the strengthening of the youngsters' self-confidence in ways which enhance their pride in their own background and enable them to face their common problems realistically and with dignity.

The range of services a family advice centre provides for the adult population of the community may be regarded as the solid basis and the supportive framework for the services to the community's youth and children. Experience shows that the one cannot succeed without the other. These services include a great variety of community action, self-help, recreational and social service activities. The value of professional guidance and support for such neighbourhood organisations as tenants' associations, parents' associations, self-help committees, mothers' groups, playground, play group and youth club management committees has been sufficiently proved and needs no further discussion. We would point out, however, that more determined attempts should be made to involve the *men* of the community, not only in community action activities and self-help groups, but also in recreational and cultural programmes, through sports activities and social clubs. The initiative taken by several of the detached centres in organising jumble sales, clothing exchanges and regular sales of secondhand clothes, toys, furniture, etc., deserve special mention because we found that such activities combine practical material help with social activities and often serve as first steps in involving the community with the functions and goals of the family advice service.

The success of the 'F' project centre in employing indigenous workers as home helpers seemed very promising. The home help service comes under the jurisdiction of the local authority health department under Section 29 of the National Health Service Act. It has been observed that 'the service is a valuable instrument for preserving family unity in times of difficulty, but that personnel is often inadequate to meet need, and development and expansion are badly needed' (Packman, 1968, p. 76).[1] While we do not believe that the family advice centre should relieve the health department of this responsibility, the centres can make an important contribution to the efficiency and range of this service by helping to select the most suitable local people and by integrating the service of the home helpers with other helping functions and with the self-help activities of the community.

Services for elderly members of the community, including personal services, material assistance and recreational activities, either provided directly by the F.A.S. worker or by community home helpers, highlight the encompassing character of a children's department service which broadens the scope of preventive work to include *all* members of the community. The rationale for providing services for the elderly in the F.A.S. setting is twofold:

1. There is a significant number of old people who remain unreached by the services, either because the latter are too overburdened to make all-out efforts to detect need, or because some old people do not know where to obtain the needed help, or else because old people are reluctant to admit that they need help. The implications for the family advice centre in terms of detection of need, on-the-spot availability for immediate help in crises situations, and mobilising community resources

[1] See also *The Home Help Service in England and Wales*, H.M.S.O. 1969, which found that 'at least 20 per cent more visits would be required to meet the full needs of people currently receiving some help from the service', and that 'half the people over 65 years of age likely to need the service did not know they were eligible for it' (reported in *Child Care News*, no. 100, July 1970, p. 7).

are clear. Here too it must be emphasised that the family advice centre should in no way seek to replace the responsible statutory service, but co-operate with these and supplement their work where this seems necessary.[1]

2. The family advice centre can play a key role in raising community concern and stimulating community activities not only in order to provide help for the older people in the neighbourhood but, and this is perhaps most important, in order to involve the 'senior citizens' in the activities, concerns and the social life of the community.

Professor Kahn (1970) writes that 'a welcome development has been the growth of a neighbourhood legal services program under the anti-poverty effort, going well beyond the traditional legal aid; this is seen as yet another component of the total effort to assure access, open opportunity, end abuse, and eliminate a dual system of law and policy that is traceable to Elizabethan Poor Law' (p. 101).

Legal advice services in the form of neighbourhood legal advice centres can be provided in a variety of ways and under different auspices. The most obvious of these are legal advice centres offered by a group of lawyers who volunteer their services and use what premises they can find in the target area, lawyers employed by a voluntary agency under some contractual arrangement, and teams of lawyers financed by voluntary or central government funds. In all these cases the family advice centres may become instrumental in introducing legal advice services to the area, help the legal advice centre to establish itself in the community, as well as maintaining close co-operation between the family advice and the legal advice centre. This co-operation would mainly consist of mutual consultation about neighbourhood problems and of a mutual referral arrangement in which F.A.S. clients who need legal advice are introduced to the legal advice staff, while the latter are able to call in the F.A.S. worker or send a client to the centre when there is need for any form of social work support. This referral relationship will, of course, be more effective if the legal advice centre is located either in the same building, or else in close proximity to the family advice centre.

The possibility of incorporating legal advice into the statutory network by gaining for it local authority recognition and financial support should be regarded as the logical next step. The detached family advice centre setting would provide a suitable basis for neighbourhood legal service, mainly because it could provide a community-oriented frame of reference within which legal advice could be co-ordinated with the range

[1] Agate and Meacher (1969), provide a useful review of the needs of the elderly and the gaps in the existing services.

of other services to the area. Many lawyers and social workers have expressed the opinion that legal advice could never become incorporated in the statutory services because local authorities would never agree to facing the possibility that local people and ratepayers could be advised to take legal action against the very authorities which have sanctioned and are financing the easily accessible availability of legal advice. If this pessimistic view is proved to be true, this would show a rather shortsighted attitude. Shortsighted because it makes sense to regard the provision of 'no-strings-attached' legal advice by the local authority itself as a big step in the direction of strengthening the confidence of the population in the fairness and integrity of the authorities, a step which would contribute significantly to closing the 'us' and 'them' gap, the perpetuation of which is self-defeating to local government endeavour as it is harmful to the population. Furthermore, it can be predicted that a local authority which is seen to encourage people to regard the legal provisions and the processes of law as binding upon everyone alike, the providers as well as the recipients of the statutory services, would thereby gain the support of the people in maintaining high standards of service, and would raise the efficiency of its own complex system.

Supervision

It has been said that 'the purpose of supervision is to ensure for the client the help he has the right to expect from the agency' (Houwink, 1967, p. 110). It is equally important to point out that supervision is the means through which the agency conveys to the worker its readiness to back him and its confidence in him as a professional. Eileen Younghusband (1964) noted that 'a distinction is often made between supervision as an educational and as administrative process', and added, 'surely this is a false distinction' (p. 144). In the often far from ideal reality of daily practice, administrative demands and educational functions are, however, frequently clearly distinguished and sometimes conflicting aspects of a process which should aim at the support of the practitioner and of the integration of the practice within the overall approach of the agency.

In the F.A.S. setting, as in other specialised settings in a social work agency which provides a range of services, the supervisor combines a number of roles and functions:

1. The supervisor functions as an educator, imparting professional knowledge helping the worker to conceptualise his experience, to

gain perspective on various aspects and processes of the work and
to develop self awareness.[1]

2. The supervisor provides support for the worker, helping him to
    cope with frustration and failure and, when necessary, giving
    the worker confidence in his own judgment and skills.

3. The supervisor acts as a resource person to whom the worker
    can turn when difficulties are encountered in making certain contacts
    or in obtaining needed equipment, funds, facilities, etc.

4. The supervisor functions as liaison between the agency and the
    worker, interpreting agency policies to the worker, stating the
    need for modification or change of agency policy when these
    seem needlessly cumbersome or incompatible with the requirements
    of the functions and goals of the special setting. In this role the
    supervisor mediates between the worker and the administration
    when established administrative procedures clash with the worker's
    'ways of doing things'.

5. The supervisor holds the worker accountable for the latter's use of
    his time and professional ability.

In all these five areas the supervision processes of the family advice
centres, especially the detached ones, encountered certain problems
and faced a number of challenges which bear further analysis. The
author of a report on a two-year training programme in supervision
for youth workers wrote:

While learning from and about the situation, the worker is looking outside himself,
but is also becoming increasingly aware of his own behaviour, feelings and values.
Perhaps an important aspect of supervision is that it should help such learning
to be an interesting process, rather than a deflating, unhappy one. Inevitably,
increased awareness brings discomfort or depression at times, and workers would
confirm this. But if learning from the situation is geared to building on to what a
worker knows and is aware of, then the awareness of new factors to be recognised
and understood can be balanced with recognition of strength, understanding
lack of skill can be seen in terms of acquiring that skill (Tash, 1967, p. 79).

This author points at the essential integration of the educational and the
supportive functions in supervision. We would go further and say that, in
structuring the relationship between supervisor and worker in a new
setting, like that of the family advice service, both must be ready to learn
from each other and to be mutually supportive. This becomes specially
important in the detached settings, when neither supervisor nor worker
have experience in group and community work, or else when the worker

[1] 'Self awareness grows from within and may be described as a process that is midway
between knowing and feeling. It is possible for a person to be aware of something without
being able to describe it. Awareness often precedes conceptualization. It is a close cousin
to intuition, a quality that cannot be translated or brought into existence through
didactic methods' (Grossbard, 1954, p. 15).

brings into the situation knowledge and experience in these social work methods, while the supervisor does not. We saw that in those centres in which a mutually supportive, co-operative relationship between worker and supervisor developed, this led to a constructive, imaginative and rewarding experience for both. Where either the supervisor or the worker or both were not able to relate to each other in this manner, the experience was at times a rather painful and futile one. As could be expected, the 'negative' relationship between supervisor and worker tended to develop most often in those detached centres in which the worker had the kind of specialised experience which the supervisor lacked.

At least as important in its effect upon the worker–supervisor relationship is the latter's liaison role. Especially in the detached centres, the F.A.S. worker needs the supervisor's help in interpreting the special requirements of the detached, community-oriented or community-based setting to the agency. An Australian report on detached youth work pointed out that:

The concept of 'Detached Worker' envisages a worker detached from the authoritarian image of the agency that employs him, or in some cases detached from the agency structure altogether. There appear to be two motives behind this idea of detachment—one is to break down the image the client usually has of a social worker in an authoritarian setting. . . . The other motive is that the worker should be given the maximum freedom and autonomy possible, and thus he needs to be detached from the red tape and traditional procedures often to be found in an established agency—particularly in a long established one (Killington, 1964, p. 1).

Our observations showed that the detached family advice centre *can* and *should* be seen as an integral part of the parent agency, and that this is to the benefit of the agency as well as the family advice service and its clients. This presupposes, however, that the agency makes the necessary adjustments to the special requirements of detached work. The supervisor has a key role in his liaison function in furthering these adjustments. The task cannot be added to the many other burdens carried by the detached worker. The degree to which the agency shows understanding and flexibility in meeting these special requirements has a decisive impact upon the worker–supervisor relationship. When a supervisor is forced to say again and again that he or she agrees with the worker that one or the other of the established agency procedures do not apply to the special situation of the detached family advice centre, but that it has proved impossible to convince the chief officer or the agency administration of this, the worker's reaction is likely to be: What does the supervisor do to further my work that I could not do just as well myself? Let us take a brief look at the effects of such a situation.

In one of the community-based centres the supervisor had to confront the F.A.S. worker with administrative decisions and directives which the worker regarded as irrelevant and obstructive. This happened, for instance, when the department insisted that the F.A.S. worker follow the same routine procedures in accounting for her working time as other child care officers, although the F.A.S. worker's consistent and conscientious recording provided a full account of the use of her time. It happened when the supervisor was instructed to make a periodic check of the worker's diary because the agency administration felt that there was cause to tighten accountability procedures for all staff. The F.A.S. worker, an experienced worker with many years of professional employment, regarded this as an aspersion upon her trustworthiness and reliability. Facing a work situation in which her self-confidence and her professional status were constantly put to the test, the worker was understandably upset and, rightly or wrongly, felt that her supervisor was expressing lack of confidence in her.

A certain amount of friction also resulted from the policy decision that all letters, proposals, requests, etc. drawn up by a child care officer must go through channels and be signed by the chief officer. This caused delays which caused difficulties for the worker in her helping relationships to a group of clients who were all too prone to regard delays as a method used by 'them' to shelve a request until the client gave up pursuing the matter. Furthermore, while the F.A.S. worker did not at any time disguise her professional identity as a social worker employed by the children's department, the community-based setting demanded a considerable degree of self-assertion in the role of the F.A.S. worker *vis-à-vis* clients and officials from other agencies. This was not furthered by conducting all written communication under the children's officer's signature.

The matter was discussed at some length and the following decision was reached:

1. Any written statement or letter concerning specific needs or issues in the client community sent by the F.A.S. worker to one of the statutory services should be addressed to the person representing that service on the consultative committee. The document should be submitted to the project supervisor before posting. After being authorised by the project supervisor and (if the latter decides this is necessary) by the children's officer, the document may go out signed by the family advice service worker.
2. Correspondence between the F.A.S. worker and colleagues from other statutory or voluntary services regarding the family advice centre's clients goes out under the signature of the F.A.S. worker.

3. Any statements, memoranda, petitions, etc. drawn up by the tenants' association or any other group representing all or part of the community served by the centre should be signed by the relevant members of the community or their chosen representatives. The F.A.S. worker, even if the said document has been drawn up with her help, will not sign such a document.

It was a compromise solution in which points 2 and 3 were quite acceptable, while the first provision seemed somewhat cumbersome and, in its wording, imbued the supervisor with an authoritative function which was bound to lead to a widening of the distance between supervisor and worker.

In situations of this kind there is a tendency to let accountability overshadow or displace the supervisor's roles of educator and his supportive and liaison functions. It is, however, essential that accountability be regarded as a useful structural tool, a technique which helps to balance the worker's use of time and skills, which is applied by mutual agreement, and which worker as well as supervisor regard as helpful to both of them. A situation in which, consciously or not, accountability is regarded as the *real* aim of all other aspects of the supervisory relationship will inevitably become detrimental to an effective service and should be avoided. To mention only one of the ways in which this negative situation can be avoided: the work load, the informality and fluidity of F.A.S. work, results in the F.A.S. worker having to assume responsibilities and tasks which may be beyond his or her capacity or in conflict with the accepted role and functions. With regard to these matters accountability should serve as a means of protection for the worker and be applied by the supervisor to guard the worker against all forms of exploitation, whether by clients, other agencies or the parent agency.

It has been said that: 'The degree to which the administrator, supervisor and practitioner are joined with the single purpose of creating the best possible service to clients is the degree to which the vitality and dynamic quality of an agency will exist' (National Association of Social Workers, New York, 1962, p. 3). Having pointed out some of the problems of supervision in the F.A.S. setting, let us add that our observations showed that this unity of purpose was indeed achieved in many instances, and that the preconditions for this achievement exist, or can be created without too much difficulty in the children's departments.

In many departments makeshift arrangements will continue for some time and senior officers responsible for the supervision of children's department sectors or areas will continue to add the supervision of family advice centres to their many other responsibilities. This may prove adequate for those F.A.S. settings which function as sub-settings of the parent agencies. It cannot be regarded as a satisfactory permanent arrangement for the detached family advice centres. We tend to the view that in those children's departments (and eventually in the unified social service departments) which are operating more than one family advice centre, an *F.A.S. sector* be set up within the department. This sector could consist of several detached community-based centres in high-need areas, or else of a combination of different settings. A children's department (or a social service department) may, for instance, operate an F.A.S. unit in one or several of its area offices, finance and supervise a family advice service in a voluntary agency in an area in which no other advice services are available, operate a community-oriented family advice centre to serve an area of 'mixed' population and housing and a community-based centre in a council housing estate or a redevelopment area. In one London borough, for example, there are now five family advice centres of different types in operation or in the planning stage. All these family advice centres would be regarded as a sector of the department and would be supervised by a senior F.A.S. worker with the appropriate experience and training. One children's department has already made this arrangement.

As so often in the past, agencies which apply new methods to meet existing needs more effectively will have to be ready to experiment with new adaptations in many areas of their service, including supervision. The supervision of an F.A.S. sector consisting of several family advice centres, or even of one detached family advice centre, will necessitate the devising of supervisory procedures which meet the needs of a range of different types of personnel, including F.A.S. youth, ancillary and indigenous workers, arts centre and play group leaders and volunteers. In order to meet the requirements of this situation, supervision will have to take place on two levels, namely in the sector and in each individual centre. This means that the F.A.S. worker who leads a team will himself assume supervisory functions. Based upon our observations we envisage the supervisory structure as follows:

1. The senior F.A.S. worker who supervises the sector meets with *each individual F.A.S. worker* once a month, and is available for emergency meetings to discuss urgent matters if the need arises.

2. The supervisor meets with *all* members of his team once a month for a group discussion.

3. Each F.A.S. worker meets with every individual member of his team once a month, and is available for emergency meetings to discuss urgent matters.

4. Each F.A.S. worker meets with *all* members of his team once a month for a group discussion.

It would be emphasised that the group meetings should include indigenous workers and volunteers, and that in individual as well as in group meetings, special care must be taken to meet the needs of these untrained workers.

This type of structured supervision will have to rely to a great degree on group supervision and some further discussion of this method of supervision is, therefore, in order. Group supervision, like individual supervision, focuses on the client, the work process and the needs of the worker. The supervisor carries out the same functions as in individual supervision.

[Group supervision] 'is not a seminar in which the leader's primary responsibility is to the whole group and where the exclusive aim is to convey knowledge. Nor is it peer supervision in which each member of the group makes a contribution, but no one helps the worker to integrate the various contributions'. Leadership is vested in the supervisor who provides guidance and direction. 'The central concern of the group is client need—it does not primarily focus on the group process [within the staff group]; it is not group therapy. The sessions are focused, and related to the worker and his helping role.' However, the supervisor must know the weaknesses and strengths of the individual workers and be aware of their patterns of interaction, and alert to the dangers which may arise for the individual worker through undue exposure to destructive, uncontrolled criticism. Workers are called upon to present their work and formulate specific problems clearly for their colleagues and for the supervisor. 'Since immediacy of response is an essential quality in the direct treatment process, the worker—in group supervision—develops flexibility and the ability to examine and test his ideas quickly when exposed to a variety of approaches and concepts. The worker is exposed to many sources of knowledge; he sorts out what is usable and integrates it for himself. This affords additional help in learning to sift ideas. Knowing the work of one's colleagues produces mutual respect and enables the worker to see the many different ways in which a client can be perceived and helped.' The supervisor determines the emphasis of discussion, synthesises, evaluates and communicates the professional approach to problem-solving. The supervisor is less protected in his authority. He must be flexible in using the roles of teacher and participant (Leissner, 1969a, p. 247; quotes from Judd *et al.*, 1962).

A final word before we leave the subject:

Throughout the supervision process, the supervisor must be aware of the ever-present temptation to take over and do the worker's job himself, or to interfere unnecessarily. The supervisor's support must at all times be given on the basis of respect for the worker's abilities and potentialities, and must neither deprive the worker of his independence, nor stunt his initiative. The worker should neither be over-protected by the supervisor and sheltered from the dangers of his profession, nor should he be exposed to the 'sink or swim' approach and made to feel inferior when he has to be saved from drowning. We might well heed the dictum of the great Russian educator Makarenko: 'The utmost possible demands on a person, but at the same time the utmost possible respect for him' (Leissner, 1969a, p. 259).

Consultation

Consultation should be regarded as important an aspect of the professional structure of the family advice service as supervision. It must, however, be stressed that consultation is a complement to supervision, *not* an alternative, or a replacement.

Joan Cooper (1965) wrote: 'It is now being recognised that organisational patterns must allow for social workers to have regular consultation with specialists in other related fields and within their own field'; and she concludes: 'The time has come for greater administrative recognition of the social worker's need for consultation' (p. 101). One of the children's departments participating in the study met this need by setting up a consultative committee which met with the F.A.S. worker and her supervisor at first every month, and then every two months. The committee was chaired by the children's officer and consisted of senior officers of the health, housing and welfare departments, and a representative of the borough's Council of Social Service. The department of education was not represented, but the area youth officer attended several meetings in order to participate in discussions of the need for a detached youth worker. One of the most interesting developments was the attendance of the chairman of the tenants' association of the community served by the family advice centre on several occasions.

The committee, while set up with the stated purpose of providing a forum for exchanges of information, discussion and consultation for the family advice centre, also served to give the represented agencies a stake in the family advice centre, to enable them to gain understanding of the F.A.S. approach and, last but not least, to guard the interests of their own services. It became apparent that the effectiveness of the committee depended to some degree upon the opportunities it afforded the F.A.S. worker and social work practitioners and officials of the participating agencies.

In evaluating the work of the consultative committee it can be said that there were many instances in which the worker benefited from factual information, as well as from professional advice provided by the members of the group. The pronounced tendency of some of the members to guard the interests of their own agencies at times inhibited frank discussion and sometimes made the F.A.S. worker unduly defensive.

Some modifications of policy by the participating agencies were discernible, but it seemed more likely that these were brought about through accommodation between the F.A.S. worker and field level practitioners and through community pressure, than through the intervention of members of the consultative committee. For example, the representative of the welfare department stated initially that her agency would object to any services to old people in the target community being provided by the centre. Although it was explained that a community-based family advice centre could neither turn away an elderly person who asked for advice, nor simply pass on requests for emergency help for an elderly person to the welfare department, the F.A.S. worker was instructed to do just that. In practice, however, field level and senior staff of the welfare department soon agreed that the family advice centre's on-the-spot availability for help to old people in the community was a welcome supplement of their own overburdened services. Reasonably good co-operation between the centre and the welfare department soon was established. In the case of the housing department, the F.A.S. worker stated the case for better communication and more readiness to provide information on policies and procedures on behalf of her clients. However, when the housing department began to introduce procedures which would enable the community to obtain at least some factual information about the department's plans and policies, this came about largely through community pressure organised with the support and guidance of the F.A.S. worker, and ensuing newspaper publicity played no small role.

While the consultative committee was not set up specifically to further the co-ordination of services in the area, it could be assumed that an interdisciplinary, interagency group of this type would indeed bring about better co-ordination. In some instances such indirect effects became apparent. That the potentialities of the consultative committee for what we might call 'co-ordinated thinking' for the benefit of all the services was not fully realised was illustrated by a development which took place towards the end of the study period. Despite the fact that the family advice centre had done pioneering work and gained much valuable experience over a period of two years, the Council of Social Service Representative on the committee initiated the setting up of a neighbourhood advice and community work centre in a sector of the borough without any consultation with the F.A.S. worker, thereby depriving her agency and its potential clients of the professional experience and the fund of knowledge which had become available.

Despite its many inadequacies the consultative committee made some useful contributions to the family advice centre and provided us with valuable learning experience. Our conclusion is that 'high level' consultative committees of this kind should become part of the F.A.S. structure in all departments which operate family advice centres. Like the consultative committee described here, such groups should consist of senior members of the statutory agencies, including the education department, which was not represented in the above described case. Our observations also indicate the importance of adding an official of the Department of Health and Social Security. Representatives of the relevant voluntary agencies should be asked to join the committee, as well as local headmasters and general practitioners; and, especially where a legal advice centre has been set up as part of, or in conjunction with the family advice centre, a solicitor could make a valuable contribution. Great emphasis should be given to ensuring the participation of community representatives, such as chairmen of tenants' associations, parents' groups, youth services management committees etc. In order to prevent the committee from becoming too unwieldy there could be a core group of permanent members, while other relevant people could be invited from time to time to discuss specific issues, so that the committee might benefit from their special knowledge and expertise. It is suggested that at least two community representatives should be appointed permanent members of the consultative committee. In order to help the consultative committee to achieve unity of purpose, establish relations of mutual confidence between its members, and to learn to regard their work as an effective and valid service to the client population, the chairman of the committee, the F.A.S. supervisor and the F.A.S. worker must combine their efforts to help the members of the committee to perceive the process of consultation as a mutually beneficial one in the perspective of the services to the people of the borough, as well as to make the meetings relevant, interesting and challenging.

The senior level consultative committee will, in all cases, have to be supplemented by the informal field level consultation between the F.A.S. staff and the social work practitioners, officials and other relevant persons. This kind of consultation is, in fact, the essential basis for the F.A.S. worker's liaison/mediation function. A link between the two levels of consultation could be maintained by inviting field level practitioners to consultative committee meetings to discuss specific relevant issues. We believe that this would be of great value in solving practical and policy problems, in communicating the views of field workers in direct contact with the family advice centres to the representatives of their own and other agencies, and in furthering the identification of needs and the co-ordination of services.

In an area in which the family advice service has taken its own specific place in the social service provisions and functions as the community work branch of the statutory services, structured and consistent consultation will, in our view, not only provide the necessary support for the F.A.S. staff, but will be of considerable benefit to all the services of the area.

Confidentiality

A recent investigation of the relations between child care officers and the police juvenile bureau reported the following finding with regard to confidentiality: 'This is an area where there appeared to be a great deal of confusion in the minds of child care officers, and some conflict between their views and those of their department' (Bilton, 1970, p. 7). There is reason to believe that this confusion is prevalent among the personnel of all the social services. Social workers, all of whom have had to face the issue from time to time, are likely to look with envy at professions, such as medicine, law or the clergy, whose members and clients enjoy the protection of a precisely worded code which lays down their rules of confidentiality for all to see. The British Association of Social Workers, only recently founded, has no doubt already put the issue of confidentiality on its list of priorities. Meanwhile the practitioner in the field, the supervisor and the chief officer, all have to continue to face the problems and conflicts posed by this issue.

The goals and functions of the family advice service make confidentiality imperative. The family advice centre cannot hope to become truly accessible unless it can establish relationships of mutual trust with its clients, and such a relationship must be based upon the assurance of confidentiality. The image of the family advice centre as a no-strings-attached service, an open door to which people can bring their problems at the earliest possible moment, depends to a large degree upon the centre's ability to demonstrate that a person's wishes with regard to the confidentiality of what he discloses will be respected. The detached worker who goes out into a community beset by problems and tensions will find full acceptance and gain real insight into causes, needs and attitudes only if the people of the community become convinced that he is somebody one can tell things to without fear of betrayal.

All this seems simple enough. After all social workers *are* taught the basic principles of confidentiality. However, they often take it for granted that confidentiality means that one doesn't tell Mrs X's neighbour about Mrs Y's problems. The trouble is that people, especially the people the family advice service seeks to 'reach', find it often even more threatening when they learn that social worker A of the children's department has regarded it as routine procedure to discuss Mrs X's problems with social worker B of the housing department whom she regards as a colleague, someone who is equally committed to helping Mrs X, and who has a right to know 'all the facts of the case'. Things become even more difficult when the matter which Mrs X has confided to the social worker A has to do with her anxiety about having rented a room of her council flat, and social worker B may be obliged to report this infringement of the rules to her agency. Whatever else happens, one may assume that Mrs X will think twice before ever telling social worker A anything again.

Our experience has shown that F.A.S. workers are well able to handle situations of this kind. The procedure is and should be a straightforward one: the client's wish must be respected in every case. If there is no urgency to the matter, the worker will regard it as part of the guidance function to 'work through' with the client the need to share certain information with another social worker or official or, in some cases, another member of the client's family. If the matter is urgent, or the client insists on his right to impose confidentiality, even though it is clear that his problem cannot be solved without the sharing of information with the relevant people, then the worker may have to state firmly and clearly that he cannot provide the help the client needs under the conditions imposed by the latter. Our observations showed that this kind of impasse rarely arises, least of all if the worker has been able to establish a positive, mutual accepting relationship with the client, or if the client is a member of a community which has learned to trust the worker. We would add that the rule of confidentiality applies to children and teenagers as well as to adults. One cannot gain the trust of children and earn the right to help them without respecting them as persons.

The question will, of course, be asked: but what of the case in which a client reveals criminal behaviour to the worker, or the situation in which the worker becomes convinced that a life may be in danger? Our answer would be that criminal behaviour should *not* be disclosed by the F.A.S. worker. There are organisations and institutions, foremost among them the police, whose function is to detect crime and bring the offender to justice. The social worker should do everything possible to prevent crime, and to help the offender face the consequences of his act to himself, his family and the community. The social worker will certainly refuse to help an offender to profit from his offence or to escape the consequences of his action. But a worker who has been told of an offence by a client who has come to the centre to be helped must in no circumstances betray a confidence. A society which gives the social worker the mandate to help people in need must be ready to extend to him the privilege of confidentiality, the same privilege extended to the priest who hears confession.[1] The situation is very different when not property or propriety, but human life is in danger. In such, fortunately rare, cases, the worker (if time permits in consultation with the supervisor) will take all necessary steps to safeguard life and this must, of course, take precedence over all other considerations.

It has been argued that clients should be able to trust the worker's judgment with regard to the use made of information they disclose, and that this general trust makes strict rules of confidentiality unnecessary. A relationship of mutual trust can indeed, in at least some instances, permit the worker to use his own judgment without the need to obtain the client's agreement in each and every case. A relationship of mutual trust may be interpreted by client and worker as an agreement between them that the worker will take all necessary steps to obtain effective help for the client and will not do anything to harm the client's interests. However, a relationship requires time to grow and become clearly defined. Every client–worker relationship has to start with the first meeting, the first request for help, the first exchange of information. We hold that this first contact must be based on a clearly defined code of conduct and procedure with regard to confidentiality.

[1] The social worker's 'privilege' as regards confidentiality is still far from established in Britain. There is *no* common law or statutory privilege, but some safeguards are provided through the privilege of confidentiality stipulated for information given by a client to his social worker 'without prejudice', although this is usually interpreted to pertain mainly to matrimonial disputes. It is interesting to note that a lecturer in law who discusses the issues involved asserts that the public interest as represented by law 'is more important than any feeling of security in the client or feeling of status or pride in the social worker'. Nevertheless the author concludes that: 'The court is aware of the possible conflict of loyalties assailing the social worker and would compel him to give evidence against his conscience only in very extreme cases indeed. Such a situation is in fact practically unknown' (Samuels, 1968, pp. 48–9).

The situation in the United States differs from state to state. Most progress has been made in the State of New York where the legislature 'passed a law protecting communications between the client and the social worker from forcible disclosure in a legal proceeding' (Arnold, 1970, p. 61). In fact, the 1965 'Privileged communications', Section 7710, Article 154 of the State Law rules that: 'A person duly registered as a certified social worker under the provisions of this article shall not be required to disclose communications made by his client to him, or his advice given thereon, in the course of his professional employment, nor shall any clerk, stenographer or other person working for the same employer as the certified social worker be allowed to discuss any such communication or advice thereon.' But exceptions are made for cases in which the client authorises the social worker to disclose information to the court. The social worker is *not* required to withhold information regarding criminal behaviour but the implication seems to be that he is *not obliged* to disclose such information. However, in cases of children under the age of sixteen having become subject of a crime, the social worker is *obliged* to testify fully during the investigation and/or court proceedings (Leeves, 1968, p. 372).

Detached F.A.S. work, especially in community-based settings, poses its own particular problems with regard to confidentiality. Our observations showed that it is sometimes very difficult to keep confidential matters from spreading. There is a certain amount of gossip in every community. Gossip increases with the degree of physical proximity in which people live, and becomes more destructive when a community is beset by conflicts and tensions. The informality of the client–worker relationship makes it more likely for conversations between client and worker to be overheard: walls are thin, doors are left open, a neighbour walks in at the wrong moment. We have known of cases in which a harassed woman broke down and confided a 'shameful' secret to her neighbour, then told the F.A.S. worker about it, saying: 'You've got to swear you won't tell anybody.' The neighbour tells a friend who tells the client and a week later the latter accuses the worker of having betrayed her confidence because: 'How else would Mrs Z know about that.' We have also seen a client shout her problems across the courtyard and then convince herself that 'everyone knows her business' because the F.A.S. worker told everyone. There have also, admittedly, been cases in which the F.A.S. worker 'let something slip' in a casual conversation when he or she should have known better. It should, however, be remembered that gossip is a reality of life in the community and, like other aspects of daily living, is accepted as such, sometimes causing frustration and anger, but also adding a little spice to a rather dull existence. The experience of the community-based family advice centres showed that accidental indiscretions sometimes caused momentary outbursts of anger, but rarely affected the client–worker relationship or distorted the image of the centre in the eyes of the community. Infringements of confidentiality involving social workers and officials of other agencies often have more lasting detrimental effects, sometimes resulting in reactions such as: 'We thought you were on our side, but you go snitching on us to "them".'

The presence of indigenous workers and community volunteers on the F.A.S. team may pose problems of confidentiality. Supervision and guidance by the F.A.S. worker as the leader of the team should be geared to guard against this. On the whole there were no significant difficulties in this area. It is interesting to note that a Dutch experiment in community-based social work reached the same conclusions: 'The district team also rely heavily on voluntary workers from the estate to assist with individual problems and do not see this as raising problems of confidentiality' (Rae-Price, 1968b, p. 1804).

One of the most frequent sources of confidentiality problems arises in the relations of the F.A.S. worker with colleagues from her own and from other agencies. Partly this is so because the lack of a unified code of conduct on confidentiality leads to a situation in which different social workers hold widely different and sometimes incompatible views on the matter of confidentiality. Social workers and officials also differ in their views of the F.A.S. worker's role. In one case, for instance, a social worker interpreted confidentiality as a device to keep the clients from finding out what the professionals were doing. Social workers and officials also sometimes take it for granted that the F.A.S. worker is an ally of authority whose primary obligation is to help the authorities to carry out their established policies, they may hint darkly at 'over-identification' when the F.A.S. worker seems to take the side of her clients and defends their right to withhold information from an official under certain circumstances. These difficulties may have very significant repercussions for the F.A.S. worker's functions as liaison person and mediator, thereby directly affecting the efficiency of the family advice centre's services. Anthony Forder (1966) rightly points out that some social workers 'take an extreme view about the binding nature of confidentiality', and adds that 'those who do can be very difficult to work with, and their attitude sometimes produces resentment among colleagues because they accept information given to them but give nothing in return' (p. 127). Clearly defined rules of confidentiality binding for all social workers would serve to alleviate this situation. Meanwhile there is need for flexibility and tact in handling the confidentiality issues with colleagues, while there must be constant awareness of the obligations to the client.

One established tool of co-ordination and co-operation, the case conference, poses some problems here. An American writer observed that:

Inter-departmental case committees and co-ordinating committees, although confidential in themselves, normally disseminate a considerable amount of confidential information without seeking the client's consent. The crucial problem seems to be whether the social worker has any mandate to agree to unconditional confidentiality or to disclose confidential information without permission even if it is in the client's best interests. It is necessary to consider the conditions under which the information was obtained. Apparently some workers inform clients that discussions are private and confidential but one must ask whether they are entitled to do so (Leeves, 1968, p. 371).

Surely the case conference or co-ordinating committee has the primary function of ensuring better services to the client and must, therefore, assign priority to the client's feelings and wishes. The social worker may have to make some considerable effort to convey to the client the beneficial role of the case conference in the helping process, and the necessity of sharing information about the client's needs and problems with colleagues. Nevertheless, the client's decision must be respected. Not to do so is a negation of a basic tenet of human dignity which would not be tolerated in any other professional relationship, whether the subject is a gall bladder operation discussed between doctor and patient, a case of litigation involving lawyer and defendant or, for that matter, the choice of material for a suit by a tailor and his customer. It should be clearly established in F.A.S., as in any other social work practice, that the consumer of social services has the same right to accept or reject a service as any other consumer. The consequences of a rejection should be carefully explained, and the social worker may have to point out that he cannot provide the kind of service the client requests, either because it is not compatible with professional standards, or else because it is not available. The client should certainly have the right to object to having his problems discussed in a case conference, whether the members of the case committee agree with his decision or not.

We might add that one way of engendering better understanding and of obtaining the co-operation of clients is to invite them to attend case conferences themselves. This has been done in some instances and, we believe, has had some beneficial effects. It may be advisable to make client participation a condition of every interdepartmental meeting which is convened to discuss a client's case for the first time, in effect giving the client an opportunity to meet the people who wish to share and discuss the information about his case, and allowing the client to express his opinions and make his own decision.

Supervision may pose additional problems. High standards of relationship and structure of supervision are essential, but where such high standards existed we found that there was no difficulty in explaining to the client that the supervisor should be regarded as a sort of 'silent but essential partner' in the client–worker relationship, a partner bound by the same rules of confidentiality and the same purpose of providing an effective service to the client.

Finally, we turn to recording. Obviously conscientious recording is an indispensable part of consistent, efficient service to the client, an essential basis for discussion and sharing of thoughts and opinions between worker and supervisor and, last but not least, an important source of information and 'household statistics' for evaluation of the past and planning for the future. Consistent and detailed recording is especially important in F.A.S. settings which combine a considerable number of different functions, a wide range of specialised services and a team of several different types of professional, indigenous and volunteer workers. Here recording becomes an essential aid to continuity and co-ordination of services. Quite frequently F.A.S. records will contain confidential material which is intended for the eyes of the F.A.S. worker and the supervisor only. Experience shows that it happens all too often that such records are accidentally exposed to the eyes of others, sometimes with very unpleasant results. This kind of accidental exposure may occur through a break-in at a detached centre when a few youngsters scatter the papers they find in a filing cabinet; in the offices of the children's department when a typist comes across some very intimate details about the affairs of someone she happens to know; or when a visiting official happens to glance at an open folder left on a desk and reads his name, or the name of his agency in a highly controversial context. Whether this occurs accidentally, through neglect or by design, the disclosure of recorded communications by, or information about a client can rightly be regarded by the latter as a breach of confidence. The most basic requirement is, of course, great care in the storing of records where they are safe from accidental exposure, illicit snoopers or delinquent tres-passers. Furthermore, we would suggest that only the essential number of copies of records be kept and that, as far as possible, all typing should be done by a permanent clerical assistant assigned to F.A.S. work and ade-quately 'vetted'. In those cases in which the worker becomes convinced that some specific information may become highly damaging or embar-rassing to a client, it may be best *not* to record these items at all, communi-cating them verbally to the supervisor, or else destroy the record as soon as its immediate usefulness has ended. This becomes specially important in cases where there is reason to assume that the record will at some time come under the scrutiny of other agencies. It seems that an apt reaction to this problem is given in the conclusion drawn in a searching analysis of confidentiality by a West German author: 'The social worker has . . . the initial duty to consider what to entrust to the files, in view of the fact that these may eventually have to be submitted to another agency. The social worker should, therefore, not enter everything in the files without prior examination' (Niclas, 1968, p. 98).

Generic approach and specialisation in the family advice service

The experience of the family advice centres, especially in the community-oriented and community-based settings, drew our attention to the relevance of the ongoing 'generic-specific' discussion. Broadly speaking, this discussion is concerned with the relations between an all-encom-passing 'generalised' social work role and the role of the social work 'specialist' (see, for instance, Stevenson, 1968). The important issues involved, and the farreaching implications for the profession, are often blurred because the problems are not formulated with sufficient precision. An example is the comparison between the generic social worker and the general practitioner which tends to ignore the fact that the latter's approach is 'generalised' only up to the point where the services of a specialist become necessary.

The case for the generic social worker can be stated in two ways, both equally important, but each with very different implications. The first of these is an argument for a *unified profession* whose members are *social workers* rather than child care, probation and welfare officers, medical, psychiatric, child guidance practitioners etc. In other words, it is argued that the social worker should be defined by his profession, rather than by his setting or employing agency, in the same way as a doctor of medicine is defined as a member of the medical profession, whether he is a general practitioner, works in a pediatric clinic, the surgery department of a hospital, or a cancer research institute. The second argument is for a *'truly generic' social worker* whose training and vocational commitment enable him to deal effectively with *any* type of social problem, be that a child-rearing or a marital problem, group delinquency, emotional stress, material deprivation or community conflict, to name only a few in a wide range of problem categories which are the concern of the social worker. This generic social worker must be equally adept at applying methods and skills of case work, group work and community work, to say the least.

Social work in this country is now beginning to take the first faltering steps towards professional unification. This means that social work is beginning to seek its identity as a profession, rather than remaining content with the present state of fragmentation and the confusing array of vaguely defined functions and roles which certain of our clients include in the laconic term 'the welfare'. The formation of a national professional association which seeks to establish one clearly defined frame of reference for social workers of all settings and specialisations, coinciding with the reorganisation of the social services in accordance with the recommendation of the Seebohm Report, has started a process which, we believe, will gain its own momentum and will prove to be irreversible. However, we are equally certain that the generic conception of social work as a unified profession, which will eventually emerge, will continue to accept and to further develop the processes of professional specialisation which the complexity of modern society demands.

The image of a generic social worker who combines all skills, applies all methods and is able to meet all needs is about as realistic as a general practitioner who is an expert on tropical diseases, removes tonsils, performs organ transplants, is a trained chiropodist and pediatrician, a skilled brain surgeon and engages in research in psychosomatic pathology besides running his general practice surgery. The unifying basis for the social work profession must be provided by a basic range of generic training requirements which are obligatory for all social workers, and in which their subsequent specialisation is founded, as well as a code of conduct and professional procedure which is binding on all members of the profession, regardless of their settings, their employing agencies or specific tasks. In accordance with this thesis, the F.A.S. worker should be regarded as a specialist who develops expertise in the methods and skills of family advice service work on a solid basis of generic social work training and a clear definition of his identity as a member of the social work profession. At present this worker carries out his specialised tasks as a staff member of the children's department. As more and more local authorities reorganise to form unified social service departments, the F.A.S. worker will take his place in the team work approach of the new departments, making his own specific contribution. As Kahn (1970) observed, different 'professional and organisational perspectives do affect the ways in which a problem is perceived and structured, the values that are held supreme, the priorities given to components of and the sequences in a solution to a family's difficulties, the "costs" to be tolerated for given outcomes or benefits' (p. 99). It is the F.A.S. worker's specific task to provide a range of services which ensures as far as possible that the people who are most in need of help in many areas of their lives do not become the foremost victims of these differences. This task is one of specialisation in such functions as liaison/mediation, co-ordination and community work, as well as advice, guidance and assistance. As a referral agent, the F.A.S. worker helps to make the services of other specialised professionals and agencies available to the client. As the leader and co-ordinator of a community oriented or community based team, he provides a range of specialised services to the community. As a community worker he enables the client community to participate creatively and, eventually, autonomously, in the processes and services aimed at creating better living conditions.

Professor Kahn (1970) pointed out that every professional and every specialist within a profession has to deal with 'organisational factors and bureaucratic realities [which] may supersede professional ethics' (p. 99). No social worker can be expected to deal with these factors without the backing of a strong, determined professional organisation which guards the interests of the worker and the profession and is ready to back the worker in situations of conflict. The F.A.S. worker's specific goals and functions, especially in the detached settings, will most likely involve him in situations in which he must take the side of his clients *vis-à-vis* colleagues and officials of other services, local authority policies and practice, or with regard to the policies and practice of his own agency. In order to carry out his tasks the F.A.S. worker who seeks to reach the 'hard-to-reach' and to serve a 'high-need' community will inevitably have to adopt the specialised roles which our American colleagues describe as those of the 'advocate' or the 'social broker'.[1] It is therefore essential that the social work profession, i.e. the professional association, should take a close look at these important new social work tasks in order to confirm their professional validity, and that the schools of social work be ready to adapt their training programmes to the requirements of detached, community oriented and community based social work settings. The remarks of a British social worker are relevant here:

The increasingly generic concerns of agencies such as the children's departments mean that they are having to accommodate increasingly contradictory functions. A growing social control role on the one hand, as they begin to supplant the juvenile court in the consultations with the police that are taking place to avoid the need for a child to come before the court . . . , and on the other hand they are beginning to develop preventive approaches based on community development and community action. Not only does the preoccupation with agency function concepts leave contradictions of these kinds undiscussed on training courses, but it also results in little or no place being found for discussion of challenging new techniques such as advocacy, now being so much debated in the U.S.A. (Price, 1968c, p. 2286).

In stating the case for the *F.A.S. specialist* our major objectives are: (1) to enable the F.A.S. worker to focus upon the specific goals of his assignment, to sharpen the definitions of his functions and to develop appropriate skills and methods; (2) to safeguard the F.A.S. worker against being used as general handyman, to prevent him from becoming a Jack-of-all-Trades who is in danger of dissipating his energies and of losing sight of his objectives by trying to be everything to all people. We are *not* aiming at a narrow specialisation, but at a generic professional approach which integrates a clearly defined range of functions, namely advice, guidance, assistance, referral and follow-up, mediation/liaison and community work, and which makes the fullest possible use of the expertise and resources of other social work specialisations and other relevant professions.

Most important of all, the community-oriented or community-based detached family advice service approach is fully in step with the

---

[1] For detailed discussions of these terms and the concepts they denote see Brager (1968), the National Association of Social Workers (1969), and other articles on the subject listed under References.

increasingly evident development towards a more integrated, encompassing focus on the family and the community as the 'client unit', and
away from the earlier tendency to regard rigid categories of clients such
as children, old people, the physically handicapped, homeless, etc., as
the main determinants of service specialisation.

We believe that, rather than perpetuating the fragmentation of social
work, this new specialisation may serve to integrate the various specific
social work tasks and approaches, making an important contribution
to a diversity which, in the words of Professor Piven (1969), 'is highly
desirable for the growth of a profession'. As this writer points out:

Clearly new theories, new policies and new programs are periodically needed
in order to meet a profession's service goals under changing conditions. Diversity
created by increasing specialization reflects the profession's effort to provide
a high level of service based on new knowledge and improved technique to meet
the complex needs of modern society (p. 89).

Implications for training

The specific requirements of F.A.S. work indicate the need for training
provisions which meet the needs of this service. At the present time
it is difficult to see how these requirements can be met without some
much needed improvements and innovations in social work education
which will affect the profession as a whole. Stevenson (1968) made some
recommendations which may point the way:

Firstly, we should attempt to establish a truly 'generic' social work education
at basic level. Despite agreement in general terms that this is desirable, we are a
long way from the reality. The implications of this must be recognised by practitioners. It means abandoning concentration on detail and attempting to paint
on a wider canvas. Much that is now uneasily included in basic training under
the heading of 'settings'—child care law, detailed medical knowledge and so on—
would be jettisoned (p. 188).

We would qualify this by suggesting that, while this generic course
should give the student the opportunity for a solid basis in the three main
approaches of social work, namely case work, group work and community
work, the student should be enabled to concentrate on one of these
disciplines and select one major subject in which he can deepen his
theoretical and methodological knowledge. Practical experience through
course-linked field placements should be geared to the student's major
subject. Furthermore, there should be some emphasis on the application
of sociological theory to equipping the student with knowledge of
socio-cultural and socio-economic differences, the social, cultural and

economic implications of dominant societal norms and expectations in relation to groups of different backgrounds and expectations.

Stevenson continues:

This leads to the second implication—the extensive development of in-service training as an outgoing indispensable part of professional education. This would equip new social workers with the necessary detailed knowledge; and it would encourage mobility between whatever formal organisational specialisational specialisations do arise (p. 188).

As regards F.A.S. work, this in-service training should take place on two levels, in the same way as professional supervision. The most economic and integrated form of this essential form of training is a merging of the supervision and staff training functions on both levels. This means that the unit supervisor and the F.A.S. team leaders would also function as tutors, giving full recognition to the maxim that supervision is largely a teaching and learning process. The teaching material is directly related to the experience of the staff in daily practice and, therefore, remains relevant and dynamic. Levels of discussion, supplementary reading and choice of subjects would have to be adapted to the participants, i.e. demanding different levels for the supervision staff training session for professional F.A.S. staff and for untrained workers.

Besides sharpening the expertise of F.A.S. staff with regard to their own specific tasks, in-service training can afford opportunities to provide understanding of the functions and methods of other social work specialisations and of other professions. For this purpose, talks by invited speakers, preferably field workers, from other agencies, as well as other professionals, such as probation officers, health visitors, child care officers, housing and Department of Health and Social Security officials, teachers, lawyers, general practitioners, etc., should be regarded as part of the staff training programme.

Stevenson concludes: 'Thirdly, universities and technical colleges should develop advanced trainings, of various lengths in different specialisations and in management' (p. 88). Advanced graduate training in community work would be especially relevant to F.A.S. staff, but there should also be graduate generic courses, group work courses and courses in administration and supervision.

At present the required range of structured professional training facilities is only partly available and, in consequence, we shall have to make do with F.A.S. workers and supervisors whose training cannot be regarded as adequate. Fortunately our observations showed that there are people available who are attracted to the challenges and opportunities of F.A.S. work and who bring with them a wealth of relevant experience, even if they lack formal training. Not only that, but we found that the type of worker who is drawn to F.A.S. work often shows remarkable abilities to 'learn through doing', even if he or she has had neither training nor practical experience in community work, group work, socio-cultural theory and other relevant subjects. It is to be hoped that, through the efforts of the professional association and in response to the requirements of the current reorganisation of the social services, more adequate professional training programmes will become available. Eventually we may look forward to a situation in which we can expect an F.A.S. worker to have undergone a basic social work course, qualifying in community work, to have the benefits of staff training, and to be able to attend specialised graduate courses, while the F.A.S. unit supervisor has, in addition to this basic training, graduated from courses in supervision and administration and community work.

Having made some statements as to the subjects and the structure of training programmes which are relevant to F.A.S. work as well as to all other types of social work, it may be useful to take a brief look at the content and the objectives of social work education as they relate to the requirements of F.A.S. work.

Case work

The report on a recent study group on field work training states the basic requirement for 'sufficient competence in social casework to make valid diagnostic assessments of families and individual and social contacts in order to determine the appropriate form of treatment'; to this the report adds: 'sufficient competence to begin to undertake social casework treatment of those individuals and families whose needs may be met wholly or partially by this approach' (Central Training Council in Child Care, 1970, p. 9). We have already discussed the difficulties encountered in trying to arrive at a generally accepted definition of case work. Competence in diagnosis and in realistic methods of help and support for social malfunctions and personal problems arising from these are, of course, essential for the F.A.S. worker, but we have strong reservations about any tendency to encourage the dominance of psychoanalytic theory which overwhelmed American social work and has, in recent years, led to strong criticism of the case work approach as such. Whether one embraces the psychoanalytic dogma or not, it should be clear to anyone that a thorough understanding of this therapeutic approach demands long and intensive study, as well as the undergoing of analysis and the acceptance of a specific view of human nature and society. A person who qualifies in this respect becomes a psychoanalyst, not a social worker. A case work course can, at best, offer some elementary principles and some samples of the intricate terminology related to this theory. The application of such half-knowledge to the helping process in social work is irresponsible. Diagnostic conclusions arrived at on the basis of some half-understood principles of psychoanalysis are sheer quackery, at best irrelevant, at worst harmful to the person who seeks help.

The tendency to equate case work with social work *per se* has, in recent years, aroused some critical attention in this country. Barbara Kahan (1970), for instance, wrote that among the changes the child care service will have to accept, 'one of the most important is the recognition that social work is something more than case work, and that case work training is only part of a wide range of skills needed by social workers' (p. 65). A more radical view is expressed by Rae Price (1968), who writes: 'It is quite clear that increasing numbers of social workers are exhausted and bewildered by the intellectual contortions involved in continuing to meet with interpersonal (i.e. case work) technique problems which are being shown to be principally the consequence of community factors' (p. 1388). The experience of the family advice centres among others, may help the profession to take another look at case work methodology. The inclusion of guidance (or counselling) techniques in case work training would be especially relevant to F.A.S. work. More attention might also be paid to teaching referral process and procedures, and to relate case work and guidance to group and community work settings.

Group work

This important subject has, as yet, barely penetrated this country's social work courses, although it is a well established fact that a thorough knowledge of group work methods and group dynamics is indispensable for effective services to groups of every description, whether they be groups of youngsters in residential care or youth clubs, street corner gangs, the inmates of therapeutic, rehabilitative or penal institutions, members of professional associations, participants in recreational programmes or community organisations such as tenants' associations, etc. The social significance of the group—'a convenient sociological designation for any number of people, larger or smaller, between whom such relations are discovered that they must be thought of together . . . a number of persons whose relations to each other are sufficiently impressive to demand attention' (Small, 1905, p. 495)— is so universal, that it is somewhat astonishing that the profession which is by definition concerned with the social situations and relations of people has not given much more emphasis to the study of group dynamics and group work. Both subjects are of decisive importance to effective F.A.S. work in the community-oriented and community-based settings.

It is our view that group work should be given considerably more scope and emphasis in social work education than it has at present. At least for the student who chooses to specialise in community work, competence in the dynamics and methodology of group work should be given precedence over case work as an essential basis for community work. Group work competence should also be regarded as an obligatory qualification for every social worker who provides services for children and youth.[1] The relevance of group work to the detached F.A.S. setting in the light of our experience as described in this report is borne out by the definition of social group work as

one of the three basic methods of social work. In the course of applying this method, all the other approaches (except group psychotherapy)[2] come into play as part of the total process. The social group work method aims at the full utilisation of forces in group life to bring about social growth in the individual members. It is in the process known as group-goal-achieving that these forces are at their maximum, the members being most fully engaged with each other and with the group as a whole. This process involves common decision and common action towards the accomplishment of common goals, shared by the members for the group as a whole. In the course of guiding this process, the group worker uses a variety of group experiences and program media, including social action, community services, and cultural, educational, social, and athletic activities. The group is involved in discussion and decision-making about the specific goals it wishes to achieve. It may also find itself, in the course of its life, discussing general matters of concern to its members or specific matters dealing with the problems of individuals, but these discussions will have arisen naturally out of the work the group has cut out for itself and the relationships that ensue (Tropp, 1968, pp. 271–2).

Community work

The importance and relevance of community work training in the detached F.A.S. setting is so obvious that it need not be emphasised any further. Unfortunately the opportunities for acquiring professional

---

[1] A report on the 'Training implications of the white paper "Children in Trouble"' speaks of 'the need for more teaching of awareness of group dynamics as part of the training of Child Care Officers', but does not mention group work (*Child Care News*, no. 84, March 1969, p. 8).

[2] The author lists group education, group counciling, group recreation as different group work specialisations. We fully agree with the exclusion of group therapy, which is a therapeutic method demanding intensive training in the use of the group as a medium for effecting the cure of sickness in the individual member. The F.A.S. worker may, under certain circumstances, refer a client to group therapy, but he should not himself undertake this task.

competence in this social work method are still highly inadequate in this country, although there are now some indications that the social work courses are beginning to pay more attention to the teaching of this basic subject. The previously cited report of the Central Training Council in Child Care tells us that: 'It was firmly held by some members that practitioners in group and community work require special skills and that it was unlikely that social workers completing basic professional training could be expected to be as competent in either of these two specialties as in casework which is their major basic method.' These members of the Training Council found that 'given the shortcomings of newly qualified caseworkers, the introduction of teaching in group of community work at a specialised level can only serve to dilute the casework expertise', a view which shows a complete lack of awareness of the many indications that case work practised in isolation from the social context of community and group is in danger of becoming highly introspective and ineffective with regard to a wide range of needs and social problem situations. However, some members of the Council did feel that the view that child care officers should be exclusively qualified for case work 'was a needlessly restricted view of the function of child care officers' (Central Training Council in Child Care, 1970, p. 10).

Another form of misconception comes from those who seem to regard social work as a whole as being synonymous with case work, and therefore conclude that community work is incompatible with social work. Robert Holman (1969), for instance, writes that social workers engaged in community work need to develop skills and strategies which are 'alien to their professional principles' (p. 144). This is seeing things rather upside down, for community work is deeply rooted in social work principles. Indeed, as any student of the history of social work in Britain and the United States will discover, social work principles grew out of the experience of community work in the early days of the emerging profession. If alienation from these principles has taken place, it has been caused by the gradually narrowing focus of casework, largely due to the influence of psycho-analytic theory. As an authoritative American statement on community work points out:

The practice of community organisation is rooted in the values traditionally associated with the practice of social work . . . The roots of sanction for community organisation practice are not only derived from the values and purpose [of social work], but also from the social conditions particular to our time. . . . Method in community organisation practice is the orderly application of a relevant body of knowledge, guided by social work values. The worker applies systematically and sequentially this coherent body of knowledge employing practice-wisdom and learned behaviour through characteristic, distinctive and describable procedures to help the community engage in a process of planned change toward community improvement (National Association of Social Workers, 1962).[1]

A British author reminds us that: 'Basically the task of the social worker, whether with individual or family, group or local community, is the same—to help the clients to deal more effectively with their needs and problems' (J. Spencer, 1944, p. 301). The Gulbenkian Report (1968) and such recent authors as Goetschius (1969) have made detailed suggestions and recommendations regarding structured teaching of community work. It is to be hoped that the academic institutions and the professional associations will combine their efforts to provide adequate training facilities for community workers and others whose functions include community work, such as the staff of detached family advice centres.

Social structure and Social administration
The Central Training Council in Child Care (1970) defines 'social structure' as 'Knowledge which will enable workers to identify problems or parts of problems which may be a function of social or political phenomena' (p. 9); 'social administration' is described as: 'A critical assessment of the function of existing social services in the light of current needs. Sufficient understanding of the administration of services and the dynamics of organisations in order to be able to act on behalf of their clients or in relation to them and/or to refer appropriately' (p. 10). This range of knowledge is, of course, essential to every aspect of family advice service work. We believe that the two subjects are closely related and should be integrated in the basic, generic, social work course, as well as in special courses in case work, group work and community work. Furthermore, this range of knowledge should be taught in more depth and detail in advanced, post-graduate courses. At present the emphasis is on providing information of agency functions. As Peter Leonard (1968) has pointed out:

This focus on formal agency functions . . . can only take us a limited way and is related to the kind of teaching on social administration, descriptive and weak in theoretical foundation, which has often characterised social work training up to the present. The teaching of social work practice to include focus on organisational structure, on decision-making, on delegation of authority, on informal group pressures, in short, on the whole gamut of organisational behaviour, prepares the student for his future role in a more realistic and at the same time intellectually stimulating way (p. 381).

[1] For a broadly conceived discussion of the value-basis of community work, see also the Gulbenkian Report (1968).

Another writer stated that: 'Present social work training generally places far more emphasis on developing casework skills rather than encouraging social workers to discover what rights and benefits are available to their clients. Training does not usually involve studies of decision making in power situations where material aid can be withheld' (Brooke, 1969, p. 96).

The implications for the need for integrating information on the social service system with a thorough understanding of socio-economic and political factors are clearly indicated. The experience of the family advice centres showed the decisive importance of such knowledge. Equally important, and as closely related, is the need for socio-cultural studies. Leonard (1968) writes:

The development of awareness of the socio-cultural aspects of clients' problems is now an integral part of the training of social workers, but it often remains at a micro-sociological level, under-emphasizing the larger questions which would be raised by an examination of political and economic structures and their impact upon certain sections of society and upon social work itself (p. 378).

Margot Jefferys (1965) stressed the grass-roots implications of this type of training when she wrote:

All social workers should be knowledgeable about the social and economic circumstances in which people live. They must appreciate the influence of kin, neighbourhood, religion, the work unit and the formal and informal groups in the formation and maintenance of community and group norms and values, and the attitudes displayed towards those who deviate from these norms.

Supervision and administration

We hold the view, confirmed by our observations of the seven family advice centres which participated in the study, that supervision and administration demands not only practical experience, but specific training. As the supervisor is, in most instances, also the administrator of a unit, sector or area team, the teaching of administrative techniques should be regarded as part of the training of supervisors. A series of lectures on supervision, linked to field-work experience in supervising junior colleagues and volunteers in the field placements during the second half of the basic generic course, are suggested. This should be followed by a series of seminars in supervision, linked to practical experience in the participants' field work settings as part of post-graduate education. On both levels, general principles of supervision and administration should be taught, followed by specialised teaching in supervision of group and community workers and of volunteers and indigenous workers. The experience of the detached family advice centres showed clearly that the assignment of, for instance, a case worker with no additional training or experience to supervise a community work oriented project can result in highly frustrating and inefficient situations. Our observations also highlighted in some instances the need to emphasise the distinction between certain casework trends and the supervision process in the training of supervisors. The following remarks by American and British writers (cited in Leonard, 1966, pp. 12–13, 63) on the subject are relevant in this context:

Since sensitivity to the motivational and emotional states of the client—perhaps the prime objective of social work training—must be preceded by self-awareness, the student is himself subjected to a near psychotherapeutic experience. He is persistently called to account for his own behaviour, not in cognitive but in emotional terms—not 'why do you think this way?' but 'why do you feel this way?' (Wilensky and Lebeaux, 1958).

Workers whose judgement frequently differs from that of their supervisors might be accused of being 'unable to accept supervision'. The practice of questioning the worker's unconscious motives tended to elevate the super-ordinate into an omniscient power. Workers found that they could not be right in any disagreement since their arguments were not accepted at their face value but dismissed as being rationalizations to mask unconscious resistance (Blan and Scott, 1963).

As we stated previously, we regard in-service training as an integral part of the supervision process and as one of the responsibilities of the supervisor. Theoretical knowledge and practical experience in staff training should, therefore, be included in the curriculae of supervision training. The supervision and in-service training of indigenous workers and volunteers demands special attention and is highly relevant to the team work approach of the detached family advice centre. Mary Richmond (1930) wrote many years ago that 'the supreme test of a trained worker is the ability to turn to good account the services of the relatively untrained'. The teaching and guidance of the untrained worker should, however, not be left to accident and inclination, but should be based on thorough preparation and training of the social work supervisor. With regard to the guidance and training for indigenous workers, a report on American Neighbourhood Service Centres stated:

Some form of preparation has always been regarded as desirable for indigenous workers. While efforts hitherto have tended to be rather haphazard, there seems to be increasing stress on the importance of some form of systematic training. This raises a difficulty, for most of the projects have also emphasized the dangers of 'professionalization' and have felt that indigenous workers should be 'discouraged from attempting to remold themselves in the professional image'. One project escapes this dilemma by stating its aim as being: 'To train the workers to utilize fully their own natural style which made it possible for them to reach their neighbors, rather than retraining them and developing another style' (Perlman and Jones, 1967, p. 56).

13

This is a subtle and sophisticated process which requires supervisors with educational preparation in community work, group dynamics and socio-cultural theory.[1] Much skill and knowledge is also essential for the supervision and training of volunteers. To this subject the Deputy Chief Social Work Adviser to the Edinburgh Social Work Services Group said:

> There is much need for our training establishments to help professionals to develop skills of easily assessing both the what and the when of the volunteer contribution in services. I mean this at the delivery point of services—the receiving end of the whole exercise, the consumer. It isn't enough to teach vaguely about volunteers alongside teaching about the history of the voluntary movement and perhaps the differing nature of voluntary organisations. We must become more skilled at enabling the professional to work with this resource of personnel as part of the plan of operation. . . . In professional training (including staff development programmes) there is much need for staff of training establishments to help professionals to develop the skill of really assessing both the what and the when of the volunteer's contribution. If we are encouraging partnership with volunteers then it is encumbent upon us to see that there is an element in training which will help the worker to use this additional resource (McInnes, 1970).

It has been rightly stated that: 'Social work education sets in motion a learning process which should continue as long as practice' (Central Training Council in Child Care, 1970, p. 9). The continuity and relevance of this learning process can be fully assured by the availability of trained supervisors. It has also been said that 'our clients have the right to demand more than good motives and enthusiastic commitment. They have the right to demand thorough knowledge, discipline and responsibility. These can only be guaranteed by intensive professional training and the watchful eye of an alert professional organisation (Leissner, 1968, p. 2408).

The family advice service and the children's department

The exploratory study pointed out that the question has been raised 'whether the family advice service should, indeed, operate under the auspices of a statutory agency, such as the children's department' (Leissner, 1967). This question has, in various forms and contexts, appeared throughout the period of investigation.

---

[1] Our reluctance to recommend formal training for indigenous workers is based upon our observations and confirmed by the alarmed rejection of a suggestion of such training by indigenous workers in one of the detached projects. Empirical evidence shows that formal training is more likely to result in the indigenous worker's alienation from the community. This does not, of course, mean that indigenous workers should be deprived of opportunities to change their status by obtaining professional training.

A number of voices have recently been raised which expound the supposition that social work approaches which focus upon the rights and the human dignity of the poor, and which uphold the concepts of community involvement and client participation, should be left to inspired amateurs because this kind of approach will never be tolerated within a statutory setting. It is especially interesting to note that the exponents of this voluntarism-versus-the-establishment attitude are to be found among the most ardent supporters of the welfare state, who are apparently unaware of the implications of what they are saying. These implications are clearly that if the services which are available *by right*, are declared unable to apply progressive, radical methods to meet the needs of their clients, this is in fact tantamount to a declaration of bankruptcy on behalf of the welfare state, the institutional framework for which there is, at the present time and in this society, no realistic alternative.

We are fully aware of the pioneering work of the inspired amateurs in the history of social work, and of the valuable services provided by the voluntary organisations. We are, however, convinced that it is of the utmost importance for the future of the social services in Britain that new concepts and methods should become integrated in the statutory system, rather than take on the permanent character of esoteric fringe activities. Family advice services or similar provisions by voluntary agencies should be welcomed and encouraged. Our observations lead us to the view that it would be preferable to operate voluntary family advice centres independently of the statutory services, so as to offer people a true choice, rather than the same service under a different heading. Voluntary agency operated family advice services should provide an alternative for the client; they should *not* be regarded as an excuse for the local authorities for not providing such services. The often heard argument that voluntary organisations are free from bureaucratic pressures and political obligations and are, therefore, more effective in advancing the interests of their clients is, we believe, a fallacy. First of all, many voluntary organisations are financially dependent upon local authorities[1] and, secondly, voluntary organisa-

---

[1] A previously cited report on Citizens' Advice Bureaux, for instance, states: 'The Bureau's workers say that the average citizen recognises the advantages of a Bureau's non-statutory status. They believe that he can tell his problems more freely to an unofficial listener and can accept unpalatable information more easily from a worker who is not a government official. The CAB staff believes that this independent status enables CAB to take whatever action is best for the inquirer without feeling the pressure of political considerations. Whether this can ever be completely true, particularly of an organisation that receives its financial support from local government, remains a question for observers' (Kahn *et al.*, 1966, p. 31).

tions have their own administrative complexities and are subject to their own specific political and ideological determinants.

The issue is closely related to that of a possible conflict between the statutory functions of the children's department and the basic principles of the family advice service. This was discussed in some detail in the exploratory study, and the points made in that initial report were seen to be so relevant in the experience of the seven family advice centres that they bear repeating:

> Apparent or anticipated conflict between statutory obligations and the advice, guidance and assistance functions of the Family Advice Service have been a subject of discussion in the field. Specifically, workers are concerned with the possible incompatibility of their statutory obligations under Section 2 of the Children and Young Persons Act, 1952 and the F.A.S. goal of creating the image of a 'safe', 'easily accessible, confidential, no-strings-attached', service, geared to inducing the widest possible range of clients to seek help and advice with their problems at a pre-crisis stage. This apprehension is based on the assumption that certain, especially unskilled, semi-skilled and new immigrant population groups regard the statutory services as powerful, threatening, authority-wielding bodies, and are likely to react to them with fear, distrust, or even open hostility.
> ▶ The assumption seems to have found some support in practical experience. A number of workers feel that many clients who would benefit from the service keep away because they identify the F.A.S. worker as a Child Care Officer, and are afraid to 'get into trouble' (Leissner, 1967, p. 64).

Our observations showed that there *is* some potential and actual conflict between the statutory and the F.A.S. functions. In almost all instances this could be overcome. More important is the possible incompatibility of what we might call the 'statutory attitude' and the informality, flexibility and permissiveness which is essential in the F.A.S. setting. While we were aware of the possibility of conflict in this sense, we found that in most cases this posed no significant problems because the kind of social worker who *wanted* to do the F.A.S. work, was also the kind of person who has suitable qualities and attitudes. The clients of the family advice centres, while sometimes initially cautious or even openly suspicious and hostile, in most cases, particularly in the detached, community-based setting, soon overcame their reserve and established relationships of mutual confidence and acceptance.

Our observations showed that, with a few exceptions, children's departments understood that certain duties carried out by child care officers would conflict with the functions and the image of the family advice services, and F.A.S. workers were usually not asked to carry out these duties. Moreover, it should be pointed out that the widely accepted emphasis on prevention and a growing interest in community work in the children's departments made the latter more receptive to F.A.S.

work than would have been the case some years previously, and more ready to exempt the worker from statutory duties and to tolerate experimentation and flexible, permissive attitudes.

Some years ago the Director of the National Bureau for Co-operation in Child Care wrote:

Early and comprehensive preventive action is now possible under the Children and Young Persons Act 1963. But it is neither inevitable nor compulsory that such action will in fact be taken. It will entirely depend upon whether the Act is interpreted in the broadest possible sense or whether it will only be used to prevent disaster such as the break-up of families or serious delinquency (Kellmer Pringle, 1965a, p. 265).

The family advice service, especially in the form of detached community-oriented and community-based centres, can be regarded as one of the most important recent manifestations of a broad interpretation of preventive work by statutory children's departments. The exploratory study carried out in 1966 concluded that:

In all the Children's Departments which were visited a positive attitude was found towards the basic concepts underlying the Family Advice Service approach. These concepts, namely that the family should be regarded as the basic client unit, and that the focus should be upon early prevention, appear to have had a decisive influence upon the overall service of the departments; indeed, they appear to have guided their work to varying extents for some years prior to the publication of the 1963 Children and Young Persons Act (Leissner, 1967, p. 79).

The present study not only confirmed the readiness of children's departments to apply the F.A.S. approach, but also showed that a growing number of children's departments are receptive to new concepts and methods which introduced detached work, community work, services for children and youth and a number of other modifications and innovations which broaden the scope and range of the statutory services considerably.

While our observations led us to conclude that, at least at present, the children's department is the most suitable parent agency for the family advice service, we also noted some of the predictable difficulties which arose when established procedures and long-held attitudes had to be adapted to new situations and different approaches. Whether an issue arose over the need to rely upon the detached F.A.S. worker's judgment in providing emergency financial assistance without going through the prescribed channels, or whether the worker's involvement with a militant client group aroused concern, it was always apparent that unless a compromise was possible without denial of basic principles the children's department had to examine its policies and procedures and make the necessary adjustments.

The experience of the family advice centres showed that the basic policies and the established administrative procedures of the children's departments *per se* do not present unsurmountable obstacles to change. On the contrary, we were often surprised at the readiness to experiment with new methods and to establish precedents. Where serious conflict between the demands of detached, community-oriented or community-based F.A.S. work and the policies and procedures of the parent agency arose, this was due to such factors as the chief officer's reluctance to risk the disapproval of the local authority power structure, his unwillingness to give offence to other statutory services, or else the department's administrative staff was too much concerned with rules and regulations and resented interference with their habitual ways of doing things. Lack of financial resources did sometimes, but by no means always, cause delays or the turning down of a request. Mainly due to lack of communication and insufficient sharing of the F.A.S. experience with colleagues in the department, there were instances of vague resentment of apparent 'special privileges' enjoyed by F.A.S. workers among the other members of the staff, and this had some impact on the overall attitude of the agency. There were also occasions where F.A.S. workers put senior staff and administrators on the defensive by being too impatient in pressing their needs and requests, and by giving the impression that they were not sufficiently aware of the many other obligations and priorities of the department. Useful lessons were learned from all this. The overall experience, however, confirmed the statement of a leading American social worker that:

With persistent attention an alert agency can adapt its structure as conditions change and can analyse administrative difficulties, not only in terms of personality attributes or shortcomings of given individuals, but also in terms of organizational arrangements—size of the agency, intake procedure, number of clientele, physical arrangements, organizational roles, supervisory systems, and the like (Stein, 1965, p. 61).

The differences between one children's department and the other must, of course, be taken into account. An observation made some years ago still holds true:

The local authority Children's Departments still differ enormously one from another. They can vary not only in size, wealth and resources, but in such matters as the personality of the Clerk of the Council, the relationship between Children's Officer and Medical Officer and the intensity of political friction (Stroud, 1965, p. 17).

It is all the more important to be constantly aware of the fact that innovation rarely succeeds because of the enthusiasm and the good intentions of the innovators, but is subject to the dictates of reality.

In the case of the children's departments this reality is usually not immutable, but it has in each and every instance its own potentialities and limitations. The task of the innovator in any profession and agency setting is to recognise the potentialities and to test the limits. To put it more concretely: the opportunity for demonstrating the benefits, as well as the challenges, of a community-based family advice service approach may present itself in a children's department which has become concerned about the severity and density of problems in a geographically and/or socially isolated neighbourhood. A family advice centre in such a neighbourhood may, in the attempt to help its clients to improve their conditions and to gain self-confidence, have to test the limits to which the department and the local authority will permit the F.A.S. staff to become the advocates of the rights of their clients. Making 'progressive' noises may be enough for the amateur. The task of the professional is to test the limits in an articulate, informed and imaginative manner if he seeks to improve a service, to introduce a new approach. The task is to find a way. An American writer described the professional obligation in another context:

The lesson concerning the tendency towards inflexibility in some social agencies, their inability to respond readily to new ideas and approaches, is one that must be kept in mind in all novel and imaginative programs. Procedures and paths must be discovered to deal with such institutional inertia—and often this is quite possible—or calculated steps must be taken to bypass such obstacles as expeditiously as possible (Geis, 1965, p. 43).

In shouldering this task, the worker is entitled to the guidance of his professional training and the backing of the professional association. This is all the more important because part of the reality that must be recognised and faced is that the social services are not solely determined by social work principles or even by the goals and concepts of the welfare state. There will always be other factors evident, ranging from the immediate practical concerns of the administrator who wishes to rationalise the service, to public opinion and political issues which determine the attitudes of local authorities. (For an informative discussion of these factors see Fanshel, 1962.) The reality that there *are* limits must also be recognised. In many situations compromise is both necessary and acceptable. However, great care should be taken not to let compromise result in the abandonment of basic concepts and goals to the point where the professional's values and principles become casualties of expediency. For instance, a family advice centre may become convinced of the need for a specific service, but may have to postpone or give up the request for such a service because the parent agency is unable to bear the cost, or is not ready to accept this further expansion of its statutory responsibilities. But if a family advice centre finds itself under pressure to use its influence and its relationships with the community to facilitate the implementation of policies which must be regarded as detrimental to the best interests of this community on the basis of social work principles, then it becomes the responsibility of the F.A.S. staff to state clearly that the situation has become incompatible with the goals and concepts of the service, and that the service to the community must therefore be terminated.

Our observations indicate that such extreme situations are unlikely to occur very often, a view which seems to be confirmed by so authoritative a writer as Barbara Kahan who tells us of the changes the children's departments will have to accept:

> The history of the child care service in particular tends to illustrate the way in which social work in general is being pushed by events to make a decision as to whether it continues to be a way of helping people to sort out and put up with intolerable situations with more equanimity than they would otherwise have done, or whether, in addition to that, it must accept the role of a pressure group within society, commenting on intolerable situations and seeking to remedy them by means of national policy as well as individual supportive work. The new legislation on young offenders and the implications of a Seebohm approach could both point child care workers further in this direction. Many are willingly looking that way already. It may, in fact, be easier for some to accept this than to modify attitudes to casework as a method, although there are encouraging signs that community work, group work, mixed field and residential work are all forming 'growing points' in some departments and will act as precedents for others to use and emulate in varied ways (Kahan, 1970, p. 65).

The limits and prospects of community work under local authority

As we have seen, a large proportion of the community work carried out in F.A.S. settings is concerned with enabling client groups to mobilise and to activate their own resources, to identify and to make constructive use of the available services, to identify or create channels of communication between the community and the services and institutional bodies and, last but not least, to persuade and, where necessary, to prod the latter into offering more effective, accessible and flexible services. While sometimes involving the need for patient and forceful arguing and negotiating, these processes do not necessarily involve situations of direct conflict with the local authority statutory structure. One or another official or agency may show some signs of discomfort or even annoyance, but we found that the powers that be are usually ready to acknowledge that the family advice service is pursuing legitimate professional goals and that in the long run this type of community work benefits the local authority itself as much as the client population. The best evidence for this is the increasing interest in detached, community-based family advice centres shown by local authorities, and the increasing number of such family advice centres which have been opened recently. We can, for instance, cite the case of Tower Hamlets, where a pioneering attempt in a community work oriented family advice centre initially caused some controversy[1] and was succeeded by a detached family advice centre which engaged in a wide range of community work with an impressive measure of success. A recent article on the work of this local authority reported that in the year 1968–9

we employed four child care workers full-time at our Family Advice Centres. The centres are situated in areas of high social need, the workers are readily accessible and people tend to ask for help at a much earlier stage than they would otherwise do. Two more new centres, one at Wapping's Pier Head and the other in a row of shops in Bethnal Green, will open shortly. This will bring our total of Family Advice Centre workers to seven (Brown, 1970, p. 4).

The fact must be faced, however, that community work in deprived areas does raise the issues of client participation, social action and advocacy. These three interrelated issues result in activities which are aimed at bringing about change by enabling the client community, the consumers of the services provided by the statutory agencies, to insist on being informed and consulted, to know and demand their rights and to recognise and make use of their own legitimate powers. This inevitably leads to some degree of conflict with the various bodies representing local authority, and the F.A.S. workers may find themselves in the uncomfortable position of having to choose between the interests of the clients they serve and the local authority structure which determines overall policy and which pays their salaries.

Conflict between the social worker, especially the community worker, and the local authority has, in recent years, become the object of increasing awareness and discussion of the issues involved. Most of the opinions expressed emphasise the inevitability and the decisive importance of conflict in bringing about social change. This valid observation is, however, usually linked to the more questionable denial that any degree or form of conflict can be tolerated and be allowed to take place within the local authority setting. Holman (1969), for instance, wrote:

Two strategies are available to bring about change: consensus (research, reports, co-ordination) and conflict (which includes encouraging claims for rights, political campaigning, rent strikes). I will argue that conflict is the method

[1] See Lapping, (1967), and Runnicles, (1967).

most likely to achieve the stated objectives in deprived areas. As institutionalised bodies, like local authorities, will not countenance conflict, the community development project is unlikely to promote radical improvement (p. 444).

Holman (1970) also notes that:

Occasionally a local authority does employ a community worker able to participate with local residents. An example is the Family Advice Centre of Birmingham Children's Department located in Brookfields. It is true to add, however, that as yet the Centre has not involved inhabitants in actions which might threaten the norms or policies of the local authority (p. 177).

These views appear to be representative of those held by a substantial number of social work practitioners and theoreticians. As we have already indicated, we fully agree that conflict is often necessary and inevitable in the process of helping deprived communities to bring about constructive and lasting changes in their social conditions. We do, however, dissent from the view that this conflict must inevitably be suppressed in the local authority setting and will not be tolerated by the statutory agency. It appears to us that writers like Holman are not sufficiently aware of that important function which consists of inducing, and if necessary of pressuring, the statutory system to carry out its own acknowledged policies, to make available its own existing provisions in more effective ways, and to draw upon its own available resources. This too may entail a certain amount of friction, but it is a legitimate professional social work function to which local authorities must and, indeed, do give recognition. Also largely ignored is the change-inducing task of interpretation, liaison and mediation. As Price (1968a) puts it:

One of the most devastating aspects of the British class system is that what have been assumed to be traditional channels of democratic expression have been quite alien to the cultural patterns of the working class. Thus . . . community work from within a statutory social work department may soon have the role of ensuring that community opinion is accurately canvassed and expressed (p. 1389).

Moreover, the critics of community work in the local authority setting seem to regard the large and complex network of local authority structure as an absolutely cohesive, self-centred and obtuse monolith in which there are no internal contradictions and tensions, no manifestations of self-doubt and soul searching, no people who are accessible to intelligent reasoning and new ideas. Our observations have *not* convinced us that this is so. As Banks (1970) pointed out: 'Local authorities, like individuals, vary; and within them, similarly, are officers who vary in their perceptions and commitment' (p. 6). Perhaps even more important, one key issue is almost completely ignored. That is the fundamentally important struggle of an as yet embryonic profession for respect and recognition. This struggle has lately been given new impetus by the formation of a professional social work association. It is a struggle which must be waged *within* the official power structure, e.g. the local authorities and central government. Only if and when social work as a profession and its professional functions and responsibilities are acknowledged within the official structure, and recognition is accorded to the fact that this professional responsibility must take precedent over the employer–employee relationship, agency policies and vested interests, then will social workers, and among them community workers, be able fully to represent the interests of their clients, even if these conflict with the traditions and established methods of local authority. Only when social workers are able to demand the same respect as other, longer established professions, such as doctors and lawyers for instance, will they be able to act, when necessary, as the advocates of their clients. Anyone who urges social workers in the statutory service or students about to enter these services to opt out and to apply their 'progressive', 'radical' ideas and methods solely outside the official structure is spreading defeatism and recommending abject surrender. The obligation to carry out the urgently needed changes is that of the official structure on the national and the local level, and it is this official structure which has the power and the resources to bring about change and to introduce innovations. It is the task of the community worker to make his contribution in inducing the authorities to meet their obligations, *not* to relieve them of these obligations by withdrawing from the statutory arena. One of the conclusions recorded at the International Conference on Social Welfare and Human Rights was: 'Social workers fail in their professional duty if they do not bring their knowledge and experience to the attention of the community and of law-makers, planners, politicians, and others and use their influence to help in the formulation of social policies which maximise the exercise of human rights' (*Social Welfare and Human Rights*, 1968, p. 387).

The strides made by the profession in recent years towards meeting the challenges within the statutory structure are best illustrated by an excerpt from the presidential address to the 1969 Annual Conference of Child Care Officers by J. Thomas:

In an effort to see our role in a wider context, the last year or two has brought increased usage of the term 'social action'. I take the term to mean an effort to influence policies and manipulate the environment on behalf of either whole communities or on behalf of an individual, in which case it could be a plan agreed in the course of casework. Social action belongs to the movement of protest and a commitment to it means that social workers must be prepared to bring conflict into the open. We can no longer be blind to policies which negate our commitment to man's worth and right to happiness. There is still considerable haziness around the term, and the time has come to be more explicit and make our social action idea operational. What are our social action models? Do we want to secure publicity, engage in protest activity, in militant action, in advocacy on behalf of clients? There is a whole new exciting prospect opening up of defining and refining ways of helping and working with fellow members of the community. We need not only think of the kinds of activities but also to examine how acceptable they are, and what the effects might be. In what guise would we become involved in social action and what would be the basis for action in any case? If we could produce a document of Citizen's Rights with which to arm every child care officer (and how I wish we would do this before we dissolve—I do not think the problems of keeping it up to date and relevant to local situations would be insurmountable)—how far would we go beyond informing the citizen of his rights? To what extent would we be prepared to become his advocate and what would be the methodological implications of this? Of course many unorthodox social workers have quietly represented clients in these ways for years, but there is a difference if this helping method is taken up in a big way by the profession. Incidentally, it would be a pity if we thought of social action only in relation to the community as sometimes we may need to be militant on behalf of our inarticulate children in care (*Child Care News*, no. 87, 1969, p. 12).

The family advice service and the unified social service department

In May 1967 a *New Society* reporter wrote that 'the Seebohm Committee on local authority personal services is likely, in its report, to recommend family advice centres as doorways to more integrated social work departments' (Lapping, 1967, p. 649). When the Report appeared about a year later it did not include such a recommendation, perhaps mainly because sufficient information about the concepts and functions and the experience gathered about the work of family advice centres was, as yet, not available. Nevertheless, the Seebohm Report contains many implications for the role of the family advice service in the new unified social service approach. In December 1968 Mr Frederic Seebohm, chairman of the committee which issued the report, stated in an address on the report:

We see a highly professional service which . . . must be sensitive but certainly not sentimental, which will be community based, designed to help people to help themselves, but caring fully for the helpless. It will, we hope, develop community activities, youth services and so forth, and in co-operation with other departments plan to meet social change and social needs. In other words, an entirely new department with new responsibilities and a new concept.

Our observations lead us to conclude that the family advice service approach fits in very effectively with the new responsibilities and concepts of the unified social service department. Moreover, the already existing family advice centres can make a valuable contribution to the new service because they have gathered a range of experience which is highly relevant to the problems and challenges the unified social service department will have to face.

Our observations of four different types of F.A.S. settings suggest two main functions for the family advice service in the unified social service department: (1) a family advice centre as an advice, intake and referral service of the new department; (2) detached family advice centres as 'reaching out' community-oriented or community-based services in priority areas.

As an advice, intake and referral service the family advice centre would function as the reception unit and the 'open door' of the social service area teams and as a kind of 'sorting-out' centre. In practice this would look something like this:

A small unit of two or three experienced social workers and a clerical assistant is assigned to the F.A.S. unit. The workers are selected from the staff of the specialised services who, according to the Seebohm proposal, will become part of the unified social service department. Social workers with children's, welfare, housing and health department experience seem most suitable, but workers of other backgrounds are not necessarily excluded. The main requirements are: social work training and experience, an easy-going, accepting, confidence-inspiring and flexible attitude towards people, a good basic knowledge of the structure and methods of the helping services and of the local authority system, the will and ability to use every opportunity to learn and to add to a growing fund of knowledge and information, and considerable diagnostic skill.

The functions of the unit are those of advice, guidance and assistance, mediation/liaison, referral and follow-up. Long-term, intensive case work is excluded from the functions of the F.A.S. unit.

This type of F.A.S. unit or family advice centre may very well be the most economical and efficient way of dealing with the inevitable confusions and adjustments of the changeover from the previous statutory services system to the new unified approach. From the very outset the family advice centre could provide a clearly identified, easily accessible entrance door to the social service department for the public, an anchorage point for the group of social workers and administrative staff who have to readjust to the new structure, and an easy-to-contact address for the field workers and officials of those statutory and voluntary agencies which are not included in the unified department. Adequate publicity would be essential. The family advice service should be made known to the public and to the services in the area by such means as advertisements in local papers, posters, circulars, etc. defining the functions of the family advice centre within the social service department and emphasising the confidential, no-strings-attached character of the service. The intake function of the family advice centre does not imply any limitations imposed upon clients who know what type of service they require and whom they wish to consult. The centre would mainly serve those who are not able, for a variety of reasons, to make these decisions unaided, and those who find it difficult or impossible to identify and articulate their problems and needs.

The F.A.S. unit would, furthermore, provide a valuable service for social workers and others in the helping professions who need assistance and advice in dealing with clients who have presented problems which do not lie within their areas of competence. The F.A.S. staff would assume the task of providing advice and consultation, and of redirecting clients to the appropriate services if necessary. In addition to this, the F.A.S. staff would offer a continuous service to people who can be helped within the limits of advice, guidance and assistance, without the need for further referral or as a supplementary supporting service.

With the aid of consistent record keeping and a general attitude of alertness to the community's needs, problems and resources, the F.A.S. staff should be able to provide a significant amount of useful information to the professional and administrative staff of the social service department and to other community services and organisations, such as statutory and voluntary agencies, tenants' associations, parent groups, local community management committees, etc. Good communications and continuous feedback should be assured through staff meetings and meetings with professional and community groups, newsletters, reports, etc. It may be assumed that the sharing and dissemination of information would serve to encourage the filling of gaps in the services, the reassessment and revision of existing provisions and methods and the more efficient distribution and supplementation of resources.

The 'detached' family advice centres need not be regarded as an alternative, but rather as supplementary services to the social service department F.A.S. It may be assumed that 'detached' F.A.C.s have specific functions and should be set up only in such areas and population groups within the area which have been specifically identified as 'priority areas', i.e. sectors of the overall community in which there is a high incidence of problems and needs which, for reasons of geographical or social isolation, are not being adequately met by the existing services.

The 'detached' F.A.C.s would be located within the client community (a housing estate, a cluster of streets populated by an unusually large number of multi-problem families, a shopping district serving a fringe sector of the area, etc.), and would be set up for the specific task of serving such a population group or community. These centres would be staffed by one F.A.S. worker, heading a team consisting of professionals, indigenous workers and volunteers in accordance with the needs of the community and adequate to provide the range of services needed. The centre may be located in a flat, a store or any other suitable accommodation easily accessible to the target community. It would have the following functions:

1. *First aid.* This means mainly being on the spot for immediate advice, guidance and assistance in crisis situations. This type of service may be expected to take up a great proportion of the worker's time and effort in a 'high-need' community.

2. *Community work.* This presupposes the developing of relationships with the members of the community, and the gaining of insight into the community's structure, its cultural and socio-economic characteristics, its needs, resources, sources of conflict and potentialities for improvement, which would enable the worker to help the community as a whole to improve its internal relationships as well as relationships with the environment, including the statutory and voluntary services of the area. The worker would use the relationship with the community, and the knowledge gained to foster and support informal and organised community activities which serve to make the community more self-sufficient, to encourage patterns of neighbourly mutual aid and to educate and guide the community in applying its own resources in finding solutions, and in obtaining the necessary outside assistance, in coping with problems such as inadequate housing conditions, the need for play facilities and delinquency. One of the worker's major tasks in this context would be the interpretation of the client community's problems, needs and characteristics to the social service department, as well as to the other statutory and voluntary service agencies of the area in order to ensure an understanding attitude and suitable methods of approach.

3. Referral, liaison/mediation and follow-up would be carried out in the ways defined above, but should be suitably adapted to the specific requirements of community work. It is important to assure the 'detached' F.A.S. worker of good and consistent lines of communication to the department. The most efficient way to do so would probably be to make 'detached' centres part of the department's family advice service unit, supervised by one senior officer with direct access to the chief officer of the department.

The F.A.C. could furnish valuable information regarding 'high-need' areas which have remained a sort of 'no-man's-land' to the staff of the helping professions in the area. F.A.C.s of this type could act as the 'eyes and ears' of the department in geographically or socially isolated multi-problem population 'pockets'. The information they provide may not only furnish much-needed factual material, but may also be of considerable educational value affecting the thinking and attitudes of all concerned. It should be included in the overall information material provided by the F.A.S. unit of the department.

Confidentiality is of the utmost importance in this type of detached, community based work. In order to make the service effective and to enable it to bridge the gulf which all too often exists between isolated communities and the helping services, the client community must learn to trust the worker. In a sense, he or she must become 'their' worker and must be seen to be 'on their side'. Only thus will this kind of population group learn to accept the fact that representatives of the social services, to which the F.A.C. is clearly seen to belong, are not necessarily agents of the not-to-be-trusted 'them', people who 'don't understand what we're up against and who don't want to know'.

One of the most frequent sources of resistance to the introduction of family advice centres is the (sometimes valid) argument that other agencies may already be providing the services which F.A.S. has to offer. As far as the function of the family advice service as the intake and referral unit of the new unified department is concerned, these objections do not seem to be relevant. As stated, F.A.S. staff would be recruited from the staff of any of the statutory services scheduled to merge into the new department. It is reasonable to assume that staff members who have done F.A.S. work in their former agencies will be given priority. In this respect it would be highly desirable if the Citizen's Advice Bureaux would become closely associated with the social service departments.

Where well-staffed and easily accessible C.A.B.s exist, providing a wide range of information, this would indicate that the social service department F.A.S. will be able to reduce time spent on providing 'simple advice' by referring such clients to the local C.A.B. However, in those cases in which the local C.A.B. is able and willing to provide more far-reaching professional social work services, this should be welcomed by all concerned. It would provide people seeking help with a choice between different services, and reduce the caseload of the department. It would not affect the role and the tasks of the family advice service as the intake and referral unit of the department.

Community work projects are a somewhat different matter. There has, recently, been a welcome upsurge of interest regarding community work and a number of activities have been initiated under various names, such as 'community work', 'community development', 'community action', etc. In many cases it is difficult to define the methods, functions and goals of these, undoubtedly well motivated and often very useful, services. So far as the detached community-based family advice centres are concerned, it can only be said that there would certainly be no point in introducing this type of service into a community where another agency is already engaged in community work. In some instances a detached family advice centre may work in conjunction with a community work project, or add the community worker of another agency to the F.A.S. team. There may also be occasions where the F.A.S. worker either participates in his or her specific function in a wider community work programme, or where a centre withdraws from a neighbourhood because worker and clients have come to the conclusion that an available community worker would better serve the needs of this particular community.

Finally, some remarks on the Seebohm Report's suggestion that 'local authority should provide a centre for housing advice and guidance' (para. 391). This very important category of advice and information should be provided by the family advice centres and, where available, the C.A.B.s. Experience shows that, no matter how well motivated, an agency which offers advice and information in matters directly concerning the policies and interests of its employing agency, will of necessity, become subjected to overt or unconscious pressures to let its advice be influenced by the interests of the employing agency. The more neutral, more objective view of a service operated under the auspices of the social service department, representing the policies and reflecting the experience of a fairly wide range of social services, is more likely to assure the client of impartial advice which takes all aspects of the client's situation into consideration.

The Seebohm Report points out that 'because of their previous departmental experience, and in some cases because of their training, the workers entering the new social service department will tend to cling to familiar ways of looking at their work' (para. 576). Especially in the initial stages of the new department, this may lead to considerable difficulties in the process of creating a truly unified service. We suggest that the setting-up of a family advice service as an 'entrance door' to the department may ease and speed up the process of unification by providing a central unifying factor and a practical demonstration of applying a unified policy in receiving and referring clients.

The Report states: 'The quality and efficiency of the personal social services also depend upon sufficient relevant knowledge. There are many social problems about which we know comparatively little; we are often unsure what form of provision best meets particular social needs or most effectively forestalls them (para. 96). Information provided by the F.A.S. and the 'detached' centres could make a valuable contribution to providing this relevant knowledge.

The Report says: 'An effective family service must be concerned with the prevention of social distress. Morally, socially and economically this makes sense. In principle, by taking timely and appropriate measures, much human suffering and family breakdown can be avoided' (para. 427). One of the main goals of the family advice service is to provide an easily accessible confidential service where people can come to seek advice, find some relief from anxiety, talk about their situation, and gain some perspective on their problems, *before* these problems have taken on crisis proportions. By functioning as the 'entrance door' to the social service department and by providing detached workers for on-the-spot availability, the F.A.S. could make a major contribution to the preventive work of the new unified services as well as helping to co-ordinate the different aspects of the new approach and to further good communication with the target population.

The concepts, goals and functions of the family advice service, especially in the detached settings, can also play an important role in fostering client participation and in pioneering the still new and daring concept of client accountability which Professor Leaper (1968) described as 'the answerability of . . . [the social] worker for the general strategy of his intervention in an area . . .'; as he points out:

In this there are the seeds certainly of dilemma for the social worker which we must do all we can to resolve, but without such a healthy tension between the large and comparatively remote local authority . . . and the people of a smaller locality 'a community based social service' is hardly likely to be anything more than a vague aspiration betrayed in daily practice (p. 2337).

In conclusion we cite the comments of an American author which appear to us to confirm the conclusions we have drawn from this study:

Beyond the question of defining the content of their activities, it seems the workers in the new social work departments will be equally challenged to go far beyond their present repertoire of helping. A thrust for more immediate and effective work with clients means increasingly a differentiation of the techniques of helping and above all, a searching out of techniques which are increasingly relevant to the clients' situation, rather than to the professional's generalised learning. It may require the social worker to seek out, learn, experiment with, and eventually to integrate additional approaches into his methodology of helping (Maier, 1969, p. 26).

Final remarks

It is something of a cliché to say that the whole is more than the sum of its parts. Nevertheless, it is easy to lose sight of this fundamental truth when one seeks to describe and evaluate the fairly wide and diverse range of functions of the family advice service. It is necessary to distinguish between the different objectives, functions and methods of the service for the sake of description and evaluation, in order to provide guidelines for the practical application of theoretical concepts, and in order to facilitate the definition of the different roles of the F.A.S. worker in different situations. It must, however, be realised that the range, the quality and the efficiency of the service depend first and foremost on the degree to which the various objectives, functions and methods interact and complement one another to form an integrated whole.

Any one of the F.A.S. functions can be, and often is, part of the routine work of a number of social service agencies. So, for instance, guidance, possibly defined as case work, is carried out by child care officers; Citizens' Advice Bureaux provide simple advice and information; any social worker may, under certain circumstances, adopt the roles of mediator and liaison person between clients and statutory services. Our observations showed that those F.A.S. settings which are *not* community-oriented or community-based can make a valuable contribution to their parent agencies, on the condition that their functions complement the services provided by the agency, do not needlessly duplicate existing agency functions and are thoroughly integrated with the overall services of the parent agency. Clearly distinguished from this type of family advice service, the detached, community-oriented or community-based family advice centres can add a new dimension to the overall service of the parent agency, whether this is the children's department or the new unified social services department, by combining and integrating a range of functions and approaches which share the common goal of providing an encompassing in-depth service to a high-need neighbourhood.

The tasks which confront the F.A.S. worker in bringing about and in maintaining the essential integration of the functions and methods of the service are complex and numerous. The problems and obstacles he faces reflect those faced by the social work profession and the social welfare system as a whole. The task of creating an integrated whole, consistent with the goals of the service, out of the needs of his clients and the prevailing environmental factors on the one hand, and the range of F.A.S. functions—advice, guidance, assistance, referral and follow-up, mediation and liaison, community work—on the other hand, demands high qualities of leadership, the ability to remain flexible and imaginative while able to maintain a disciplined structure, as well as a thorough understanding of the wider issues which impinge upon social work in modern society. The task is that of a generic social work approach based on specialised knowledge and skills. Our observations lead us to conclude that the detached family advice centre may serve as a model of this approach, and as a reaching-out service which applies this approach where it is most needed. McCormick (1970) has pointed out that the dimensions of social work 'appear to shift and change, not only with changing times but with every refinement of the knowledge, understanding, and skill that characterize professional performance' (p. 3). The detached, community-oriented or community-based family advice centre may be regarded as one of the responses to the growing awareness of the need for new concepts and approaches, such as community work, client participation and social work advocacy, helping to introduce a new dimension to the statutory social services in this country by integrating these approaches in a preventive reaching-out service.

Collis (1966) said that:

For effective diagnosis and treatment it is important to look at the total needs of the individual within his family and community setting. When this is done the number of social issues and the number of services involved increases: and it increases as our understanding of the intensity and depth of need increases, the boundaries of responsibility become more difficult to draw and effective co-operation and co-ordination become more difficult to achieve (p. 70).

It is the avowed goal of the newly emerging unified social service departments to ensure a more comprehensive understanding of need. As this goal is achieved, the services will be faced with the challenge of providing more effective, arranging and co-ordinated services. Our observations lead us to anticipate an important role in the identification and interpretation of need, as well as in the provision and the field level co-ordination of services. There is no doubt that the implementation of the F.A.S. approach will require investments in resources and manpower. We have seen that a number of local authorities were willing and able to make these investments, and there are indications, especially regarding the detached family advice centres, that these investments were found to be profitable in the widest sense of the term. To those who feel that the rules of economy should provide the yard-stick for investment in social service approaches, we offer for consideration the following statement:

The current vogue is to stress 'cost effectiveness'. This gives the impression of scientific rigour but in fact ignores the central issue of fundamental goals and values. It is these which should determine how to choose from possible alternative courses of action. Cost effectiveness as the main criterion is a poor instrument for determining priorities: it is short-sighted and restrictive (Kellmer Pringle, 1970, p. 7).

One of these fundamental goals, and one of the major objectives of the new unified social service departments, is that of accessibility. Our observations showed that community based and community oriented family advice centres are effective in furthering the accessibility of services to those strata of the population who have, traditionally, found the services least accessible, and who have been found to be hardest to reach by the services. We believe that this is one of the most significant findings of the F.A.S. study, and that it should be regarded as one of the determining factors for the application of the F.A.S. approach. Professor Kahn (1970), who has for some years been involved in the structuring and the evaluation of community-based services, points out that it has been argued that 'the creation of access services draws off pressure and resources necessary for the development of basic programs of income maintenance and social service'. He gives three answers:

First, the provision of access is of itself a significant social service. Many people need information, application forms and advice and can then proceed on their own. Second, an access service system with adequate feedback and reporting machinery can contribute to identifying qualitative and quantitive lacks in the service system and can contribute significantly to the planning process. Finally, even given continuing service gaps, decent access services can end the conspiracy of silence or the organizational obfuscation that perpetuate inequality of usage. If there are to be shortages, why solve the problem by ignoring the need of the most needy? The social services today can hardly justify adopting a philosophy of the survival of the fittest, yet this is what present practice often offers in fact, if not in rhetoric (p. 97).

We conclude our report by asking the reader *not* to regard the descriptive material and the observations we have presented as the final word on the family advice service, but as a basis for further discussion and as an impetus for further experimentation and innovation. We have tried to provide an overall view of the service based on the experience of seven family advice centres and, of necessity, limited by this experience. There is ample room for further investigation. The Seebohm Report speaks for us when it states:

> We cannot emphasise too strongly the part which research must play in the creation and maintenance of an effective family service. Social planning is an illusion without adequate facts; and the adequacy of services mere speculation without evaluation. Nor is it sufficient for research to be done spasmodically however good it be. It must be a continuing process, accepted as a familiar and permanent feature of any department or agency concerned with social provision (para. 473).

As the Director of the National Bureau for Co-operation in Child Care pointed out, the family advice centres themselves can contribute to this essential ongoing process of investigation and evaluation:

> In addition to being itself an experimental project, a Family Advice Service could sponsor, or possibly itself undertake, some investigations. It would have unique opportunities for certain kinds of studies: for example, an examination of the composition of families who seek its advice, the kinds of questions, relating to children's growth, that are most commonly raised by mothers; the problems which are specific to the incomplete family, especially the mother who is without a husband's support; the effect of having a physically handicapped child in an otherwise normal family; and the kind of situations that spark off crises, threatening the break-up of the family as a viable unit (Kellmer Pringle, 1965a, p. 287).

As the present study ends, we have been offered the opportunity to take advantage of the wide range of possibilities for further study provided by the family advice service by carrying out an investigation of services for children and youth based on detached family advice centres as part of a range of experimental treatment services.

UNIVERSITY LIBRARY
NOTTINGHAM

References

ABEL-SMITH, B. (1968) 'The need for social planning', in P. Townsend *et al.*, *Social Services for All?* The Fabian Society, London.

AGATE, J. and MEACHER, M. (1969) *The Care of the Old*, Fabian Tract 278.

ARNOLD, S. (1970) 'Confidential communication and the social worker', *Social Work* (U.S.A.), **15,** no. 1.

BANKS, J. (1970) 'The role of central government', in A. Lapping, ed., *Community Action*, Fabian Tract 400.

BELL, K. (1969) *Tribunals in the Social Services*, Routledge & Kegan Paul, London.

BENJAMIN, J. (1961) *In Search of Adventure*, The National Council of Social Service, London.

BERELSON, B. and STEINER, B. A. (1964) *Human Behaviour*, Harcourt, Brace & World, New York.

BERNARD, S. E., KURTAGH, E. and JOHNSON, H. R. (1968) 'The neighborhood service organisation—specialist in social welfare innovation', *Social Work* (U.S.A.), **13,** no. 1.

BILTON, K. (1970) 'Report of a working party appointed to examine the relationship between the Child Care Service and the Police Juvenile Bureau, South East Region', *Child Care News,* **97.**

BIRMINGHAM CITY (1967) *Report on the Work of the Children's Department, three years ended 31 March 1967.*

BLAU, P. M. and SCOTT, W. R. (1963) 'Formal organisations', in P. Leonard, *Sociology in Social Work*, Routledge & Kegan Paul, London, 1966.

BRAGER, G. A. (1968) 'Advocacy and political behaviour', *Social Work* (U.S.A.), **13,** no. 2.

BROOKE, R. (1969) 'Civic rights and social services', *The Political Quarterly*, **40,** no. 1.

BROWN, S. D. (1970) 'Tower Hamlets 1970', *Child Care News,* **97.**

CENTRAL TRAINING COUNCIL IN CHILD CARE (1970) 'First report of the study group on field work training' *Child Care News*, no. 100.

CLOWARD, R. A. and OHLIN, L. E. (1960) *Delinquency and Opportunity*, The Free Press, Glencoe, Illinois.

COLLIS, A. T. (1966) 'The structure of social services—principles and practice', The Association of Children's Officers, proceedings of the Seventeenth Annual Conference, 14–16 September, 1966, *Focus on the Family*, Norwich (mimeographed).

COLLORD, J. C. ed. (1930) *The Long View, Papers and Addresses by Mary E. Richmond*, Russell Sage Foundation, New York.

COOPER, J. D. (1965) 'The role of social work: administration and practice', in M. L. Kellmer Pringle, ed., *Investment in Children*, Longmans, London.

COOPER, J. D. (1969) 'Social disadvantage and social help', *Approved School Gazette*, **62,** no. 12.

DEPARTMENT OF EDUCATION AND SCIENCE AND THE YOUTH SERVICE DEVELOPMENT COUNCIL (1967) *Immigrants and the Youth Service*, H.M.S.O., London.

DONNISON, D. V. (1970) 'Action research', paper presented to the Social Administration Conference at Nottingham University, 10–11 July, 1970 (mimeographed).

DOWNES, D. M. (1966) *The Delinquent Solution*, Routledge & Kegan Paul, London.

FANSHEL, D. (1962) 'Administration in social work', in D. Fanshel, ed., *Research in Social Welfare Administration*, National Association of Social Workers, New York.

FITZWILLIAMS, M. (1969) 'Neighbourhood work on a pre-war council estate', paper given to the A.P.S.W. Meeting, London.

FOGELSON, F. B. (1970) 'How social workers perceive lawyers', *Social Casework* (U.S.A.), **51,** no. 2.

FORDER, A. (1966) *Social Casework and Administration*, Faber, London.

GEIS, G. (1965) *Juvenile Gangs*, President's Committee on Juvenile Delinquency and Youth Crime, Washington, D.C.

GIBBENS, T. C. N. (1966) 'Family situation and delinquency', The Association of Children's Officers, *Focus on the Family: Proceedings of the Seventeenth Annual Conference, 14–16 September 1966* (mimeographed).

GOETSCHIUS, G. W. (1969) *Working with Community Groups*, Routledge & Kegan Paul, London.

GOLAN, N. (1969) 'When is a client in crisis?' *Social Casework* (U.S.A.) **50,** no. 7.

GOULDNER, A. W. and MILLER, S. M., ed. (1965) *Applied Sociology*, The Free Press, New York.

GRANT, J., LIPP, K. and SHERMAN, S. (1968) *The Arts, Youth and Social Change*, Department of Health, Education and Welfare, Washington, D.C. (mimeographed).

GREVE, S. (1969) 'Financial help as part of social work', *Social Work*, **26,** no. 2.

GROSSBARD, H. (1954) 'Methodology for developing self-awareness', *Social Casework* (U.S.A.), November 1954.

GROVES, D. (1969) 'Community self-help groups', *Case Conference*, 16, no. 4.

GULBENKIAN REPORT (1968) *Community Work and Social Change*, the report of a study group on training set up by the Gulbenkian Foundation, Longmans, London.

HANDLER, J. (1968) 'The coercive children's officer', *New Society*, no. 314, 3 October 1968.

HASTINGS, S. and JAY, P. (1965) *The Family and the Social Services*, Fabian Tract 359.

HODGES, M. B., ed. (1951) *Social Work Year Book*, American Association of Social Workers, New York.

HOLMAN, R. (1969) 'The wrong poverty programme', *New Society*, no. 338, 20 March 1969.

HOLMAN, R. (1970a) 'Combating social deprivation', in R. Holman *et al.*, *Socially Deprived Families in Britain*, Bedford Square Press, London.

HOLMAN, R. (1970b) 'Handsworth Adventure Playground', in A. Lapping, ed., *Community Action*, Fabian Tract 400.

HOLMAN, R. and RADFORD, E. (1969) 'Social work in the '70s', *British Hospital Journal and Social Service Review*, **79**, no. 4134.

HOME HELP SERVICE IN ENGLAND AND WALES, THE (1969) H.M.S.O., London.

HOUWINK, E. (1967) 'Supervision is teaching and enabling', *Case Conference*, **14**, no. 3.

HUNTER, D. R. (1970) 'Social action to influence institutional change', *Social Case Work*, (U.S.A.), **51**, no. 4.

INTERNATIONAL CONFERENCE ON SOCIAL WELFARE, *see Social Welfare and Human Rights*.

IRVINE, E. (1967) 'The hard-to-like family', *Case Conference*, **14**, no. 3.

JAY, P. (1962) 'A plan for family bureaux', in D. Donnison, P. Jay and M. Stewart, *The Ingleby Report*, research series 231, The Fabian Society, London.

JEFFERYS, M. (1965) *An Anatomy of Social Welfare Services*, Michael Joseph, London.

JUDD, KOHN and SCHULMAN (1962) 'Group supervision: a vehicle for professional development', *Social Work* (U.S.A.), **7**, no. 1.

KAHAN, B. (1970) 'The child care service', in P. Townsend *et al.*, *The Fifth Social Service*, The Fabian Society, London.

KAHN, A. J. (1969) 'Perspectives on access to the social services', *Social Work* (U.S.A.), **26**, no. 3.

KAHN, A. J. (1970) 'Perspectives on access to social services', *Social Work* (U.S.A.), **15**, no. 2.

KAHN, A. J. *et al.* (1966) *Neighbourhood Information Centers*, Columbia University School of Social Work, New York.

KAIM-KAUDLE: 'Selectivity in family allowances', in P. Townsend *et al.*, *Social Services for All?* The Fabian Society, London, 1968.

KELLMER PRINGLE, M. L. (1965a) *Deprivation and Education*, Longmans, London.

KELLMER PRINGLE, M. L. (1965b) 'The challenge of prevention', *Investment in Children*, Longmans, London.

KELLMER PRINGLE, M. L., ed. (1965c) *Investment in Children*, Longmans, London.

KELLMER PRINGLE, M. L., ed. (1969) *Caring for Children*, Longmans, London.

KELLMER PRINGLE, M. L. (1970) 'Co-operation in child and family care', *Concern*, no. 5.

KEMENY, P. J. and POPPLESTONE, G. (1970) 'Client discrimination in social welfare organisations', *Social Work*, **27**, no. 2.

KILLINGTON, G. (1964) 'The history and development of the streetwork project initiated by the Service to Youth Council, Inc.' in Paper delivered at the seminar on 'Streetwork' held at the University of Adelaide, 30 May 1964, *Streetwork in South Australia*.

LANCE, E. E. (1969) 'Intensive work with a deprived family', *Social Casework* (U.S.A.), **50**, no. 8.

LAPPING, A. (1967) 'How not to help Wapping', *New Society*, no. 240, 4 May 1967.

LEAPER, R. A. B. (1968) 'Seebohm Report', *British Hospital Journal and Social Service Review*, 13 December 1968.

LEEVES, R. E. (1968) 'Problems of confidentiality', *Case Conference* **14**, no. 10.

LEISSNER, A. (1967) *Family Advice Services*, Longmans, London.

LEISSNER, A. (1968) 'Association of Community Workers', *British Hospital Journal and Social Service Review*, 27 December 1968.

LEISSNER, A. (1969a) *Streetclub Work in Tel Aviv and New York*, Longmans, London.

LEISSNER, A. (1969b) 'Family Advice Service', *British Hospital Journal and Social Service Review*, 17 January 1969.

LEISSNER, A., RUBIN, N. and BORS, S. (1967) *Research Project on Forces Acting in Street Corner Groups*, vol. 1, report prepared under a grant from the Department of Health, Education and Welfare, U.S.A., and carried out under the auspices of the Israel Ministry of Social Welfare and the Tel Aviv Municipality.

LEONARD, P. (1968) 'The application of sociological analysis to social work training', *The British Journal of Sociology*, **19**, no. 4.

LEVIN, J. and TAUBE, G. (1970) 'Bureaucracy and the socially handicapped: a study of lower-status tenants in public housing', *Sociology and Social Research* (U.S.A.), **54**, no. 2.

LOEWENBERG, F. M. (1968) 'Social Workers and indigenous non-professionals: some structural dilemmas', *Social Work* (U.S.A.), **13**, no. 3.

LOWRY, P. (1969) *Ancillary staff in Children's Departments*, Home Office, London.

McCORMICK, M. J. (1970) 'Social advocacy: a new dimension in social work', *Social Casework* (U.S.A.), **51**, no. 1.

McINNES, N. (1970) 'Partnership of the professional and the volunteer in social service', paper presented at the seventh British National Conference on Social Welfare, Swansea, 11–15 April 1970.

MACIVER and PAGE (1962) *Society*, Macmillan, London.

McNEIL, C. F. (1951) 'Community organisation for social welfare', in M. B. Hodges, ed., *Social Work Yearbook*, American Association of Social Workers, New York.

MADGE, J. (1965) *The Tools of Social Science*, Longmans, London.

MARRIS, P. and REIN, M. (1967) *Dilemmas of Social Reform*, Routledge & Kegan Paul, London.

MAYER, M. W. (1969) 'New Wine for New Bottles', *International Social Work*.

MAYS, J. B. (1965) 'The role of social work—theory and policy', in M. L. Kellmer Pringle, ed., *Investment in Children*, Longmans, London.

MOBILIZATION FOR YOUTH, INC. (1961) *A Proposal for the Prevention and Control of Delinquency by Expanding Opportunities*, New York.

MOSS, P. (1969) *Welfare Rights Project '68—an examination of poverty in a small area of Liverpool*, Merseyside Child Poverty Action Group (mimeographed).

NATIONAL ASSOCIATION OF SOCIAL WORKERS (1962) *Professional Competence in Supervision*, New York City Chapter.

NATIONAL ASSOCIATION OF SOCIAL WORKERS, ad hoc Committee on Advocacy, (1969) 'The social worker as advocate: champion of social victims', *Social Work* (U.S.A.), **14**, no. 2.

NATIONAL COUNCIL OF SOCIAL SERVICE, THE (1965) *Research in the Personal Social Services*, London.

NICLAS, I. D. (1968) 'Schweigepflicht und Aussageverweigerung des Sozialarbeiters', *Nachrichtendienst*, **48**, no. 4, Frankfurt am Main.

O'DONNELL, E. J. (1968) 'The Neighborhood Service Center', *Welfare in Review*, **6**, no. 1.

OWENS, J. K. (1969) 'The Seebohm Report and the future role of the voluntary bodies', *Social Service Quarterly*, **42**, no. 4.

OWTRAM, J. (1969) 'The right to help?' *Case Conference*, **16**, no. 3.

OXFORDSHIRE COUNTY COUNCIL CHILDREN'S DEPARTMENT, *Report to the Secretary of State under Section 1 (4), Children and Young Persons Act 1963*, September 1964.

PACKMAN, J. (1968) *Child Care: Needs and Numbers*, Allen & Unwin, London.

PARAD, H. J. (1966) 'The use of time-limited crisis intervention in community health programming', *Social Service Review*, September.

PARKER, R. A. (1968) *The Rents of Council Houses*, Occasional papers in social administration, no. 22, London, Bell, 1962, cited by K. Spencer, 'Housing and socially deprived families', in R. Holman *et al.*, *Socially Deprived Families in Britain*, Bedford Square Press, London, 1970, p. 72.

PERLMAN, R. and JONES, D. (1967) *Neighborhood Service Centers*, U.S. Department of Health, Education and Welfare, Washington, D.C.

PIVEN, H. (1969) 'The fragmentation of social work' *Social Casework* (U.S.A.), February 1969.

POLANSKY, N. A. (1960) *Social Work Research*, University of Chicago Press.

POWER, N. S. (1965) *The Forgotten People*, Arthur James, Evesham, Worcs.

POWLEY, T. A. (1970) 'Intermediate treatment services', *Concern*, no. 5.

RAE PRICE, J. (1967) 'The social pathology—a dilemma for social work', *Case Conference*, vol. 13, no. 12.

RAE PRICE, J. (1968a) 'Social workers as social planners?' *British Hospital Journal and Social Service Review*, **78**, no. 4084.

RAE PRICE, J. (1968b) 'The Netherlands—some models for Britain?' *British Hospital Journal and Social Service Review*, **78**, no. 4093.

RAE PRICE, J. (1968c) 'Reactionary past? Radical future?' *British Hospital Journal and Social Service Review*, **78**, no. 4103.

RAPOPORT, L. (1961) 'The concept of prevention in social work', *Social Work* (U.S.A.), **6**, no. 1.

REX, J. and MOORE, R. (1967) *Race, Community and Conflict*, Oxford University Press.

RICHMOND, M. E. (1930) *The Long View: papers and addresses by Mary G. Richmond*, J. C. Collard, ed., New York Russell Foundation.

RODMAN, H. and KOLODNY, R. L. (1965) 'Organisational strains in the researcher –practitioner relationship', in A. W. Gouldner and S. M. Miller, eds., *Applied Sociology*, The Free Press, New York.

ROSS, M. G. (1955) *Community Organisation: Theory and Principles*, Harper Brothers, New York.

RUNNICLES, D. S., 'Family Advice Centre in a high problem area', *Case Conference*, vol. 14, no. 7, November 1967.

SAMUELS, A. (1968) 'Privilege and the social worker', *Social Service Quarterly*, Autumn 1968.

SEEBOHM REPORT (1968) report of the committee on local authority and allied personal social services, H.M.S.O., London.

SEEBOHM, FREDERIC (1968) Address to the Seebohm Report Study Conference, Association of Municipal Corporations and County Councils Associations, London, 4–5 December 1968.

SHORT, R. and McCULLOCH, J. W. (1968) 'Health, welfare and advice centre', *Case Conference*, **15**, no. 3.

SINFIELD, A. (1969) *Which Way for Social Work?*, Fabian Tract 393, London.

SMALL, A. W. (1905) *General Sociology*, University of Chicago Press.

SOCIAL WELFARE AND HUMAN RIGHTS (1968) Proceedings of the XIVth International Conference on Social Welfare, 18–24 August 1968, Helsinki, Finland.

SOCIETY OF CONSERVATIVE LAWYERS (1968) *Rough Justice*, Conservative Political Centre.

SOCIETY OF LABOUR LAWYERS (1968) *Justice for All*, The Fabian Society, London.

SPENCER, J. *et al.* (1964) *Stress and Release in an Urban Estate*, Tavistock Publications.

SPENCER, K. (1970) 'Housing and socially deprived families', in Holman, Lafitte, Spencer and Wilson, *Socially Deprived Families in Britian*, Bedford Square Press, London.

STACEY, M. (1969a) *Methods of Social Research*, Pergamon Press, London.

STACEY, M. (1969b) 'The myth of community studies', *The British Journal of Sociology*, **20**, no. 2.

STEIN, H. D. (1965) 'Administration', in H. L. Lurie, ed., *Encyclopedia of Social Work*, National Association of Social Workers, 15th issue, New York.

STEVENSON, O. (1968) 'Specialisation within a unified social work service', *Case Conference*, **15,** no. 8.

STEVENSON, O. (1970) 'The problems of individual need and fair standards for all', *Social Work Today*, **1,** no. 1.

SAMUELS, A. (1968) 'Privilege and the social worker', *Social Service Quarterly*, Autumn.

STROUD, J. (1965) *An Introduction to the Child Care Service*, Longmans, London.

TASH, M. J. (1967) *Supervision in Youth Work*, The National Council of Social Service, London.

THOMAS, J. (1969) Presidential address, Annual Conference of Child Care Officers, 1969, *Child Care News*, no. 87.

THOMAS, E. J. (1960) 'Field experiments and demonstrations', in N. A. Polansky, ed., *Social Work Research*, The University of Chicago Press.

TIMMS, N. (1964) *Social Casework*, Routledge & Kegan Paul, London.

TIMMS, N. (1968) *Language of Social Casework*, Routledge & Kegan Paul, London.

TITMUSS, R. M. (1968), *Commitment to Welfare*, Allen & Unwin, London.

TITMUSS, R. M. and ZANDERS, M. (1968) *Unequal Rights*, Child Poverty Action Group and London Co-operative Education Department, London.

TOWNSEND, P. (1954) 'The meaning of poverty', *British Journal of Sociology*, **5,** no. 2.

TOWNSEND, P. *et al.* (1968) *Social Services for All?*, The Fabian Society, London.

'Training implications of the White Paper', (1969) *Child Care News*, no. 84.

TROPP, E. (1968) 'The group: in life and in social work', *Social Casework* (U.S.A.), **49,** no. 5.

TURNER, J. B. (1968) 'Report of the pre-conference working party', *Social Welfare and Human Rights*, proceedings of the XIVth International Conference on Social Welfare, 18–24 August 1968, Helsinki, Finland.

WAKEFORD, J. (1968) *The Strategy of Social Enquiry*, Macmillan, London.

WHITAKER, B. (1968) 'Wanted: Lawyers for the poor', *New Statesman*, 27 September 1968.

WILENSKY and LEBEAUX (1965) *Industrial Society and Social Welfare*, The Free Press, Glencoe, Ill.

WILLARD, J. W. (1968) 'Social change, human rights and social welfare', *Social Welfare and Human Rights*, proceedings of the XIVth International Conference on Social Welfare, 18–24 August, 1968, Helsinki, Finland.

YOUNGHUSBAND, E. (1964) *Social Work and Social Change*, Allen & Unwin, London.

YOUTH SERVICE DEVELOPMENT COUNCIL (1969) REPORT, *Youth and Community Work in the '70s*, Department of Education and Science, H.M.S.O., London.

YOUTH SERVICE DEVELOPMENT COUNCIL (1967): *see* DEPARTMENT OF EDUCATION AND SCIENCE AND THE YOUTH SERVICE DEVELOPMENT COUNCIL (1967).

ZANDERS, M. (1968) 'Poverty and the legal profession', in R. Titmuss and M. Zanders, eds., *Unequal Rights*, Child Poverty Action Group and London Co-operative Education Department, London.